CW01024544

To Tony

Glad to have met you

Good luck.

John Duffell Canbray.

1992

WAR
AT SEA

J. DUFFELL-CANHAM.

WAR AT SEA

South African Maritime Operations during World War II

CAPTAIN CJ HARRIS

ASHANTI PUBLISHING
(PTY) LIMITED

P.O. Box 10021 Rivonia 2128

Published in 1991 by Ashanti Publishing (Pty) Ltd
A Division of Ashanti International Films Gibraltar
P.O. Box 10021
Rivonia 2128

ISBN   1 874800 16 2 Standard Edition
       1 874800 27 8 Collector's Edition
       1 874800 28 6 De Luxe Edition in full leather

First published 1991
© CJ Harris 1991
© Richard Wood

End paper photograph of HMSAS *Southern Barrier*, leader, mine clearance flotilla. (Author)

Designed and typeset by Adcolour, Pinetown
Printed by CTP Book Printers, Cape Town

This Book is copyright under the Berne Convention in terms of the Copyright Act (Act 98 of 1978). No part of this book may be reproduced or transmitted in any form or by any means, electronic or mechanical including photocopying, recording or by any information storage and retrieval system, without permission in writing from the publisher.

BK2540

A unique action photograph of a German U-boat being depth-charged from the air; part of the stricken submarine can be seen at the base of the explosion. The U-boat was sunk with heavy loss of life.

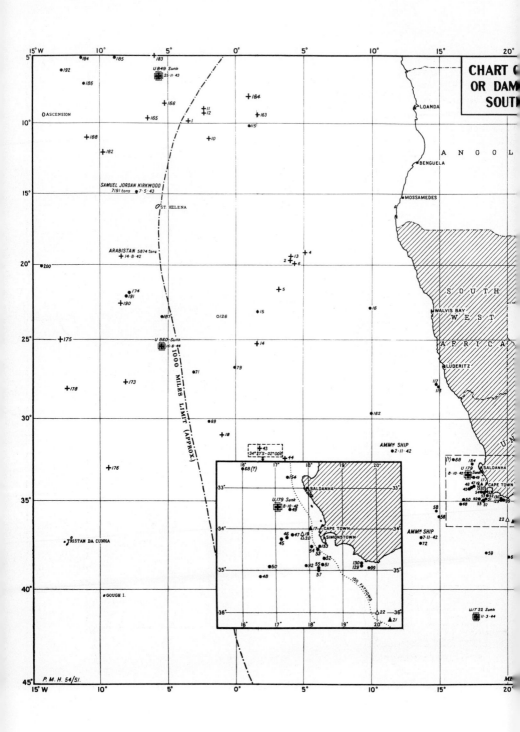

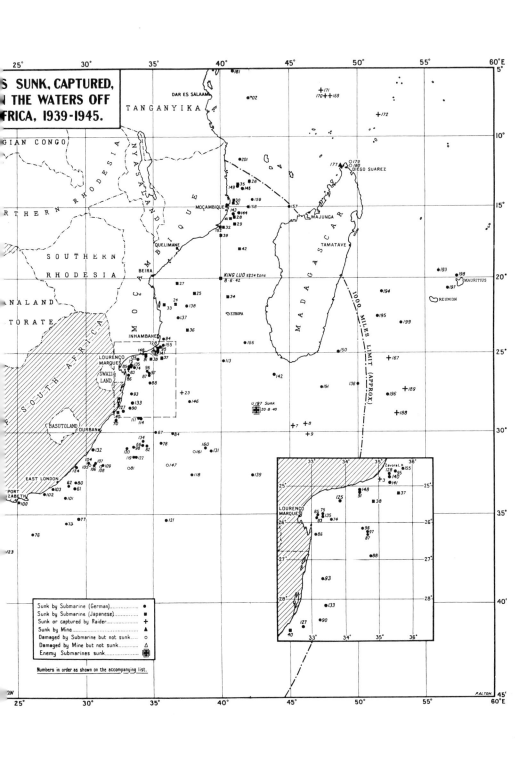

LIST OF SHIPS (INCLUDING WARSHIPS) SUNK, CAPTURED, OR DAMAGED, WITHIN 1000 MILES OF THE COAST OF THE UNION AND SOUTH-WEST AFRICA. 1939-1945.

No.	DATE	NAME & TONNAGE		COUNTRY	LAT. & LONG.	HOW SUNK
1	7-10-39	ASHLEA	4222	BRIT.	9°52'S–03°28'W	RAIDER (GERMAN)
2	22-10-39	TREVANION	5299	"	19°40'S–04°02'E	"
3	15-11-39	AFRICA SHELL	706	"	24°48'S–35°01'E	"
4	2-12-39	DORIC STAR	10086	"	19°10'S–05°05'E	"
5	3-12-39	TAIROA	7983	"	21°36'S–03°13'E	"
6	3-5-40	SCIENTIST	6199	"	19°55'S–04°20'E	"
7	27-8-40	FILEFJELL	7616	NOR.	29°38'S–45°11'E	"
8	27-8-40	BRITISH COMMANDER	6901	BRIT.	32°05'S–46°06'E	"
9	27-8-40	MORVIKEN	5008	NOR.	30°08'S–46°15'E	"
10	18-1-41	SANDEFJORD	8038	"	11°S–02°W (est.)	"
11	20-1-41	STANPARK	5103	BRIT.	20°22'S–02°20'W	"
12	20-1-41	BARNEVELD	5597	DUTCH	09°00'S–02°20'W	"
13	14-5-41	RABAUL	6809	BRIT.	19°26'S–04°05'E	"
14	24-5-41	TRAFALGAR	4530	"	25°17'S–01°35'E	"
15	28-10-41	HAZELSIDE	5297	"	23°10'S–01°36'E	SUBMARINE (GER)
16	1-11-41	BRADFORD CITY	4953	"	22°55'S–09°49'E	"
17	16-3-42	ALCYONE	4534	DUTCH	33°59'S–18°03'E	MINE (GERMAN)
18	23-3-42	PAGASITIKOS	3942	GREEK	31°S–01°W (est.)	RAIDER (GERMAN)
19	2-5-42	DALFRAM	4558	BRIT.	34°10'S–17°49'E	MINE (DAMAGED)
20	4-5-42	MANGKALIHAT	8457	DUTCH	34°10'S–17°49'E	"
21	15-5-42	SOUDAN	6677	BRIT.	36°10'S–20°22'E	" (GERMAN)
22	15-5-42	H.M.S. HECLA	10850	"	S – 20°E	" (DAMAGED)
23	5-6-42	ELYSIA	6757	"	27°33'S–37°05'E	RAIDER (JAPAN)
24	5-6-42	MELVIN H. BAKER	4998	AMER.	21°44'S–36°38'E	SUBMARINE (JAP)
25	5-6-42	ATLANTIC GULF	2639	PAN.	21°03'S–38°03'E	"
26	5-6-42	JOHNSTOWN	5086	PAN.	13°12'S–42°06'E	"
27	6-6-42	WILFORD	2158	NOR.	20°20'S–36°47'E	"
28	6-6-42	SUSAK	3889	Ju-Sla	15°42'S–40°58'E	"
29	6-6-42	AGIOS GEORGIOS IV *	4847	GREEK	16°12'S–41°00'E	"
30	11-6-42	MAHRONDA	7926	BRIT.	14°37'S–40°58'E	"
31	11-6-42	HELLENIC TRADER	2052	PAN.	14°40'S–40°53'E	"
32	12-6-42	CLIFTON HALL	5063	BRIT.	16°25'S–40°10'E	"
33	12-6-42	SUPETAR	3748	Ju-Sla	21°49'S–35°50'E	"
34	28-6-42	QUEEN VICTORIA	4937	BRIT.	21°15'S–40°30'E	"
35	29-6-42	GOVIKEN	4854	NOR.	13°25'S–41°13'E	"
36	30-6-42	EXPRESS	6736	AMER.	23°30'S–37°30'E	"
37	1-7-42	DE WEERT	1805	DUTCH	25°12'S–35°36'E	"
38	1-7-42	ALCHIBA	4427	"	25°25'S–34°49'E	"
39	1-7-42	EKNAREN	5243	SWED.	17°S–40E(Approx)	"
40	6-7-42	MUNDRA	7341	BRIT.	28°45'S–32°20'E	"
41	6-7-42	NYMPHE	4504	GREEK	15°48'S–40°42'E	"
42	8-7-42	HARTISMERE	5498	BRIT.	18°00'S–41°22'E	"
43	10-9-42	AMERICAN LEADER	6778	AMER.	34°27'S–02°00'E	RAIDER (GERMAN)
44	13-9-42	EMPIRE DAWN	7241	BRIT.	32°27'S–03°33'E	"
45	7-10-42	CHICKASAW CITY	6196	AMER.	34°18'S–17°11'E	SUBMARINE
46	7-10-42	FIRETHORN	4700	PAN.	34°13'S–17°21'E	"
47	8-10-42	PANTELIS	3845	GREEK	34°09'S–17°31'E	"
48	8-10-42	BORINGIA	5821	BRIT.	35°09'S–16°32'E	"
49	8-10-42	CITY OF ATHENS	6558	"	33°32'S–17°26'E	"
50	8-10-42	CLAN MACTAVISH	7631	"	34°55'S–16°48'E	"
51	8-10-42	SARTHE	5271	"	34°53'S–18°24'E	"
52	8-10-42	SWIFTSURE	8206	AMER.	34°43'S–18°27'E	"
53	8-10-42	GAASTERKERK	8679	DUTCH	34°30'S–18°15'E	"
54	8-10-42	KOUMOUNDOUROS	3598	GREEK	34°26'S–18°04'E	"
55	9-10-42	EXAMELIA	4981	AMER.	34°53'S–18°16'E	"
56	9-10-42	COLORADAN	6557	"	35°53'S–14°57'E	"
57	9-10-42	BELGIAN FIGHTER	5403	BELG.	35°00'S–18°16'E	"
58	10-10-42	ORCADES	23456	BRIT.	35°34'S–14°44'E	"
59	13-10-42	EMPIRE NOMAD	7167	"	37°57'S–18°26'E	"
60	17-10-42	EMPIRE CHAUCER	5970	"	38°12'S–20°04'E	"
61	23-10-42	CITY OF JOHANNESBURG	5669	"	33°27'S–29°10'E	"
62	26-10-42	ANNE HUTCHINSON	7176	AMER.	33°18'S–28°37'E	"
63	29-10-42	LA SALLE (?)	5462	"	40°S–21°30'E(est)	"
64	29-10-42	ROSS	4978	BRIT.	39°05'S–22°06'E	"
65	29-10-42	LAPLACE	7327	"	40°39'S–21°52'E	" (DAMAGED)
66	31-10-42	EMPIRE GUIDON	7041	"	30°48'S–34°11'E	"
67	31-10-42	REYNOLDS	5113	"	30°02'S–35°02'E	"
68	31-10-42	AEGEUS (?)	4538	GREEK	32°30'S–16°E(est)	"
69	31-10-42	ALDINGTON COURT	4891	BRIT.	30°10'S–02°00'W	"
70	1-11-42	MENDOZA	8233	"	29°13'S–32°13'E	"
71	2-11-42	LLANDILO	4966	"	27°03'S–03°08'W	"
72	3-11-42	EAST INDIAN	8159	AMER.	37°23'S–13°34'E	"
73	3-11-42	PORTO ALEGRE	5187	BRAZ.	36°34'S–28°33'E	"
74	4-11-42	TREKIEVE	5244	BRIT.	25°55'S–33°35'E	"
75	4-11-42	HAI HING	2561	NOR.	25°46'S–33°20'E	"
76	8-11-42	PLAUDIT	5060	PAN.	36°10'S–26°05'E	"
77	10-11-42	K.G. MELDAHL	3799	NOR.	35°15'S–29°28'E	"
78	13-11-42	LOUISE MOLLER	3764	BRIT.	30°37'S–35°44'E	"
79	13-11-42	STAR OF SCOTLAND	2290	AMER.	26°45'S–00°02'W	"
80	13-11-42	EXCELLO	4963	"	33°05'S–29°15'E	"
81	15-11-42	ADVISER	6348	BRIT.	32°10'S–33°10'E	" (DAMAGED)
82	19-11-42	SCOTTISH CHIEF	7006	"	30°10'S–33°10'E	"
29A	8-6-42	KING LUD *	5224	"	20°S–40°E(Approx)	(JAPAN)
83	19-11-42	GUNDA	2241	NOR.	25°52'S–33°10'E	SUBMARINE (GERMAN)
84	20-11-42	PIERCE BUTLER	7191	AMER.	30°10'S–36°25'E	"
85	20-11-42	CORINTHIAKOS	3562	GREEK	25°48'S–33°12'E	"
86	22-11-42	ALCOA PATHFINDER	6797	AMER.	26°20'S–33°07'E	"
87	24-11-42	DORINGTON COURT	5281	BRIT.	26°20'S–34°40'E	"
88	24-11-42	MOUNT HELMOS	6481	GREEK	26°55'S–34°47'E	"
89	27-11-42	JEREMIAH WADSWORTH	7176	AMER.	39°33'S–22°55'E	"
90	28-11-42	NOVA SCOTIA	6796	BRIT.	28°30'S–33°15'E	"
91	28-11-42	EVANTHIA	3551	GREEK	34°S–34°25'E	"
92	29-11-42	ARGO	1995	"	34°53'S–17°54'E	" (ITALIAN)
93	30-11-42	LLANDAFF CASTLE	10799	BRIT.	27°30'S–33°20'E	" (GERMAN)
94	30-11-42	CLEARYHIS	4153	GREEK	24°10'S–35°44'E	"
95	2-12-42	AMARYLIS	4328	PAN.	24°33'S–35°30'E	"
96	4-12-42	SARONIKOS	3548	GREEK	26°10'S–34°30'E	"
97	17-12-42	EMPIRE GULL	6408	BRIT.	26°15'S–34°40'E	"
98	17-12-42	SAWAHLOENTO	3085	DUTCH	30°55'S–33°30'E	"
99	11-2-43	QUEEN ANNE	4937	BRIT.	34°57'S–19°46'E	"
100	11-2-43	HELMSPEY	4764	"	34°17'S–25°04'E	"
101	17-2-43	LLANASHE	4836	"	34°00'S–28°30'E	"
102	17-2-43	DEER LODGE	6187	AMER.	33°46'S–26°57'E	"
103	27-2-43	H.M.N.S. COLOMBIA	10780	DUTCH	33°26'S–27°34'E	"
104	3-3-43	HARVEY W. SCOTT	7176	AMER.	31°54'S–30°10'E	"
105	3-3-43	TIBIA	10356	DUTCH	31°54'S–30°10'E	" (DAMAGED)
106	3-3-43	NIRPURA	5961	BRIT.	32°03'S–30°33'E	" (GERMAN)
107	4-3-43	EMPIRE MAHSEER	5087	"	32°03'S–30°33'E	"
108	4-3-43	SHEAF CROWN	4868	"	32°03'S–31°05'E	" (DAMAGED)
109	4-3-43	MARIETTA E.	7628	"	32°04'S–31°05'E	" (GERMAN)
110	7-3-43	SABOR	5212	"	34°33'S–22°58'E	"
111	8-3-43	JAMES B. STEPHENS	7176	AMER.	29°05'S–33°53'E	"
112	9-3-43	TABOR	4768	NOR.	37°20'S–23°06'E	"
113	10-3-43	RICHARD D. SPAIGHT	7177	AMER.	29°05'S–40°10'E	"
114	11-3-43	AELYBRYN	4986	BRIT.	29°08'S–34°05'E	"
115	19-3-43	LULWORTH HILL	7628	"	10°10'S–01°E(Approx)	" (ITALIAN)
116	20-3-43	NORTUN	3663	PAN.	28°00'S–14°55'E	" (GERMAN)
117	24-3-43	CITY OF BARODA	7129	BRIT.	27°S–13°E(Approx)	"
118	5-4-43	ALOE	5047	"	32°37'S–37°50'E	"
119	17-4-43	SEMBILAN	6566	DUTCH	34°30'S–33°30'E(est)	" (ITALIAN)
120	18-4-43	MANAAR	8007	BRIT.	30°59'S–33°00'E	"
121	18-4-43	CORBIS	8132	"	35°20'S–35°57'E	" (GERMAN)
122	21-4-43	JOHN DRAYTON	7177	AMER.	31°30'S–33°40'E	" (ITALIAN)
123	26-4-43	DORYSSA	8078	BRIT.	37°03'S–24°03'E	"
124	11-5-43	KAILSEA MEADOW	4962	"	32°04'S–29°18'E	" (GERMAN)
125	11-5-43	TINHOW	5232	"	25°25'S–33°55'E	"
126	11-5-43	CAPE NEDDICK	6797	AMER.	23°21'S–01°22'W	" (DAMAGED)
127	21-5-43	NORTHMOOR	4392	BRIT.	28°40'S–32°45'E	" (GERMAN)
128	21-5-43	SICILIA	1633	SWED.	34°45'S–35°20'E	"
129	29-5-43	STORAAS	7886	NOR.	34°52'S–19°33'E	"
130	29-5-43	AGWIMONTE	6679	AMER.	34°52'S–19°33'E	"
131	29-5-43	HOPETARN	5231	BRIT.	31°10'S–39°20'E	"
132	1-6-43	SALABANGKA	6586	DUTCH	31°02'S–30°30'E	"
133	5-6-43	DUMRA	2304	BRIT.	28°10'S–33°25'E	"
134	6-6-43	WILLIAM KING	7176	AMER.	30°30'S–34°15'E	"
135	7-6-43	HARRIER	193	BRIT.	25°50'S–33°20'E	"
136	27-6-43	SEBASTIAN CERMENO	7194	AMER.	27°00'S–50°00'E	"
137	4-7-43	MICHAEL LIVANOS	4774	GREEK	40°55'S–36°50'E	"
138	4-7-43	BREIVIKEN	2669	NOR.	21°54'S–37°30'E	"
139	6-7-43	JASPER PARK	7129	BRIT.	32°40'S–42°18'E	"
140	6-7-43	HYDRAIOS	4476	GREEK	24°44'S–35°20'E	"
141	7-7-43	LEANA	4743	BRIT.	24°55'S–35°20'E	"
142	10-7-43	ALICE F. PALMER	7176	AMER.	26°22'S–43°53'E	"
143	11-7-43	MARY LIVANOS	4771	GREEK	15°36'S–40°50'E	"
144	14-7-43	ROBERT BACON	7191	AMER.	15°48'S–41°10'E	"
145	23-7-43	CITY OF CANTON	6692	BRIT.	13°40'S–41°40'E	"
146	23-7-43	PEGASUS	9583	SWED.	28°05'S–37°40'E	"
147	30-7-43	WILLIAM ELLERY	7181	AMER.	32°S–36°E(Approx)	" (DAMAGED)
148	1-8-43	MANGKALIHAT	8457	DUTCH	25°06'S–34°25'E	"
149	2-8-43	CITY OF ORAN	7323	BRIT.	13°31'S–41°12'E	"
150	5-8-43	EFTHALIA MARI	4195	GREEK	24°58'S–48°35'E	"
151	17-8-43	EMPIRE STANLEY	6921	BRIT.	27°12'S–47°25'E	"
152	23-10-43	FANEROMENI	3404	GREEK	16°21'S–40°04'E	" (JAPAN)
153	1-4-44	DAHOMIAN	5277	BRIT.	34°25'S–18°19'E	" (GERMAN)
154	16-4-44	COLUMBINE	3268	"	32°44'S–17°22'E	"
155	18-6-44	DIRECTOR	5107	"	24°30'S–35°44'E	"
156	13-8-44	RADBURY	3614	"	24°25'S–35°48'E	"
157	16-8-44	EMPIRE LANCER	7037	"	15°S–45°E(Approx)	"
158	18-8-44	NAIRUNG	5414	"	15°3–42°E (est.)	"
159	19-8-44	WAYFARER	5068	"	14°30'S–42°20'E	"
160	20-8-44	BERWICKSHIRE	7464	"	30°58'S–38°50'E	"
161	20-8-44	DARONIA	8139	"	31°10'S–38°00'E	" (DAMAGED)
162	23-8-44	POINT PLEASANT PARK	7136	"	29°42'S–09°58'E	"
163	15-7-42	GLOUCESTER CASTLE	8006	"	09°22'S–01°38'E	RAIDER
164	16-7-42	WILLIAM F. HUMPHREY	7982	AMER.	08°00'S–01°00'E	"

133 Merchant ships lost by Submarine, 6 damaged by Submarine = 139 ⎫
20   "   "   "   Raider,   0   "   Raider = 20 ⎬ 163
2   "   "   "   Mine,   2   "   Mine   = 4 ⎭
(1 Warship lost by Submarine & 1 Warship damaged by Mine)

P. Alton

LIST OF SHIPS (INCLUDING WARSHIPS) ON MAP SUNK, CAPTURED, OR DAMAGED, OUTSIDE THE 1000 MILE LIMIT.

No.	DATE	NAME & TONNAGE		COUNTRY	LAT. & LONG.	HOW SUNK
165	5-10-39	NEWTON BEECH	4651	BRIT.	09°35'S–06°30'W	RAIDER (GERMAN)
166	10-10-39	HUNTSMAN	8916	"	08°30'S–05°15'W	"
167	12-9-40	BENAVON	5872	"	25°20'S–52°17'E	"
168	16-9-40	KOSMOS	17801	NOR.	11°S–01°W(Approx)	"
169	20-2-41	BRITISH ADVOCATE	6994	BRIT.	03°48'S–41°E	"
170	20-2-41	GRIGORIOS C.II	2546	GREEK	07°00'S–47°40'E	"
171	21-2-41	CANADIAN CRUISER	7178	BRIT.	06°36'S–47°18'E	"
172	22-2-41	RANTAU PANDJANG	2542	DUTCH	08°24'S–51°35'E	"
173	17-4-41	ZAMZAM	8299	EGYPT	23°S–08°08'W	"
174	13-1-42	SAGADAHOC	8175	AMER.	21°50'S–07°50'W	SUBMARINE
175	30-3-42	WELLPARK	4649	BRIT.	25°S–13°W (Est)	RAIDER
176	10-4-42	KIRKPOOL	4842	"	27°17'S–49°00'W	"
177	5-5-42	H.M.S. AURICULA		"	12°17'S–49°00'E	MINE (FRENCH)
178	26-5-42	KATTEGAT	4245	NOR.	28°07'S–12°27'W	RAIDER (GERMAN)
179	30-5-42	H.M.S. RAMILLIES		BRIT.	DIEGO SUAREZ	SUBMARINE (JAP) (DAMAGED)
180	30-5-42	BRITISH LOYALTY	6993	"	"	"
181	8-6-42	CHRISTOS MARKETTOS	5209	GREEK	05°05'S–40°53'E	SUBMARINE (JAP.)
182	11-6-42	LYLEPARK	5186	BRIT.	12°04'S–09°47'W	RAIDER (GERMAN)
183	17-7-42	ARAMIS	7984	NOR.	05°S–06°W(Approx)	"
184	12-9-42	LACONIA	19675	BRIT.	05°10'S–11°25'W	SUBMARINE (GER)
185	14-9-42	BREEDIJK	6861	DUTCH	05°05'S–08°54'W	"
186	10-10-42	DUCHESS OF ATHOL	20119	BRIT.	07°03'S–11°12'W	"
187	6-11-42	CITY OF CAIRO	8034	"	23°30'S–05°40'W	"
188	29-3-43	SAWOKLA	5882	AMER.	28°52'S–52°51'E	RAIDER (GERMAN)
189	11-12-42	EUGENIE LIVANOS	4816	GREEK	27°21'S–53°30'E	"
190	2-1-43	EMPIRE MARCH	7040	BRIT.	22°35'S–08°30'W	"
191	8-9-42	ROGER B. TANEY	7191	AMER.	22°05'S–08°05'W	SUBMARINE
192	20-5-43	BEAKAT	4763	DUTCH	06°05'S–12°56'W	"
193	2-7-43	HOIHOW	2798	BRIT.	19°30'S–56°00E	"
194	15-7-43	EMPIRE LAKE	2852	"	20°56'S–51°47'E	"
195	16-7-43	FORT FRANKLIN	7135	"	22°50'S–57°30'E	"
196	29-7-43	CORNISH CITY	4952	"	27°40'S–52°15'E	"
197	4-8-43	DALFRAM	4558	"	20°55'S–56°40E	"
198	7-8-43	UMVUMA	4419	"	19°55'S–57°20E	"
199	12-8-43	CLAN MACARTHUR	10528	"	23°00'S–53°11'E	"
200	25-7-44	ROBIN GOODFELLOW	6885	AMER.	20°03'S–14°21'W	"
201	5-8-44	EMPIRE CITY	7295	BRIT.	11°33'S–41°12'E	"
202	7-8-44	EMPIRE DAY	7242	"	05°05'S–42°08'E	"

Dedicated to all those who served at sea in the Second World War and to their loved ones who endured the agony of separation and uncertainty

Recruits literally 'learning the ropes' while being taught to splice wire at the RNVR base àt the Castle, Cape Town.

Contents

Foreword

I am greatly honoured to have been invited to contribute these few introductory lines.

My association with the author dates back some fifty-eight years when we served together as cadets in the training ship *General Botha,* and subsequently when we were shipmates in ships of the South African Navy.

I can think of no one better equipped to compile this book; he is a professional sailor with wide experience in peace and war and who in latter years has become a prolific and successful writer.

Although many books have been written about the war at sea they have generally been official histories, or of a biographical nature.

The author has departed from this format in preparing a book in which some of the men who took part tell their stories in their own words.

These men came from all walks of life, yet so well did they adapt to their new and strange environment that their services were in great demand by experienced Royal Navy officers who wanted the best.

Since few lower-deck ratings ever managed to get their experiences into print, this book which is largely anecdotal, has broken new ground.

In the past very little has been written about South Africa's wartime naval force and these pages fill a long overdue need.

During the 1939 – 45 war South African naval forces reached a peak of 504 officers and 4 696 ratings. A further 786 officers and 2 151 ratings were seconded to the Royal Navy.

It is on these latter that the book mainly concentrates, for their story has never been recorded in any significant detail.

These men served in all theatres of war and in many and varied ships. At least two of their number qualified for the maximum number of campaign stars and medals it was possible to receive. A South African naval officer was the only member of the country's armed forces privileged to be present at the signing of the Japanese surrender on board USS *Missouri* in Tokyo Bay on 2 September 1945.

Their overall record was second to none.

This book tells some of their achievements and I have no hesitation in recommending it to those interested in South Africa's great contribution to the war.

HH Biermann, SSA, SD, OBE
Admiral SAN (Retd)
Former Chief of the Defence Force

Acknowledgements

The author would like to express his sincere appreciation and gratitude to all those who helped to facilitate his task by contributing so generously towards the compilation of this work.

Regrettably there are reasons why certain material cannot be acknowledged individually, but wherever possible it has been listed below.

For the others their experiences recorded in the following pages speak for them. To those who inadvertently or through circumstances beyond the author's control have not been recognised, he tenders his apologies.

The latter include former honorary editors of school magazines, MOTH newsletters and other magazines and periodicals now long out of print. In that category we may include wartime letters written to parents or loved ones, the recipients of which at this remove cannot be traced.

Many of these letters, treasured through the years, have come to hand. They reveal the euphoric feelings of youth written immediately after battle. Their natural exuberance is marred only by the scissors and rubber stamp of strict wartime censorship.

Personal interviews within a limited range were conducted whenever and wherever circumstances permitted. But alas, the passage of time has taken its toll on the many who fought so valiantly to preserve decency and freedom and who have lost the last great fight.

The author acknowledges with deep gratitude the help and co-operation given throughout by Commander WM Bisset, Senior Staff Officer SA Naval Museums, and custodian of much naval material of historical interest.

For many years Commander Bisset has been accumulating a vast amount of information on South Africans who were seconded to the Royal Navy and its auxiliary services. These findings, including photographic material, he generously placed without reservation in the hands of the author, and constantly kept him up to date him as further material came to hand.

With the utmost courtesy and patience at all times he has sought out information, checked detail, taken part in copious correspondence and shared his efforts with no thought other than to place it all on permanent record.

Much of the information so obtained has had to be presented either in abridged form or, in some cases, regrettably discarded altogether. Nevertheless, the author trusts that his benefactor, and the reader, will approve of the final presentation.

I must also thank my wife who through the years grew to accept her husband's ship as her greatest rival, only to find a new contender in the form of a word-processor! I am much obliged to her for long months of patience and understanding.

While every effort has been made to obtain copyright clearance, that has not always been possible and the author trusts that any inadvertent infringement will be viewed tolerantly by those concerned.

WS Adams, HSJ Adlam, JN Barfield DSC, M Bartholemew, Adm HH Biermann SSA SD OBE, Cmdr EL Bingham VRD, P Brooke, (Mrs) S Bryant, (Mrs) I Burnwood, Col JA Combrinck (Senior Staff Officer, Documentation Service, SADF), (Mrs) D Cullis, Director SA Library Cape Town, Director SA National Museum of Military History, PH de C de Kock, Cmdre RP Dryden-Dymond SM ED, JG Duffell-Canham, A Duffell-Canham, FE Evans, (Mrs) P Fraser, H Fourie, Cmdre J C Goosen SM, Capt GF Gower SM, Cmdr HR Gordon-Cumming OBE, D Green, (Mrs) E Grogan, (Mrs) E Hamilton, Cmdre WD Hogg SM, Dr AL Jackson, P James, V/Adm J Johnson SSA SM DSC KStJ, Cmdre EW Jupp SM, Cmdre DK Kinkead-Weekes SM, IL Knock, DE Lagerwell, CH Loots, AH Maccoy DSC, RM Maud, GG Middleton, W/O1 R Miller (SA Naval Printing Press), Dr FK Mitchell JCD, AT Morain, SJ Munton, W Nielson, (Mrs) E Payne, E Pretorius, LB Ribbink DSC, MJ Schoeman, W/O1 R Slater (Personnel Info Bureau, SADF), DH Smulian, EL Shaw, (Mrs) AW Solomon, DJL Smit DSM, DR Stephens DSC, R Stuart, C Stuckley, G Upton, (Mrs) AE van der Vyver, HH McWilliams, DD Will, RD Williams, Lt-Cmdr AH Winship JCD DSC, HC Woodhouse and George Young.

I would also like to express my gratitude to Mrs Naomi Musiker for compiling the index to this book, and to Dr Richard Wood for supplying maps.

Please note: The cryptic SANMMH accompanying certain illustrations indicates the South African National Museum of Military History.

Author's Preface

There was a huge explosion underneath Gribb *and it seemed as if some giant was lifting her up out of the sea. A mighty column of water arose from both sides, and although it must have been happening quickly it seemed to the Bosun, Charlie the Gunner on the stern decking, and to those on the boat deck, as though they were viewing it in slow motion as the water, blackened by the explosive debris, went climbing higher and higher above the ship, blotting out everything for'ard of the funnel from view. As hands reached out for Mae Wests hanging nearby, Charley exclaimed,'Christ! The whole for'ard end's been blown off'. All those aft thought so too, but they held their positions watching the tower of water begin cascading downward and,because of the vessel's momentum, it was now pouring down on them also. Through it all the gunner could see the bridge structure begin reappearing and then slowly as he picked himself up, the coxswain's head and shoulders appeared as he got back on to the steering platform.*

The *Gribb* mentioned in this extract from the personal memoirs of John Duffell-Canham was in peacetime a modest vessel of 280 tons. She was built in 1930, owned by Thor, Dahl & Co, and designed for the now generally execrated hunting of whales. Requisitioned by the Seaward Defence Force (SDF) in May 1941, she entered into service the following month, was converted into an LL (magnetic mine) sweeper at Beirut in April 1942, and was finally laid up in 1945 to be sold back into commercial service the next year.

The story of how this little ship came to be in such a desperate situation, and those of her sisters both large and small and of the men who manned them, will be told in part in the pages that follow.

It must be appreciated that the whole story of the vast theatre of a worldwide conflict can never be adequately recorded within the limitations of a single volume. Moreover, the last great war ended nearly half a century ago. Assuming enlistment age to have been seventeen, simple arithmetic proves that even if he joined at the very end of hostilities, no one under the age of sixty-three now (1990) would have been old enough to serve. It also means of course that many naval veterans have 'gone over the side'. It follows, therefore, that many a stirring yarn has died with them.

Fortunately for those of us who remain, many of our former comrades-in-arms and shipmates left records of their adventures and experiences either in the form of diaries (strictly *verboten* in time of war but practised nonetheless), letters home preserved by relatives or published in school magazines and other journals. Some have even written books for their personal satisfaction or for family interest that have never seen the light of day. Despite the passage of time, books written by professional authors about the 1939 – 45 war are still as abundant as if those momentous years were a recent event and not vanishing into the mists of history.

The author has made use of all the sources mentioned and whenever possible he has personally interviewed those who served at sea. For many of these men, especially those recruited from civilian life, the war years proved to be the most exciting time in their entire lives and were therefore vividly remembered.

Since he is descended from two of the greatest seafaring nations in the world, the British and the Dutch, it is not surprising that the average South African should have responded to the stirring call of the sea and felt the bite of the sea bug. His immediate forefathers looked to the hinterland for their living rather than to the sea, but their love of the sea was only dormant. Many years were to pass before South Africa acquired a navy and a merchant fleet offering opportunities to youngsters keen to embark on seafaring as a career.

Such an opportunity presented itself with the outbreak of war.

The new sailors came from all walks of life. It is doubtful whether many of those young men joined up with high moral intent or with a burning desire to defeat Hitler and his Nazis. They left their desks and their farms to take part in what promised to be a great adventure. And of course because the call to arms was 'a strong one that could not be denied'.

At this stage it is appropriate to describe the main sources of manpower that formed the nucleus of the wartime navy.

The various Royal Naval Volunteer Reserve (South African Division) – RNVR – bases had long been the training ground for so-called 'weekend sailors', young men who spent a couple of nights each week undergoing basic naval training that was put into practice during an annual cruise of a fortnight in vessels of the South Atlantic Squadron of the Royal Navy based in Simon's Town or, before that, in the short-lived South African Naval Service. Many RNVR personnel had also gained previous experience in such bodies as the Sea Cadet Corps or the Sea Scouts.

Another source of manpower was the training ship *General Botha* gently rolling on her fixed moorings in Simon's Bay. This old cruiser, built in 1886, had been bought in 1921 by a Mr TBF Davis, a wealthy Durban businessman, and presented to the country to train young men for entry into the Mercantile Marine, now known as the Merchant Navy.

Cadets in the *General Botha* received officer training, and their record is second to none. For example: in 1937 the Royal Air Force let it be known that they had vacancies for five commissioned officers.

Thousands of applications were received. These were whittled down to two hundred and of the five selected, four were former cadets from the *General Botha*. Another former cadet who joined the RAF, John Nettleton, won the Victoria Cross.

In 1942 the Captain-Superintendent of the *General Botha* stated that of the more than one thousand cadets who had passed through the ship, eight hundred were on active service and twenty-six had been killed. The final number on the Roll of Honour when hostilities ended was eighty-three. Former cadets had also gained sixty-two decorations awarded for valour or meritorious service. It was a proud record.

The *General Botha* was thus a rich source of trained men of officer timber, and as cadets left the ship so they were appointed to almost every branch of wartime marine activity.

The Royal Naval Reserve (RNR) must not be confused with the RNVR. The RNR consisted of professional seamen, mostly Merchant Navy officers and men who had elected to join the reserve and do spells of duty with the Fleet. As professional seamen, of course they had the advantage over the men of the RNVR.

Then came the Merchant Navy itself in which South Africans, many of them former training ship cadets, were well represented. Since these men were employed by various shipping companies it has been difficult to gain comprehensive information about their personal careers in wartime, but in general the Merchant Navy war record is a tale of sheer guts and glory.

When the war ended British Merchant Navy casualties totalled 43 582 of whom 32 279 had been killed, 4 215 injured and 4 088 taken prisoners of war. These losses were proportionately higher than in any of the other services on land, at sea, or in the air.

By comparison the German U-boat arm, which was responsible for most sinkings of merchant ships, lost a total of 781 submarines as a result of direct anti-U-boat action. Over thirty thousand German submariners lost their lives.

The overall number of South Africans serving at sea in the 1939 – 45 war is not known with any accuracy but it was several thousands.

They served in almost every theatre of war: In the Battle of the Atlantic, the grim convoys to Russia, the Mediterranean, the vastness of the South Atlantic and the Indian oceans, and in the fever-ridden 'chaungs' of Burma. In their ships, ranging from the greatest of battleships to small motor launches, and in the Fleet Air Arm, they fought the Germans, Italians and Japanese. Two of them, Lieutenant WH Olds and Leading Seaman Bruce Graham, qualified for the maximum number of campaign stars and medals that it was possible for a South African serviceman to get. These young men, many of them mere boys, were never found wanting.

This is not a history of the war, which has been covered in innumerable volumes. It is a collection of personal anecdotes and recollections of a few of those who took part. The author has found it difficult to plan a satisfactory sequence of chapters. Ships constantly moved from one hemisphere to another and from one ocean to another. A story that began in the Mediterranean might continue into the Arctic and end in the Far East. The reader is therefore requested to treat with indulgence any apparent lack of coherence in what follows.

Captain CJ Harris

HMSAS *Immortelle* and *Sonneblom* in company. Both were paid-off and returned to the Royal Navy in March 1934.

1

The Birth and Death of a Navy

Standing in a post-office queue recently a friend of the author's was accosted by an elderly gentleman who pointed at the RNVR blazer sported by the former and said that it was a long time since he had seen that badge. 'Do you remember,' he asked, 'how we waited and waited to be drafted in 1914?' Since my friend had not even been born at the time he did not feel greatly flattered!

Apart from a brief history of the RNVR in the 1914 – 18 war there is little information on South Africans serving at sea before then. The first volunteer naval unit to be established and to flourish in this country had its origin in Durban. The year was 1885 and the unit, known as the Natal Naval Volunteers (NNV), was intended for the defence of Port Natal during a period of tension between Great Britain and Russia as a result of the Afghan War. It was feared that a Russian man-o'-war might hold Durban to ransom!

Subsequent members of the NNV joined the naval brigade during the Boer War and saw action in several engagements. One of its officers, Lieutenant Chiazzari, was awarded the DSO for his achievements during the crossing of the Tugela. He also made history by being the first non-regular officer to receive that decoration.

During the Zulu rebellion of 1906 the NNV were once again called into action. Naval in name and uniform only, they lacked ships of their own; but in the course of time they acquired some small boats, and from 1903 underwent periodic training in visiting ships of the Royal Navy.

In that year (1903) Great Britain passed an Act of Parliament that was to have far-reaching effects on South Africa. The Bill was to establish a Royal Naval Volunteer Reserve (RNVR), and a Cape Colonial Division of the RNVR was established on 1 February 1905.

The new unit had a difficult course to steer, especially when in 1908 financial difficulties caused the Colonial Government to order its disbandment. However, public protest was so vehement that alternative financing was found, and on 1 August 1908 a Naval Volunteers Act was passed by the Cape Parliament placing the unit on a permanent footing.

A similar Act was passed by the Natal Legislative, and the British Government accordingly sanctioned both acts, thereby creating both Cape and Natal Colonial Divisions of the RNVR.

With the creation of the Union of South Africa on 31 May 1910, both Colonial Acts fell into abeyance and the two divisions reverted to their original standing – and so remained until July 1913.

Meanwhile the South African Defence Act was passed in 1912. This provided for a body of naval volunteers to form part of the RNVR and to be known as the South African Division of the RNVR. Although the Union Government was responsible for the divisions, training would be carried out by the Admiralty through the Royal Naval Commander-in-Chief at Simon's Town.

Accordingly, two companies were formed at Cape Town known as 'A' and 'B'; and a 'C' company was formed in Durban. Seniority of officers was effective from 1 July 1913. A permanent staff of one retired Royal Navy officer and one rating was then appointed for administrative and instructional duties. The authorised establishment was 303 with nine officers and a further five officers and one rating as Divisional Staff.

Training then began in earnest with 6-inch and 12-pounder guns provided by the Admiralty. Boathouses were erected at Cato Creek in Durban (still there as SAS *Inkonkoni*) and at Cape Town on Woodstock beach. Each volunteer was expected to attend a minimum number of parades a year, but so keen were the members that the figure was invariably exceeded.

HMSAS *Protea* (ex HMS *Crozier*) 500 tons, 2 200 hp, 16 knots; coal-burner. Original CO Commander DE St M Delius OBE RN. Became pleasure craft on paying off and subsequently Spanish War blockade runner. Ultimate fate unknown. (SA Navy Hydrographic Office)

With the outbreak of the First World War in 1914, all three companies were mobilised and reported a strength of twelve officers and 267 men. The Cape Town detachment was ordered to Simon's Town, where forty-three of their number were drafted to the cruiser HMS *Hyacinth*. HMS *Astraea* joined forces with a contingent of 'C' company on board. Those men were the first body of South Africans to serve afloat on board warships on active service.

They saw service on convoy duty, blockaded the Tanganyikan coast and took part in the search for the elusive German cruiser *Königsberg*. They also manned port defences in the Union and were employed in naval dockyards. Some were drafted to the 10th Heavy Battery in East Africa, while others supervised the landing of troops in German South West Africa.

SAR & H tug *Ludwig Wiener*. Became HMS *Afrikander* during the South West Africa campaign in World War I.

It is recorded that since there was no other means of communication, the RNVR signalmen proved their worth in passing messages between shore parties and the ships lying offshore in the naval roadsteads.

At the end of the South West African campaign the Union Government ordered partial demobilisation of the RNVR and those serving afloat were recalled and discharged in August 1915. A short while later, however, approval was obtained for volunteers to serve

3

with the Royal Navy. From October 1915 to September 1917 a total of five officers and 159 men volunteered for service overseas. They earned a good name for themselves and several were commissioned. One officer, Lieutenant Penny, actually rose to command a gunboat on the River Tigris. The eighty-five South African RNVRs who were present at Scapa Flow on 21 November 1918 when the Grand Fleet of the German High Seas Fleet steamed in to surrender were fortunate.

It is a little known fact that the war of 1914 – 18 also introduced the first South African quasi-warship. She was the (then) SAR & H harbour tug *Ludwig Wiener,* a 658 ton vessel with a horsepower of 2 400, which made her the most powerful and the best-equipped tug in the world at that time. At her maximum speed of twelve knots she consumed thirty tons of coal a day.

The Admiralty took her over and used her for patrolling local and German South West African waters during that successful campaign.

She was given a couple of small guns and flew the White Ensign of the Royal Navy. But, since her name was scarcely acceptable in a time of war with Germany, their Lordships of the Admiralty decreed that she should be renamed HMS *Afrikander.* Her career as a warship was short-lived but she performed good service.

After the war the last man was discharged from active service in 1919. During the Kaiser's war twenty-four officers (twelve having been promoted during the war) and 388 men saw service in various theatres. There were eight casualties, only three of which were the direct result of enemy action. One officer, the late Commander LR Heydenrych VRD

HMSAS *Protea* passing through Knysna Heads outward bound.

RNVR, served in Arctic waters and with the White Russian land forces in Southern Russia, and was awarded the Russian Orders of St Anne and St Stanislav (with swords).

As a reward for its services in time of war, the RNVR (South African Division) was allowed to expand. Two more bases were established: 'D' company at Port Elizabeth (there had been a short-lived volunteer unit as early as 1861) and 'E' company at East London, both in 1921.

Ship's Company HMSAS *Protea*. (Probably taken in 1920s.) (SANMMH)

In the Hitler war U-boats wrought havoc along the South African seaboard; but in the 1914 war German submarines had not ventured so far south, although surface raiders had laid mines off the coast which probably induced the Union Government to decide that they should not rely solely on the protection of the Royal Navy. That led to the establishment on 15 November 1921, of the South African Naval Service.

The British Admiralty accordingly allocated three vessels to form the nucleus of this new force. These were the sloop HMSAS *Protea* (ex HMS *Crozier*), Cmdr DE St M Delius OBE RN, fitted out as a hydrographic survey vessel, and the minesweeping trawlers HMSAS *Sonneblom* (ex HMS *Eden*), Lt-Cmdr AE Buckland DSO DSC RN, and HMSAS *Immortelle* (ex HMS *Foyle*), Lt-Cmdr LE Scott-Napier DSO RN. Except for a few key ratings of the Royal Navy the ships were now manned by South African crews.

This new service was placed under the command of a retired officer of the Royal Navy, Cmdr NH Rankin, who was also Instructor Commander to the RNVR. For the next ten years the minesweepers were employed as training ships for the RNVR while *Protea* carried out extensive surveys of coastal waters.

The then Secretary for Finance, while declining to grant £100 for a special commissioning ceremony, agreed to the sum of £20 for re-painting of the ships' names! Then came the great depression of 1929 – 1934, which caused the Union Government to order *Protea* to be sold and the two minesweeping trawlers to be laid up.

The establishment of the SANS at that time numbered 164. Of those, two officers and three ratings from *Protea* were retained for survey duties using the fishery research vessel *Africana* for six months of

Lt-Cmdr LE Scott-Napier DSO RN – later to become wartime Deputy Director, SDF. (SANMMH)

Commander DE St M Delius OBE RN, Commanding Officer of HMSAS *Protea*. (W Nielson)

the year. Another officer, a petty officer and five ratings continued full-time training and administering the affairs of the RNVR(SA).

The minesweepers were paid off at the end of March 1934 and returned to the Royal Navy to make their way back to Britain. The short-lived South African Naval Service, which had begun in a modest way, yet with such high hopes of future development, had now virtually ceased to exist.

One of the officers of the *Protea* who remained in service was Lt-Cmdr James Dalgleish. The part that he was to play in the naval affairs of this country was outstanding, as will be seen as the story unfolds.

The three SANS personnel retained to carry out hydrographic survey duties when Service disbanded. This early pic shows Lieutenant FJ Dean (later Commodore), Leading Seaman JCM Germishuys (later Commander) and Lieutenant-Commander (later Commodore) James Dalgleish setting up a theodolite station. (SANMMH)

CHAPTER

2

The Navy Ressurected

Thus, when the clouds of war gathered in 1939, the South African naval forces consisted of only two officers, three ratings and a flourishing RNVR. In 1939 the government had sent a scratch crew of permanent force personnel to Britain to man a monitor, HMS *Erebus,* intended to strengthen the coast defences, which were considered inadequate for the new Table Bay harbour. But the expedition ended in something of a fiasco. In the event, the ship was retained by the Admiralty and the South African contingent was sent home to face much disciplinary action.

On the outbreak of war the RNVR and its war reserve were immediately mobilised. The Union Government agreed to their being directed by the Royal Navy on a voluntary entry basis for local defence, and at the same time agreed to a limited number embarking for service overseas. Fortunately there were enough volunteers for the immediate needs of the Admiralty.

Local trawlers and whale-catchers were requisitioned to be converted into auxiliary warships by various engineering firms, the chief of these being the (then) SAR & H workshops.

The trawlers *Disa, Richard Bennett* and *Bluff* were in commission and flying the White Ensign of the Royal Navy with the South African flag

Whale-catchers and trawlers being taken in hand and converted into minesweepers and anti-submarine vessels (left) and the finished product, HMSAS *Brakpan* (right). (SANMMH)

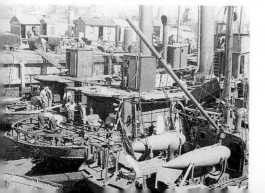

Rear-Admiral GW Hallifax CMG RN (Retd). First Director of Seaward Defence Force (SDF). (SANMMH)

at the fore by 15 September, and were already busy sweeping the approaches to Table Bay. By the end of the year a further dozen had been completed and were in service.

Meanwhile the Union Government had decided to create its own naval force for the duration of the war. General Smuts offered a retired officer of the Royal Navy, Rear-Admiral GW Hallifax, CMG RN (Retd), the post of Deputy Director of Coast Defence and OC SA Naval Service, which he accepted.

Himself the son of a Rear-Admiral, GW Hallifax was a good choice for the new post. He had had a distinguished naval career as Naval Adviser in Turkey before the First World War, for which service he had been awarded the Order of the Medjideh (3rd Class) in 1914. Throughout the 1914 – 18 war he served in HMS *Ajax* and was present at the Battle of Jutland. A further honour came in 1919 when he was made a Commander of the Order of St Maurice and St Lazarus (Italy) in 1918. In 1919 he was sent to South Africa to carry out an inspection of wireless stations.

He commanded HMS *Carlisle* on the China Station (1926 – 28) and was Naval Attaché in Paris (1928 – 31); and he commanded the battleship HMS *Malaya* (1932 – 34) before being appointed Director of the Signal Division of the Admiralty in 1934, a position he held until his retirement in 1935.

In 1936 Admiral Hallifax was appointed Secretary to the Governor General of the Union of South Africa, the Earl of Clarendon, and held that post until 1937 when he settled in Cape Town. In September 1939, on accepting General Smuts' offer, certain legal problems arose concerning the transfer of the RNVR (SA) to his command.

These necessitated the establishment of a new active citizen force unit, the Seaward Defence Force (SDF), of which he became Director. Thus it came about that early in 1940 the newly formed SDF took over mine-sweeping and anti-submarine patrols, the port war signal stations and the examination service (inspecting the bona fides of visiting ships) at all the Union's ports.

HMS *Erebus* was to have been manned by South Africans but the project was abandoned. (SANMMH)

In other words the SDF, now a unit of the Union Defence Force, would be responsible for all local naval commitments. This innovation was viewed with a jaundiced eye by the Royal Navy Commodore-in-Charge at the Cape who suspected that it would interfere with the plans he already had in mind. His suspicions might easily be appreciated, but he could not have foreseen the enormous expansion that was to follow and that proved to be far more effective than if those tasks had been confined solely to the RNVR.

For the manning of this new force it was found necessary to recruit from the RNVR, who were given the option of transferring to the SDF permanently, or on temporary loan. The response was poor. The RNVR was associated with the Royal Navy and the fact that the SDF came under the Army was not an attraction. Besides which, the name of Seaward Defence Force was unfortunate; it was usually referred to as the Seaweed Defence Force.

Admiral Hallifax had therefore to rely on the small remaining SANS team of two officers and three ratings, and on such of the former *Erebus* crew as were deemed suitable, and some of the RNVR who had opted for the SDF, the SANS War Reserve, and a few retired Royal Navy officers. But most of the officer cadre was composed of other suitably qualified men with seafaring experience. That was where the recruits of the *General Botha* proved valuable.

On 15 December 1939 approval was obtained for an establishment of 526, this figure being the men needed for thirteen minesweepers

The author's ship at the time of joining the SDF. It was later sunk leaving only two survivors. (Author)

(M/S) and five anti-submarine (A/S) vessels. That allowed for no reserves in the event of illness, leave and so on. The Military Discipline Code also proved to be unsuitable for application to matters maritime and radical amendments had to be made, applicable to the SDF only.

The larger and faster vessels were fitted out in Simon's Town with ASDIC (Asdic) equipment, and their crews were trained by an anti-submarine specialist officer and his team on loan from the Royal Navy. The first two A/S trawlers, *Mooivlei* and *Blomvlei* were ready for service in April 1940.

From the earliest days after the declaration of war, local mine-sweepers had been clearing channels in the approaches to the harbours and carrying out anti-submarine surface patrols. The largely amateur crews of these vessels were keen but their task was undoubtedly boring.

But then, without warning, things began to happen; and the balloon went up. On 13 and 14 May 1940, two explosions were seen and heard about 5 – 10 nautical miles (nm) from Cape Agulhas lighthouse. Since the area had been mined by German surface raiders in the First World War the event was not entirely unexpected. Shipping round that busy promontory was diverted by the Royal Navy while the Director SDF ordered four of the six minesweepers then in Cape Town to the scene with all despatch. The senior officer of this clearance flotilla was Lt-Cmdr FJ Dean, one of the two SANS officers retained in service.

The flotilla arrived in position early on 15 May. That evening another explosion occurred some distance from the ships, and on the

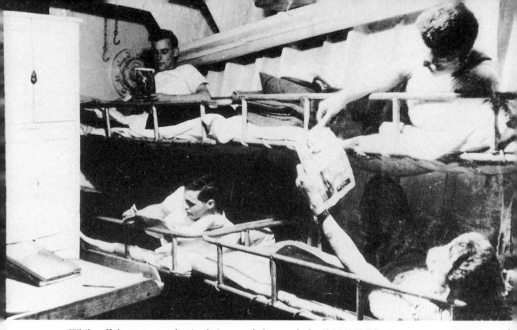

While off-duty, crew relax in their crowded mess deck. (SANMMH)

following morning a mine exploded in HMSAS *Aristea*'s sweep, and yet another was sighted soon afterwards. For his leadership in this and other operations, Dean was awarded the OBE.

Up to 7 June eleven mines had been accounted for: eight swept at sea and three seen to explode. Although only four more were subsequently swept, the operation continued, for the sea route was important and nothing could be left to chance.

Down below the 'Black Squad' at engine control station. (SANMMH)

Commodore FJ Dean who, as a Lt-Cmdr, commanded the mine clearance flotilla in sweeping the Agulhas Bank. Awarded the OBE. (SANMMH)

Much later Royal Navy Intelligence revealed that ninety-two mines had been laid by the German raider *Atlantis* on 9 May 1940. Sweeping continued until March 1941, backed up by occasional searches when the mine clearance flotilla was not needed elsewhere.

The Cape Agulhas area is notorious for its boisterous and often dangerous weather. Sweeping was frequently interrupted by gales with accompanying high seas and heavy swells. It was a testing time for both men and ships. Seasickness, especially among stokers in the coal-fired ships, was a problem causing loss of steam and difficulty in maintaining station which was so important when sweeping in a group.

Nevertheless morale remained high and it might be said that the SDF won its spurs on the Agulhas Bank. The success of this operation had a marked effect on its members and recruiting picked up.

Examination vessel *Buffalo* alongside a merchantman. (SANMMH)

The author was himself one of the early entries into the SDF and recalls some of his impressions on leaving a well-regulated passenger liner to embark on a new way of life in the fledgling SDF. It was from my younger brother, then based with the RNVR at Port Elizabeth (and destined later to win the DSC in Burma), that I was first told of the formation of the Seaward Defence Force.

At the time I was serving as a Deck Officer in a passenger liner on the United Kingdom-Cape route and I had already had a taste of war by being machine-gunned by the *Luftwaffe* in the North Sea. When I joined the SDF I must have been the only locally based member to have actually encountered the enemy in the 1939 war.

At any rate, on my arrival in Durban, I visited the naval base, only to be told that all appointments were made in Cape Town. When in due course my ship arrived there, I duly made my number at headquarters where I was interviewed by Lt-Cmdr Scott-Napier.

After discussing the need to obtain sea-time for my Merchant Navy certificates of competency, for which naval service was a doubtful qualification, I convinced the interviewer that I was prepared to let the future look after itself.

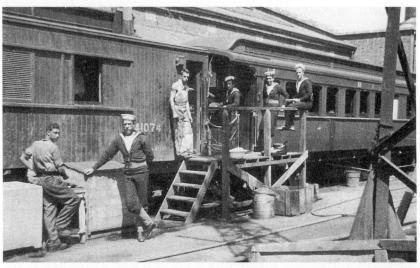

Two railway coaches provided sleeping accommodation for the new Navy. Cold and cheerless in winter. (SANMMH)

Having filled in numerous forms, I was then told there was no immediate vacancy, but that I would be kept informed. There was nothing for it then but to continue my voyage to the United Kingdom. On arrival there I was handed a cable telling me that there was a vacancy for a sub-lieutenant and that the appointment would be effective on the date of assuming duty.

That was all very well, but in those days (this was in June 1940) obtaining a passage to South Africa was not easy. However, I persuaded my company to give me a passage to the Cape as Fifth Officer at a token pay of a shilling a month. Alas we didn't get very far, for the ship was taken over by the Admiralty at Dover and scuttled as a blockship at nearby Folkestone!

The second attempt proved more successful and after experiencing many of the vicissitudes of wartime voyaging, my ship at last arrived safely in Cape Town on 9 August 1940. I reported to naval headquarters and was sent to the Castle for a medical examination.

Returning on board to sign-off, I mentioned to the captain that it had been hinted that I would soon command an anti-submarine vessel. He looked me up and down. 'Good God!' he said. Not very complimentary, but then I remembered that I was only twenty-three and it had taken him as many years to achieve command.

The next move was to go to a naval tailor to get the straight ring and diamond of the Merchant Navy replaced by the gold stripe and curl of the Navy. The so-called orange flash signifying willingness to serve outside South Africa was also added. At that time no ruling seems to have been made about where this flash was to be worn, and many and varied were individual tastes. Eventually it was worn above the curl, and on shoulder-straps at the pointed peak.

This orange (or red) flash caused some confusion among men of other navies and, since navy surgeons wore a red strip between the gold lace on their sleeves, we were assumed in New York to be members of the medical fraternity!

I now had a weekend free to collect my thoughts. Reporting for duty on Monday morning, I found that the naval base in the docks consisted of a portion of the railway workshop known as Shop 17 (now the site of the National Maritime Museum), adjacent to the Robinson dry dock. Drawn up outside this building were two second-class railway coaches providing sleeping accommodation. Cold and cheerless they were too.

I was told to report to a certain very imposing gentleman with an impressive air of authority. As a new hand I treated him with some awe. Later in the day we were visited by Commander Dalgleish, then Second-in-Command to Admiral Hallifax, who promptly told my companion that it was high time he got into uniform. When he did so I was mortified to discover that he held the same rank as myself.

Coming from the Merchant Navy, with its traditional cut and dried routines, into a service that was still finding its feet was bewildering. Apart from quasi-naval training in the *General Botha* a few years earlier, I had had no training for the fighting navy and was destined, despite twelve years' service, never to undergo even the most elementary instruction. My newly joined colleagues and I had to learn the hard way.

Officers enjoy moderate comfort in a tiny wardroom. (SANHHH)

We soon found ourselves detailed as night duty officers and responsible during the silent hours for administering a service that we knew nothing about. During the day we were each allocated a whale-catcher in the course of conversion to minesweeping, which we were supposed to supervise. Again, we knew nothing of what that entailed, but soon learned that the harbour café nearby offered a safe refuge and that, if we emerged from time to time with a purposeful air and armed with a clipboard, a sheaf of papers or some sort of instrument in hand, High Authority was none the wiser.

Those whale-catchers, by the way, were just as their crews had left them. They stank. Rotting food had been left on the tables, and they were infested with flies and fleas. My hosts at Sea Point were none too pleased when I carried such vermin home with me.

Amidst all this we found our names on a roster detailing us to go to sea on alternate days in the local sweepers engaged in keeping the approach channels clear. That meant rising before dawn, and in my case a long walk from Sea Point to the docks in the bitter cold of early morning.

We were greeted on board with a chipped enamel mug of steaming coffee liberally laced with sugar and condensed milk. Never since those days have I been able to stomach sugar with my tea or coffee.

Nor shall I ever forget that first short voyage. I felt very uneasy and attributed it to early rising and the coffee. The thought of seasickness never entered my mind for, after all, I had already been at sea for five years. It was only when the minesweeper turned at the end of the

Handling the sweep-gear. Note the constricted space. (SANMMH)

searched channel and made for home with the wind astern, making for a comfortable ride and a certain lightening of spirit, that it dawned on me that I had felt the first qualms of *mal de mer*. That knowledge produced a psychological effect that persisted on every subsequent voyage until I grew accustomed to the often violent motion of those sturdy little craft, which lacked even bilge-keels to damp down the rolling.

They were uncertain times. Uniforms for the ratings were in short supply, as indeed were the men themselves. It was not uncommon for a ship returning from patrol to lose some members of her crew transferred to another ship outward-bound. There were chronic cases of seasickness to be weeded out, and discipline was not all that it should have been. Many of the trawler crews elected to remain with their ships under the White Ensign of the Navy, and fishermen have always been a notoriously independent breed. This prompted Lt-Cmdr Scott-Napier to call the officers together for a homily on the need to enforce discipline. In making a point he alleged that discipline in the Merchant Navy was maintained through fear of unemployment.

At this distance of time I feel that perhaps he was right, but at that time I thought he was being very unfair for, like so many starry-eyed youngsters, I had gone to sea in a spirit of loyalty to the owners, the captain and the ship. And my generation was not so rebellious as those that followed.

At any rate, things gradually sorted themselves out. Some newly joined officers had been fortunate enough to undergo a few weeks' basic training at the RNVR base in Port Elizabeth, and from then on any new entry could expect to be taught the ropes.

Then followed various specialised courses, with emphasis on the all-important Asdic equipment designed to seek out submarines lurking in the depths. These courses were conducted by a very large, black-haired and beetle-browed RN lieutenant known to all as The Black Death. Lt Burton (rumoured to be a scion of the famous Burton's Fifty-Shilling Tailors) succeeded in making his classes shiver in their squeaky new shoes and was held in great awe. Not the most patient of instructors, he had been known to throw a bridge chair across the wheelhouse at an inattentive pupil.

This is only a faint outline of the early impressions formed by a newcomer to naval service. And I was indeed appointed in command, not of an anti-submarine vessel, but of a minesweeper operating from Durban, at the age of twenty-three.

In signalling that I had taken up the appointment I used the expression 'wish to advise', and stated the time as 0900 hrs. This brought a reproof from the local SANOIC, Cmdr HR Gordon Cumming RN, who pointed out that 'advise' was a commercial term and that 'inform' or 'submit' would have been preferable. Also that, in the Navy, 'hrs' following the usual four-figure notation was not used for indicating time. And that practice has been observed in the pages which follow.

Much as I would have liked to confront my former Merchant Navy captain in my new capacity, it was fated not to be for his ship had been torpedoed off Freetown, leaving only two survivors to tell the tale.

Another early entry into the SDF who is happy to relate the lighter side of his wartime service is former Lieutenant JL (Louis) Ceronie.

On leaving the training ship *General Botha* in 1936 with a very sound record, he was offered an appointment as a cadet with the Blue Funnel Line. However, with the depression barely over, his parents could ill afford the expenses of a premium, outfitting, and a voyage abroad to join his first ship, so he opted for service in a local coasting firm, and in 1939 took employment with the SAR & H in their shipping section in Johannesburg. There he was joined temporarily by the present Admiral

HH Biermann, who at the time had been serving as a deck officer in a fleet of steamers controlled by the South African Government.

One of the first to join the new Navy, Louis Ceronie, found himself at Port Elizabeth in company with Biermann and that lovable character known to all Navy men as Uncle Jack Netterberg (now a Captain DSC SAN, Retd). The three of them, all sub-lieutenants, were billeted in considerable comfort at the select St George's Club. Ceronie believes that if there had been a seniority list at that time he would have been ranked about fourth.

Shortly afterwards, they were joined by a squad of newly appointed officers drawn mostly from the Royal Cape Yacht Club, who were given a six-week course in naval procedures and minesweeping.

Ceronie's next appointment should have been as watchkeeping officer to the big whale-catcher-cum-anti submarine vessel *Southern Seas,* but in the general confusion of those early days, that was suddenly cancelled, and instead he found himself in Cape Town as First Lieutenant of the armed trawler-minesweeper *Aristea,* commanded by a flamboyant trawlerman, Skipper William J Chesterfield.

Many of the trawler skippers of the day came over with their vessels when they were requisitioned by the Navy, given the traditional rank of skipper, and in most cases later elevated to full commissioned rank.

William J Chesterfield was a large man brimming over with self-confidence and (let it be whispered), self-importance. He lost no time in regaling his 21-year-old first lieutenant with stories of his experiences in the Battle of the Dogger Bank in the First War to end all Wars. He stressed that the most important thing in any captain's life was

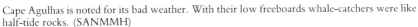
Cape Agulhas is noted for its bad weather. With their low freeboards whale-catchers were like half-tide rocks. (SANMMH)

his ship, and he was a firm supporter of the tradition that, when all else failed, a captain should go down with his ship.

Just before New Year's Day, 1941, *Aristea* was carrying out a surface patrol off Cape Town on a line between Robben Island and Blaauwberg Strand. Ceronie handed over the watch to his captain at midnight and turned in. Scarcely had he done so when there was a tremendous shuddering, and all the lights went out. Everyone streamed on deck, some very frightened (for there was a war on), only to find that their ship was hard and fast aground with even the propeller visible at low tide.

Skipper Chesterfield reached for his megaphone. 'Every man for himself!' he bawled. 'I will go down with my ship.' The first (and only) man to obey the order broke a leg landing on the hard-packed sand. Seeing that, the crew, huddled along the deck, decided that discretion was the better part of valour and stayed where they were.

It was strongly suspected at the time that the gallant captain had dozed off, but if that was ever proved at the subsequent inquiry, it was never made public and it did not affect his position in any adverse way. It was no doubt written off as one of the many wartime hazards that the new navy would have to face. At high water, the next morning, two harbour tugs pulled HMSAS *Aristea* off the sand.

After a short minesweeping refresher course, *Aristea* next found herself one of six vessels comprising the mine clearance flotilla and sailed for the Cape Agulhas area where, as has been already observed, the German raider *Atlantis* had laid a minefield.

German mines were washed ashore near Cape Agulhas in 1940. (SANMMH)

Towards the end of the third day of sweeping, and while busy retrieving the gear, those on deck were horrified to find that the sweep had fouled a mine, which was bobbing about under the stern. As one man they made for the fo'c'sle head as being the farthest point from the threat of violent destruction.

Ceronie was trampled underfoot in the rush, but he did manage to yell to the crew to get outboard of everything so that if the mine exploded they would be blown clear.

The captain observed all this, framed by the small wheelhouse window in which he appeared to have become stuck. He was a big man and it was a small window. The cook, Laity, with great presence of mind emerged from his galley with a butcher's cleaver in his hand and hacked through the sweep wire, thus releasing the fouled gear and the mine.

Aristea returned to Simon's Town to replace her sweep gear and her captain made his report on the incident. Ceronie was shown the report, and he took umbrage to the fact that, while the skipper stressed the point that he alone had remained at his station, his first lieutenant was up for'ard, 'hanging on to the jackstaff like a piece of bunting.' Summoned to attend the court of inquiry, Sub-Lieutenant Ceronie was asked why he had deserted his post while the captain had remained in control at his recognised station in the wheelhouse.

Ceronie replied that he had been concerned with the safety of the crew and the reason why the captain had stayed was that he couldn't get out! Anyway, Senior Skipper WJ Chesterfield was given the DSC for his services in assisting in the clearance of the Agulhas minefield.

His citation read: 'When in charge of his vessel during the mine clearance operations off Agulhas a mine was caught foul in the sweep and hauled up to the gallows. Lt Chesterfield handled his ship and gear with great coolness and promptitude and by his action undoubtedly saved his vessel from becoming a casualty. His conduct in the face of grave danger on this occasion was an outstanding example to his officers and men.' Petty Officer F Gassner received the DSM for the same operation together with a similar citation.

In 1942 Louis Ceronie, by this time in command of the mine-sweeper HMSAS *Florida,* took part in the rounding up of a Vichy convoy (described more fully later in these pages). Having intercepted the convoy, his ship was passing under the stern of one of the Vichy ships when there was a bright flash, an explosion and a cloud of smoke. At first it was thought they were under attack but it later turned out that an act of sabotage had taken place on board; the French crew had attempted to blow up the ship's steering gear.

Ceronie took a boarding party away to board the Vichy merchant-man *Cap Padaran* and when climbing up the side of the pilot ladder his party was bombarded with every kind of rubbish and boiling water.

When they got on deck the filth was indescribable. Pigs and fowls with all their feed and accompanying mess, and even an emaciated cow showing her ribs like an inmate of Belsen and so weak that she could not get up.

Later, on 15 October 1942, his ship came upon several rafts, the legacy of a torpedoed ship. One of these was hove alongside and found to contain biscuits, flares, lanoline and all manner of life-preserving commodities, even bottles of gin and whisky. This was too good an opportunity to let slip, and the crew accordingly spent six hours rounding up the rafts and plundering the contents. The whisky so acquired would have lasted many a month.

But meanwhile, having reported the sighting, a signal was received ordering them to bring in the rafts 'at all costs'. Reluctant to part with their loot they held an earnest discussion, the outcome of which was to restock two or three of the rafts and sink the others with the ship's Oerlikon guns.

That was duly done, and three rafts were taken in tow. On the homeward voyage it occurred to Ceronie that, although the tanks in the abandoned rafts had been punctured, the rafts themselves were constructed of wood and therefore unlikely to sink.

This was subsequently borne out when a fortnight later the press reported 'typical acts of Hun frightfulness' with pictures of the bullet-riddled rafts. Ceronie and his merry men kept a discreet silence, which has probably remained unbroken until this account of the incident.

Other events recalled by Lou Ceronie, some actually recorded in notebooks at the time and still preserved, give a good idea of day-to-day events as experienced in the local minesweeping flotillas. It was not all sheer boredom. For example, a log entry for Saturday, 16 January 1943 records:

> Sighted enemy submarine 45 degrees on starboard bow at 1100. Ship's position 34,22,24S, 18,20,48E. Slipped sweep and went in to attack. *Soetvlei* [a sister minesweeper] instructed to dispose herself 8 cables on my port quarter and await further instructions. 1225, discovered large patch of oil at 34,25,54S, 18,19,54E. Was about to drop depth charges when a large bubble was observed on port beam. Put wheel hard over with intention of ramming but lost all way and unable to drop depth charges. Missed target. Organised a search of an area 10 miles square. Took command of flotilla of six ships, *Hektor, Soetvlei, Brakvlei, Krugersdorp, Randfontein* and *Oostewal. Soetvlei* made depth charge attack on oil patch and bubbles at 1300.

Even earlier, on 24 December 1940, the following report was received from Port War Signal Station: 'Submarine sighted between Robben Island and Blaauberg. Keep vigilant look-out'. The ship went to action

Captain and crew of HMSAS *Hektor*. (SANMMH)

stations and was blacked out. In his zeal the Hotchkiss gunner fired and perforated the funnel. It is not on record, but the odds are even that the bridge crew threw themselves on their faces!

Still referring to notes kept by Lou Ceronie: Friday, 15 November 1940 saw the mine clearance flotilla hard at work on the Agulhas minefield. At 1130 HMSAS *Hektor*'s sweep cut loose a German XX mine which proved to be rusted and barnacle-encrusted. Trying to sink or explode it by rifle fire proved frustrating in the seas running at the time so the Lewis gun was brought into action. By the time the mine sank, the ship was only forty yards away. Luckily none of the horns was hit.

A few days later, at 0700 on Tuesday, 19 November, *Hektor* cut loose another mine and was ordered to destroy it by gunfire, and did so – but only after five hundred rounds had been fired by Lewis gun in atrocious weather.

In another area a few weeks later, on 20 January 1941, *Hektor* reported passing a floating mine between Dassen Island and Robben Island. Unlike the weatherbeaten mines sighted off Agulhas, this one was shiny red and obviously new. In April 1942 Ceronie's ship responded to a report made by a Greek steamer that they had sighted several waterlogged lifeboats, numerous corpses and floating wreckage, but a search over three days revealed nothing more than a mass of empty boxes.

About that time the crew had many complaints about the poor quality of their rations. The cooking also left much to be desired, and it was truly a case of 'Who called the cook a bastard?' and 'Who called the bastard a cook?' So moved were the crew that the coxswain appeared on the bridge wearing a gas-mask while carrying a plate of food! We shall meet Lou Ceronie again in a chapter on Vichy convoys; but before leaving him it is worth mentioning a most unusual part played by his ship, HMSAS *Florida*.

Unaccustomed as the mostly civilian lower-deck personnel of the new navy were to naval discipline, their frequent minor breaches of good conduct resulted in numerous cases of being confined to barracks more commonly known as CB.

Since this was a very mild punishment, its infliction did not bother the culprits in the least. This don't-give-a-damn attitude persuaded the authorities to earmark HMSAS *Florida* as a punishment ship. Accordingly, men undergoing CB were drafted to her and except for brief spells in harbour to replenish stores and bunkers she was permanently at sea.

This was an exceedingly unpopular move for her officers and key members of her crew for, despite their innocence of any misdemeanour, they had to share a routine especially designed for those who had sinned against authority. This means of retribution lasted about two months and it was practised by both Durban and Cape Town bases.

CHAPTER

3

Neutrals and Vichy Convoys

In the previous chapter mention was made of the Vichy convoys intercepted by units of the SDF. In the early days of the war, and up to 1941, consideration had to be given to the interception and subsequent handling of either neutral shipping or vessels operating from enemy-occupied territory. In particular, traffic between Vichy France and its colonies made a serious breach in Allied control of contraband. Most of such ships were rounded up by prowling Royal Naval cruisers, but on their arrival in South African ports and waters the SDF played an important part in providing steaming parties from one port to another, and in maintaining armed guards on board on arrival in port.

Among vessels so taken and subsequently requisitioned for the use of the Allies was the French *Sontay*, delivered at Durban by a cruiser on 28 January 1941, followed on 7 March by the *Ville de Strasbourg* which had been stopped at sea with a shot across her bow by the cruiser HMS *Shropshire*. *Ville de Strasbourg* had a 300-lb bomb on board to be set off if intercepted but, despite the unco-operativeness of her officers, they drew the line at blowing up their own ship. Yet another captive brought into Durban in May that year was the *Lieutenant St Loubert Bie*, taken by the armed merchant cruiser HMS *Pretoria Castle*, one of the famous Union Castle liners in unfamiliar guise.

A month later she brought the captured 10 000 ton *Desirade* into Walvis Bay, with her engines sabotaged. She was carrying 6 000 tons of cargo and 212 passengers among whom there was a French general. East London acted as host to the *D'Entrecasteaux* and the *Ville de Rouen,* brought in on 22 July and 1 August respectively. The *Jean LD* was held at Cape Town.

This wholesale seizure of valuable ships persuaded the Vichy Government to order such as they still possessed to sail in convoy. When Intelligence reported that such a convoy had sailed from Madagascar on 12 August, an operation was devised to intercept it. The cruisers HMAS *Australia* and HMS *Hawkins* were detailed for this operation as was the SAAF. Five SDF whalers also joined the expedition: the A/S vessels *Blaauwberg, Cedarberg* and *Sydostlandet* from Cape Town and the *Odberg* and minesweeper *Southern Barrier* from Durban. This operation was given the name of 'Kedgeree'.

Stationed between three hundred and five hundred miles from the coast and carrying out broad sweeps, the Cape Town whalers sighted three ships steering east on the evening of 22 August and began shadowing. In the sighting signal the words 'course east' were inexpli-

HMSAS *Blaauwberg*. Senior ship in 'Operation Kedgeree' seeking out Vichy convoy. (FW Neave)

cably omitted in coding and the Flag Officer Simon's Town, quite reasonably, assumed that the ships were on a westerly course. By 2115 the convoy had increased speed, and in the heavy head sea the whalers could not keep up and lost contact. Dense fog and extremely bad weather added to the difficulties. *Sydostlandet* had to return to base with engine trouble and, with *Cedarberg*'s radio broken down, contact could not be maintained.

Operation Kedgeree was a washout. Poor handling and lack of endurance of the Maryland aircraft taking part in the search were contributing factors. But another opportunity for interception presented itself, the outcome of which gave the small ships of the SDF a most timely and well-deserved morale-boosting shot in the arm.

It happened barely two months after Operation Kedgeree when, on 27 October, the Dutch liner *Tegelberg* reported that a convoy of five Vichy ships escorted by a sloop, *Francois d'Iberville,* and possibly a submarine, had sailed from Fort Dauphin in Madagascar three days earlier.

The French sloop *Francois d'Iberville* lost her convoy to capture by combined RN and SDF forces. (JL Ceronie)

Another interception plan was mounted and this time given the code name 'Bellringer'. The major warships involved in this new venture were HM cruisers *Devonshire* (senior ship), *Colombo,* and the armed merchant cruisers *Carthage* and *Carnarvon Castle*. Apart from the many South Africans among the crews manning these ships, others in Marylands of the SAAF made aerial sweeps up to six hundred miles from the coast. The mine clearance flotilla from Durban also joined in the search. This group consisted of *Southern Barrier* (senior officer), *Nigel, Florida, Terje, Steenberg* and *Stellenberg*.

The SDF flotilla left Durban at 1735 on 29 October for a rendezvous four hundred miles SSE of Durban, but head-winds and a heavy sea delayed their arrival until dawn on 1 November. By that time the weather had moderated somewhat and visibility was good.

At 1545 *Terje,* the starboard wing ship, sighted smoke and turned towards it at full speed. Soon afterwards she sighted several columns of smoke and made dense black smoke herself, a signal for the flotilla to close her position.

Southern Barrier reported the sighting by radio through the SAAF station at Durban but there was no acknowledgement and it was later learned that the message was never received. By 1730 *Southern Barrier* was well within sight of the convoy and asked the sloop for her name. Shadowing continued and for the rest of the night the flotilla rode herd on the convoy, closing in to about half a mile in rain squalls.

HMSAS *Southern Barrier* (Lt-Cmdr RLV Shannon OBE RN). Senior ship of mine clearance flotilla on interception of Vichy convoy. (SANMMH)

Meanwhile the convoy and sweepers had been sighted by SAAF patrols and at 1800 *Devonshire* arrived on the scene, took over command of the operation and signalled congratulations to *Southern Barrier*. The French sloop had meanwhile indicated to the cruiser that he could not countenance a diversion from his route to a port in South Africa.

Vichy convoy vessel with French sloop in foreground and AMC *Carnarvon Castle* 'riding herd'.

During the night the weather continued to improve and, by dawn on the 3rd, the gathering of ships had been joined by the light cruiser HMS *Colombo* and the AMCs *Carthage* and *Carnarvon Castle*. After an exchange of signals the captain of the sloop indicated that his convoy would return to Madagascar, and the ships accordingly made a full 180 degree turn in that direction. *Devonshire* then fired two rounds of blanks followed by a live round across the bows of the *Compiegne*

She then trained her guns on the French sloop and threatened to sink her if she did not order the convoy to stop within five minutes. She did so at 0710 and then lay off and took no further part in the affair. That evening she set course for Madagascar with *Devonshire* following her until nightfall.

Doubtless acting on instructions from the sloop, sabotage was carried out on a large scale, and the crew of one ship actually lit the fuses of the scuttling charges. The crew of the *Bangkok* set their ship on fire but when attempting to abandon her, were driven back by *Colombo*, machine-gunning ahead of the boats. They reboarded and had to put the fires out themselves. *Cap Padaran*'s engines were completely put out of action and she had to be towed by *Carthage*.

At 1145 HMS *Colombo* and HMSAS *Nigel* set off for East London escorting *Compiegne* and *Bangkok,* arriving there on the 6th. *Carnarvon Castle* and *Florida* had arrived with *Commandant Dorise* on the day before, while *Devonshire* rejoined on the 4th, and reached Port Elizabeth with *Steenberg* and *Cap Tourane* on the 6th. For the rest,*Carthage* with *Cap Padaran* in tow and screened by *Southern Barrier, Terje* and *Stellenberg,* arrived in Port Elizabeth on the 7th, after calling for tug assistance during the later stages of the passage.

The Vichy ships were claimed by the Royal Navy as prizes on the grounds of 'resistance and sabotage', and their crews and passengers were either interned or deported. SDF detachments took over the care and maintenance of the captured ships.

Thus ended a most successful operation with the honours shared by both the SDF and the SAAF. Lt-Cmdr Shannon, Senior Officer in HMSAS *Southern Barrier,* received an OBE in recognition of his handling of the flotilla.

The whole operation was neatly summed up in a cartoon prepared by Jock Leyden of the *Natal Daily News* in which, if memory serves me right, he depicted a burly bell-bottomed Royal Navy sailor hand in hand with a very small companion in tropical rig representing the SDF, while over his shoulder he carried a fishing rod with five toy ships hanging from the end of the line. The caption read: 'This week's best Vichy story!'

As a postscript: a year later *Cap Padaran* was sunk by a U-boat in the North Atlantic while serving the Allied cause.

Sub-Lt JL (Louis) Ceronie. (JL Ceronie)

As was said in the last chapter, Sub-Lt Lou Ceronie took part in Operation Bellringer and duly noted events in his pocket book. At the time he was in command of HMSAS *Florida*.

He records that, after sailing from Durban, the ships steamed in line ahead at 9 knots heading into a choppy sea accompanied by frequent rain squalls. On Friday, 31 October the wind reached gale force with visibility reduced to zero and heavy seas breaking, not only over the fo'c'sle head but also clean over the bridge. With the driving spray and rain, keeping a look-out was more a token gesture than serving any useful purpose. It was bitterly cold too, and amidst all this unpleasantness five storm-battered swallows flew on to the bridge seeking shelter from the elements. Contact was lost with the rest of the flotilla but regained at about 0230.

The weather eased on Saturday, 1 November and the vessels formed a search pattern spread out six miles apart. At noon *Nigel* raised an alarm which proved to be false, and then at 1600, as mentioned earlier, *Terje* made the first confirmed sighting. Her signal read: 'Convoy 5 ships one

Lt-Cmdr RLV Shannon OBE and some of the officers and men involved in the Vichy convoy interception. Sub-Lt Ceronie is ninth from left in the back row. (JL Ceronie)

sloop position course and speed 36,04S, 34,44E. 250 degrees true. 8 knots'. This message was passed to all ships in the group. Course was altered to intercept and at 1810 the smoke of three ships was seen, fifteen to twenty miles distant.

At 1930 the French sloop signalled 'Français' and this was repeated five times. Course and speed were then adjusted to shadow the convoy, which at times was lost in heavy rain squalls. Indeed the flagship HMSAS *Southern Barrier* and *Nigel* lost both the convoy and the flotilla.

Until they rejoined, *Terje* assumed the role of flag and guide. At dawn the guns' crews were closed up and guns trained on the sloop. At this time, and trailing about four miles astern of the convoy, there appeared a Royal Navy cruiser; but she soon disappeared over the horizon only to show up again at 0800. At 1420 an aircraft was sighted, which circled the convoy three times and was then lost to sight. At 1850 the AMC *Carnarvon Castle* took up a position with the convoy.

At 0545 on Monday, 3 November the Royal Navy made its presence felt in no uncertain manner and doubtless the small South African whalers were relieved to see the major warships and armed merchant cruisers arrive to keep them company.

Ceronie's account continues: At 0720 a cloud of smoke was observed coming from abaft the bridge of the *Bangkok,* the result of arson on the part of her crew, who then manned and lowered both boats. While the boats were being lowered *Colombo* steamed close alongside and directed machine-gun fire ahead of the port lifeboat. This soon persuaded the crews to scramble back on board. *Colombo* then signalled *Florida*: 'Tow my whaler to SS *Bangkok*'. This was duly done and a boarding party from the cruiser clambered on board at 0750. In due course, a message was received to the effect that *Bangkok*'s crew had attempted to scuttle their ship but it was considered that the vessel could be saved.

Boarding party *en route* to Vichy ship. (JL Ceronie)

The whaler-towing operation was repeated at 0750, when the *Colombo*'s whaler and a second boarding party left for the *Commandant Dorise,* from which two explosions had been heard. By 0840 the whaler was alongside the merchant-man when a message came to Florida from *Colombo*: 'Instruct our whaler this is *Devonshire*'s bird. Bring whaler to my starboard side'.

The rest of the story has already been told, except that by using bread crumbs as bait the crew of *Florida* enticed into captivity a carrier-pigeon that appeared to have come from the Vichy ship, *Commandant Dorise*.

From the foregoing it will be seen that life in minesweepers was not all monotony. Minesweepers were sometimes used for other purposes such as target towing; and the following story is worth telling. After all, it just may have happened.

'. . . nothing that suggested the old school tie about a minesweeper.' – Winston Churchill. Some crew members HMSAS *Kommetjie*. (W Gleave)

It seems that on one occasion, a Durban minesweeper was towing a huge battle target for the battleship HMS *Revenge*. The latter was over the horizon with only her fighting top visible, and the fall of shot was being recorded by a circling aircraft. The crew of the tiny minesweeper, commanded by a junior sub-lieutenant, became rather alarmed and put on their steel helmets as the fifteen-inch shells landed nearer and nearer until it seemed that they were almost bracketing their ship and certainly falling well clear of the towed target. The captain of the minesweeper is said to have sent the following signal to the battleship: 'Respectfully submit that I am towing targets, not pushing them!'

Since the battlewagon was wearing an admiral's flag it is doubtful whether this message was received with any degree of enthusiasm. And if it did indeed happen, it is perhaps as well to draw a veil over the consequences of this example of *lèse-majesté*.

We shall learn more about the humble minesweepers and their exploits as this book proceeds. Meanwhile it would be appropriate to recall the tribute paid them by Sir Winston Churchill: 'The service of minesweeping,' he wrote, 'is one of peculiar danger, calculated to try the strongest nerves because of the slowness and constant uncertainty of destruction on which those who engage on it must dwell. There was nothing that suggested the old school tie about a minesweeper. They were fellows of the college of hard knocks and graduates of the university of experience.'

CHAPTER

4

The SDF Heads North

In November 1940 the South African Government received a request from the Admiralty for anti-submarine vessels to be sent to the Mediterranean at the urgent instance of the Commander-in-Chief in that theatre, Admiral Sir Andrew Cunningham.

At the time there were only four suitable units available in South African waters, and Admiral Hallifax proposed the acquisition of four larger vessels already earmarked for conversion and commissioning. These were the *Southern Sea* and *Southern Isles* lying in Durban, where they were joined by their sisters, *Southern Maid* and *Southern Floe* from Cape Town. The ships were hastily prepared for service overseas, the first South African warships to be so engaged – and as the 22nd Anti-Submarine Group of the British Mediterranean Fleet, they arrived in Alexandria on 11 January 1941.

HMSAS *Southern Isles* in full warpaint some-where in the Med. (SANMMH)

HMSAS *Southern Sea* at Port Said. (P James)

MAID LEAVING ALEX
FOR HOME. PROTEA INFORCED
LANGEBAGES ALREADY MOVED

Admiral Cunningham expressed himself fully satisfied with the ships and was impressed by the youthfulness of their crews. He told them that they would be used to guard the northern supply route to Libya and that, since the Italians had many submarines in the area, there would be plenty for them to do.

These were no idle words, for almost immediately the group was involved in brushes with the enemy in what became known as the

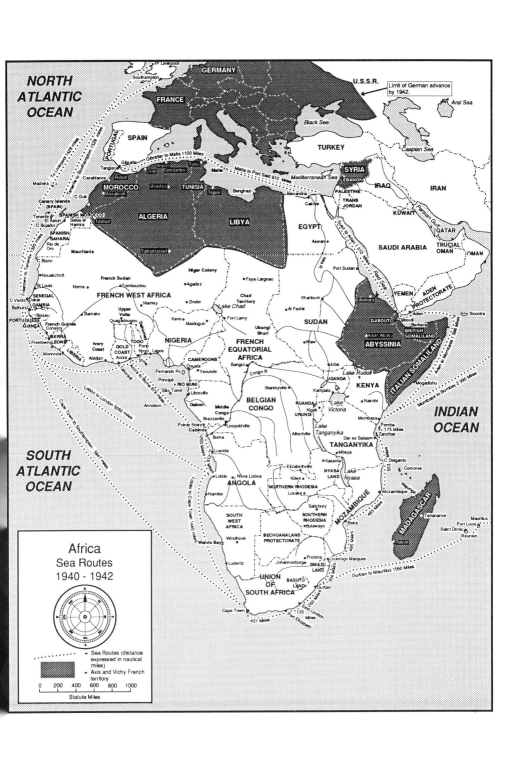

NORTH
ATLANTIC
OCEAN

SOUTH
ATLANTIC
OCEAN

INDIAN
OCEAN

Africa
Sea Routes
1940 - 1942

- Sea Routes (distance
  expressed in nautical
  miles)
- Axis and Vichy French
  territory

0   200   400   600   800   1000
Statute Miles

Lt-Cmdr AF Trew DSC. (Author)

Tobruk Run, or Bomb Alley. Operations began on 20 January with the *Southern Maid* (Lt DA Hall) and *Southern Isles* (Lt AC Matson) escorting a troopship to Sollum.

The brave story of these little ships has been recorded in detail in various official histories of the war and in *South Africa's Navy: the First Fifty Years* by Commodore JC Goosen, SM. Suffice it therefore to give only a few brief examples of their activities.

Lt-Cmdr AF Trew, Senior Officer of the group, tells of the entry into the newly captured harbour of Tobruk, a port that was to feature so prominently in the fortunes of the South African forces 'up north'.

In the early hours of next morning we [*Southern Maid*] joined the remainder of the naval ships westward bound and at dawn were off Tobruk. It was amazingly interesting. A heavy pall of black smoke from burning oil tanks covered the sky ahead of us, and as we closed the shore we saw the Italian cruiser *San Giorgio* burning fiercely. A large liner, *Liguria,* burnt out and scuttled, was a fine landmark for the approach. We were second ship of the line, a fine little M/S trawler *Moy* sweeping ahead of us. It was delicate work. We knew the approximate position of the Italian minefields, but our own 'Eagles' magnetic mines were more of a problem. There was a boom to be negotiated and baffle nets – however, *Moy* nosed about and finally found a way in, and on a very lovely clear day we steamed into the inner harbour of Tobruk and, negotiating many sunken wrecks, secured to a buoy with the Union flag flying jauntily where the Italian ensign had flown not so many hours previously.

We have been here – Tobruk – for three days and . . . the men are in fine spirits, heavily armed with souvenirs and thirsting for more excitement. However they have still not fired our guns in anger, nor have we been fired at or bombed, so there is much still to come.

HMSAS *Southern Maid* homeward bound passes the troopship *Mauretania* in the Suez Canal. (SANMMH)

Never was a truer word spoken! A few evenings later three JU 88s selected the two ships as targets for bombs and machine-gun fire. Completely taken by surprise, they failed to get off a single round in return but fortunately escaped damage or casualties. Further raids soon induced the necessary alertness and experience. Enemy action was almost entirely confined to the air. Except for a few unconfirmed submarine contacts, all the action was against aircraft and floating mines adrift from as yet unlocated minefields.

GUN FIRED! NOTE FULL RECOIL CAUGHT BY CAMERA.

Gun's crew closed up on board *Southern Sea* somewhere in the Med. (SANMMH)

JD-C
↓

The late Vice-Admiral James Johnson who, as a young RNR officer also saw service in the Mediterranean, always said there were two wars at sea: air war in the Mediterranean and a submarine war in the Atlantic.

Misfortune was soon to strike the 22nd A/S Group. On the morning of 11 February, a month after their arrival in the Mediterranean, *Southern Sea* arrived at a patrol rendezvous, two miles east of Tobruk, but there was no sign of her consort *Southern Floe*. The latter was never seen again and was assumed to have been sunk by a magnetic mine. Such an event was, unhappily, not an unusual occurrence in those grim days but, with the loss of *Southern Floe*, a human drama was played out.

Stoker CJ Jones, a South African serving in the cruiser HMS *Gloucester*, suddenly found himself transferred to the much smaller *Southern Floe* to replace a man drafted elsewhere. By a strange quirk of fate he, a temporary appointment, was the only one to survive the sinking.

The explosion, on striking the mine, broke *Southern Floe* in two and Stoker Jones found himself carried upwards together with a great quantity of oil and debris. In the process he suddenly found himself opposite an open skylight and somehow managed to pull himself through it to break surface.

It was pitch dark (the ship had been mined at precisely 0405), his ship was gone and there was nothing left even to hang on to. He then discovered that he was one of about nine members of the ship's company floundering in the water. These included his commanding officer, Lt John Lewis of Fish Hoek and a former winner of the *General Botha* Gold Medal.

Leading Stoker CJ Jones, sole survivor of HMSAS *Southern Floe*. (SANMMH)

While they were struggling to keep afloat, Lt Lewis called the swimmers together and said a prayer, after which they all sang a hymn. He then wished them good luck and told them that it was now a case of every man for himself.

During the night they drifted apart in the darkness, and when at last he came across a piece of drifting plank Stoker Jones clung to it for dear life. When the sun came up over the Mediterranean all his shipmates had disappeared and there was no sign of any ship or aircraft. Throughout that long day he clung to his piece of timber until at some time in the afternoon, under a blazing sun, he lost consciousness.

'I came to,' he says, 'in the sick-bay of an Australian destroyer HMSAS *Voyager*. They told me that at 1830, just as he sun was going down, a lookout on the ship's fo'c'sle spotted me in the water and I was picked up.'

Voyager called at Tobruk before returning to Alexandria, where Stoker Jones was transferred to the shore base, HMS *Nile,* and held in custody for three weeks until his story was verified! It was soon confirmed and he, the sole survivor of a ship's company of forty, could thus consider himself one of the luckiest men alive. After recovering from his ordeal he was posted back to HMS *Gloucester* and ended the war as a Chief Engine-room Artificer.

Back in civilian life after the war he was employed with the SAR & H and the Division of Sea Fisheries. After his first retirement in 1971, he was offered a civilian post at the Naval College in Gordon's Bay.

Sitting with his wife as a guest at the prize-giving ceremony on 5 December 1980, he was summoned by the then Chief of the Navy, Vice-Admiral RA Edwards, to stand by his side on the saluting base. It was a moving tribute to a man whose experience is still spoken of among those who go out to sea in ships.

The other three ships of the 22nd A/S Group carried on, seldom working together, but kept fully employed on individual tasks. In May 1941 they were due, under the original agreement, to return to the Union.

HMSAS *Protea.* Replaced lost *Southern Floe* in the Med. (SANMMH)

However, a further six months were requested by the C–in–C Mediterranean who referred to 'these fine ships and their outstandingly efficient ships' companies'. His request was approved and the extra six months' grace was later extended to the end of the war, in the course of which the group roamed the whole expanse of the Mediterranean. This extension of service made it necessary to replace the loss of *Southern Floe* and restore the group to its original strength.

Accordingly HMSAS *Protea,* of very similar design to the 'Southerns', was sent to the Mediterranean under the command of Lt RP Dryden-Dymond, and she sailed from Durban early in August. She was the second of four vessels to bear a name honoured in South African naval circles and was destined to win fame.

Meanwhile, however, the SDF had suffered yet another grievous loss. On 28 March 1941 a Lockheed Lodestar aircraft in which Admiral Hallifax was returning from a tour of inspection of the newly established Walvis Bay base, in thick mist struck a hill near Baboon Point, about fifty miles north of Saldanha, and all nine men on board were killed.

Rear-Admiral GW Hallifax, Director SDF addressing the ships' companies of the first SA warships to serve outside SA waters at the RNVR base, Durban, 6 December 1940. (SANMMH)

Admiral Hallifax's naval and diplomatic ability, his optimism, resourcefulness, and fair degree of independence from the apron-strings of Pretoria, enabled him to ensure that the second attempt by South Africa to establish a navy did not fail, and his loss was therefore a serious blow to the Navy in its early formative years.

Fortunately there was another able man to step into his shoes. Cmdr James Dalgleish who, it may be recalled, was the senior of the two SANS officers retained when the service was disbanded. Born in Leith in Scotland on 8 July 1891, James ('Jamie') Dalgleish joined the Merchant Navy at the age of sixteen and served with the Royal Navy during World War I attaining the rank of Lieutenant, RNR.

During the latter part of the war he was employed on surveying duties, which included preparations for minelaying along the Belgian coast and the Straits of Dover. That was followed by some field work in Belgium and France, erecting range lights and preparing firing maps for monitors.

After being demobilised he came to South Africa to join the Department of Mines and Industries as Navigating Officer of the survey vessel *Pickle* and he was transferred to the hydrographic survey section of the SANS. Later, he commanded the hydrographic survey ship HMSAS *Protea* until that vessel was disposed of in 1933, thereafter sharing the fisheries survey ship *Africana* for hydrographic survey work.

Commodore J Dalgleish. (SANMMH)

After the death of Admiral Hallifax, Commander Dalgleish was appointed Director of the SDF on 28 March 1941 and promoted Captain the same day. The only other permanent force officer to be retained from the old SANS days, Lt-Cmdr FJ Dean, was made Commander. Dalgleish retired on 30 November 1946 having been promoted Acting Commodore on 1 May 1946 on the formation of the SANF (PF), and confirmed in the rank on 1 August 1946.

'Blackie' Swartz, Scott and mascots HMSAS *Protea*. (SANMMH)

During his time as Director SDF (later SANF) Commodore Dalgleish had seen his force grow from its small original numbers to a total of 8 090 officers and ratings, of whom 2 937 had been seconded to the Royal Navy. In addition 316 Swans (SA Women's Auxiliary Naval Service) had been enlisted. For this outstanding achievement and for his services to the country generally, he was awarded the OBE in 1944 and CBE in 1946. On his retirement he was succeeded by Commodore FJ Dean, OBE.

But, back to the war, and the adventures of HMSAS *Protea*. The date was 11 July 1942, the scene the eastern Mediterranean and the two ships concerned were the *Protea* (now commanded by Lt Gordon Burn Wood) and *Southern Maid* (Lt J Bangley).

On a glorious day of bright sunshine, a clear sky and smooth blue Mediterranean waters, the two ships were steaming in company bound for Famagusta. They were carrying out an A/S sweep with *Southern Maid* stationed four cables on *Protea*'s starboard beam.

Lt Burn Wood was relaxing in a deck-chair on the bridge with a copy of the *Reader's Digest* when his officer of the watch (OOW), with a pair of binoculars to his eyes, suddenly exclaimed: 'My God! A submarine!'

Burn Wood's first response was one of disbelief. He could not believe that a submarine would surface in daylight under such clear conditions. The ship was immediately brought to action stations and *Southern Maid* informed. The submarine, which was about two and a half miles away, submerged within a minute.

That was at 1500 and the two ships carried out an extensive Asdic search without result until 1610, when *Southern Maid* gained an A/S contact at short range and became directing vessel. *Protea* immediately made contact too and went into the attack.

At 1615 a pattern of depth charges was released with 250 and 350-feet settings. The only apparent result of this attack was a slight yellowish discoloration of the water and contact was lost, to be regained again ten minutes later at 1615, when *Protea* became directing vessel for *Southern Maid*. The latter, however, lost contact.

At 1635 *Protea* again attacked and dropped a second pattern of charges with settings of 350 and 500 feet. This time oil was seen to bubble up with the explosion. At 1647 while she was running in for her third attack, a Walrus aircraft that had been sent from Beirut was sighted ahead. *Protea* then dropped a six-charge pattern with the same settings and a calcium flare to mark the position.

This last attack produced results immediately, and at 1652 the submarine was blown to the surface, stopped, and lying well over to starboard in a sinking condition. As she slowly righted herself, her crew could be seen pouring out of the conning tower, and some of them dived overboard.

Gun crew of *Southern Maid* who helped in the destruction of the Italian submarine. (SANMMH)

Protea then closed the submarine at maximum speed, opening fire with the 4-inch and Oerlikon guns at 1 000 yards. The first and third shots from the 4-inch straddled the target, and the other five registered hits on the conning tower, the gun position and the hull.

The Oerlikon meanwhile kept up a rapid fire to prevent the submarine's gun crew from closing up. Simultaneously, with the gun action, the Walrus aircraft dived low and dropped two 250-lb bombs which straddled the submarine. One of these appeared to register a hit.

Having closed to 250 yards, and with the submarine badly holed, her ready-use cordite ablaze and her gun out of action, the order to cease fire was given. By this time the submarine was sinking rapidly by the stern with the last of her crew taking to the water. Eventually, at 1655, she sank some six miles from the position where she was first sighted.

Protea lowered her boat and began to pick up survivors while *Southern Maid* provided an A/S screen. Twelve survivors were put on board *Southern Maid* and the remaining twenty-nine on *Protea*.

Next morning the two ships entered Famagusta harbour, where *Protea* landed two seriously wounded survivors and took on board the twelve from *Southern Maid*. Depth charges were replaced and the ship took on water. At 1022 a guard of seven soldiers embarked, and the ships sailed for Beirut, where the prisoners were landed.

The complement of the submarine was made up of five officers and forty-one ratings. Two men lost their lives and three others were wounded.

Wreck of Italian cruiser at Benghazi. (G Nash)

Depth charge explodes in attack on *Ondina*. (G Nash)

Some interesting information was obtained from the surviving officers. The submarine, the Italian *Ondina,* had intended to torpedo *Southern Maid* but found that she was not in a suitable firing position for that method of attack so she decided to surface and engage with gunfire. Only on surfacing did the captain discover, to his dismay, that he would have to deal with two A/S vessels, and not a merchant ship with escort as he had thought. He therefore decided to dive again immediately. He was later interested to know how the attacking whalers had estimated his depth.

He listed damage caused to his submarine in the attacks, in which he had been on the receiving end, at about 7 200-lbs of TNT. On the first attack all the lights had been put out and an oil tank (or tanks) possibly damaged. In the second attack *Ondina* rolled completely over, and leaks were started. All watertight doors jammed and arrangements for blowing tanks put out of action. After that attack they made no further attempt to get under way. With the third and last depth-charge attack the watertight doors were blown open and the submarine herself was actually blown to the surface.

The navigating officer also revealed that when they surfaced the gun-crew was closed up, only to find that the gun barrel had been distorted by the explosions and was useless. Since the submarine was obviously sinking, the gun-crew then took to the water.

Capt J Dalgleish chatting to Lt Gordon Burn Wood DSO on the bridge of a SANF ship. Lt Burn Wood has just returned from service with the SANF in the Mediterranean area.

Lt Burn Wood later told the author that when he entered port and reported to the SNO, he was told that they hoped he had kept the prisoners separated from his crew.

'Oh yes, of course, sir,' he replied. 'Good.' said the SNO, 'I think I will accompany you back to your ship.' He did so and found, much to Burn Wood's chagrin, both captors and captives having a convivial sing-song in the mess deck!

Burn Wood was awarded the DSO for this action. Other awards were distributed to both ships, including a DSC for Sub-Lt AW Solomon 'whose efficient leadership and calm resourcefulness as officer in charge of the depth-charge firing and reloading party did to a very large extent contribute to the successful outcome of the action'. The ship herself was later granted more battle honours by the Royal Navy than any other ship of the SANF.

Letters from Burn Wood and Solomon to their mothers have been preserved. Reading these one can vividly recapture the excitement of the occasion, and also sense the extreme youthfulness of the participants.

Solomon records that one of the survivors was either German or German-trained. The author recalls Burn Wood telling him that this man was the first into the water and the first to be picked up, from which it seems likely that he was some sort of political commissar.

In Commander Gordon-Cumming's unpublished official history of the SANF he said of the 22nd Anti-Submarine Group:

Ships' Company HMSAS *Protea*. Their ship earned more battle honours than any other SA ship. (Mrs A W Solomon)

Operationally, the history of the 22nd A/S Group in 1941 and 1942 is chiefly that of the 'Tobruk Run' on which the ships were employed, with those of the Royal Navy, except for occasional periods on local patrol off Alexandria, and on convoy duties to Famagusta [Cyprus], Haifa and Beirut. These comparatively restful trips were known as 'Cook's Tours'.

The ships were particularly well adapted to survive and repel the continual air attacks, usually by dive-bombers, which made up nine-tenths of the fighting; they had a fair turn of speed and answered the helm rapidly; they presented a very small target and, for their size, their AA armament was great in volume if not in range. Owing to these advantages; to their good sea-keeping qualities, and to the determination with which they were handled and fought, the 22nd A/S Group were given considerably more than their share of what was perhaps the most hazardous and trying small-ship work of the war – if its intensive nature over so long a period is taken into account.

The compliment thus paid to our ships by the RN authorities (which was confirmed in writing on several occasions) was fully justified by results; it was not only good fortune - although the hand of Providence was evident at times - which brought them through the remainder of the year 1941 with but slight damage and a handful of casualties, at a time when Libyan waters became a veritable graveyard for British ships.

These losses created such a shortage of escort vessels that a 'Southern' was often the sole guardian of a small convoy and had to fight off the bombers single-handed.

During the height of the Blitz period one of the 'Southerns' was taking a convoy out of Alexandria *en route* for 'Bomb Alley' and Tobruk. Outside she met HMS *Auckland* (an old friend and one of the big RN escort vessels) and signalled: 'Are you joining the party?' *Auckland* replied: 'Not bloody likely'. She was sunk by bombing soon afterwards.

Further details of operations affecting the 22nd A/S Group can be derived from publications already mentioned. But now it is time to turn our attention to the minesweepers. The scene is the same: the hard-fought battle for control of the Mediterranean Sea.

In addition to the 22nd A/S Group, the Union Government in May 1941 also agreed to despatch eight LL minesweepers for service with the Royal Navy. They were to be fitted with equipment for dealing with acoustic and magnetic mines, but since it was not available in the Union they were to be fitted out at their destination.

Accordingly, on 1 July HMSA ships *Gribb, Seksern, Treern* and *Imhoff* sailed from Durban. Others were to follow early in 1942. Of the first quartet two were sent to Haifa to be fitted out and the other pair to Beirut. *Imhoff* at the time was commanded by Lt HH Biermann, later to become South Africa's first Admiral and Chief of the South African Defence Force.

Lt PA North DSC receiving Major-General Frank Theron on board HMSAS *Bever* in the Med. (SANMMH)

It was not until April – May 1942 that these ships came into service, and in the meantime two other sweepers, *Bever* and *Boksburg,* had arrived from Durban in February, followed by *Langlaagte* and *Parktown* in May. *Boksburg* was the first to begin operations, and on a passage to sweep mines off Tobruk in March she managed to rescue thirty-one of a total crew of thirty-nine from a burning sea; their ship *Christa* having been torpedoed and bursting into a towering mass of flame. Again in June, *Parktown* rescued twenty-eight men from a burning sea after their ships carrying petrol and ammunition were torpedoed. The first South African ship to detonate an acoustic mine was *Seksern,* while on passage to Haifa.

Lt PA North, Commanding Officer HMSAS *Bever,* was awarded the DSC. (SANMMH)

On 10 May HMSAS *Bever* (Lt PA North) arrived in Tobruk to carry out LL sweeps and she endured the usual intensive air raids and shelling, which resulted in some damage and one casualty. A month later, after the rescue referred to above, *Parktown* (Lt LJ Jagger) joined *Bever* at Tobruk.

On the afternoon of 20 June, with Rommel's Afrika Korps hammering at the defences of the town, shell-fire greatly increased and at 1800 all ships were ordered to embark personnel for evacuation. At 2000, while they were busy with that, enemy tanks entered the town and *Bever* cast off after receiving a hit from a tank which killed one man. Meanwhile enemy motorised troops had arrived at the end of the jetty and opened fire with machine guns. *Parktown* was also hit and, with one army NCO killed, she too cast off. Both ships left harbour through a smokescreen laid by an MTB, which partly protected them from a heavy barrage of shells and bombs.

During the night the two ships became separated. *Bever* was fortunate and arrived at Mersa Matruh next day without further mishap.

But luck ran out for *Parktown* which had the dubious distinction of being the last ship to leave Tobruk harbour before it fell to the Germans.

Once clear of the harbour she was ordered to take in tow a disabled tug which, like herself, was overloaded with troops. With her speed reduced to 5 knots, *Parktown* was only about fifty-seven miles from Tobruk at daybreak the next day. Her officers were relieved to see a dense fog-bank ahead which promised at least some shelter from the inevitable air attacks that were bound to follow.

HMSAS *Bever* which made good her escape from Tobruk. (SANMMH)

However, at 0654 her look-outs sighted an enemy E-boat and half an hour later she was attacked by four of them. The enemy obviously had the advantage in speed, weight of armament and superior numbers. *Parktown*'s heaviest gun was a 20mm Oerlikon as against the three-pounder of the E-boats.

They made the most of their advantage by fanning out and attacking from all directions. Within a few minutes *Parktown* was rendered helpless. A direct hit in the boiler caused the hurried evacuation of the boiler-room. At the same time, a shell exploded on the bridge and killed the captain, Lt LJ Jagger, the navigator, and wounded most of the men there.

The sole surviving *Parktown* officer was her First Lieutenant, Ernest Raymond Francis. Born on 26 October 1908, he received his nautical training in the SATS *General Botha* as a member of the 1923 – 25 term. On 3 February 1941 he joined the SDF at Port Elizabeth as a Sub-Lieutenant.

During the E-boat attack he manned one of the Oerlikons, and found that it had been damaged by enemy fire; so he abandoned it and made his way to the Vickers gun whose crew of four had been wounded. He then opened fire on the enemy until a shell exploded in the vicinity and blew him down a hatch opening. He was seriously injured in both legs. Despite great pain he once again clambered aloft and fired the Vickers until it ran out of ammunition.

By this time the ship was hove-to, burning fiercely, and with steam blasting from the holed boiler. Out of a complement of twenty-one,

Parktown had suffered thirteen casualties. Four killed, one missing and eight seriously wounded. It was then that he heard that the captain's last order had been to abandon ship.

That was easier said than done. All the boats had been damaged either by shell-fire or burning, so there was nothing left for it but to jump overboard. Once in the water he swam to one of the floats upon which the wounded had been placed, while he and other survivors clung to the sides. The E-boats then began to fire on the few survivors but were driven off by a German fighter aircraft. This humane act by the enemy has never been satisfactorily explained. But, whatever it was, that unknown *Luftwaffe* pilot certainly saved the lives of those in the water.

Fortunately the E-boats did not attack the tug which, overloaded with troops, drifted helplessly in the vicinity. Just as urgent temporary repairs had been effected to get the small craft moving, a torpedo boat arrived on the scene and proceeded to pick up the survivors.

A striking photo of HMSAS *Protea* in full warpaint. (P James)

The burning *Parktown* was sunk by depth charges from the MTB. In due course Sub-Lt Francis was transferred to the Mersa Matruh Hospital where, as a result of the grievous injuries that he had suffered, one leg was amputated.

For his gallantry Ernie Francis received the Distinguished Service Order. Many thought that his coolness and fortitude while seriously wounded qualified him for the supreme award of the Victoria Cross. In April 1944 he was promoted Full Lieutenant.

The Captain of the ill-fated *Parktown,* Lt Jagger, received a posthumous mention in despatches, the citation of which reads as follows:

> Lt Jagger, Commanding Officer of HMSAS *Parktown,* for skilful and courageous handling of his ship while on passage to Tobruk on June 10th, when he succeeded in saving a large number of the crew of SS *Havre* which had been torpedoed and was burning, and later he endeavoured to rescue the crew of SS *Athene* without success, but did succeed in saving some of the crew of *Bramble Leaf* which had been torpedoed and was burning fiercely, and more particularly for the resolute and courageous way he handled his ship under heavy fire during the evacuation of Tobruk.
>
> This officer was killed on the bridge of *Parktown* by a bursting shell during an action with E-boats which resulted in *Parktown* being abandoned on fire and later sunk with depth charges by our own MTBs.

A man who had a narrow escape from the inferno of Tobruk was Lt Biermann in *Imhoff.* He was due to relieve Jagger within the week and also replenish the dwindling stock of potatoes, but Tobruk fell before he got there.

Commodore John Goosen, now living in retirement in Fish Hoek, remembers those days well. At the time he was a Paymaster Lieutenant on the staff of SDF headquarters at Alexandria.

Group of *Protea*'s company at Tobruk. (P James)

In June 1942 the Royal Navy were growing increasingly concerned over the information they were receiving about Rommel's advance on Tobruk and, when his inexorable progress continued, the C-in-C decided to vacate Alexandria. The ships, all except the minesweepers, which were instructed to remain behind as a rearguard and continue their sweeping operations, were despatched east of Suez, some of them transporting Wrens and other shore personnel.

John Goosen was on board paying a ship's company when he was told to leave Alexandria forthwith. The office was abandoned and, having filled a safe with money drawn from the army paymaster, he set off in a temperamental truck lent by the paymaster at the South African base accompanied by Sub-Lt Jock Beyers who had only arrived from South Africa for service 'up north' the previous day, and PO Writer Roy Glegg.

GE Wilman stands by his gun on board HMSAS *Protea*. (SANMMH)

It took them four days to reach Port Said via Cairo, whereupon they were told to turn round and return to Alexandria. That they did in one day, having left Beyers to join a ship in Port Said. Most of the SDF documents had been taken out with the staff, and business was soon resumed as usual.

The minesweepers continued to serve in the Mediterranean, and the last to leave reached Durban only in December 1945. In the early days of their commission they had to clear the thousands of mines laid to hold up the advance of the Eighth Army in the desert campaign. *Imhoff* and *Treern* were among the sweepers engaged in clearing the approaches to Mersa Matruh, while *Boksburg* swept off Bardia and *Treern, Seksern* and others swept the Tobruk area.

It gave the hard-working flotilla a boost when, on 11 February 1943, General Montgomery visited HMSAS *Boksburg,* then sweeping for magnetic mines off Tripoli.

By the middle of 1944 the sweepers were largely employed in the Levant and by October that year *Bever, Seksern, Treern, Boksburg* and *Gribb* were in the Gulf of Athens preparing to clear the numerous minefields there. The dangers of minesweeping were brought forcibly home when, on 30 November, a day of rain and mist, the number of mines exploded in the sweeps had gradually slowed down operations and brought the minesweeping trawlers to a halt.

Bever, stationed astern of the sweepers to deal with unexploded mines, was likewise stopped, with just an occasional engine movement to maintain station when, at 1430, she struck a mine. In the violent explosion her bridge collapsed and the afterpart disintegrated. When the steam and spray had subsided the forepart was seen to roll over and sink.

It was common practice on sweepers for all hands not on duty to stay on deck and that was the case with *Bever.* Nevertheless it is remarkable, considering the force of the explosion and the rapid disintegration of the ship, that seven survivors should have been picked up out of a ship's company of twenty-three. Most of them, including the captain and his first lieutenant, had been blown overboard.

More misfortune was to follow. On Christmas Eve ,1944 *Treern* left Piraeus for Volo to relieve her sister ship *Seksern* but found the harbour empty. The arrival on board of a representative of ELAS caused the captain (Lt P Byrne) some uneasiness, and he took his ship to the island of Skiathos, and later into the Gulf of Volo.

At 0830 on the morning of 12 January 1945, while towing a caique laden with fuel for motor launches at Volo, there was suddenly a huge explosion, attributed to a mine, which blew the little ship apart. This time history was to repeat itself again, and *Treern* sank leaving only one survivor, Stoker JJ Bosch. He found himself somersaulting through the air and into the sea. On surfacing he found a lifebuoy floating nearby, and he was in time to see the bows of the ship disappearing. At the same time another mine exploded about a hundred yards away. One of his legs had been hurt but he was picked up by the caique, which had escaped damage, and soon afterwards he was transferred to HMS *Musketeer.*

To make up for these losses two other ships, *Langlaagte* and *Imhoff* were diverted from the coasts of Egypt, Cyprus and Syria to the Aegean Sea. The war in Europe ended on 8 May 1945, but the sweepers carried on; and it was not until three months after the fall of Japan that the last South African minesweeper, HMSAS *Langlaagte,* arrived home on 12 December 1945.

The Commanding Officer of *Boksburg* (Lt DK Kinkead-Weekes) made the following report during those post-war mine clearance operations:

The help, conduct and efficiency of the ship's company during operations were excellent. Ships were under way at dawn and frequently did not anchor or secure alongside until an hour or two after dark. Nine or ten hours of Dan-laying and mine destruction, with another three or four hours of steaming through unknown waters, often followed by a two-hour anchor watch at night, is strenuous work, but never was there any sign of complaint.

He also noted that 'the bitterly cold gales during the winter months gave the ships a violent shaking and caused them to ship tons of water.'

It should not be forgotten that the crew lived under extreme tension, never knowing when their ship would strike a mine. For those of them cursed with a vivid imagination, it must have been an ordeal bordering on sheer torture. All the more credit to them for never flinching.

CHAPTER

5

Seaman Gunner Do Not Weep

A young sailor who served on the lower deck of minesweepers during those stirring times kept a comprehensive record of his experiences and impressions. It is the only account written by a rating who served in one of our ships in the Mediterranean and the Aegean, and its 263 pages give a remarkably detailed picture of life in our ships not found in any of the official accounts.

The book was never published but the title, *Seaman Gunner Do Not Weep* will be familiar to any navy man worth his salt. It is derived from a song, familiar to most sailors, about a seaman who, driven to desperation by the bleak solitude of Scapa Flow and lack of feminine company, sought consolation by carnal intercourse with a sheep. As a

Maria with SANF minesweeper men – mostly from HMSAS *Gribb* – at Piraeus, 1945. (J Duffell-Canham)

Seaman Gunner John Duffell-Canham in Greece, early 1945. (J Duffell-Canham)

Maria Xanthopoulou. Picture taken in Piraeus, Greece, 1945.

result any member of that particular ship's company was greeted with loud bleatings until the practice was discontinued by order of the Admiralty.

Despite its indelicate title, the book is dedicated to a young girl, Maria Xanthopoulou of Piraeus, Greece, who adopted one of the minesweepers, HMSAS *Gribb*. She was in turn 'adopted' by the ship's company and became their pet and mascot. In recent years the author of the book, John Duffell-Canham, has been seeking in vain for news of Maria. Early in his book John Duffell-Canham philosophises thus:

> Many of us, anyway, have experienced changes in our lives since those far-off days. It must also be borne in mind that the men involved were the products of a very conservative – perhaps even puritanical – South African society and many of the things that shocked or amazed us in the Middle East and elsewhere would probably not even raise comment today. But it is cause for wonder that so much that we considered degenerate then has spread into our Western society – or has it merely just come out into the open?

John was the youngest of three brothers, all serving at sea. One survived the sinking of the battleship HMS *Barham*. As a young recruit into the SDF, John sailed from Durban in a troopship and was sung out of the harbour by the famous Lady in White, Perla Siedle Gibson. Her rendering of 'Wish Me Luck As You Wave Me Goodbye' brought lumps to the throat and tears to the eyes of many of the young men leaving home for the first time.

For the first time too, he was to discover the mysterious galley wireless, the nautical equivalent of the bush telegraph. Rumours abounded, yet it was remarkable how often the content proved to be accurate. An RAF contingent on board was berthed far down below with only one ladder to the upper decks. Near panic ensued during a depth-charge attack.

Duffell-Canham's description of the 'heads' will be confirmed by all who sailed in the troopers. A long trough ran below seats facing one another through which ran a continuous stream of water. This gave rise to a bright idea. Seeing the row of 'sitting ducks', jokers crumpled up old newspapers, set them on fire, and sent them drifting along the stream!

After nineteen days his contingent was decanted at Port Tewfiq and after many vicissitudes they duly arrived at Alexandria, where they were accommodated in barracks that had formerly been King Farouk's stables, and where they received the numerous mandatory doses of inoculations.

John was then drafted to the minesweeper HMSAS *Bever,* and he noted that her armament consisted mainly of 20mm AA guns, .303 machine guns and a German MG 34 Spandau with a plentiful supply of ammunition collected at points along the coast.

It was then that he experienced his first air raid. Called out in the early hours of the morning and told to take shelter, he found that the whole of the crowded Alexandria harbour was completely ringed by

Searchlight displays over Alexandria that so impressed young Duffell-Canham. (G Nash)

A gunner keeps an eye on his target (SANMMH) and (inset) a Stuka dive bomber is caught fair and square in the sights. (G Nash)

[handwritten annotation] NOT A STUKA. PROBABLY ME 110 DOING A MACHINE GUN/CANNON ATTACK. UNLESS LINED UP BY BACK SIGHT WITH PLANE FLY TOWARD CENTRE OF CROSS ON FORESIGHT SHOTS FIRED WILL MISS?

anti-aircraft fire. Heavy fire was coming from the batteries of the two battleships that had earlier been damaged by Italian Charioteers (two-man semi-submersibles). A blast farther along the quay wrecked a small RN minesweeper. He was greatly impressed by the arcs of exploding shells and tracers criss-crossing the night sky, but was brought back to earth by shrapnel falling back and clanging on to his ship.

Next morning he had his first experience of sweeping when, in company with an RN sweeper and a South African sister ship, they put down their 'hammers' and electric 'tails' to sweep the channel outside Alexandria. After a night raid it was usually found that mines had been laid in the approaches. I should perhaps explain that the 'hammer' sent out sound-waves ahead of the ship to explode acoustic mines, while an electric current passing through the 'tails' towed astern of the vessel activated the magnetic mines. The ships themselves had been degaussed, or demagnetised, to avoid the magnetic mines. These so-called LL sweepers would then be followed by ordinary Orepesa sweepers whose job it was to cut the cables of moored mines.

Although not fitted with Asdic, the sweepers often formed part of convoy escorts, together with the bigger 'Southerns', and so received their full share of attacks by enemy aircraft, often Stuka dive-bombers escorted by Messerschmitts. The main targets were of course the supply ships in the convoy, but none was immune. 'The noise,' Duffell-Canham wrote, 'of a Stuka dive-bombing, and the scream from the

59

whistles and gadgets they had attached to their wings and bombs, was at times nerve-wracking and once heard never to be forgotten.'

In John's ship the oldest men on board were the coxswain and the chief engine-room artificer. The crew were mostly in their early twenties; the writer himself being still in his teens and by far the youngest. An able seaman, who could not have been more than thirty-two, was named Pop.

John was at Alexandria when the Navy vacated the port and, like the other minesweepers, his ship was left behind. A commanding officer of one of the Royal Naval minesweepers was moved to compose the following:

> They took their guns and shiny ships,
> They took their Wrens with rosebud lips
> East of Suez, as usual on the booze.
> They left Alex to the whalers
> Those glorious South African sailors.

Not a literary gem, but a sincere tribute to the men in our little ships from a member of the senior service. The verses went on to say some uncomplimentary things about higher authority, which were seized on by the Egyptian press, which at that time was beginning to show distinctly pro-German leanings. It was printed in full in the newspaper *El Gon*. They were all saddened when many of those 'Wrens with rosebud lips' were lost when the big submarine depot ship HMS *Medway*, with a large number of Wrens on board, was torpedoed between Alexandria and Port Said with severe loss of life.

The ill-fated submarine depot ship HMS *Medway* with her brood. (G Nash)

Coinciding with the advance of the Eighth Army John found himself drafted to one of the 'Southerns' and in that ship they followed up the advance, and in due course saw service the length and breadth of the Mediterranean. Before that they had carried out anti-submarine exercises with a former Yugoslav submarine affectionately known as 'Hubbly-Bubbly'. They never learnt her real name.

Throughout his book John Duffell-Canham carefully avoids naming people, but in telling certain mess-deck yarns he breaks that rule. A debate was in progress as to who really deserved most praise for setting the new navy on its feet. Certain senior officers were mentioned, but by far the most agreed that it was the former RN and RNVR instructors to whom all credit was due. These men, it was considered, had been the backbone of training and the real fathers of the South African Navy.

Gunnery in-structors such as Dick Bland, Mickey Forbes, Tom Vincent, Dick Whittington, and other men such as CERA Nic Carter, Seamanship Instructor CPO Leo Barret, and the Chief Yeoman of Signals and Chief Telegraphists, all made it their business to turn raw

Ships on fire following attack on convoy in the Med. (G Nash)

material into fighting men imbued with a keen sense of discipline and pride in the service. Certainly those who passed through their hands will never forget them. According to Duffell-Canham:

> With the whole of Africa in Allied hands the anti-submarine vessels from the Eastern Mediterranean were now finding themselves moving along to the more exotic ports (in peacetime) such as Bizerta, Oran, Algiers, etc. and one of the SA ships even went as far as Casablanca. But mostly their convoy runs would cease at these ports, or alternatively, at Gibraltar. However, for some time to come they were still to experience bombing attacks from enemy aircraft based in Sicily.

Another development was that their own anti-submarine group was gradually finding itself separated; and the author's Southern, for example, found herself the only converted craft on escort with a group consisting of frigates and corvettes. Duffell-Canham continues:

> When going through the Skerki Channel [they were] usually also accompanied by one or two special anti-aircraft cruisers, which gave the South Africans their first introduction to anti-aircraft fire, controlled at night by radar.

Typical gun platform on board a minesweeper. (SANMMH)

The Germans were taking more to night bombing through this stretch because in daylight hours Allied fighters were soon among the enemy shooting them down. The first warning would of course be the noise of aircraft engines in the darkness, and everyone would be watching out for the flares to begin dropping which lit up the sea almost like daylight for the German JU88s, which either bombed or came in from the sides of the convoy with torpedoes. Against the torpedo bombers the Southern would often be using her old 4-inch gun to fire star-shell out to the horizon, to light up or silhouette the enemy bombers coming in at low level. That would give the escorts and the merchant ships the opportunity to wait for the plane to come within range and then let it have it with everything they had as she lifted from low level to clear the convoy after dropping her tin-fish.

A toll was taken of the enemy bombers in this way, and also it was quite a delight when the anti-aircraft cruisers, using radar, would somehow, to our amazement, shoot down in flames the odd bomber out of a pitch-black sky into which they seemingly appeared to be firing at nothing.

Unfortunately, with the convoys now being increased in numbers, only a narrow channel could be swept clear, by minesweepers from Malta, through the Skerki Channel into which the Germans and Italians kept dropping mines. Invariably convoys would form a single file stretching for miles with the escorts tucked in close down

the sides; with no possibility of trying to 'comb' incoming torpedoes, the Germans exacted quite a heavy toll. In some cases the
escorts would have to run alongside, taking the crew off a torpedoed
ship as it was going down, or alternatively if it showed no sign of
sinking fast enough, shallow-set depth charges would be dropped
right alongside to blow holes in the bottom so that the vessel would
go down faster and thus clear the channel for the ships following
astern.

Corvette in trouble after air attack in the Med. (G Nash)

Moving into the new
zone at the western
end of the Mediterra-
nean, John records
that the small South
African flag flown
from the yardarm,
and widely known
at the other end of
the Mediterranean,
aroused some curios-
ity among ships of
which many were
seeing the flag for the
first time. South African crews were indignant when they were asked
what flag they were flying, the ships of other navies probably supposing
it some special signal of which they were not aware!

In due course the Southern arrived at Gibraltar with a number of
other A/S trawlers of the RN and was sent to patrol the Straits to ensure
that no U-boats in the Mediterranean could escape to harry the huge
convoys making for the invasion of Normandy. Of their visit to
Gibraltar John writes:

At this stage of the war, if not from actual enemy attacks, then from
strain and fatigue, many of the chaps were beginning to behave as
though they were slightly 'bomb happy' and sleeping below decks
in Gibraltar was not exactly peaceful, as about every twenty minutes
there would be a terrific thump under water as the harbour defence
ML patrolling just outside the bay dropped a depth charge. There
had been what would now be called 'frogmen' attacks by the Italians
in the same style as they had scored their spectacular success back in
1941, when they badly damaged the giant battleships *Queen Elizabeth* and *Valiant* in Alexandria harbour. Here in Gibraltar they had
attacked vessels anchored in the bay when the docks were too
crowded for them all to get in, and they scored quite a few
successes. It was easy to guess that they were enjoying the assistance

Alexandria suffered many air raids. (G Nash)

of the Spaniards, and it was learnt after the Italian surrender that they were, in fact, launching them from an Italian tanker anchored in neutral Spanish waters off Algeciras where she had fled when Italy joined in the war on the side of the Nazis.

These frogmen rode astride their underwater chariots of which the warhead of their torpedo-like vessels was detached and hung by clamps underwater from the ship's bilge-keels and set to go off within a certain time, which would allow the frogmen to swim away and, in most cases, they managed to reach the safety of nearby Spanish beaches. It was suspected that the Germans had taken over this job after the Italian surrender and preventive measures had to be maintained.

HMSAS *Gribb*, LL minesweeper, at Volos, Greece, 1944.

A particularly arduous and unusual task performed at this time by one of the Southerns and a large RN A/S trawler, was the escorting of a large floating dock capable of lifting a battleship, and destined for the Far East via the Mediterranean. The main towing was done by a powerful American diesel-powered tug sailing under the White Ensign of the Royal Navy and assisted by two smaller tugs, one of which rejoiced in the name of *Josephine*. This gave rise to many rude signals bandied back and forth on the theme of 'Not tonight, Josephine!' The tow was the longest continuous escort duty carried out in the Mediterranean during the war and it took twenty-four days from Gibraltar to Port Said.

Since it was obvious that the Germans were not going to allow the passage of this slow-moving target, the escorts were kept on their toes.

Sure enough, a submarine attack developed; but since the escorts could not leave their convoy, Catalina flying-boats took over the hunt. And, as if threatened enemy action were not enough, a furious gale caused the towing cable to part, and with heavy seas thundering along the length of the floor of the floating dock, recovery could not be made for the next five or six days.

John records at this time: 'While sweeping the Corinth area not far from Nauplia, the SA minesweeper HMSAS *Bever* had struck a mine (some observers said two mines) and sank with most of her crew killed by the explosion. There were about seven survivors. It was like losing members of the family.'

It was about that time, too, that John was transferred from his Southern to the minesweeper HMSAS *Gribb*. That introduced him to a new way of life: a smaller ship with the added prospect of being blown up at any moment.

He breaks off his record here to express his admiration (shared by all who served at sea) of the engine-room crews. These men had only a slim chance of surviving if bombed or torpedoed and were the real heroes in any theatre of the war at sea, a

A/B van den Berg of HMSAS *Gribb* finds time for some dhobey. (SANMMH)

'Sparks' keeps his lonely vigil at the radio. (SANMMH) *Roy Munro of Durban died 8.1.90.*

degree of danger shared only by those whose action stations were down in the magazines and shell-rooms. His admiration for these men, who had only a narrow steel ladder as a means of escape, grew with the long hours in minefields during the months that followed.

The *Gribb* headed north towards Greece with other sweepers, including her sister *Treern* and encountered wintry weather on the way. Cold seas continually swept the decks and even the bridge. The movement was violent. When they were approaching the Gulf leading to Athens and Piraeus they were ordered to sweep and, except for the engine and boiler-room crew, all hands were ordered on deck. Large scale sweeping round the coast to clear channels for the invasion forces now began in earnest. At first the LL sweepers had only moderate success but the Orepesa sweepers cut mine after mine, to be destroyed as they bobbed up to the surface.

It is with regret that we must leave John Duffell–Canham at this point and branch out into a broader field.

CHAPTER

6

The Armed Merchant Cruisers

In both great wars the British Admiralty adopted the practice of requisitioning large passenger liners for conversion into armed merchant cruisers. These costly vessels were used to back up the protection of Allied shipping along the trade routes of the world, to carry out ocean patrols, intercept any doubtful ships for contraband, and to blockade any possible enemy traffic in far northern waters.

Lacking protective armour these ships were extremely vulnerable to attack and, armed as they were with often obsolete weapons, they were more of a deterrent than a serious challenge. Intended to combat surface attack, when on convoy escort duty they were stationed in the middle of the massed columns of ships as a precaution against submarine attack. It was hardly a comforting thought to those in the labouring vessels on the outer fringes of the convoy, yet such an armed merchant cruiser (AMC) was often their only protection.

On the outbreak of the Hitler war the Admiralty commissioned fifty of these large liners, or cargo-passenger liners, for conversion into AMCs. That was necessary because of the lack of foresight that had resulted in an acute shortage of proper cruisers.

That they had their uses is beyond question. The heroic story of HMS *Jervis Bay* in challenging the German pocket-battleship *Admiral Scheer* was a typical example. By so doing she distracted the enemy warship to the extent of enabling several of the convoy she was escorting to scatter and escape. *Jervis Bay* herself was soon reduced to a charred and twisted wreck, but her gallant stand earned her undying fame, and her captain a posthumous Victoria Cross.

Another noteworthy action was the occasion on which the AMC *Rawalpindi* encountered the German battle-cruisers *Scharnhorst* and *Gneisenau* in far northern waters. The outcome was a foregone conclusion and the battered *Rawalpindi* sank, but not before transmitting a useful sighting report.

HMS *Carnarvon Castle* being shepherded into Simon's Town naval dockyard by tug *St Dogmael*. (SANMMH)

However, such were the grievous losses suffered by AMCs – fifteen of these valuable ships were lost to enemy action, mainly as the result of U-boat torpedo attack – that the whole system was ultimately abandoned.

On original requisitioning of these liners, workmen stripped them of all their finery and inflammable material. Formerly opulent staterooms were gutted and public rooms cleared of all ornament. All surplus material was removed from above and below decks to make the ship less vulnerable to fire, and accommodation was provided for naval ratings. Magazines were built to house ammunition and decks were strengthened to accept heavy guns, and extra protection was fitted to key points such as the bridge, the radio office, the engine-room, and so on. Naval equipment was installed and naval stores embarked, not forgetting a plentiful supply of rum for the issue of the daily tot; a practice now, alas, defunct.

The Red Ensign was replaced by the White Ensign and a Royal Naval officer assumed command, bringing with him a staff of key officers and ratings. At the same time a number of the ship's original complement were retained and given temporary naval ranks. South Africans serving in the RN, RNR, RNVR and MN, representative of all the many departments of a fighting ship, were drafted to these vessels.

To the people of the Union of South Africa, by far the best-known liner to be so requisitioned was the former Royal Mail motor vessel *Carnarvon Castle*. Built in 1926 she had been recently refurbished at considerable cost, and was one of the most popular of the mail ships, the forerunner of the magnificent fleet of Union Castle motor ships. Thousands of South Africans had trodden her spacious teak decks

Cargill and Waldren at 6-inch gun HMS *Carnarvon Castle*. (SANMMH)

between Southampton and their own country in peacetime. Many were to serve on board her in time of war.

Carnarvon Castle arrived in Table Bay from Southampton during the second week of September 1939. During the outward voyage passengers had heard Prime Minister Neville Chamberlain's momentous broadcast announcing that a state of war existed between Great Britain and Germany. Now, on arrival at Cape Town all, even those booked coastwise, were compelled to leave the ship, which had been requisitioned by the Admiralty.

Workmen lost no time in stripping her public rooms. Furniture and fittings were removed and stored against better days in a pre-cooling shed on the East Pier in Table Bay harbour. This gave rise to an amusing consequence, for in the South African Navy immediately after the war, invited guests would find that the wardroom tables would be laid with crockery and cutlery bearing the mark of many a famous company whose ships had been stripped for wartime conversion.

Whether such trophies had been acquired by fair means or by foul is uncertain; but it is safe to assume that after the war such ships that survived must have found their catering stocks sadly depleted.

At 1800 on 8 September 1939 the Red Ensign was hauled down and the White Ensign of the Royal Navy run up. Next day the ship sailed for Simon's Town for drydocking and to receive her armament. She emerged again on 25 October, and a brief entry in the bulky dockyard register confirms that she was 'converted to AMC: emergency equipment 2 000 tons stone ballast added in dock.'

A party of twenty-eight RNVR(SA) officers, petty officers and ratings was also added to her complement. Under the mobilisation exchange the RNVR(SA) was to have provided a large proportion of the crews needed for four armed merchant cruisers that were fitted out by the Admiralty in South Africa. As the RNVR(SA) was not mobilised that was not possible. Three officers and eighty-two ratings (mainly seaman gunners) were, however, drafted to these ships while they were fitting out. The rest of the ratings needed to complete the crews were sent from the United Kingdom by the Admiralty. So successful was the conversion of the *Carnarvon Castle* that three other prospective AMCs, *Comorin, Bulolo,* and *Esperance Bay* received similar treatment – and their share of South African seamen.

First Port Elizabeth draft of RNVRs to join HMS *Carnarvon Castle,* 11 September 1939. (SANMMH)

On the morning of 5 December 1940 HMS *Carnarvon Castle* was some seven hundred miles south-east of Montevideo, Uruguay, and steaming towards the River Plate at 18 knots. Captain WHM Hardy, DSO, RN had kept his crew on full alert, for German commerce raiders were known to be in the area. These were usually innocent-looking merchant ships, disguised and posing as neutrals. But in an instant they could change into formidable fighting men-of-war when flaps in their sides clanged down to reveal heavy armament.

A group of SA sailors on board HMS *Carnarvon Castle*. (SANMMH)

At 0642 *Carnarvon Castle*'s look-outs sighted a ship some eight or nine miles sway. The stranger was steaming directly away but Captain Hardy was suspicious and ordered an increase in speed to overtake and intercept her. He then signalled 'SC' (What ship?), but received no reply.

Now convinced that the stranger, a long low freighter of about 10 000 tons, painted dark grey or black, with two masts, a single smoke-stack, straight stem and cruiser stern, was an enemy, he signalled 'K' (Stop immediately). Still the stranger did not reply; and at 0737 with the enemy coming within range he ordered *Carnarvon Castle*'s gunners to fire a warning shot from one of their old 6-inch guns across the other vessel's bows.

Only then did the stranger respond. Two stern guns flashed, side-plating vanished and a big swastika flag was hoisted at her main. Then, turning to starboard, she unmasked her whole gun battery. Suddenly the sky was full with hurtling shells.

Hardy was now confronting the German commerce raider *Thor*. He duly turned the bulk of the 20 000 ton *Carnarvon Castle* to close the gap between the two ships and bring his own starboard battery of 6-inch guns to bear.

On board the *Thor, Frigattenkapitän* Otto Kahler watched in dismay as the big liner turned to challenge him. Earlier he had been in a quandary as he observed the AMC emerging from the morning haze. It was no business of his to take on such a formidable adversary, and in fact he had been instructed to avoid such an encounter. She was far greater

71

in size and speed than his own comparatively modest command and his first impulse had been to run. It was only when he saw her alter course and begin to overtake him that he decided to stand and fight.

But who knows? It is possible that German Naval Intelligence had told him that, should he be forced into such a situation, he could assume that the armament of the AMCs was mostly of an old pattern with plenty of bark but not much bite.

Hardy was all too aware of the age of his guns. Some of them had been used in the 1914 war. Some had been cast even before the Boer War! He also knew that for these ancient weapons to have any significant effect he would have to close the range as much as possible. He therefore moved rapidly upon *Thor*.

At 15 000 yards he was able to open fire; but by this time both ships had the range, and a devastating fire erupted from *Thor* that immediately blasted the AMC's electrically operated fire control communication system. That made salvo firing difficult, as the guns now had to be trained by hand.

At 0838 *Carnarvon Castle* was still closing the gap when two torpedoes were sighted from the bridge. Hardy flung the huge liner to starboard under full helm to comb the tracks and anxiously watched as they passed by, a mere 50 yards on either side. Four minutes later the range had been brought down to 8 000 yards. *Thor*, with British shells passing harmlessly overhead, now turned to bring her port battery to bear and scored repeated hits on *Carnarvon Castle*'s superstructure

White Watch 6-inch gun's crew HMS *Carnarvon Castle* included some RNVR (SA) ratings. (Unknown)

Shell-fire damage to *Carnarvon Castle* after a brush with an enemy raider. None of her shells hit their mark! (SANMMH)

causing fires to break out in several places. By now all the big liner's control circuits were out of action and the guns were all firing independently.

With his ship being mercilessly hammered, Captain Hardy was now in serious trouble and had to find a quick way out of his predicament. Accordingly he swung his ship away and opened up the range to assess the damage. He could not know that *Thor*'s guns were also giving trouble, with recoil cylinders leaking and barrels that would not train properly. But *Carnarvon Castle* was in a far worse plight and a reluctant yet necessary decision was made to break off the engagement and make for Montevideo to carry out urgent repairs.

He was in radio contact with the cruiser HMS *Enterprise* which was somewhere in the area and asked her to take over while he set course for the River Plate. *Enterprise* found nothing – *Thor* had retired under cover of a smoke screen to lick her own wounds and escape.

The damage suffered by *Carnarvon Castle* in this brief encounter was severe. Thirty-eight hits had marked a trail of destruction along her hull and upperworks. All her electrical and voice-pipe communication systems had been shot away. Her engine-room telegraphs and telephones had been riddled, her galley was completely wrecked, the main exhaust pipe from her engines extensively cut, and her forepeak flooded. This extensive damage necessitated docking on arrival at Montevideo where, ironically, some of her injuries were repaired with steel taken from the wreck of the scuttled German pocket-battleship *Admiral Graf Spee* defeated earlier in what became known as the Battle of the River Plate.

Carnarvon Castle's casualties after her ninety-minute battle were six dead and thirty-two wounded. *Thor* made it safely back to Germany and after the war, when the full story could be told, it was learned, with not a little chagrin on the part of the Royal Navy, that of the five hundred shells fired by the *Carnarvon Castle,* not a single one had found its mark!

Reaction in naval circles to the outcome of the engagement, and the subsequent news that no damage had been inflicted on the enemy, was shock. The fact that a much smaller German raider had successfully outfought, outgunned and badly damaged a British armed merchant cruiser was unpalatable. Certainly this failure must have brought home even more forcibly to the Admiralty a situation of which they were already doubtless well aware: that the weakness of the AMCs lay in their big silhouettes, old short-range weapons, primitive fire control methods and lack of protective armour-plating. Their days were numbered.

Close-up of damage incurred by *Carnarvon Castle* – note hands fallen in for entering harbour. (SANMMH)

A photocopy of a scribbled note written by Chief Petty Officer H Heynes RNVR(SA) who was on board *Carnarvon Castle* at the time, has come into the author's hands. It must be borne in mind that this was written before the facts were known. In places time has made the writing barely legible. But interest lies in the fact that it records events and impressions on the spot. CPO Heynes writes:

On watch, from 4 a.m. to 8 a.m. on Dec 5th. Sighted ship at 6.45 a.m. Challenged at 07.19 a.m. w/'K'. No reply so Capt gave orders for 1 round to be fired over her bows. Enemy ship replied with 2 rounds and put up a smoke-screen. She increased speed and we chased her. Action started at 0800 and broken off owing to shortage of ammunition at 0912. 5 ratings were killed, 1 steward, 1 ship-wright, 1 stoker and 2 A/Bs. 27 injured and wounded, some very badly burnt when cordite went up. Comm Pegram gave us high praise. On morn of 6th Dec buried our dead with highest naval honours, 4 C-of-E, and 1 RC. We scored 17 hits approx. They scored 23 hits approx. We used 418 rounds.

Messages of congratulation poured in from the Admiralty, South Africa and the British Press. By hindsight it was all rather premature. But Captain Hardy's message to his ship's company in the ship's news-sheet of Saturday, 14 December 1940 was justified:

> I should like to thank every one of our officers and men for the way they all pulled together in the recent action.
>
> For most of us it was the first time under fire; from what I saw and from the reports I have received, it can safely be said that the old hands showed the quickness and zeal of youth, and the youngsters the steadiness and discipline of veterans.
>
> We have had a good try-out and we know now that we can trust one another in any emergency which may occur. I personally am proud to command, as you are to belong to, this ship.

Many of the officers and men who manned the armed merchant cruisers were members of the Royal Naval Reserve. That is, Merchant Navy men who had joined the RNR in peacetime and undergone regular periods of training with the Royal Navy, and also bona fide merchant seamen who joined the RNR for the duration of hostilities only. Because these men were so widely dispersed, and because many of them had almost severed connection with South Africa, any information about their wartime activities has been difficult to obtain.

However, it is known that the South African training ship *General Botha* provided a regular flow of officer material, represented by both former cadets and those under training. As a result of the high professional standard achieved by *General Botha* the services of these boys and men were much in demand by captains who wanted the best. And what captain did not?

Apart from those already serving at sea, the first cadets from *General Botha* to join the RNR on the outbreak of war did so in October and November 1939 without waiting to pass their final examinations. Next year the captain-superintendent put his foot down and declared that

Commodore EW Jupp SM SAN (Retd). He served as a midshipman RNR on board the AMC HMS *Asturias* during her capture of the SS *Mendoza*. (SANMMH)

before any further appointments were made the two-year course would have to be completed. As had been the practice for several years, towards the end of the cadets' second year on board, four of them were selected for appointment as midshipmen RNR.

One of those so nominated at the end of 1940 was the present Commodore EW (Ted) Jupp, SM SAN (Retd).

Aged sixteen and a Senior Cadet Captain (similar to a school prefect but with greater responsibilities), he had from an early age made up his mind to make a career in the Merchant Navy. However, persuaded by the captain of the training ship, and after discussing the matter with his parents, he chose the RNR appointment and duly appeared before a Royal Naval selection board in Simon's Town on 5 December 1940. He still regards the interview as a mere token formality for, as we have already hinted, the Navy were only too anxious to recruit lads from the *General Botha*.

On 8 December 1940 the four who had been selected, Powell, Stephens, Power and Ted Jupp, and nineteen other South Africans, joined the former Royal Mail liner *Asturias,* now an armed merchant cruiser, one of HM ships flying the White Ensign. The boys' official designation was Temporary Probationary Midshipmen RNR. A modest rank indeed, but one that in the case of Ted Jupp eventually led to his flying the broad pennant of a Commodore before his retirement in 1978.

In 1942 members of the RNVR(SA) were given the choice of joining the newly named SA Naval Forces. In May 1943 South Africans serving in the RNR were offered a similar opportunity. Jupp (for this is his story) duly applied but heard nothing further until late 1944 or early 1945, when news of confirmation brought a welcome bonus in the form of backleave and backpay, both of which were on a far more generous scale in the South African forces than those pertaining to the Imperial forces.

He best remembers the occasion when he was standing watch while *Asturias* drifted with engines cut, about six miles south-east of Punta del Este off the South American coast in the vicinity of Lobos Island.

It was a dead calm summer night when the distant barking of seals came clearly across the waters. The date was 14 January 1941. Jupp recalls:

> The previous evening, we were patrolling the sea east of the River Plate when *Asturias* was ordered to intercept the Vichy French ship *Mendoza* which had recently sailed from Montevideo.
>
> Just after 0200 *Mendoza* was sighted between Punta del Este and Lobos Island. We immediately closed in and ordered her to stop her engines. This she did, but only after protest, and an armed boarding and anti-scuttling party were sent away to board her.
>
> At this stage *Asturias* intercepted radio transmissions from *Mendoza* in which she was attempting to inform the Montevideo port authorities that she was being attacked inside the territorial waters of the neutral country.
>
> We ordered her to stop immediately, but the orders were ignored and *Mendoza* got under way and turned back to Montevideo. Once again she was ordered to stop, and this time she obeyed, being finally brought to anchor not far from Lobos Island.
>
> The armed boarding and anti-scuttling parties were then able to board the ship and duly reported that her captain claimed to be within Uruguayan waters and consequently refused to weigh anchor and proceed as ordered.
>
> A check of the ship's position by *Asturias* confirmed this and our captain said that, under the circumstances, he was not prepared to take her. Our boarding parties had therefore to be reluctantly withdrawn and recalled. Of course, for the whole time since our first contact till *Mendoza* let her anchor, she had been cleverly edging back into territorial waters and slyly outwitting us.
>
> *Asturias* herself now had to withdraw to outside territorial waters and *Mendoza* steamed triumphantly back to Montevideo.

Just before this encounter *Asturias* had also put into Montevideo. It was customary at that time for warships in that part of the world to be allowed to enter a neutral port for a stay of twenty-four hours. That was the maximum time allowed for refuelling and provisioning and *Asturias* followed this practice once a month. A situation often arose on such occasions when Allied merchant ships had perforce to secure at a berth adjacent to an enemy vessel. Jupp writes:

We docked at Rio de Janeiro some time after the *Mendoza* incident, making fast astern of a German ship flying a large swastika. And here is an interesting point. If you should happen to arrive in port while there was an enemy ship there, they could stay as long as they liked providing they were merchant ships.

We on the other hand as a warship were only allowed 24 hours. But, if one of those ships had sailed while we were there, then we would have been forcibly held for a maximum of 24 hours to enable them to get away to a head start.

I do believe that on occasions seamen from the countries fighting one another would meet. There was an incident in Rio when some of the ship's officers attending a night-club met officers from this particular German ship and the encounter was not at all cordial!

When *Asturias* put into Montevideo on 7 January, there was a strong possibility of her being in port at the same time as *Mendoza*. That, combined with the boarding incident, and of course the fact that the young South African recruits had been at sea for only a month and had already made contact with the enemy, will help to explain the state of tension on board HMS *Austurias* as she waited off Lobos Island expecting *Mendoza* to make a second attempt to run the British blockade. And that is exactly what she did.

On 14 January *Mendoza* was again reported to be at sea, and she was closed by *Asturias* in the area where she had been intercepted before. Once again, however, she anchored within the three-mile zone of territorial waters between Punta del Este and Lobos Island.

From the diary he kept, Ted Jupp is able to reconstruct the three-day pursuit of the Vichy ship before she was taken:

We were being fed information from ashore because, well, both countries had very good spy systems going for them and so we knew in advance that the elusive Vichy ship with her cargo of contraband was coming out again.

I made a note in my diary at the time that on 15 January she plucked up courage, weighed anchor, and started to move off up the coast; but still remaining within the three-mile limit. On that particular Wednesday night a tremendous deterioration in weather conditions set in and there was a heavy swell running with an easterly wind. That meant a lee shore, which made it a hair-raising situation for the captain. Then the next day I again noted in my diary that the wind had increased. Not only was the weather bad, but the visibility too. I think the captain of the *Mendoza* had some narrow escapes, almost to running aground because of the presence of several reefs extending from the coast. To avoid them he was coming pretty close to leaving the security of the three-mile limit – which factor he had, of course, to balance against the risk of falling into our clutches.

So it really was a very trying time for him.

After three days, during which we lost sight of *Mendoza* through bad visibility and the fact that we were six to seven miles seaward of him, we eventually managed to board her because of a tactical error on the part of her master.

As I recall, the name of the bight was Portobello Bay, which has a wide sweep. By rights, to keep inside the three-mile limit the captain should have followed the natural contours of the coast, but he failed to do that.

In the early hours, just after dawn, *Mendoza* was observed to be steaming out across the bay. Our officer of the watch, with great presence of mind, noticed that in so doing she was coming outside territorial waters. With a rapid alteration of course, and at full speed, we managed to get between her and the land.

We signalled her with an Aldis lamp ordering her to stop; at the same time firing a shot across her bows with one of our guns which, incidentally, were antiquated things. In fact we had some with the year 1902 stamped on the breech!

When at last we put our boarding party on board there were no difficulties because by that time *Mendoza*'s captain was ready to give up anyway. He was a nervous wreck after three days without sleep. Once our chaps had gained her decks they found her crew very co-operative.

We then had to escort her to the narrows of the central Atlantic where a cruiser, HMS *Dorsetshire,* took over.

A Reuters press release in London at the time, surprisingly frank in those days of strict censorship, confirms the foregoing as follows:

The French steamer *Mendoza*, 8 199 tons, has failed in a third attempt to run the British blockade. The *Mendoza* sailed from Montevideo on Tuesday but returned to Uruguayan waters, where she rode at anchor near Punta del Este, east of the city. Her captain told local authorities that he was waiting for orders.

A British warship, believed to be the auxiliary cruiser *Asturias*, formerly the Royal Mail liner of that name, is reported to be lying at sea.

The *Asturias*, 22 048 tons, intercepted the *Mendoza* on Friday after she had left Buenos Aires with a general cargo for unoccupied France and compelled her to take refuge in Uruguayan waters.

'No grounds exist for protest from Uruguay over the interception of the French steamer *Mendoza*,' declared a Ministry of Economic Warfare spokesman today.

It was disclosed that *Mendoza* is one of five French ships which have been loading in River Plate ports. The others are *Katiola, Formosa, Campana* and *Aurigny*. No navicerts have been applied for, and it is learned that there is no question of the British blockade being lifted in their favour should they decide to sail.

It was emphasised that all ships bound for Europe which are not provided with navicerts are liable to interception and detention. The British authorities have no information regarding *Mendoza*'s cargo, but it is believed that it comprises mainly meat and wool.

At 1521 on 1 November 1942, the German submarine U-178 (*Kapitän-zur-See* Ibbeken) cruising off the Natal coast, submerged to attack what he described, according to *War in the Southern Oceans* (Oxford University Press), as a 'Big passenger ship; nice present after so long a time.' He fired two torpedoes at five hundred metres but recorded: 'Nothing happens. Enough to drive one mad.' A third torpedo hit the stern and put the ship out of control. After a further fifteen minutes, when she showed no sign of sinking, a fourth torpedo set the oil tanks on fire.

The victim of this attack was our old friend *Mendoza*. That last torpedo also struck the boiler-room causing a spectacular explosion just as the large number of troops, civilian passengers and crew on board the stricken ship were collecting their belongings. Her master, Captain BT Batho, one of the survivors of the torpedo attacks, lost his life while stepping from a lifeboat into an Air Force rescue launch.

The sinking of the *Mendoza* was the nearest to Durban during the war, only seventy miles east north east of the Bluff. When this became known, ten ships in the outer anchorage were hurriedly brought into port and the remaining twenty-five warned that an attack might be imminent.

Her earlier captor too, became a victim of war. After refitting in Belfast, *Asturias* likewise suffered damage inflicted during a torpedo attack by the Italian submarine *Ammiraglio Cagni*, which cost four or five lives. However, the ship herself managed to remain afloat and to reach Freetown in Sierra Leone, where she was beached and temporarily repaired, and later served as a floating barracks.

As the youngest officer on board *Asturias*, in which he spent three years, Ted Jupp traditionally had to reply to the time-honoured toast, 'Sweethearts and Wives'. Despite his long service, and the fact that he had already spent two years in the *General Botha*, it was still as a midshipman that he was eventually drafted ashore to undergo various courses before being appointed to the destroyer HMS *Ferne* at Harwich. Promotion to Sub-Lieutenant only came at the age of twenty – later

HMS *Asturias* shown here in peacetime colours. (Author)

reduced to nineteen and a half. As an RNR midshipman he received a warm welcome on board the destroyer. This he found refreshing after being a mere nobody in a big ship. He regards his time in *Ferne* as being his happiest in the wartime navy.

There followed operations on the east coast of Britain, escorting North Sea convoys, and memories of freezing winter months spent on exposed bridges. There were encounters with E-boats in which *Ferne* narrowly escaped being torpedoed; the track of the tin-fish passing ahead of the ship. With D-Day imminent, secret documents began to pour on board marked 'For Captain's Eyes Only', and to be opened on receipt of signal ON1 – Operation Neptune. The captain soon realised he could never deal with the huge pile of bumf, and he called on his First Lieutenant and Navigator (Ted Jupp) to assist him. For the next fortnight the three of them worked on chart corrections and so on, somtimes until 2 or 3 a.m. The ship's surgeon dosed them with Benzedrine to keep them going, and no one was allowed outside the dockyard, to avoid any breach of security.

On 4 June 1944, HMS *Ferne* escorted a coastal convoy from Southend and passed through the Straits of Dover during the night to arrive off Portsmouth at 0700 on the 5th. Then, as is well known, there was a twenty-four hour postponement. The convoy was turned round to head back for Southend the same afternoon, but was back again at Portsmouth at 0600 on the 6th, by which time forces were already landing at the Normandy beachheads. Like all others who took part in that momentous occasion, Jupp recalls hundreds of landing craft milling about like water-beetles.

Anchoring her convoy off Spithead, *Ferne* sailed again with a newly composed convoy and arrived off Normandy just twenty-four hours after the first landing had been made.

All were surprised at the lack of enemy air activity. The scene on the beaches was unbelievable, with everything being enveloped in smoke and the rattle and thunder of gunfire.

The arrival of the convoy was duly reported to 'Captain South-bound Convoys', whose presence on board his base ship was advertised by a huge black and white striped banner displayed across the bridge, and they were dispersed to their various beaches. *Ferne* then underwent the same procedure, in reverse, reporting to the similarly marked 'Captain Northbound Convoys', and spent the next three weeks escorting laden convoys south and empty ships back north.

On the third such voyage they had tussles with prowling E-boats and with aircraft laying pressure mines, against which there was no known antidote. *Ferne* carried a VHF gadget (known as 'The Headache') that could monitor the German radio frequency. There was also a Dutchman on board who was fluent in German. On this particular trip, with the convoy in two lines led by a captain-class frigate, the Dutchman reported that he had overheard the leading E-Boat say: 'Let's pick off the southern escort'. Conditions precluded zigzagging but *Ferne* went off at full speed from the port quarter to the van to intercept. But before she had got halfway down the line of convoy, the frigate had been torpedoed, her bow being blown off almost to the bridge.

Ferne gave chase to the E-boats then heading back to Le Havre, and although they rounded on the pursuing destroyer, they were probably out of torpedoes and their stand was merely a bluff.

The captain of *Ferne* then elected to stand by the stricken frigate and closed her to take off her wounded. With the wardroom turned into a hospital her surgeon managed to save many lives. The destroyer then took what remained of the frigate in tow, stern first, and headed for Portsmouth until met by a tug.

After several adventures on the 'Normandy run', Ted Jupp was transferred in July 1944 to the East Indies Fleet; and thereby hangs a most refreshing tale of compassion on the part of a senior commander at the Admiralty responsible for the drafting of RNR sub-lieutenants and midshipmen.

Jupp approached this commander with a request for leave in South Africa, and he was told to carry out his orders, while the commander would see what could be done. Jupp accordingly embarked in the troopship *Mooltan* bound for Suez. Just before its arrival at Port Said a signal was received ordering that he was to be landed at Port Tewfik to go home on leave. He still marvels at the request of a very junior officer being considered and acted upon in the midst of a war involving hundreds of thousands of men.

In the event he was driven to a Fleet Air Arm station and by truck to Cairo, where he embarked in an Empire flying-boat for the five-day flight home via Wadi Halfa, Khartoum, Kisumu, Mozambique, Durban and finally by train to Cape Town, where he was reunited with his parents for a three-week holiday after nearly four years away.

He then took passage in the cruiser HMS *Newcastle* from Simon's Town to Trincomalee via Mombasa, followed by a train journey to Colombo to join HMS *Scout*, a 1914 – 18 war destroyer engaged in target-towing.

A few months later he was appointed to the frigate HMS *Swale*, and left her in South Africa just as the war ended and, somewhat paradox-ically, just as that ship was being manned by a South African crew.

The End of the *Bismarck*

The following is a letter written by Commander CW Byas, then of HMS *Dorsetshire*, to his mother. Commander Byas came to the Free State from England with his parents as a child and lived in the Tweespruit district until the age of thirteen and a half when he joined the Royal Navy as the Natal Naval Cadet in 1915. He was later posted to the Fleet Air Arm and eventually became a Wing Commander.

In 1931 he flew solo from England to South Africa in a Comper-Swift aircraft. In the years before the war he served in several British aircraft carriers and in 1938 he was promoted Commander. In March 1941 he was serving as Executive Officer in the heavy cruiser HMS *Dorsetshire* and survived her sinking.

This letter originally appeared in *The Friend* newspaper. To refresh the reader's memory, the events immediately preceding the sinking of the *Bismarck* are as follows.

After a patrolling aircraft had reported that the battleship *Bismarck* and her escorting cruiser *Prinz Eugen* had left Bergen, HM heavy cruisers *Norfolk* and *Suffolk* were ordered to the Denmark Strait, and on the evening of 26 May they caught sight of the enemy in a sleet storm north of Iceland. Next morning the great battle-cruiser HMS *Hood* and the *Prince of Wales* got within range.

The outcome of the brief but costly action off Greenland was that *Prince of Wales* was damaged by gunfire and the *Hood* got a direct hit in the magazine, blew up and sank leaving only two survivors out of a ship's company of about 1 500 men.

Suffolk and *Norfolk* shadowed *Bismarck*, which had been damaged sufficiently to leave an oil slick. This was spotted by an aircraft and it enabled the carrier HMS *Victorious* to deliver a torpedo attack that scored at least one direct hit.

Next day all contact with the German warships, which were making for Brest, was lost. On 27 May aircraft resumed contact with the now crippled battleship, and her speed was reduced by air and destroyer attacks by day and by night. Commander Byas' letter takes up the story:

We had been at sea for about ten days when we heard that the *Bismarck* had got out. We were then several thousand miles away, and wondered how it would affect us, or whether we might not be involved in an attack if she got away. We watched the progress of her escape with mixed feelings, and we were somewhat depressed when we heard that the *Hood* had been lost. Then the *Bismarck* disappeared and I must say we were most distressed about it all.

In the forenoon of the second day I was down in my cabin when I felt the ship put on speed. I wondered what it was, and had a vague thought of the possibility of having made contact with an unknown ship. I went up to the bridge and at once read a signal from an aircraft reporting having sighted an enemy battleship. She was between 800 and 1 000 miles distant, but the captain had decided to leave the convoy to try to head her off from the south.

I then went down and fell the sailors in for work. Their looks of surprise when I ordered final preparations to be made to prepare the ship for action will always be in my memory. Most of them had been in the ship all of the war and had covered tens of thousands of miles without any action. Now, on their way home, it seemed that something was going to happen.

All that day and that night we dashed across the ocean wondering whether we would manage to head her off, whether she would get beyond us, whether we would be on the spot before she was brought to action, or whether we would arrive too late. All the morning of the second day we expected that we should sight her about ten o'clock that night, and during the day we began to be over-optimistic.

As the day wore on however, we doubted whether we would do that day, until later in the afternoon when we could not, and at best we would not do so until early next morning. During the afternoon she was attacked and that night we heard that her speed had been reduced and she had turned north. We knew then that we were sure of intercepting her in the morning.

We went to dawn action stations, from which we were able to send all the sailors off for relays for breakfast. We began to wonder whether we would arrive after all was over because we realised that at least two of our battleships were on the scene and would presumably soon be in action.

About 9 a.m. we sighted one of our destroyers, and we were told that the enemy was in sight about six miles ahead of him. We closed and very soon sighted the *Bismarck*, which was then being engaged by the *Rodney* and *King George V*. We opened fire at a range of about eight miles and evidently some of our early salvoes were good ones.

The *Bismarck* was making a heavy smoke screen and obviously trying to escape the punishment, but it was no good. She was being engaged from four directions and the end seemed inevitable. About 1030 she had been pretty well silenced and was burning fiercely. By then we had closed our range to about four miles. I remember thinking then that we would look very silly if she managed to get off even one salvo at us at that range.

However, we soon saw that her guns were just anyhow, so we closed to about three thousand yards and fired two torpedoes at one side and one at the other. I think they all hit; certainly two did.

All the time I was at my action station, which was high up about halfway above the ship. I had a front-row view of everything. When we got close to the ship and saw that our torpedoes had hit we also saw many of her crew on the upper deck getting ready to save themselves. The ship soon began to settle, and she slowly turned on her side. Then she turned turtle and sank in about five minutes.

We steamed up to the position and threw lines over the side: we managed to save eighty Germans, but we could not stay there. We were too vulnerable, and reports of bombing came in very soon after. We had to get out of the danger zone, so we left many of her crew in the water.

Those whom we saved we wrapped in blankets and fed and we let them sleep off their ordeal.

For the rest of that day and up to late in the evening we stayed with the two battleships, and parted company about midnight.

Next morning was foggy, but we managed to get on slowly. In the afternoon we were told to get into harbour that night, so we had to increase speed and we actually came on through very poor visibility at practically full speed. We got in just before dark and I got to bed at 0200, only to turn out again at 0500 to turn the prisoners over to the military.

After that we had the ordeal of the press on board, added to the business of having got home and trying to make arrangements for leave and so on.

★ ★ ★ ★ ★

Of the fifteen armed merchant cruisers lost in the 1939 – 45 war, one was sunk by aircraft, ten by submarine, three by surface craft, and one by fire. The last was HMS *Comorin*, a former P & O passenger liner.

On 5 April 1941 she rendezvoused with the convoy she was to escort, bound from the River Mersey to the Middle East. Captain DLC Evans, master of the *Glenartney,* one of the ships in the convoy, was startled to observe on the following day clouds of smoke erupting from *Comorin*'s funnel.

At 1430 he received a signal from her: 'Have serious fire on board. Stand by me.' Soon afterwards *Comorin* was seen to be fiercely ablaze amidships. The fire spread rapidly, and it was soon apparent that the ship would have to be abandoned.

Despite heavy seas lashed by a south-easterly gale, *Glenartney,* although rolling through an arc of 60 – 70 degrees herself, manoeuvred to windward of the burning ship, spreading oil as she did so. By superb seamanship she managed to rescue 109 of the crew from two lifeboats and seven rafts under fearsome conditions. The standard of seamanship displayed by the captain of the destroyer HMS *Broke* was likewise not forgotten by the survivors.

The officer ranged his ship under the lee counter of the burning ship over and over again in the raging seas, and by that means rescued a further 180 of the crew. Another destroyer HMS *Lincoln*, a former American four-stacker, picked up another 121. Altogether 310 of the complement of 330 of *Comorin* were saved.

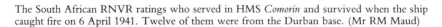

The South African RNVR ratings who served in HMS *Comorin* and survived when the ship caught fire on 6 April 1941. Twelve of them were from the Durban base. (Mr RM Maud)

About fifteen South African seconded RNVR ratings and two South African RNRs, Midshipmen P Macpherson and PEJ Ives, were there too. In a letter to his parents in Port Elizabeth, young Billy Lochhead described his experiences:

The ship has gone and I have had a wonderful escape. I cannot give any details as to how the sinking came about just yet, but I can tell you of our escape.

By 7 p.m. the ship was a mass of flames and there were 125 of us on the after end trying to invent a way of getting off to an American-type destroyer that was standing by. There was an increasing gale blowing and a terrific sea running. All the boats had gone and so had most of the rafts.

My raft, meant to carry twenty could only take nine owing to the weather, so I sent the petty officer off in it hoping there might be some way of getting it back. This, however, was impossible.

About 7 p.m. another destroyer turned up. This was a British one and a little bigger than the other. After trying a few methods of rescue, all of which failed, everyone was about to give up hope. If the destroyer had tried to come alongside she would have been reduced to scrap-iron in a few seconds, so her commander decided to run his ship up under our quarter and away again as close as he dared, giving us a chance to jump for it.

Of course the rolling and pitching of the destroyer was terrific and often she came smashing with terrific force against us. Sometimes she disappeared right under our stern so that we came down on top of her as if to break her to pieces. The order 'Every man for himself' was passed and we started jumping. Some had terrible falls, as much as forty feet. At other times the destroyer came right up to the level of 'A' deck and some just walked off.

When she came past for about the eighth or ninth time I was on 'A' deck looking for N– (this must have been about 9 or 9.30 p.m.). The destroyer's bridge came crashing against 'A' deck and I thought I saw N– jump on to it. He then shouted to me to follow. The bridge was about forty feet below and the destroyer had rolled about thirty feet away from the ship.

However, the next wave brought it back and I jumped across and managed to grab the rail on the bridge. As we rolled away from the ship I quickly worked myself hand over hand round to the front where I found a place to climb to the forecastle. I then went into the forecastle where our men were being collected together. It was terrible in there. Everytime we came alongside passing the old ship we were simply flung off our feet.

After about twenty of these trips all on board, including the captain, were picked up. Some missed in jumping, but I am not allowed to give details of casualties. It was just about midnight now, and the destroyer was in a bad state. Water leaking everywhere and the motion terrific (it was still blowing gale force).

Everything was wet and miserable, and we did our best to sleep on anything we could find. We had to hang on tight all the time, even chairs and armchairs in the wardroom being lashed down.

The forecastle (men's quarters) was as much as three feet deep in water, and we had to keep it and the wardroom dry by baling by hand. It must have been terrible for the badly injured. In that way we spent three nights before being landed.

There was no fresh water for washing for the first two days. Unfortunately I was wearing my old suit on coming away, because when the order to abandon ship was given I couldn't get to my cabin. I was wearing your blue polo-necked jersey, no shirt, sea–boots and cap.

I also saved all my negatives of photos taken since I've had the camera – the camera you gave me. I had my overcoat on but threw it off rather than risk my jump. I also saved my sheepskin coat by giving it to one of the stokers to wear. He returned it to me; I had to leave the gloves. When we landed we were each given a pair of socks. Mine came from the Society of St George, Port Elizabeth!

An interesting fact about the destroyer (HMS *Broke*) which picked us up is that she was the one that took the *Empress of Britain* in tow. Her First Lieutenant is Peter Scott, RNVR, son of Captain Scott, the Antarctic explorer. He is a most delightful fellow. He is a professional artist and is going to try and make sketches of the scene. For this purpose he has asked me for photos of the ship. He is a great small-boat sailor and has won the International Dinghy Race, etc.

He also represented Britain at the Olympic Games. He showed me all his photos and we had long chats about sailing, etc. I took about forty photos of the scene and rescue and am taking them to the Admiralty for developing and censorship.

Another survivor, Lt RM Maud, likewise gives a detailed account of the incident in the following edited version of a letter to his father dated 15 April 1941:

We sailed from a Scottish port late one Thursday night. Until Sunday the trip was uneventful. Sunday 6 April was a dull sort of day with a heavy sea running and a cold wind blowing.

There were no church divisions that morning. We also broke out from two watches as we were now past the danger zone. I had an early dinner and afterwards went on deck to have a smoke before turning in as I had the 'first' that night. Aubrey Griggs came along and said he was glad we were out of the danger zone. He also said he would hate to get torpedoed or bombed on that trip particularly. I said, 'You're telling me – well, it won't be long now before we're home'. Another fellow came along and wanted to know if I was turning in and I said, 'In all probability, but every time I sleep in the afternoon something happens!'

Sub-Lt RM Maud whose description of the sinking of HMS *Comorin* is given in this chapter. (SANMMH)

He agreed and said, 'Something is bound to to turn up.' For you see, on our ship everything happened on a Sunday. I then left him and turned in to my hammock and began to read a book. I put the book down after a while and for some reason couldn't sleep.

At a quarter to three I heard a commotion, then the call, 'Hands to fire stations'. I grabbed my lifebelt, a pair of trousers (with half a seat), two jerseys and a pair of snow-shoes – the nearest clothes to hand at the time.

We did our best to check the fire but it was in the bottom of the stokehold. Owing to the steam having to be shut off we could coax no water out of the valves. Well, by half-past three the flames were pouring out of the funnel and hands were piped to 'Abandon ship stations'.

I was on a raft which was on the after poop-deck – right at the stern of the ship. Watty's station I know was in a lifeboat but I never saw him. Alf, too, I knew was on a float somewhere. For some time I couldn't bring myself to realise that we really had to leave the old tub which had been my home for so long and carried me for 62 000 miles. It was all so sudden.

We were carrying a number of military passengers, these were sent away in the first boat. I saw three people lose their lives (seamen) on this trip, but the remainder managed it.

A photographic reconstruction of the loss of HMS *Comorin*. Many of the survivors jumped from the stern of the sinking ship onto the fo'c'sle of HMS *Broke*.

The remaining boats I saw lowered but wasn't able to watch their progress as there was such a lot of work to be done. I took off my boots and sheepskin coat – the latter I forgot to mention I grabbed as I dashed from my hammock.

I started work then, helping to pass a grass-line between our ship and a destroyer that had been escorting us. To this we attached the rafts and they were hauled backwards and forwards.

A very slow job and only four to six men able to go at a time. Each trip took roughly twenty minutes. While I was thus engaged other fellows were heaving ammunition over the side. By then the ship was well alight, especially the top deck. Someone realised the AA shells had not been thrown overboard, so volunteers were called for. They got more than enough as the work wasn't too dangerous. I was among the crowd that went up and, believe me, I was like a cat on hot bricks because I had bare feet and the planks and plates were so darn hot. By the time we had finished I was covered in oil fumes and soot – like all the others. By that time too, the funnel was more than just red-hot and there was a continuous roar.

The grass-rope had broken for the rafts and it was getting dark. Several fellows I saw in the water crying for help, but nothing could be done. Indeed, and unfortunately, I saw many fellows killed but I will not relate the manner of their deaths. It shook me up a bit and I don't like recalling the scene.

The last I saw of Alf – or rather who I thought was he – was on a raft making its way to a destroyer. I'm sure they all reached it safely as the order came through to 'haul away'.

Another destroyer which we had signalled for had now come up but from all appearances it was too rough for her to come alongside without sinking herself. The rest of us on board went as far aft as we could and just waited to see what would happen.

I will admit that I thought, like the others, that there was no hope for us. My thoughts were very full of home just then. Thousands of cigarettes and chocolates were lying on deck but of no use to anyone – some fellows had broken open the canteen. I did at one point try to reach my locker, but as the place was filled with smoke the chances were against my ever finding the opening out again, and I therefore gave up the idea.

I was on the upperdeck when a signal came through from the newly arrived destroyer. I was standing next to the captain when the signalman gave him the message, which read: 'Attempting to reach your stern'. I heard the skipper say it couldn't be done. Nevertheless I decided to get as far aft as possible and if a chance presented itself I would jump for it. By this time it was totally dark and the ship roaring for all it was worth. Thank goodness the magazines were flooded.

The destroyer did crash alongside (thirty times). I jumped with Aubrey and a stoker the second time she came near enough. When I landed safely I believe I said a silent prayer. Everyone said afterwards we were mad to do it. It was our only hope though, and instinct told me the distance I could manage with a big enough spring. I could have jumped the first time, only I was fouled up with the sheepskin coat I had picked up to wear again. It was so cold.

Eventually, thank God, everyone had left our ship, not however without a few fellows misjudging the distance and falling between the two ships. One, a fellow of seventeen was picked up. The CPO was going mad so our commander socked him and he was thrown on board the destroyer. When we had all left our ship the destroyer torpedoed her and she was left sinking.

From crashing alongside so many times, the ship we were now on had stove in practically the whole of her port side with big holes in several parts of the foredeck. For three days we were on board this craft, crowded together on the starboard side. One was very lucky if room could be found to sit down, and even if you did your feet would still get wet. Fellows, many of them, had broken limbs. Water was rushing through the holes and every able-bodied man was kept busy for all he was worth baling the water out night and day to stop her from flooding. The two foremost compartments were flooded altogether and shores had to be rigged to stop the bulkheads giving in.

No one had any sleep for those three nights and days except for a few of the injured who were given hammocks. Food was scarce, but tins of ship's biscuits were opened which satisfied everyone.

Water was very short and we were unable to wash. A pretty sight we must have looked when we landed. This was at Greenock. Many sympathetic remarks were passed by civilians who saw the sixty odd of us.

We were given a suit, shoes and cap, and that evening went on our way to Portsmouth, being given many meals along the way. Since we travelled all night with eight to a compartment, we were unable to sleep – for the fourth night!

We spent eight hours at Pompeii during which we received an emergency kit, some money, a train warrant and two weeks' survivor's leave. By this time we were pretty well all in and I felt rotten.

The next day I awoke to find I had spots all over me and, fearing the worst, sent for a doctor. He declared I had measles and packed me off to Chatham Royal Naval Hospital. I have only German (unpatriotic!) measles, so will be leaving here in two days' time. Before leaving London I sent you a cable, but had great difficulty in wording it – hope it was clear enough.

Don't you think I've had the most remarkable birthday anyone could have? By the way, when I landed I had no seat to my pants but had my watch and cigarette case. You see I lost everything I had, but I am thankful I have my life. I think Watty was picked up by an outward bound merchant ship so there is a possibility he may be on his way home.

Fire at sea, a hazardous abandonment of one's floating home, loss of all one's personal effects, hunger, thirst, to top it all off, a dose of German measles. Our boys certainly experienced some variety in their wartime travels.

The following is an address given by Captain DCL Evans, Master of the freighter MV *Glenartney*, to some of the survivors of HMS *Comorin* on Sunday, 13 April 1941:

These are just a few passing words addressed to you by one of yourselves – a sailor. This is no Sermon on the Mount. It gives me an opportunity of telling you what is in our thoughts, and to show our sympathy with you in what you have gone through. I speak for the whole of my ship's company – officers and men.

Jack Curtayne and shipmate, survivors of HMS *Comorin* meet the Queen at SA House 1941. Between them is Mrs S Waterson, wife of the High Commissioner for SA in London. (RH Maude)

We are glad that it was our privilege to do the little we did at a time of need. It was only a helping hand, but behind that hand there lay a willingness deep from our hearts.

However, here we are today, sailing over strange waters to many of you, and under strange skies.

You stand here now, a battered crew in a battered ship, and we are glad to have you here.

We have read a few prayers and sung a hymn together – maybe it is a simple thing to do.

I saw you tossed, scattered and tumbled about over an angry sea – flotsam – and it looked a difficult undertaking to render assistance to you all – for less than all would not be good enough.

From boats and floats I saw the friendly, confident wave of your hands as I approached; as friendly and confident a wave as I have met with when walking down the Strand, or Union Street, Plymouth.

I thank you for your well-behaved manner on board my ship. For I know only too well the effect of reaction. I know too well the boredom of having nothing to do; to have to come in relays for your meals; no proper place to rest; and to have to live in dry, salt-soaked clothes.

To be brief, we like you. We admire the wonderful spirit you have shown in dire danger, and in its aftermath of apparent safety, also the genuine praise you have given me of the Chinese crew.

I cannot but feel very proud of them indeed; but the explanation is simple. They like you too, and any little thing they can do to help is done with a ready willingness that springs from their hearts. The people who go down to the sea in ships have always had willing hearts, whatever their colour or creed. In times of danger they can always be relied upon to play the game by their brothers in distress.

But, sad to say, an ugly, bloody hand has arisen to soil the honour of the sea. Standing here amongst you I say that this evil hand will be destroyed.

I know that your thoughts have been with those you love at home – England – Australia – South Africa and Newfoundland.

Good luck, and God's blessing to you – a gallant remnant of a brave crew.

CHAPTER

7

The End of the *Hecla*

HMS *Hecla*, designed as a depot ship, could care for two dozen destroyers. She was built at a cost of over one million pounds: she displaced 14 000 tons, had an overall length of 585 feet and accommodation for forty-eight officers and 770 ratings. She was exceptionally strongly built but, since her role was to service and not to fight, her armament was light.

Hecla left Greenock with Convoy WS 18 bound out via the Cape of Good Hope to join the Eastern Fleet. On 15 May 1942, when crossing the Agulhas Bank, she struck a mine that tore a great hole ($125 \times 65 \times 45$ feet) in her starboard side forward of the bridge. Steaming cautiously at $10 - 12$ knots, with strained bulkheads creaking and groaning, and escorted by HMS *Gambia*, she managed to reach Simon's Town in safety. Next day she landed a hundred wounded, while to *Gambia* fell the sad task of burying at sea the twenty-four killed by the explosion.

HMS *Hecla* had fallen foul of a minefield laid by the German surface raider *Doggerbank* (*Oberleutnant* Schneidewind). His ship had been captured from the British as *Speybank* and it was a nice touch of the German irony to give her a name ending in 'bank' like her seventeen sisters in Andrew Weir's fleet.

Later that year the ill-fated *Hecla* was to be mortally wounded. On board her at the time was a young South African officer who recorded his impressions in vivid detail.

Herbert Hastings McWilliams was born in Walmer, Port Elizabeth and joined the Royal Navy as an Ordinary Seaman in 1940. Like so many other young South Africans he was first drafted to the heavy cruiser HMS *Shropshire*. In 1942, having been selected for commissioned rank, he passed through the training establishment HMS *King Alfred* at Hove in Sussex and served for a few months as a Sub-Lieutenant in the North Sea Coastal Forces, and in due course he was promoted to Lieutenant and sent to Simon's Town to join the destroyer depot ship HMS *Hecla*.

Being an architect by profession, and also an accomplished artist, he ended up as naval editor, cameraman, and artist on the staff of the service publication *Parade*. After the war he held many exhibitions of his works and gave the proceeds of several sales to Navy League funds.

He also became a yacht designer of note: Sprog, Extra, Winger, Ultra, Echo, Billy-oh and Kitcraft were some of his designs and he also represented South Africa at the Olympic Games in 1948.

He is now residing in retirement in Port Elizabeth, and has given his permission to quote the following letter that he wrote home when the incidents were still fresh in his mind and that was subsequently published in the *Reader's Digest Illustrated Story of World War II*. The following extract has been slightly edited here and there, with the more personal passages omitted:

It is almost a week since we lost our ship and this is the first chance I have had to set down an account of it. It seems only yesterday since we were all together on board *Hecla*. Everything is still vividly clear, but it will fade from my memory. Just as well perhaps that I have the faculty of remembering only the pleasant things that happen to me and forget so soon the unpleasant ones . . .

On November 11th I had got up for the first time after a couple of days in bed with 'flu and still felt weak. Although I did my afternoon watch I was thankful when the first lieutenant arranged for someone else to do my middle watch (2400 – 0400) so that I could have 'all night in'.

It was our last night at sea; the voyage from the Cape had been uneventful, although we had had frequent reports of submarines in the vicinity.

We were due to arrive in Gibraltar next afternoon and the feeling of runnning the gauntlet was almost over. I turned in early and had been asleep for an hour or so.

The first torpedo struck us at 2316, practically underneath my cabin. My first reaction was one of annoyance at being awakened so violently! But as the ship immediately took on a considerable list and the air was filled with the stink of burnt oil, explosives and steam, I realised at once what had happened and leapt out of bed. Fortunately the lights did not fail. My cabin was a shambles and everything loose was scattered about. One's first movements in an emergency like this are interesting. I had a vase with some flowers I got in Freetown and the water in this had shot up and all over a drawing on my desk. The first thing I did was mop up the mess and move the drawing to a dry place. Then I began to dress. I decided that if I was to be found floating in the sea, at least I would be properly clad. I put on my battledress over my pyjamas with a white cashmere scarf. I combed my hair and got a clean handkerchief out of my drawer. I then decided on rubber-soled canvas shoes instead of leather shoes. Only then did I put on my lifebelt.

Meanwhile the hum of the engines had died down, a sad sound, and there was a great deal of hurrying about, but no panic. I didn't feel a bit nervous, but my mouth was very dry.

I went up on deck and spoke to a couple of officers on the way. I didn't really know where to go or what to do as no orders had been given. Just then 'Hands to action stations' was piped and I made my way forward to 'B' gun which was my station as Officer of Quarters. I had my torch and turned it on for a second but such a shout of 'Put that light out!' went up that I realised there was a general fear that our position would be revealed.

That, however, was groundless, because it was not a dark night and our plight would have been conspicuous to anyone within a mile radius. Once at the gun I found the crew mustered and correct; the routine drill was carried out and we waited about feeling rather chilly. Owing to the list the guns would only have been useful in firing to starboard but I think the real purpose in piping us to action stations was to get everyone to do something and to account for the hands.

I blew up my lifebelt and wished I'd put on an overcoat. I allowed several ratings to go, one at a time, to collect oilskins or greatcoats; some of them were clad only in vests and underpants. About 2345 word was passed to fall about but to remain handy. There was nothing to be seen, except that occasionally two of our destroyer escorts would send up starshell to illuminate the sea as they searched for the submarine. The *Vindictive* which was in consort with us dashed ahead by herself – a wise but rather selfish move.

I then went up to the bridge to find out what was happening and found that we were to prepare for being taken in tow and that our motor launch would probably be needed for the evolution. So I decided to make my way to the boat-deck in my capacity as Second Boat Officer, to see if I could help my friend Spring who was in charge of all the boats. I found him there getting the first and second launches fuelled. He asked me to go below and find out what power was available for the 10 ton crane so that the boats could be hoisted out when necessary. I duly rushed off, glad to have something to do.

Down below there was a scene of great activity. Electrical parties were running emergency mains along the alleyways and shipwrights were busy shoring up bulkheads. Those hurt in the explosion were being taken to sick-bay. I was told that the standby power-plant was working and that we could use the crane, and went back to the boat-deck. Poor old Spring was shivering with cold since he only had on sea-boots and pyjamas. I offered to go back to his cabin and get him some clothes and, as there was nothing to be done till the boats were ready, I dashed off again to do so.

While I was getting his things I thought I might as well get my overcoat and anything else I could think might be useful from my cabin. I'm glad I went back as I'd forgotten my watch (waterproof) and I took the opportunity of collecting my wallet containing £15 in traveller's cheques and four £1 notes, my fountain pen, and post office savings book – the latter as proof that I had deposited some £130. I also pocketed my Lipsal, a stick of biltong and a slab of chocolate. Finally I took my overcoat and went back to the boat-deck.

No sooner had Spring put on his clothes than we spotted the phosphorescent track of another torpedo coming for the port side, apparently about to hit the ship just below us. We both ran inboard, covered our heads with our arms, and ducked under one of the motor boats. This torpedo struck just abaft the bridge, some distance forward of where we stood. The actual shock of the explosion was less than I had expected as I imagined we would be thrown to the deck. There was a terrific orange flash shooting up as high as the mast, above which rolled a billowing cloud of ruddy smoke studded with flying debris. Then a great column of water went up and presently bits of steel and wood began raining down all round with a fearful clattering.

We shrank back against the overhanging boat until that was over, then ventured out to be caught in a shower of water coming down like rain. The ship had taken a list in the opposite direction, so of course all those clustered along the port side scrambled across to starboard. The plight of the ship now seemed desperate, and the unfortunate thing was that all power had now failed. The crane could no longer be used.

However, I doubt if the boats would have been of any use. They had been standing in chocks with chains holding them firmly in position. These chains were fitted to the sides of the boats, hooked to ring-bolts on the deck and tightened with heavy turn-buckles.

When the ship was hit the first time, the impact of the deck rising sharply and violently and then falling again put such a strain on the chains that they simply pulled the boats apart. If they had not been so tight the boats would have risen sharply on their chocks and fallen back again with no more damage than a few cracked ribs. I climbed among the boats and was amazed at the enormous havoc. It looked as if someone had just lashed out with a sledgehammer or pickaxe – even the light cabin tops were smashed to pieces.

When I saw that the boats were useless (the second explosion having completed what the first began) I went up to the shelter-deck to see about casting off the lashings of the timber stack.

Abaft the after funnel there was a large quantity of planks and baulks secured in iron frames and lashed down, to be used for repairs to destroyers and so forth. I found that the list, which had now increased, had caused the timber to shift and burst its lashings so that it was free to float off when the ship sank. But the wood was so splintery I didn't fancy clinging to any of it in the water myself.

Meanwhile the Carley floats, or rafts, each capable of supporting twenty men, had been lowered into the sea. There were about thirty of these and of course not nearly enough for everyone. I decided I'd stick to my lifebelt and not bother about a raft. I did look round the debris for something in the way of wreckage in addition, but could see nothing suitable.

The ship was obviously sinking fast but, because of the angle of heel, the water seemed just as far from the rail on the starboard side. There was still no panic, though I noticed several chaps sobbing quietly. It was quite useless to attempt to organise any sort of 'abandon ship' drill; it was just a case of every man for himself. I decided to wait till the ship had settled a good deal further, as I did not want to jump from a height, chiefly because of the chaps already swimming below, and because of the rafts and other obstructions; but also because I could see we were surrounded by floating oil fuel, and I didn't want to get it in my face. I also figured that, as she settled, a lot of floating wreckage would be washed overboard and that perhaps some of the boats might still afford a useful perch if they did not sink under the weight of their engines. So I climbed to the highest part of the shelter-deck, next to the after funnel, which was tottering drunkenly over and leaning against the tripod of the mainmast.

I had lost Spring, but at that point I found him standing next to me, also Cox, one of the officers I liked immensely but who, alas, was eventually lost. We were all quite calm. Cox and I were giving a few extra puffs at our pneumatic lifebelts when another torpedo which we didn't see coming struck somewhere below where we were standing. Up till this time I had a sort of idea that the ship might remain afloat, at any rate until daylight though she was probably almost awash, but I couldn't help being overcome by a feeling of helplessness.

More at being unable to get the boats over the side and relieving the plight of those less able to look after themselves than I felt for myself. I was not scared – much to my surprise – but after the last torpedo I thought that perhaps it would be wise to leave. I had visions of getting entangled in stray mines, or being laid out by falling structures. The wireless aerial fell down in leaping coils and as the ship took a greater list there were ominous rumblings and crashes between decks as heavy objects broke loose and slid to port. For some reason there was no shower of falling fragments after this explosion, and I did not see the flash.

There was a blast of air and spray, however, that nearly blew me overboard; and, as the torpedo had struck the after magazine, there were various muffled secondary explosions. Spring and Cox climbed over the side and went down one of the many ropes. I rather hoped they would suggest that we should stick together, but they didn't even say goodbye. I reckoned, however, that we would meet in the water, and prepared myself to go after them.

The water, because of our great list, still seemed a long way down and as I peered over I saw the enormous hole made by the first torpedo (it turned out that *two* had struck us simultaneously) that gaped in the ship's side immediately below. I noticed some of the chaps being sucked into it and decided that this was no place to go overboard so I worked my way farther aft. Reluctantly I laid aside my overcoat. I then thought my scarf might be in the way too, so I took that off as well. Then I scrambled over.

The steel stanchions supporting the shelter-deck and boat-deck were bent outwards in the middle so there was less space between each deck and it was fairly easy to scramble down. From the main deck there were several ropes hanging down and the angle of the ship's side was now so great that by holding the rope I could almost walk down.

You may be sure that I had a good look about me, chiefly to see that I was well clear of the hole. All along the ship's side men were making their way down to the water. Most of the rafts had shoved off and the water was full of swimmers. There was a good deal of shouting, and every now and then a roaring and hissing as imprisoned air burst out of the hull.

Well, when I got to the waterline I took good care not to cut my knuckles on barnacles, or to slip on the slimy part. There was another twelve feet or so of hull to negotiate covered in slippery growth.

At last I came to the water and dreaded it because I remembered noticing on the chart that there was a cold current running south along the coast of Morocco. There was quite a rough sea too, although the oil floating about fortunately helped to keep it down. I was thankful to find it quite warm and, getting in very carefully so as not to get oil in my face, I let go and struck off at right angles to the ship's side. All round me others were doing likewise, many of them making for floats and rafts that were already obviously overcrowded.

After swimming vigorously for a bit I was horrified to find I had gone no distance at all, and although I reckoned that if she capsized away from me (as she threatened to do), to stay near the ship was still rather dangerous because of the suction. I decided to swim aft and clear the stern which was a sensible move since I found that I could make good progress in that direction. As I swam I looked up at the poor old ship. It was my last clear view of her. She lay over at an alarming angle and down by the bow. The quarter-deck was lined with chaps and as I floated by they began to sing the Volga Boat Song – of all songs!

The water was bright with phosphorus but thick with oil. It burnt my lips and tasted abominable. In struggling to get out of my gym shoes I got some in my mouth and was nearly sick. The swells were so big that in the troughs the ship was lost to sight.

I decided to stay near a cluster of rafts as I reckoned the chances of being picked up were greater. But then I saw a destroyer slowly moving along, obviously picking up survivors. I made up my mind to swim across to intercept her. By that time I was a good hundred yards from the sinking ship and I swam till I was about fifty yards from the destroyer. She was surrounded by men in the water – easily seen silhouetted against the oily scum which seemed to reflect the starlight. I could see that on board they were letting ropes, nets and ladders over the side so that we could climb up.

How my spirits rose! I hadn't been in the water more than twenty minutes and here I was, as good as saved! As I swam nearer I saw to my distress that the destroyer was under way again and rapidly moving off. Great clouds of smoke belched from her funnel; but what a stroke of luck that she did move in view of what happened – otherwise sixty of our people, including the captain, would never have been saved.

While I watched my sole hope of salvation slipping away, not more than thirty yards off, there was a most fearful explosion. A torpedo struck the stern of the destroyer and blew it sky-high. Two sections of the quarterdeck rolled up like bits of stair carpet, flinging some men into the air, while vertical spurts of orange flame showed up the jagged pieces of metal hurtling upwards. The destroyer seemed to sink lower and I thought she was done for. But what immediately entered my mind, and really did frighten me, was the thought that her quarterdeck would have been loaded with depth charges and that when they had fallen into the water and sunk to the depth at which they were set they would explode. And if they could crush a submarine like an eggshell, I didn't see much hope for my own frail body.

At that point I was more occupied in dodging fragments that began to rain down all round, hitting the water with great smacks and splashes. I reckon it was these death-dealing splinters that accounted for the loss of many of our fellows. I tried to duck under water – oil fuel or not – but of course the lifebelt made that impossible and I merely covered my head with oil. Something pretty substantial fell into the water next to me and I hoped it wasn't a depth charge. I may say, however, that I did not do any praying for help to God at any time. I simply thought, 'Well, if this is the end, nothing can be done about it.' But I did think afterwards that it would have been nice to have some sort of belief in God so that I could offer up a word of thanks for deliverance.

Well, it wasn't long before the depth charges began to go off. I can't describe the terrible sensation – the pressure on all parts of the body – just like a giant squeezing me in his fist. Great mountains of spray and solid water shot up at each explosion. After the first one I lay flat on my back and floated as high in the water as I could to relieve my body of the awful pressure, and found that it helped a lot. Fortunately only four depth charges exploded at that time. More went off later, but luckily I was not in the water then.

A new horror was now added to the scene. The destroyer was burning furiously aft and the cordite magazine began to go off. Shells of all sizes began bursting, scattering and burning material far and wide. It was sheer hell and I really thought it was the end of me. But I continued swimming steadily away from the conflagration until I was no longer surrounded by other survivors, and then I decided to wait and keep a look-out for the other destroyer which I hoped would be cruising about.

The *Hecla* was by now practically awash with her bows sticking high out of the water. The burning destroyer showed up crowds of swimmers and rafts. The sea was dotted with them over a large area. But the situation was not altogether devoid of humour. I had to laugh at one sailor who was helping a companion along with a certain amount of bullying. 'Come along, Drowning,' he called, as he lugged his chum towards a raft.

I remembered noticing that the destroyer was lowering a boat before she was hit, so I kept a sharp look-out to see if it was anywhere about, though I imagined it would be crowded with her own people by now. Imagine my relief when I saw it coming directly towards me – in fact I was almost run over by it. They were rowing hard to get away from the burning ship as the ammunition had begun to go off in good earnest.

I grabbed one of the lifelines hanging from the gunwale but a voice from the crowd on board told me, very firmly, that there was no room for me. I said I only wanted to hang on for a spell to rest, and considered myself lucky not to be shoved off forthwith.

By good fortune I was protected by this boat for the poor old *Hecla* received yet another torpedo, and this in her already sinking quarterdeck where there were several depth charges.

These apparently blew up on deck, and as each contained 500 lbs of high explosive, the air was soon filled with hundreds of flying splinters. I was thankful to cower closer to the side of the boat and to be on the far side of it.

By now I was beginning to feel the cold and my teeth were chattering. The chap sitting in the boat directly above me seemed a good sort so I begged him to find me a corner to wedge into and he helped me – much to my relief. But what a crowd! We had to bale all the time as the waves broke inboard continually.

There appeared to be a warrant officer from the destroyer in charge of the boat and giving the necessary orders to keep the bows into the seas. I was glad of that because I was in no condition to take charge. All I wanted to do was to be left alone to shiver and vomit in peace. Once I'd got rid of the oil fuel I felt better and, looking about, saw that we were heading away from the scene of disaster at such a rate that we were almost out of oil-slick.

The seas became more broken and dangerous so I passed word along to the coxswain to turn back. Fortunately this difficult manoeuvre was carried out without the boat being swamped. I should say she was a 27-foot whaler with a life-saving capacity of thirty, but there were many more than that in it and, in addition, there were at least two feet of water swilling about in the bottom. The gunwales were only a foot above water amidships. I was in the bows, and now and then the seas broke right over. We began baling with anything handy, shoes, oilskins, etc. but could hardly keep pace with the water.

We were now heading back towards the destroyer, for the fire had gone out and she appeared to be unlikely to sink after all; so the prospect of sheltering under her lee was our best hope of respite. There was no sign of *Hecla*, but now and then lights flickered here and there.

We hoped they were rescue craft, but I believe they were torches shown by the rafts.

The cries and shouts for help that had been almost continuous hitherto, were now less noticeable. In fact, after I had got into the boat myself only two more chaps came along to hang on; one of whom swam off again. The other we pulled in as he was hurt and pleaded so piteously for help.

My feelings were curious. I wasn't expecting that we should be picked up, but it was such a relief to be out of the water and especially to be with some other fellows. I think one of the worst things was the loneliness – swimming about with no one near, or at anyrate nobody I knew. I did try talking to some of the men but they were looking for their own friends, and when they found that I was an officer they swam away again!

I was just beginning to get warm, or rather to stop shivering, when a particularly heavy sea broke into the boat and almost swamped it. The only thing to do was for half of us to get out and hang on while the rest baled for dear life. I led the way, and half a dozen got out too, but I had to swear at the rest to get a few more overboard.

While the baling was in progress we spotted another destroyer heading slowly towards us – in fact threatening to ram us. We got back into the boat – some of the original crew of the boat who had not been in the water produced dry matches, and these were struck and flung into the air while we alternately shouted and listened.

What a wonderful feeling it was to discover that the destroyer was actually slowing down and coming nearer to us. We knew then that we had been spotted and we were all so keen on watching this promise of help that we failed to watch the boat. When we were still about fifty yards away it began to sink, and then very quickly capsized so that we were all thrown into the sea. The boat rolled towards me, so everybody fell on top of me which resulted in a few ghastly minutes of being trampled under water, with some of the panicky ones trying to cling on to me. I'm afraid a number were lost in the boat, as it rolled right over, and I know there were several lying down under the thwarts who could never have got out in time.

When I got to the surface I could see that the destroyer had put her engines astern and had almost stopped. However, it was no easy matter to swim to her as the propellors had produced a seething whirl of water that just carried one farther and farther away. Up till now I hadn't really struggled as I was conserving my energy, but I realised that this was my last hope and struck out for all I was worth. After what seemed an eternity I grasped the scrambling net flung over the side, but by now I was so weak that I hadn't the strength to climb up it, so I just clung on grimly while the others trod on my shoulders and head and climbed over me.

Then, to my horror, I found the destroyer was off again. No doubt it was not considered safe for her to remain stationary lest she suffered the same fate as the others. As she rolled I was alternately plunged under and lifted out of the sea, and as she gathered speed I braced myself for the last spurt and just managed to scramble high enough for someone to grab me. Of course we were all so slippery with oil fuel that it was difficult for anyone to hold on to us. As we left the capsized boat I heard the cries and curses of those who had to be left behind – a horrible sound. The destroyer's crew shouted to them to hang on and promised that we would come back, but I fear most of them must have given up.

At first I expected the destroyer to be torpedoed any minute and didn't want to go below but, deciding at last that anything was preferable to shivering on deck, I found my way forward to the seamen's mess-deck. To my great pleasure and surprise I found my friend Spring and another of the officers there. They had been in the boat too, and were pretty well all in, and just as surprised as I was to find that I was also safe.

We peeled off our dripping clothes, and someone gave out blankets. Soon cups of tea were handed round and odd garments appeared. My, but those destroyer chaps were marvellous. They must have lost a lot of their kit and I know that for the next forty-eight hours they were on the go continually.

All the time more survivors were being picked up as the destroyer (which turned out to be HMS *Venomous*) stopped for a moment every now and then. The mess-decks got more and more crowded. Some were being sick where they stood. The place was a seething mass of oily clothes and seawater, and the atmosphere was thick enough to lean against.

I found a locker to crawl into and lay there getting warm. I wondered how long it would be before we were hit by another torpedo, but it was so wonderful to be out of the water that I didn't worry too much. I was right up in the bows and it's just as well I didn't know what was going on. Apparently a submarine was spotted on the surface and the captain tried, but failed, to ram her. Depth charges were dropped – ten at a time – until the very lightbulbs were shattered in their sockets. What a din! They reckon they sank the sub as the charges were dropped right on her while her periscope was still above water. They also reckoned to have sunk another. One certainly was sunk because some of the survivors found strangers coming to their rafts who, when questioned, could not give a satisfactory answer. They were whacked over the head with a paddle and pushed off!

Well, the air began to get so foul that I simply couldn't stand it; and as I felt better, I decided to make my way to the wardroom. I enjoyed being in the mess-deck with its coarse friendliness and good nature. It was grand seeing men I knew and being greeted by them. But I felt out of place, so off I went with a bundle of sopping clothes and clad only in a pair of long woollen pants, full of holes, and a towel.

I was delighted to find a number of our officers in the wardroom although some were in a pretty bad state. I was also glad to find a bottle of whisky being passed round.

Another depth-charge attack was made and our shattered nerves were tortured again as the whole destroyer trembled and shook under the explosions. I found that I had been in the water for about four hours – from 0045 until about 0500 – and I was lucky, for some were not picked up until noon, after spending over twelve hours adrift in the sea. It was impossible to sleep, and we all longed for the dawn, feeling it to be safer as it got lighter. With my fountain pen and a throat brush borrowed from the sick-bay I made rough sketches of the sinking ship, checking details with other survivors. These were done on odd sheets of signal pad and when I ran out of ink I used a mixture of iodine and lime juice!

I was given another blanket and a pair of felt slippers and when it got fairly light I went on deck and saw the work of rescue going on. What sad sights there were! The sea was still covered with patches of oil and dotted with wreckage – mostly planks from the timber stack. Familiar doors and gratings floated about and here and there would be seen floats and rafts with pathetic little figures desperately waving and calling. Now and then a body floated past still supported by its lifebelt, arms and legs in grotesque positions, but the face always peaceful. It took all the morning to pick up those who had the fortitude to cling on in the hope of being saved. One fat stoker on a door raised a cheer – 'Good old Tubby – stick it Tubby', our chaps shouted at him.

I couldn't help shedding a tear or two as he cheerfully replied, 'You lucky bastards!' as we went past to pick up somebody else first. But, back we went and got him eventually.

One Carley float contained three men who were so far gone that they didn't understand that they had been saved. They wouldn't hold the rope thrown to them, nor put the loop over their heads so that they could be hauled on board with it under their arms. They seemed to think it was a Hangman's noose and it took ages to get them on board.

Some were absolutely black with oil and while some were cheerful and enthusiastic, others seemed hardly to care whether they were rescued or not. Gradually the deck of the destroyer filled up with these survivors, the rails lined with sodden garments and yet more rafts were sighted. It seemed as if we would never pick them all up. All the time there was this awful suspense, the fear of a submarine lurking ready to put a torpedo into us. The last man to be picked up was hanging on to two planks, and as he came alongside we saw a huge shark nosing about. Thank goodness I didn't think about that additional danger while I was in the drink.

The torpedoed destroyer, HMS *Marne*, was still afloat, but she had drifted some fifteen miles south. We now made off towards her as our instructions were to circle and protect her until an escort arrived, when we were to make for Casablanca 120 miles away. I suppose it was about 1400 when we picked up the last survivor and steamed back to the stricken *Marne*. Thank goodness the weather was fine. The wardroom stewards were wonderful in producing tea from time to time and cutting slices of spam or cheese for us to eat with the biscuit.

Venomous was running dangerously short of fuel so it was decided to try to refuel from *Marne*. After cruising slowly round her we went alongside. Except for the after twenty feet she was perfectly sound and we were delighted to see our captain, commander, several officers and about sixty men safely on board her.

There was still a heavy swell running and the two ships crashed into one another as they lay moored together. The oil pipeline was rigged and the pumps started. But after a quarter of an hour it was decided to give up the idea since the heavy pounding of the ships might weaken the already sorely tried bulkheads of *Marne*. So we cast off and continued patrolling in circles until a corvette arrived at about 0430, when we instructed her to carry out protective sweeps until the arrival of the tug that was to tow *Marne* to Gibraltar. Then we headed for Casablanca, the nearest port, but which we were not sure of reaching with our small amount of fuel, but it was worth trying.

Marne was eventually safely towed to Gibraltar. In *Venomous* there were seventeen officers and 473 ratings – and in *Marne* nine officers and sixty ratings. Thus we lost about 230, the total ship's company being approximately 810.

When it got dark our nerves were pretty jumpy. I couldn't sleep, so I sat on deck in my blanket. There was a moon, and every shadow looked suspicious.

About midnight, however, I was so fatigued that I went below and stretched out on the deck in the ship's office. The next thing I knew it was morning and we were entering the harbour of Casablanca. By steaming slowly and carefully the oil had been made to last. We finally moored alongside the American flagship USS *Augusta* with about seventy *gallons* of fuel left!

The Americans looked down on us from their spick and span ship with great curiosity. It was not long before they put nets and ladders over the side and invited us on board. My, but they were wonderfully kind. The officers were taken along and provided with soap, shaving gear, towels, etc. and how grand it was to wash away that evil-smelling oil and get cleaned up again. Then they took our collar and shoe sizes so that by the time we were bathed there was a complete US Navy uniform for each of us – including underclothes, excellent shoes, and even tie, belt and forage cap. The uniform is not khaki, but rather more sand-coloured so I am now dressed in this outfit, and very comfortable it is too, though I'm afraid it won't be warm enough when we get farther north. I took my battledress into the hot shower with me and managed to wash most of the salt and oil off it, so I can wear the upper part of that too.

The harbour of Casablanca was most interesting, being wonderfully spacious and equipped with well-designed concrete warehouses, etc. To take the port a certain amount of damage was inflicted by the Americans. The big French battleship *Jean Bart* was in harbour and tried to defend it with her 14-inch guns, so most of the American fire was directed at her.

Jean Bart, which was alongside a quay, was surrounded by sunken and capsized ships and the sheds on the wharf were still smouldering. There were a lot of ships in the docks, still intact, among which were some useful-looking liners.

We left at 0800 next morning for Gibraltar and spent an uneventful day getting there. I began to feel the effects of the ordeal and had to be given Benzedrine tablets. But, considering that I had recently been laid up with 'flu, I think I came out of it all extremely well. A lot of chaps had cuts and abrasions, and we had to leave about a dozen in hospital when we got to Gib. While on the way there we buried four men who had died of shock or exposure; a sad business.

I have nothing but the clothes I stand in, my battledress trousers, a razor given to me on the cruiser, a toothbrush and some soap. Last night I washed my socks and hankie; but we are only allowed a basin of fresh water twice a day, and the hot baths are salt, so I expect to be somewhat grubby by the time we arrive. At the moment we are in a convoy bound for the United Kingdom and ploughing through a cold grey sea in the 20 000 ton troopship *Reina del Pacifico*. The suspense never lets up for a moment and we never let our lifebelts out of sight.

And there we must leave Lieutenant McWilliams for the time being, but we shall meet him again later in these pages.

Finally, for the record, both ships had been torpedoed by U-515 commanded by *Korvetten-Kapitän* Henke. On 9 April 1944 U-515 was herself destroyed in the Atlantic, near Madeira, by aircraft from the carrier USS *Guadalcanal* assisted by US warships *Pope*, *Pillsbury*, *Chatelain* and *Flaherty*.

CHAPTER

8

The Cruisers

In 1933 the naval base at Simon's Town welcomed the heavy cruiser HMS *Dorsetshire,* the new flagship of the Commander-in-Chief, South Atlantic, Vice-Admiral ERGR Evans, the famous Evans of the *Broke* and a member of Scott's ill-fated Antarctic expedition.

The arrival of the *Dorsetshire* created a sensation for she was the largest warship to be based on this station and far surpassed her more modest predecessors, the handsome light cruisers *Calcutta, Carlisle* and *Cardiff.* During her spell in these waters she officially opened the first berth at the Charl Malan Quay in the developing dock complex at Port Elizabeth.

In 1921 the so-called Washington Naval Treaty established the relative overall size of five navies: those of Britain, the United States, Japan, France and Italy, for the next fifteen years, together with maximum tonnages and main armament for various classes of ships. The highest tonnage allowed for cruisers was 10 000 displacement in light condition, while the largest gun was set at a calibre of eight inches.

For the Royal Navy the first of these 'treaty cruisers' as they were called, was laid down in 1925. Thirteen were ordered, and in appearance, and for all practical purposes, they could be considered sister ships.

Final displacement proved to be just under the 10 000 ton limit, and each had a waterline length of 590 feet. Quadruple screws gave them a maximum speed of 32 knots, while their armament consisted of eight 8-inch guns and eight 21-inch torpedo tubes. Peacetime complement was between 650 and 680 officers and men.

Two of these new cruisers were destined for the Royal Australian Navy and the other eleven (with the exception of the *Shropshire,* often mentioned elsewhere in these pages) were named after English maritime counties, so they were commonly referred to as the 'county-class cruisers'.

They were designed for long range cruising (13 000 nautical miles at economical speed) and for service in the tropics, and their high sides and three tall smoke-stacks made them instantly recognisable. Lack of armour protection gave rise to some adverse criticism in the early days, but it was soon realised that in this respect they were no worse off than the cruisers designed for other major naval powers, and in some ways perhaps even better.

HMS *Dorsetshire* built by the Portsmouth dockyard was the last of her class to be completed. She was delivered on 30 September 1930 to be commissioned as flagship of the 2nd Cruiser Squadron, Atlantic (Home) Fleet which included her sister HMS *Norfolk* and the smaller cruisers *York* and *Exeter*. Her first captain was AJ Power who was relieved after his customary two years in command by Captain PLH Noble.

With the German Navy virtually impotent under the terms of the Versailles Peace Treaty of 1919, and with the French and Italian 'treaty cruisers' keeping watchful eyes on each other in the Mediterranean, there was little point in the Royal Navy retaining such powerful units in home waters. Accordingly it was decided that these heavy cruisers would make good flagships on foreign stations and they therefore were gradually replaced in the 2nd Cruiser Squadron by newer and smaller vessels.

Dorsetshire had been allocated the Cape Station. On completion of duty in those waters she returned to the United Kingdom, and after a refit she was sent to the China Station. She was there when war broke out in September 1939.

With the powerful German pocket battleship *Admiral Graf Spee* at large on the trade routes of the world an answer had to be found; and among the many vessels chosen to hunt down the *Admiral Graf Spee* and other German raiders known to be at sea, together with their supply vessels, were the *Dorsetshire* and her sister, *Cornwall*. Both were withdrawn from the China Station and sent to South African waters. On arrival they embarked many South African volunteers, drawn mainly from the RNVR (SA) divisions.

Dorsetshire, now under the command of Captain BCS Martin, became a unit in a small force partly successful in immobilising the powerful new French battleship *Richelieu* at Dakar after the collapse of France.

That action was to prevent the possibility of *Richelieu* falling into German hands and thus threatening the main convoy routes round Africa to the Middle East and India.

For the next eighteen months *Dorsetshire* patrolled the Freetown/Cape route with occasional calls at the United Kingdom. While escorting a homeward-bound convoy in May 1941 she won a place in naval history by torpedoing a cornered German battleship, the mighty *Bismarck*. Pausing to pick up some eighty survivors, *Dorsetshire* was interrupted in her mission of mercy by a submarine alarm.

On 1 December 1941, now commanded by Captain AWS Agar, VC, DSO, RN, she intercepted the U-boat supply ship *Python,* which promptly scuttled herself. Once again *Dorsetshire* did not hang about. U-boats were known to be in the vicinity, and in fact were to play a vital part in rescuing not only the *Python*'s crew but also survivors from the sunken raider *Atlantis* that had been succoured by *Python*. Because of that successful action *Dorsetshire* was responsible for the withdrawal for some months of U-boats in the South Atlantic.

At the end of 1941 the big cruiser returned to the Indian Ocean in charge of a large troop convoy bound for Bombay and Singapore. With Japan now an enemy, and after many months at sea, *Dorsetshire* went to Colombo for a long overdue refit.

She was there at the beginning of April 1942 when intelligence reports indicated that the same formidable Japanese force of five aircraft-carriers that had caused such grievous losses to the American fleet at Pearl Harbour was preparing a strike against the weak British East Indies Fleet under Admiral Somerville. This fleet, supposedly based on Colombo, was in fact operating from a secret anchorage at Addu Atoll.

On 4 April aerial reconnaissance reported the Japanese approaching Ceylon from the south-east. *Dorsetshire* and *Cornwall,* the only major units in Colombo, were sailed immediately to join Admiral Somerville, then some 600 nautical miles to the south-west and hoping to get in a night attack against the Japanese. However, when still 200 nautical miles short of the rendezvous point, the cruisers were sighted next day by Japanese reconnaissance aircraft.

Without air cover themselves they were soon attacked by a strike of over fifty Japanese dive-bombers, hit repeatedly, and sunk within twenty minutes, leaving the survivors clinging to a few boats and rafts.

Aware from signals of the loss of the cruisers, but uncertain of their position and facing imminent attack himself, Admiral Somerville could give no immediate help. Next day, however, he despatched the cruiser

HMS *Cornwall* – typical county-class cruiser. (G Upton)

Enterprise and two destroyers to search to the north, but to turn back by 1600 if nothing were found. When that time expired the navigating officer of *Enterprise* persuaded his captain to continue for another fifteen minutes. With only *one minute* left, they sighted the survivors and picked up 1 122 men, including both captains, from the sea; a miracle if ever there was one.

Altogether 424 lives were lost between the two cruisers. During the previous two years, as has been already noted, South African volunteers had replaced many Royal Naval men due for relief in ships calling at South African ports, and by April 1942 there were 104 South Africans serving in *Cornwall,* of whom twenty-three were killed or missing in the sinking, and exactly a hundred in *Dorsetshire* of whom sixteen did not survive. Total deaths were 191 in *Cornwall* and 233 in *Dorsetshire,* of whom nineteen were officers.

So many South African naval volunteers served at one time or another in the *Dorsetshire,* both in peace and in war, that the following is included for their information and general interest:

The *Dorsetshire* that they knew was only the third to bear the name in the annals of the Royal Navy, and was fated to be the last. During her lifetime of less than twelve years she was associated with particularly distinguished senior officers. Evans of the *Broke* retired as a Full Admiral, became a Regional Commissioner for Civil Defence in 1939 and was rewarded with a peerage in 1945. Through his example and inspiration he did much to sustain the people of London through the worst of the Blitz.

AJ Power commanded the naval contingent that drew the gun-carriage bearing the coffin at the funeral of King George V in 1936 and went on to command the new aircraft-carrier *Ark Royal* in 1938. In 1944 he became Commander-in-Chief East Indies Fleet, and of the Mediterranean Fleet in 1945. Knighted in 1944, he retired as an Admiral of the Fleet in 1952 and died in 1960.

PLH Noble became Fourth Sea Lord at the Admiralty in 1935 and a Rear-Admiral, Commander-in-Chief, China Station, in 1937, and then of Western Approaches during the Battle of the Atlantic. Knighted in 1936 he ended his career as head of the British Admiralty delegation in Washington and died in 1955.

BCS Martin, having joined the Royal Navy as a boy entrant on the lower deck, became one of the very few to reach the rank of Captain RN and retired in 1946 as Rear-Admiral with a knighthood. He then settled in Natal and died at Port Shepstone in 1957 at the age of 66.

AWS Agar won the DSO as a Lieutenant in World War I and the Victoria Cross in 1919 for torpedoing a Bolshevik battleship at Kronstadt, near St Petersburg, in a daring attack in a coastal motor boat. Still a Captain he left the service in 1946 after commanding the Royal Naval College at Greenwich and died in 1968.

Sinking of Raider by HMS *Cornwall*

The following is a letter written by JP Jordi in August 1940 for the St Andrew's College (Grahamstown) school magazine:

A year ago I was at College and never dreamed then, of all the interesting and exciting places that I have seen in the last few months.

Outstanding among my experiences was HMS *Cornwall*'s action with a Nazi raider (*Pinguin Kapitän-sur-Zee* Krüger) in the Indian Ocean on 8 May 1940.

'Hands will go to tea at seven bells and must be prepared to go to action stations shortly afterwards.' It was a sultry afternoon and we were all dozing in the mess-deck, but this piped order, broadcast throughout the ship by means of loudspeakers, allowed of no more sleep. It was a sign that the reported raider for which we had been searching for nearly two days had been spotted.

Aerial view of HMS *Cornwall*. (Mrs P Fraser)

Half an hour later when I reached my post at an anti-aircraft gun, I found that *Cornwall* was travelling at high speed with a huge bow-wave fanning out on either side.

When our quarry was clearly visible, many grumbled: 'A washout – nothing more than an ordinary merchant packet.' Nevertheless she did not reply to our signal and kept edging away. We fired a blank and a few minutes later a shot across her bows.

Only then did she reply – but not by hoisting an identifying signal, nor by heaving-to for us to examine her – no, her answer was to slew sharply to port so that she was travelling on a course parallel with ours, hoisted the Nazi flag and, dropping huge flaps which concealed her guns, belched forth a full broadside.

Never have I been so taken aback – like the others near me I stood quite still for a moment or two hardly believing my eyes. Then the splash of shells landing unpleasantly near and the whine of fragments flying overhead convinced me that I would be better off treating this business as a reality.

Our anti-aircraft guns were not needed so, with fifteen others, I crammed myself into what little shelter there was on the exposed deck. If the gun crew had tried to fit into that corner at some quieter time we should have found it well-nigh impossible. But we managed then! It was thrilling to hear our heavy guns blazing forth salvo after salvo. It was fine too, to see our huge battle ensigns flying aloft, with signalmen standing by with more in case the others should be shot away.

The holocaust and confusion lasted about nineteen minutes; most of that time I was sheltering but I made occasional sorties into the open to see how things were going.

At last a salvo of ours must have pierced her magazine, for with an enormous explosion the raider was suddenly no more. All that remained was a column of smoke rising higher and higher, and a few score survivors clinging to pieces of wreckage.

The Englishmen – there were many prisoners on the raider – began singing 'Roll out the Barrel' as we drew near and lowered our boats. There were lascar seamen there too – pathetic in their gratitude and admiration. The Germans were of a haughty, sturdy type.

It was late in the evening before we were under way once more, and the natural reaction seemed to be a great ability on everyone's part to tell everyone else all about it; especially when tongues were loosened by the material results of the captain's order to splice the main-brace!

Cornwall did not escape unscathed in this encounter. A hit by *Pinguin* put her steering gear out of action and for a few minutes the cruiser was unmanageable. Then, during rescue work, a power failure in *Cornwall* put all the fans out of action so that the engine-room temperature rose to 200° F forcing the occupants out temporarily and causing the death of an engineer officer through heat-stroke, the only casualty besides a quartermaster wounded by a shell splinter. *Cornwall* also suffered an ugly gash just above the waterline.

Durban men serving in HMS *Cornwall*. Christmas day 1941. (G Upton)

About two hundred British and lascar prisoners were lost in *Pinguin*. *Cornwall* managed to rescue sixty German survivors, fifteen lascars and nine British seamen, but not *Kapitän* Krüger who went down with his ship.

★ ★ ★ ★ ★

The loss of the cruisers *Dorsetshire* and *Cornwall* is aptly described in the following account which was first published in the United Kingdom magazine *Illustrated* of 12 September 1942 and subsequently broadcast by the BBC.

It is doubtful whether the narrator, Chief Naafi Canteen Manager, AG Elsegood, is a South African; but nevertheless his vivid description of events as related to Carl Olsson will be familiar to all those who survived the sinkings:

Sailing steadily through the warm calm ocean in company with *Cornwall*, *Dorsetshire* was hunting for surface raiders and an enemy fleet. Reconnaissance aircraft from Japanese aircraft-carriers were searching for us. British carriers were too far away to afford a fighter escort.

Three hundred miles west of Colombo, at dawn on 5 April, the bugle sounded 'Action stations' through the ship's loudspeakers. This was customary at dawn, and although the time passed slowly, stations were maintained. Gradually a feeling of excitement spread throughout the ship. It was Easter Sunday, but there was little thought spared for this holy day – instead there was an awareness of increasing tension in which all shared.

My action station was in the sick-bay amidships where I was in charge of a medical party. I went along there and reported to the surgeon-commander and saw that instruments, bandages and lint were laid out in proper array. Neil-Robinson stretchers (cane and canvas folding contraptions that can carry a wounded man through the narrow confines of a ship) were stacked in the sick-bay.

Then we sat down to wait. 7 a.m. came, the time when we usually opened the canteen for the first morning sales, cigarettes, soft drinks, toothpaste, chocolate and hundreds of other things.

We waited there through the morning, cooped up under the electric lights. The waiting, the suspense, is the worst part of it all. Conversation palled after a while and some of us played cards or Ludo.

There were the usual reliefs for food and a drink of tea or coffee. I went on deck once or twice and saw the guns' crews wearing their flash hoods, tensely alert at their pom-poms, waiting like us.

About mid-morning we had word from a rating passing through the sick-bay that a Jap scout plane had been sighted. Then, about 1 p.m. we heard that more enemy planes were near.

At 1.40 p.m. we heard the muffled toll of our pom-poms and other AA fire. We looked at one another and I thought, 'This is it'.

A tough Cockney rating whom I knew well, one of the repair parties on an inspection round, grinned at us cheerfully as he passed through the sick-bay and said, 'Blimey, here's the slit-eyes at last, bringing us a nice packet of Easter eggs.' He had no sooner gone through the doorway at the end of the sick-bay than there were two terrific explosions from somewhere aft.

Gunfire ceased and then started again in slow individual gun-bursts. Lamp bulbs flickered twice off and on and then dimmed. The explosions felt exactly as if some giant hand had seized the ship and shaken her bodily. In the pause that followed I felt the even vibration of the engines falter and slow down.

I learned afterwards that Jap bombers from two carriers had come at us in waves of seven out of the sun. Some actually tried to crash themselves on our decks. The guns had not much chance; they were just overwhelmed and we got two direct hits. Just before the bomb blasts Captain Agar gave instructions to hoist the silk Battle Ensign. Great efforts were made to do so, and although the ensign did not reach the top of the mast, it was flying when the ship sank.

These waves of bombers were followed by fighters which dived, machine-gunning the decks and gun stations, and shattered most of the boats with explosive bullets.

It all happened in a few minutes. As the first wounded came in they were attended to at once by the surgeon-commander and two other doctors – my party still had nothing to do. A bomb then came clean through the deck and passed through the dispensary at the end of the sick-bay and exploded in the marines' mess-deck. It came in diagonally and I only saw the flash. The next moment I found myself on my back outside the sick-bay door where I had been flung by the blast.

All the lights went out, because our power was hit and the place was full of fumes, smoke and dust. The emergency lighting however (two single lights), came on immediately. I picked myself up, and we got to work again. Some men in the sick-bay had been killed by the blast and others wounded. Working in the semi-darkness I wished I was on deck with the guns.

But now we could all feel the ship listing heavily. The engines had stopped and the deck seemed to be falling away beneath our feet. Since the power system had been cut off we could not get any orders through the loudspeakers. The first thing I heard was some men calling from the gangway, 'She's going!' Quite unhurriedly the surgeon-commander gave orders to get the wounded up and clear of the sick-bay. We got them up.

Boats hung shattered and burning from the davits. Through the smoke clouds that drifted across the water I could see stabbing flashes of flame from the distant guns of *Cornwall*. The Japs had left us and were now making a concentrated attack on her, and she was going down fighting. Against the smoke among the gun-flashes there were long streaks of flame as Jap aircraft went diving into the sea.

The thing that struck me was the coolness of everyone. I don't know what I expected, but I know they helped me a lot. There we were, one side listing almost to the water, and you might have thought they were cheerfully waiting for the liberty boat for shore leave. No panic, no pushing or shoving, less rush and excitement than at a normal 'Action stations'.

The order came to abandon ship, and the men began throwing Carley floats, Denton rafts and any floatable wreckage overboard. Except for two whalers and a skiff the boats were useless. We got the wounded into those. I saw Commander Byas on the upperdeck. Severely wounded and holding his hand to his side, he was calmly giving orders through his chief boatswain's mate and getting the men away. All I thought was how warm the water felt, and a vague regret about the canteen I was leaving behind, newly stocked and as good as any in the Navy. That's the effect of other men's coolness and courage when you are all together.

We got to rafts and wreckage, pushing and swimming to get away from the suction as the ship went down. I saw her go. She slid under easily, only half-an-hour since I had first heard her guns in the sick-bay. She was a grand ship with a great record.

The smoke lifted a bit, and as I clung to the edge of the raft there was a mass of bobbing heads and clusters of men perched on rafts and wreckage. There was also the murmur of men's voices over the water, calling to each other and talking. Men were shouting from raft to raft after their pals, 'Has anyone seen so-and-so?', 'Is so-and-so with you?' and similar queries. One crowd started singing 'Roll out the Barrel', and other voices took it up till singing echoed over the water. Those of the Jap aircraft that survived had gone. We were alone except for *Cornwall*'s survivors, also in the water some miles away.

We got ourselves organised, as far as men swimming and floating in the ocean can do. Captain Agar was going round in one of the whalers with the wounded, rounding up swimming stragglers and others clinging to wreckage and towing them in until we were all together in one big bunch. That was a good move. Men could help each other and it would be easier for the rescue vessels to find us.

When that was done he came among us and spoke to us, his voice coming clearly across the water as if he was on his own bridge. He told us, among other things, that Commander Byas, though badly wounded, was alive, at which everyone cheered. He told us that help was coming and advised us to take shirts and underwear or other garments off and drape them turbanwise on our heads as protection against the broiling sun. It was mid-afternoon and we were only a few degrees above the Equator. That wise advice saved a lot of us from sunstroke or worse.

With our faces blackened with oil fuel floating everywhere (several survivors believed that the oil on the water enabled many to keep afloat and substantially reduced casualties) and our turbanned heads, we looked a funny sight. There was plenty of wisecracking, and one bunch of wags on a raft started a nasal Eastern singsong, chanting and hand-clapping.

We took turns on the rafts and in the water, just clinging to them. When each man's turn came for a rest on the raft he handed his Mae West over to a man who had to swim (some of them hadn't been able to get their Mae Wests before our ship went down). Once or twice I thought about sharks (the Indian Ocean is full of them) but I don't think any of us saw one. At any rate there were no alarms. One of the men said, I don't know with what truth, that fuel oil keeps them away.

Night came with everybody still cheerful and keeping together. I heard parties singing comic songs on some of the rafts. How they kept it up I don't know because I was beginning to suffer a bit from thirst. They found some water and condensed milk, but that was for the wounded. We had a biscuit each the next morning. Though mine was flavoured with fuel oil and salt water it still tasted good. During the night we kept watches to look out for rescue ships, and the brilliant stars of the tropics started several false calls.

Fortunately the night did not last long – and then came that biscuit breakfast! I didn't feel so good but, believe it or not, some of the men were still so fresh that they were swimming races from raft to raft! One crowd of young stokers actually started a sort of water polo match using a rolled-up vest for a ball.

That second day dragged a lot. I had gone over from my raft hand-hold to a floating wooden spar from *Dorsetshire*. It was 4 p.m. and I was just making myself comfortable when I heard a shout of 'Plane!' We eyed the tiny speck very tensely for a moment, wondering if it were a Jap. But in the next few seconds there was a yell: 'String-Bag!' – the Navy slang for the Swordfish reconnaissance plane of the Fleet Air Arm.

In no time it was sweeping low over our heads. I could see the pilot waving. Within an hour there was more cheering as smoke from two destroyers and a cruiser showed up on the horizon. Within an hour I was being hauled on to the deck of a destroyer and being given a sip of barley water. While our destroyer searched for any other straggling survivors we were led to hot baths and our oil coating was removed with some special solution.

Those who could not walk were carried. The destroyer's crew did everything for us, including giving up their own bedding while the officers gave up their cabins to the wounded and turned the wardroom into a sick-bay.

It was dark by then, and after the bath and a rest there were buckets of hot sweet tea to wash away the taste of fuel oil and the Indian Ocean, followed by a huge meal that they called 'breakfast'. I found myself professionally wondering where they had got all the food – but the Navy can usually manage everything.

Other accounts given by survivors say that in the shell-room the crew had not fully realised what had happened as the ship lurched and shuddered. Fumes choked everyone, and a marine corporal scrambled up to the deck with the aid of an electric torch. He found the ship almost deserted, with hundreds of men already in the water. Near him Lt Geoffrey Berlyn of East London (who received a mention in despatches) calmly lit a cigarette and took a few puffs before jumping. His coolness and courage were an example to everyone. He and two other officers

Ian Keith of Port Elizabeth. Lost with HMS *Cornwall*. (Mrs P Fraser)

later swam to the groups of swimmers to say a few words of encouragement, which did wonders for their shipmates' morale.

The corporal had only to step into the water quite calmly and start swimming, for the ship was already well down. He had lost his lifebelt but found a piece of wood to help keep him afloat. He felt no fear then, but there was a spasm of fear when the Japs flew very low in formation, spitting machine gun bullets towards the helpless men. The corporal 'beat the record for a surface dive', but when he broke water again the planes were gone. But two officers and a stoker petty officer were killed in this wanton attack.

From then on his story follows the lines of that already told. Of the general relief of being picked up – the rescue ship whose crew could not do enough for the survivors – the battleship to which many were transferred and treated in the same warm generous way – until they were yet again transferred to a troopship, and left for an unknown destination.

The first request from practically every survivor was for word of his safety to be cabled home. In dozens of letters sent as soon as the transport reached port there was the same casual attitude towards the ordeal, and the same heartfelt regret expressed that 'all my gifts for you went down'. Very little was saved but for few things, for most of the ship's silver, plate, etc., had been landed before the last cruise. In every man too, there was a fierce desire to get another ship as soon as possible and to have another go at the Japanese.

Yet another account of the sinking was taken from the pages of the *Diocesan College Magazine* of June 1942, by Able Seaman RK (Dick) Martin, who wrote thus to his old school:

I am enjoying my leave very much but feel a bit of a fraud at times as I came to no physical harm. The time spent in the water was quickly compensated for by the marvellous treatment we received from the various ships that picked us up and brought us home. Here is a summary of what happened. *Dorsetshire* and *Cornwall* left a harbour in Ceylon steaming at 27 knots to join the Far Eastern Fleet.

HMS *Cornwall's* action against a German raider. The enemy vessel suddenly blows up with smoke and debris rising to about 2 000 feet (above); the excited crew, viewed from *Cornwall's* bridge, discusses the action (left) and survivors from the dreadful explosion in a lifeboat (below).

About 0900 the following morning aircraft kept bobbing up on the horizon. We remained at action stations throughout the day allowing small parties to go to dinner at half-hourly intervals. At 1340 the navigator shouted: 'Cornwall has been hit by a bomb'. A few seconds later our HA opened up; then there was a terrific explosion followed by several others. The door of the plotting office was blown in and through the opening I could see clouds of steam and black smoke. Dorsetshire soon took on a heavy list to port and started to go down by the stern. Orders to abandon ship came about 1.50 p.m.

When I got into the water, which was calm and warm, I found that my lifebelt kept me up admirably and it was with a feeling of complete confidence that I, with hundreds of others, swam away from the rapidly sinking ship. I looked towards the Cornwall, which appeared to be stopped but was quite upright in the water.

Just then the Japs came over us with their machine guns blazing, the bullets churning the water all round us. A friend of mine got a bullet across the seat of his pants as he, emulating the ostrich, had his head under the water but his stern up in the air.

They killed the surgeon-commander and several others, one chap surviving five bullets in the chest. When the Japs left we collected everything that floated, allowing the wounded into two boats. Those of us who couldn't find a place just swam about or hung on where we could. About 5 p.m. two of our planes appeared, signalled us to 'hang on' and then made off. We heard later that one was shot down and the other crash-landed. Just before dark a Jap passed over us flying very high. It seemed they were waiting to bomb the rescue ships.

The night seemed devilish long, but we got through it at last. Thick black oil had come to the surface to add to our troubles, making those of us in the water look like nothing on earth. The rising of the sun, however, cheered us up a bit and the time seemed to pass quite quickly.

At 5 p.m. two more planes appeared and an hour later we saw, just too grand for speech, a light cruiser and two destroyers racing towards us. We were soon picked up, given food and drink, and a place for much-needed sleep.

After two days on the destroyer all South African ratings, plus about six others, were transferred to a light cruiser whose crew didn't seem to be able to do enough for us. After about a week at sea we were landed at an East African port where transport to South Africa was awaiting us.

★ ★ ★ ★ ★

With further regard to the loss of Dorsetshire and Cornwall, the following from the Medical History of the Second World War, Royal Naval Medical

Service, Volume 11 (HMSO) should be of general interest and give an indication – if any were needed – of the devotion to duty displayed by the medical staffs afloat:

In HMS *Cornwall* the sick-bay received a direct hit early in the action and all its occupants were killed, including one medical officer. The three first-aid posts were badly damaged and a sick-berth rating killed in each case.

The after dressing station was flooded, but the surgeon-lieutenant and sick-berth attendant managed to escape.

When the first bomb struck, the *Cornwall*'s senior medical officer was making his way from the sick-bay to the after dressing station. He turned to go back to the sick-bay but was prevented from doing so by an explosion in the fore-cabin flat.

The ship had quickly taken a sharp list to port and this, together with the absence of light between decks and the violent concussion of rapidly consecutive explosions, made useful action almost impossible.

However, a sick-berth attendant returned to the flooded after dressing station against a stream of escaping men and managed to retrieve a 2-oz bottle of morphia, a hypodermic syringe and a small case of surgical instruments.

By now it was obvious that *Cornwall* was sinking rapidly, and her captain gave the order to abandon ship. Nearby wounded were lowered into a whaler, the only boat which it was possible to launch, though five Carley floats were got into the sea. The ship then sank bows first, and as she sank one of her motor boats fortunately floated off and remained upright.

About two-thirds of *Cornwall*'s complement had been able to abandon ship, totalling over 500 officers and men. These survivors were scattered over an area of about one square mile and they included many injured. Morphia injections were given to those within swimming distance. Three of the ship's officers had been supplied with tubunic ampoules of omnopon. One of these officers survived, and his ampoules were made good use of.

Wreckage was gradually gathered together in the sea to make rafts, and the survivors formed themselves into about a dozen groups. The floating motor boat was reserved for those badly wounded, and bit by bit the floats and rafts were brought alongside it and the worst cases transferred. The wounded who were able to sit or remain propped up were placed in the motor boat's engine-room and after cabin. The remainder, most of them unconscious, were laid in the forepeak and on the canopy.

The number of persons in the motor boat was maintained at about forty wounded, three medical staff, three men at the pump and three others baling. The boat's gunwale was within a few inches of the water, but fortunately the sea was calm and with care it was possible to keep the boat afloat and on an even keel.

Men with simple fractures were left on the Carley floats and although lying in twelve inches of water they were surrounded and supported by uninjured men and were thus less liable to further injury than they would have been in the motor boat.

By the evening the wounded had been catered for as far as possible and the various craft had been manoeuvred into a 'snake', kept head to wind by the whaler, with the motor boat lying second.

The surviving surgeon-lieutenant attended to the wounded in the after part of the motor boat and the senior medical officer and an LSBA attended to those in the fore part. This sick–berth rating had done valuable work in hauling the wounded aboard and his competence and cheerfulness were remarkable – he was subsequently mentioned in despatches for his devotion to duty on this occasion.

Two of the wounded had died during the afternoon and they were passed overboard. Three of those in the forepeak were obviously dying, so they were hoisted out on to the boat's canopy and three from the canopy transferred to the shelter of the forepeak.

During the night eight wounded died and were lowered over the side. Their clothing was retained to be used to make dressings and coverings for the others.

After sunrise on April 6 the heat began to be troublesome and the men in the water passed their clothing into the motor boat to be used as coverings for the wounded, who were kept cool by repeatedly soaking their clothing in sea water. Those wounded who were able to do so were instructed to dip their burns and wounds into the sea at frequent intervals. Some of the serious cases of burns were lowered into the sea from time to time, and that gave them great relief.

Sharks were present in great numbers, but fortunately the sea was clear and they could be easily spotted, especially when preceded by 'pilot' fish. Vigorous splashing invariably made them turn away.

At 0800 the senior medical officer made a 'round swimming tour' of the survivors. Many were suffering from blepharitis, due probably to a combination of blast, oily salt water and strong sunlight. A small quantity of clean cotton wool had been saved and this was used to wipe their eyes, and it gave them an unexpected degree of relief. Attention was given to fractures, and a dislocated shoulder was reduced.

On the whole, those in the water and on the floats were much cooler and more comfortable than those in the motor boat. A large amount of wreckage had by now been collected and lashed together, and many of the men had slept 'strap-hanging' on to these temporary rafts, supported in the water by their lifebelts. Suitable cases were selected to fill the vacancies inboard during the forenoon.

A ration of three drachms of water was issued to each survivor at 0900, and at midday a further ration was issued to the wounded. The remainder were issued with a teaspoonful of corned beef. Many found that this made their mouths swell and it was difficult to swallow. But when rubbed on the lips, the fat greatly eased the dryness and cracking from which a large number were now suffering.

The surgeon-lieutenant organised and supervised the issue of all rations in the boat. In addition, he had throughout been dealing single-handed with the wounded in the after part of the boat. Many of these were in considerable pain and needed continual care. At about noon he collapsed from exhaustion and was made as comfortable as possible propped up against the legs of his patients. After half an hour he recovered and carried on with his work as before. This surgeon-lieutenant, an RNVR officer, was later honoured by being made a Member of the Most Excellent Order of the British Empire. He worked with the wounded for thirty hours in the motor boat, and again for another twenty-four hours after being rescued. He continued with undiminished zeal even after they had been landed.

At about 1400 shouts were heard in the distance and two men were seen to be swimming in the sea. The whaler was sent to pick them up and it was revealed they had swum from a point four miles away where there were thirty-three more *Cornwall* survivors on a home-made raft with the surgeon-lieutenant (D) in charge. This officer too received a mention in despatches for his courage and devotion to duty.

There were wounded among these men who needed further attention, and the whaler was sent out to bring them in. In the meantime patients were transferred from the motor boat to the floats to make room for these new casualties. When the whaler returned the six worst cases were taken into the motor boat and the rest distributed among the floats and rafts.

The whaler reported that there were more survivors who had been sighted even further afield, and again she set out to attend to them, this time with the surgeon-lieutenant on board.

At 1500 a ration of peaches was issued, a third of a peach to each man who could chew, and the juice distributed among the remainder. At 1530 an aircraft was sighted and as it came nearer it was seen to bear British markings. In the excitement of the next few minutes the motor boat almost capsized. Hopes of rescue now ran high, and a further ration of peaches was issued followed by a ration of water. However, the aircraft made no signal so it was thought unwise to issue more than a mere ration.

At 1730 smoke was sighted on the horizon and once more the motor boat nearly capsized! Fruit was now issued as fast as the tins could be opened.

The smoke soon gave way to the outline of a British cruiser, HMS *Enterprise,* and as she approached she was signalled by semaphore that there were wounded in the motor boat and that Neil-Robinson stretchers would be needed for about twenty of them. Within a short time the survivors of HMS *Cornwall* had been rescued and their long ordeal was at an end.

In the case of the *Dorsetshire* only one medical officer survived the sinking. He too, was a surgeon–lieutenant RNVR, and he likewise received an award of the OBE.

Perfect discipline prevailed in the water until the survivors were picked up by HM destroyers *Paladin* and *Panther.* Ten men died during the night and another two the next morning. In all, 1 120 were rescued from the crews of the two cruisers.

The following observations made by the ship's medical staffs are of interest. The senior medical officer in *Cornwall* had told his captain that ship's biscuits and bully-beef were not suitable fare for survivors and that tinned fruit should be substituted. That was done, and the benefit reaped. Also, while it had been the practice at sea to wear shoes, socks, shorts and cap, the Admiralty recommended that men should get accustomed to the sun by not wearing any head covering at all. In *Cornwall* the engine-room personnel were encouraged to come on deck to accustom themselves to the sun. That this paid was made clear by the fact that during their ordeal there was not a single case of heatstroke or severe sunburn. Gone forever now, were the days of sun-helmets and spine-pads – and it was discovered that a good tan helped to prevent prickly heat.

A South African sick berth attendant, CW Thorne was mentioned in despatches for devoted service in the care of the wounded when HMS *Dorsetshire* was sunk.

HMS *Shropshire*

One of the many South Africans serving from time to time in the heavy cruiser HMS *Shropshire,* was Gerald Middleton of Pretoria. In the November 1989 issue of the MOTH magazine *Home Front* he recalled some of his experiences. Referring to earlier material published in the same magazine in which mention had been made of the Royal Navy bombardment of Kismayu before the arrival of the troops, he gave this (slightly edited) version:

Heavy cruiser HMS *Shropshire*. (SANMMH)

The 'RN' mentioned was in fact the county-class cruiser HMS *Shropshire* which at that period was a household name from Cape Town to Durban, as she was part of the naval force that operated off East Africa during the early months of 1941.

When a bombardment was in progress it was advantageous to have a spotter. The ship's Walrus aircraft was not suited to dog-fights, so the SAAF was engaged to direct the gunfire.

The *Shropshire* had a special significance because on board, and forming no less than ten per cent of the complement at the time of the action, were ninety members of a little known past unit of our Defence Force, viz the Royal Naval Volunteer Reserve (SA Division). These men were manning guns, engine-rooms and signal stations. One must not forget them, or the pilot of the aircraft, when the operation at Kismayu is discussed.

In May that year a further fifteen Boks joined the vessel at Simon's Town. My messmates will remember our many months on board that wonderful ship.

With a fine Captain (JR Borrett OBE, RN) and a good ship's complement, we were content. Three meals a day, fresh bread (cake some afternoons), and 'Kye' (cocoa) late at night. All that, with sport, concerts and Vera Lynn, made life worth while and helped us to forget the constant action drills and the lurking U-boats that were particularly active in the Atlantic at that time and later in the Arctic Circle. This euphoric fat cat style of life was par for the course in larger naval ships and was certainly not a front for Prince Philip of

127

Mess-deck scene on board HMS *Shropshire*. (Shaw)

Greece, HRH the Duke of Edinburgh, who was then nineteen and serving on board as a Midshipman.

But, as all good things come to an end, fate dealt us a bad hand when HMS *Shropshire* was ordered to leave the sunny South Atlantic.

On arrival in the United Kingdom ominous changes began to take place. The one that caused the most apprehension was the changing of her coat from light Mediterranean grey to a glimmering Arctic white and dark moss-green. The design was a zigzag pattern and most sinister-looking.

Our curiosity was soon to be satisfied. One evening in the North Atlantic the weather was particularly bleak with a heavy sea running. The Old Grey Mare, as she was affectionately called, behaved like a rocking horse with an added rolling motion, and two hoof-kicks when the propellers became exposed by the high waves and then crashed back into the sea with a resounding thud. It was one of the worst places on this planet on which to receive bad news.

Captain Borrett told us that we were heading north, not south (as persistent optimistic rumours had suggested), to join our sister ships *Devonshire* and *Suffolk* and replace HMS *Cumberland* which had passed us in the Thames Estuary a few days before looking rather battered, with rust all over her forecastle – indicative of having recently shipped many tons of seawater. At the time she was *en route* to Chatham for a comprehensive refit.

Heavy cruiser HMS *Cumberland*. (E Redgrave)

We knew that she had been attached to the First Cruiser Squadron escorting the well-documented PQ convoys to the Arctic with such destinations as Archangel and Murmansk. RNVR men were usually issued with tropical gear and helmets but, paradoxically, no clothing for cold climates.

Thanks to the efforts of members of a library at Evesham in Worcestershire, I received a pair of socks, gloves, and a Balaclava cap. The authorities at South Africa House obtained a supply of naval greatcoats which were presented to us. That, I believe, was in response to a complaint. Another cause of dissatisfaction was the disparity in the rates of pay (recruit SDF 3/6d – RNVR 2/- per day). That was one of the main reasons for the amalgamation that took place between the SDF and the RNVR.

Our introduction to the Group was unsettling. Our sisters looked the picture of gloom. Obviously they had recently encountered bad weather.

The last vestige of conceit that we had retained was soon to disappear, for almost immediately we were confronted with our first 'Hell Ferry' assignment: Scapa Flow – Iceland – Spitzbergen – Bear Island – Murmansk.

That is another story: for instance the rush to Akureyri, in Iceland with a whale entangled in our paravane and swopped for a supply of frozen fish!

After many months fate again took a hand in our destiny. HMAS *Canberra* had been sunk in the battle of Savo Island in the

Pacific, and HMS *Shropshire* returned to Simon's Town to disembark the Boks before being transferred to the Royal Australian Navy as a replacement for *Canberra*.

The Admiralty offered the men Fairmile motor launches then being built in Cape Town docks and intended for service with Combined Operations in the Persian Gulf and the steamy jungle rivers of Burma. Most volunteered with alacrity. After all, anything must be better than dodging icebergs on the Murmansk run!

The known South African casualties are as follows: HMS *Gloucester* – thirty killed. HMS *Dorsetshire* – sixteen, HMS *Cornwall* – twenty-five, HMS *Hermes* – sixteen. Others were lost in the battleship *Barham* – seven and in HMS *Neptune* – eighteen. These were serious losses – the sad list goes on and covers almost every aspect of the work of the Royal Navy in many parts of the world. The men who joined DEMS and who kept lonely vigils at their guns in defensively equipped merchant vessels should not be forgotten.

HMS *Gloucester* – sunk in the Battle of Crete. (Morain)

Loss Of HMS *Neptune*

HMS *Neptune* (Captain RC O'Connor RN), sister to the cruiser famous for her part in the battle of the River Plate, HMS *Ajax*, was a ship of the same Leander class. *Neptune* was to be a popular naval unit during her long pre-war commission on the Cape Station where she became a familiar sight to those interested in maritime affairs, and a temporary home to many local RNVRs doing their annual fortnight's sea training with the squadron.

During her voyage home on completion of that commission Italy declared war on the Allies, and *Neptune* was accordingly diverted to the Mediterranean. She soon distinguished herself and gained immortal fame by being the first ship since the days of Nelson to report 'Enemy battle fleet in sight', which report marked the opening of the action off Calabria on 9 July 1940. On the previous day, during a high-level bombing attack by Italian aircraft, the cruiser *Gloucester* received a direct hit on the bridge, and the captain and seventeen others were killed, including at least one South African officer serving in the ship: Lieutenant Ronnie Basford RNVR (SA) of Port Elizabeth and RNVR (SA) ratings.

Gloucester was later sunk at the Battle of Crete and one of the members of her former RNVR (SA) crew, Mr AT Morain, also of Port Elizabeth, received certification of his service awards (campaign medals) exactly ten years after he left the Navy; the document was made out in favour of 'the late AT Morain'. It was assumed that he had been lost with the ship, whereas he had in fact left her a few days before. At the grand age of eighty-five Mr Morain is still hale and hearty and living in Edenvale.

Able Seaman Morain relaxing with guide in Alexandria. (Morain)

But back to HMS *Neptune*. At the naval action off Calabria the Italians were routed and in October *Neptune* resumed her interrupted homeward voyage. But this time she had to go the long way home round the Cape, thus virtually retracing her earlier track in May 1941 with a new ship's company but the same captain, Rory O'Connor – 'a

UNION DEFENCE FORCES.

The Chief of the General Staff expresses his deep regret that ̲T̲h̲e̲ ̲l̲a̲t̲e̲ ̲A̲.̲T̲.̲ ̲M̲o̲r̲a̲i̲n̲ did not live to receive the enclosed award(s) for service during the war of 1939-1945.

Order in which the Awards should be be set up, e.g., for framing.	Description of Ribbon.	Clasp or Emblem (if awarded)
1 1939-45 Star ✗	Dark blue, red and light blue in three equal vertical stripes. This ribbon is worn with the dark blue stripe furthest from the left shoulder.	Battle of Britain
2 Atlantic Star	Blue, white and sea green shaded and watered. This ribbon is worn with the blue edge furthest from the left shoulder.	Air Crew Europe or France and Germany
3 Air Crew Europe Star	Light blue with black edges and in addition a narrow yellow stripe on either side.	Atlantic or France and Germany
4 Africa Star	Pale buff, with a central vertical red stripe and two narrower stripes, one dark blue, and the other light blue. This ribbon is worn with the dark blue stripe furthest from the left shoulder.	8th Army or 1st Army or North Africa, 1942-43
5 Pacific Star	Dark green with red edges, a central yellow stripe, and two narrow stripes, one dark blue and the other light blue. This ribbon is worn with the dark blue stripe furthest from the left shoulder.	Burma
6 Burma Star	Dark blue with a central red stripe and in addition two orange stripe. .	Pacific
7 Italy Star	Five vertical stripes of equal width, one in red at either edge and one in green at the centre, the two intervening stripes being in white.	
8 France and Germany Star	Five vertical stripes of equal width, one in blue at either edge and one in red at the centre, the two intervening stripes being in white.	Atlantic
9 Defence Medal	Flame coloured with green edges, upon each of which is a narrow black stripe.	Silver laurel leaves (King's Commendation for brave conduct. Civil)
10 War Medal, 1939-45	A narrow central red stripe with a narrow white stripe on either side. A broad red stripe at either edge, and two intervening stripes in blue.	Oak leaf
11 Africa Service Medal	Orange in colour with green and gold of the Springbok Colours in vertical stripes on either side. The green stripes being on the outside.	Protea

NUMBER OF STARS, MEDALS, CLASPS or EMBLEMS ENCLOSED.

Medal award in respect of 'The late AT Morain'. Authorities assumed he had been lost with HMS *Gloucester* whereas he had been transferred prior to the sinking.

man of great charm, always approachable, yet withal a fierce determination to succeed.' He had a fine rapport with his crew and knew every man by name.

In August 1941 *Neptune* was once again ordered to join the Mediterranean Fleet at Alexandria. On the long outward passage routed round the Cape of Good Hope, and while escorting a convoy, she was detached to deal with a German merchant vessel which, on close approach, looked remarkably like a Hipper-class cruiser. Tension eased however, when the stranger turned out to be the British battleship HMS *Nelson*! The merchant ship was sighted later, promptly scuttled herself, and was helped on her way down by some gunnery and torpedo practice by *Neptune*.

Back in the Mediterranean on the night of 19 December 1941, a task force (Force K) consisting of the cruisers *Neptune, Aurora* and *Penelope* were steaming in line ahead screened by the destroyers *Kandahar, Lance, Lively* and *Havock*. They were about twenty miles north of Tripoli, steaming at 28 knots and expecting to intercept a reported convoy.

At 0125 *Neptune,* in the van, ran into a minefield and was instantly crippled. Immediately afterwards *Aurora* and *Penelope* were almost lifted clear of the sea by mines exploding in their paravanes. *Aurora* was holed and her speed reduced to 10 knots, but both ships managed to steam clear. *Penelope* was the least damaged of the three.

Neptune, severely damaged and immobilised, prepared to be taken in tow by the flotilla leader *Kandahar*, which edged in very carefully towards the cruiser. Despite her caution, however, she too was mined, and *Neptune* thereupon ordered the other destroyers to stand clear. Meanwhile, in her helpless condition and driven by the wind, she drifted on to a second mine, and then a third.

Aurora (Commodore WG Agnew, who later commanded HMS *Vanguard* on the royal visit to South Africa in 1947), decided that with his loss of power he should return to Malta with minimum delay.

Accordingly he departed, taking with him the destroyers *Havock* and *Lance* as escorts. *Penelope* remained in attendance on the two stricken ships. Since it was obvious that nothing could be done to help *Neptune* and *Kandahar* (Commander WGA Robson KBE CB DSO*,DSC RN, who in 1956 – 57 as Vice-Admiral became C-in-C South Atlantic), while they remained in the danger zone of the minefield, a frustrating and hopeless situation had developed. At dawn therefore, *Penelope* (Captain AD Nicholl) reluctantly left the scene, taking with her the remaining destroyer, *Lively*.

Meanwhile *Neptune* fouled yet another mine, rolled over, and sank taking with her almost the entire ship's company. It turned out later that some of her crew, including the captain, had survived and were seen on a raft. But all HMS *Neptune*'s wartime complement of 767 were lost save for one man who later died of exposure. This sole survivor (how often records reveal this to be the case) of the sinking, in which eighteen South Africans, including the brothers Thorp of Port Elizabeth, were killed, eventually managed to get ashore and was captured. He was later exchanged with other prisoners of war but died soon afterwards. As for *Kandahar,* after many anxious hours she drifted clear and twenty-four hours later HMS *Jaguar* (Lt-Cmdr LRR Tyrwhitt) rescued eight officers and seventy ratings.

As a fitting tribute to the South Africans who lost their lives in HMS *Neptune* the following report from their divisional officers and from the captain, addressed to the appropriate naval authorities in South Africa, is worth quoting:

General Remarks by Divisional Officers dated 2 November 1940.
There has been a remarkably high standard set by the 22 RNVR (SA) ratings who joined HMS *Neptune* on 5 October 1940. Without exception they have shown themselves to be anxious to learn their jobs and it has been a great surprise to all who have come into contact with them to observe how quickly they have adapted themselves to what must be for them a very different life.

Neptune in the past month has experienced nearly every type of weather, from extreme cold to extreme heat; on some days the ship rolled more than on any previous occasion during the commission. All ratings stood up to these conditions remarkably well, with the exception of one who suffers from chronic seasickness.

During the forenoons at sea both able seamen and ordinary seamen have been undergoing gunnery training classes. Instructors have noted that a keen interest has been maintained throughout and intelligent questions continually asked.

It is observed that the majority of men have left well paid jobs in civil life and in only a few cases is their RNVR pay made up to their peacetime rate by their old employers.

If this initial keenness continues they will prove a real asset to the ship. Their general smartness and intelligence have on more than one occasion put to shame young active service ratings. All are good mixers with both young and old, and are helped a lot by the senior ratings.

Captain Rory O'Connor's summing up of the same date is addressed to the Naval Officer in Charge, Simon's Town, with copies to the Officers Commanding RNVR Divisions at Cape Town, Port Elizabeth, East London and Durban. This is what he said:

The following report (with two enclosures) on the general conduct and efficiency of the RNVR(SA) ratings now serving in HMS *Neptune* is submitted for information:

HMS *Neptune* – one man survived her sinking only to die later. (Author)

These ratings joined HMS *Neptune* on 5 October 1940, and have today completed four weeks' service in the ship. I would not normally consider this short period adequate to form an opinion of their capabilities, but I have been so favourably impressed by their high standard of conduct and general ability that I have no hesitation in rendering this report after such brief experience.

It was only possible to give them 48 hours to shake-down before the vessel sailed on a long patrol. The ship was continuously at sea from 7 October to 26 October (nineteen days), and again from 28 October to 2 November (five days), a total of twenty-four days' sea-time out of their first twenty-eight days. The conditions experienced at sea were often extremely arduous – spells of heavy weather and extremes of temperature. During the whole period these ratings were undergoing training during working hours, and took their places in the defence organisation of the ship in two watches by night.

This routine, carried out continuously for such a long period, and under severe weather conditions, with the attendant discomforts of life in a crowded ship, must have imposed a severe physical and mental strain on these men, many of whom are drawn from sedentary occupations in civil life and have had no experience of long periods at sea. I consider that it reflects great credit that at all times they carried out their duties cheerfully and alertly.

★ ★ ★ ★ ★

While the county-class cruisers seem to have taken most of South African RNVRs, many were allocated to other units of the cruiser squadrons. In 1988 the *Argus* ran a series of personal recollections of experiences during the Second World War. Mr EN Harrison of Table View was one who responded to the invitation.

When war was declared he was nineteen years old and had just started an apprenticeship in the building trade. When he tried to enlist he was told he would have to complete at least two years of his apprenticeship before any application for active service could be considered. When the two years were up he joined the RNVR in Cape Town, and after only a month's training was sent to Simon's Town where he was drafted to the cruiser HMS *Mauritius*.

In this ship he spent several months on patrol duties in the Indian Ocean. Later she called in at Singapore for a boiler clean and refit. This visit coincided with Japan's entry into the war and the arrival at that port of the battleship HMS *Prince of Wales* and the battle-cruiser HMS *Repulse*. Oddly enough, despite the war, their arrival provided a major talking point and made headlines in the local press.

They berthed astern of *Mauritius* but slipped quietly out to sea one morning and, except for the Japanese bombers that spotted and sank them, they were never seen again.

Survivors from the two ships were later taken on board the passenger liner *Empress of Russia* to be escorted to Durban by HMS *Mauritius* which then resumed the refit so rudely interrupted by the Japanese. The refit took six weeks after which *Mauritius* escorted about forty ships to the Cape where Mr Harrison enjoyed a week's leave with his family before his ship sailed north again, bound for the Mediterranean via the Red Sea.

After her arrival there she was engaged in several invasions and bombardments, the first being the invasion of Sicily, Syracuse and Anzio. For his services in these Mr Harrison was mentioned in despatches.

On that occasion *Mauritius* was close inshore giving fire cover for landing craft, when she came under heavy fire from shore batteries. Two shell hoists in the gun turret jammed, and Harrison had to keep his own gun firing and at the same time pass shells (which weighed more than 100 lb) to each of the other two gun crews so that they could keep firing until the ship got out of range of the batteries.

Service in the Mediterranean for HMS *Mauritius* was curtailed when she was ordered into the Atlantic to search for a German naval unit believed to have sailed from Brest. The search, which lasted about ten days, proved ineffectual and the ship was ordered to Portsmouth.

Her next assignment was the Normandy landings in which she acted as flagship to the ships bombarding enemy installations and as covering fire for the hundreds of landing craft assembled and ready to move in to the beaches.

The cruiser HMS *Mauritius*. (SANMMH)

On her return to Portsmouth most of the crew were drafted to barracks for long leave, while Harrison was sent to the gunnery school at Whale Island for a six-week course.

After completing the course he was drafted back to the main barracks to await passage home in the troopship *Andes,* and he was duly discharged back into civvy street at HMSAS *Bonaventure 1* in Cape Town docks in November 1945. For him the war was over and, like so many fellow South Africans who had followed the wartime call of the sea, he had acquired memories of ships and shipmates that would never fade.

★ ★ ★ ★ ★

Another South African to serve in a cruiser was Norman Macdonald who was born in Johannesburg of New Zealand parents on 23 May 1919. He was a brilliant scholar and a keen sportsman, and graduated from Wits University in 1940 with a BSc Mining and Metallurgy. He joined the Royal Navy early in 1941, despite his academic attainments, as a second-class stoker!

When Singapore was taken in 1942 he was serving in the old light cruiser HMS *Dragon*, which had managed to escape the clutches of the Japanese. In December 1987 Norman Macdonald recorded some of his wartime memories in the MOTH magazine *Home Front.*

HMS *Dragon,* built in 1917, was fitted with neither radar nor Asdic, yet was employed escorting troopships to Singapore. She had been ordered to remain incognito and to use the codename Box O.

Like EN Harrison in HMS *Mauritius,* Macdonald was in Singapore when the *Prince of Wales* and *Repulse* arrived to strengthen the Far Eastern Fleet. At the time he too was puzzled as to why, contrary to current practice, the movements of these two great warships should have been given such conspicuous coverage by the press. Only in later years did he read in *War in the Southern Oceans* of an incident that occurred during a call at Cape Town by HMS *Prince of Wales* on 16 November 1941.

It reads: 'As Mr Churchill had suggested to Rear-Admiral Sir Tom Phillips, C-in-C designate of the Eastern Fleet, he flew to Pretoria to interview Field Marshal Smuts. On his return he told his chief of staff that Smuts agreed with the policy of sending two capital ships to Singapore as a deterrent against further Japanese aggression, and in order to accomplish such a purpose he considered it essential to give publicity to the movement.'

According to the same source, Smuts could hardly criticise the strategy of Churchill and Roosevelt but he thought there was much more at stake than a mere deterrent and he cabled Churchill expressing his serious concern at the division of Allied strength between Singapore and Pearl Harbour. 'If the Japanese are nippy,' he said, 'there is here an opening for a first-class disaster.'

Two days after the Japanese attacked Pearl Harbour on 7 December 1941 both capital ships were sunk off Kuantan by Japanese aircraft, an historic event that marked the end of the formerly invincible battleship. Their resting place is clearly marked on Admiralty navigational charts of the area to this day. South Africans lost with HMS *Repulse* were Lieutenant (E) L Wood and Ordinary Seaman WD Adamson.

HMS *Dragon* was to gain two additional members in her engine-room branch as a result of the sinking: a chief stoker from the *Prince of Wales* and another from *Repulse.*

When *Dragon* originally sailed from Simon's Town and her ship's company learned that she was bound for romantic Singapore there was much satisfaction. Singapore was at peace while the war raged in the Atlantic and the Mediterranean. Their dreams of a tropical paradise were soon to be dispersed. But before that happened *Dragon* had escorted many troopships to Singapore, among them the *West Point, Wakefield, Duchess of Bedford* and *Empress of Canada.* For the troops they landed it must have proved a futile and demoralising voyage, since most became prisoners of the Japanese. Macdonald described the fall of Singapore in clear detail. The following is an edited version:

While lying at anchor in Keppel Harbour, Singapore, in February 1942 we were startled one morning by the sounds of bombs exploding.

Attack on Singapore as seen from HMS *Dragon* on 5 February 1942 during the evacuation of women and children. (Macdonald)

Through the portholes we could see the bombs falling in the dock area where ships were embarking civilian evacuees. On the upper deck we were able to see a force of some twenty-seven silver bombers flying in perfect formation and looking like baby goldfish in an inverted bowl of blue.

Admiral Tom Phillips had gone down with his ship, HMS *Prince of Wales*. Admiral Geoffrey Layton, based on Singapore, decided that we should move to Java, where it would be safer to direct the operation of British ships.

Our ship, HMS *Dragon,* was given the honour of transferring the Admiral. With HMS *Durban* in company we travelled at high speed (about 28 knots) through the night with all six boilers at maximum burning capacity. *Durban* tied up astern of us in Tanjon Priok, the port for Batavia, and we noticed that the paintwork on her funnel was badly blistered. It had been a hot trip.

When the invasion of Java became imminent the Dutch women were offered passage to safety in our ship. They refused, much to our regret. The South African sailors in our ship became the envy of the British seamen when they heard us speaking to the girls in Afrikaans!

Two members of the ship's company who were not very happy when the bombs began to fall [on Java] and the guns began to fire, were a duck that had been rescued from the water at Singapore and a goat that a stoker, after a wild run ashore in Java, had brought on board.

HMS *Dragon*. An aged light cruiser but a happy ship. (Macdonald)

Norman Macdonald makes frequent references to impromptu rugby matches played here and there. In Singapore they beat a New Zealand team 12-0 and among the South Africans who occupied key positions in the team were Stoker Drysdale, a former fullback at Michaelhouse, Stoker Wiltshire, a former hooker at Hilton College, and Able Seaman Whipp, centre three-quarter and later father of Peter Whipp, the Springbok centre.

Rugby Team HMS *Dragon*. In the group are South Africans Norman Macdonald, Basil Drysdale and John Whipp (father of rugby Springbok Peter Whipp). This was HMS *Dragon*'s rugby team challenging that of HMS *Exeter* in Batavia. (Macdonald)

In the battle of the Java Sea HMS *Dragon* formed part of the Western Strike Force, together with the cruisers HMAS *Hobart* and HMS *Dane*, and the destroyers *Scout* and *Tenedos*. After an attack by Japanese aircraft, *Hobart,* the senior ship, signalled asking if *Dragon* had been hit. She replied, 'No, we thought you had.' Bombs had fallen uncomfortably close.

With the invasion of Java imminent, HMS *Dragon* sailed from Tanjon Priok after midnight on 27 February, slipped out through the Sunda Straits and set course for Colombo. She was the lucky one, for of the other ships that had survived the Java Sea battle, HMAS *Perth* and USS *Houston* were both later sunk trying to escape. Both captains went down with their ships. *Dragon* had escaped with only hours to spare.

While *Dragon* was later converted into an anti-aircraft cruiser, seconded to the Polish Navy and destined to play a part in the D-Day landings at Normandy, other adventures had befallen Norman Macdonald.

It is strange that a man with his qualifications should not have been considered earlier for commissioned rank. Whatever the reason for the delay it did not come about until after his service in East Indian waters, when he was selected to attend courses in the United Kingdom and duly embarked in the 19 695 ton liner *Laconia*.

She was torpedoed north-east of Ascension Island on 12 September 1942 by the German submarine U-156. The commander of the submarine, on learning that the ship he had sunk had been transporting over

The transport *Laconia* in which Norman Macdonald experienced one of the most unusual events of the war at sea. (SANMMH)

fifteen hundred Italian prisoners of war, took it upon himself to radio a message in plain language to all stations giving the position of the sinking and the boats that he had in tow. As a result of his signal other U-boats, both German and Italian, were diverted to the scene from their war stations and Vichy warships were sent from Dakar. Despite his humane action his submarine was attacked by a Liberator bomber from Ascension with the result that the tow was abandoned and the lifeboats were scattered.

Macdonald was picked up three weeks later by the French Navy and interned in Morocco. When American and British forces invaded North Africa he was released and sent to the United States for onward passage to South Africa, where, at long last, he was commissioned and posted to the Mediterranean. In those waters he served with MLs and MTBs, mainly in the Aegean, until the Germans withdrew from the area in late 1944.

After demobilisation, Norman Macdonald had a distinguished professional career and became a prominent member of ex-servicemen's associations. He died on 28 March 1989 while serving as Transvaal Regional Chairman of the South African Legion.

★ ★ ★ ★ ★

Other South Africans engaged in the battles in the Java Sea at that time were Cyril Grenfell and four others, all serving in the cruiser *Exeter* of River Plate fame. Only Grenfell and Johnny Campbell survived to tell the story of the Java Sea battle and the subsequent treatment of those unfortunate enough to suffer the hardships and indignities of Japanese prison camps.

It is generally not known that *Exeter* was not sunk by the Japanese but, after suffering severe damage, was scuttled by her own crew to avoid capture. She was well down in the water when the Japs, at close range, fired the torpedo that helped her on her way.

In her first engagement with the Japanese fleet on 27 February 1942 in the Java Sea, *Exeter* was hit by an 8-inch shell that not only put one of the starboard guns out of action but went on to explode in the boiler-room and destroy six boilers. Ordered to return to Surabaya for repairs, she was attacked on the way by an 8-inch gun cruiser but she was able to drive off her attacker.

In the evening of 28 February, *Exeter,* accompanied by the destroyers HMS *Encounter* and USS *Pope,* left Surabaya hoping to pass through the Sunda Straits and gain the comparative safety of the broad Indian Ocean. But that was not to be, and a little before noon, having fired all her shells, including smoke-shells as a last defiant gesture, she went down to her watery grave.

★ ★ ★ ★ ★

Seventeen seems a very young age to be thrust into the maw of a merciless war, yet that was the lot of many a South African boy, among whom was one who signed a letter 'Atholl'. The letter was addressed to his parents in Cape Town, and it appeared in the *Cape Times* of 12 August 1942. While his surname is not known it has been established that the name of his ship (left blank in the newspaper because of wartime censorship) was the cruiser HMS *Birmingham*. She was well-known in Cape waters like her predecessor of the same name, and she is doubtless remembered by many old enough as the four-funnelled coal-burner on the Cape Station in the 1920s and famous for being the first to sink a submarine in World War 1. It is said that the Kaiser personally issued an order to his fleet to 'Get the *Birmingham*.'

HMS *Birmingham* – 'Atholl's' ship. (Author)

The unknown Atholl's letter is quoted in full because his experiences were shared by so many duration-of-hostilities seamen.

Well, I have now a lot of news for you as we have been told we are allowed to say that we have been in action in the Mediterranean while *en route* escorting a convoy to Malta. No doubt you have heard and read about it in the newspapers and on the wireless. Madagascar was an easy show to us, but this last trouble was a bit different.

We left Alexandria on a Saturday evening and steamed out to sea to pick up our convoy. At about two o'clock in the morning enemy planes were overhead and started dropping parachute flares all over the convoy. No bombs were dropped and they soon shoved off.

I was on look-out on the bridge and wondered when they would come again. However, they did not come until the following afternoon. The planes were Ju 88 dive-bombers, and the RAF tried to intercept them before they got to us. But there were more than enough to cope with our fighters, and so on came the Jerries. Then the guns of our convoy opened up and the sky was filled with puffs of AA fire. The noise of pom-poms, machine guns and [censored] was deafening and the enemy planes were diving all over the place. You have no idea what it was like.

The merchant ships got the brunt of it. What wonderful people must be on those ships!

Bombs seemed to be dropping everywhere and coming straight towards us. I felt really frightened and then I thought, well, I am the only South African on the top deck so I must not show that I am different from the rest. But it was really hot. We shot down five of the enemy planes. I think I helped in putting one down. The RAF claimed two.

Even though you know the enemy are attacking, you feel sorry for the way they meet their death, either blowing up in mid-air or crashing down into the water in flames as I saw many do.

These attacks went on all through the night, and we on the bridge were dead tired and hungry. We felt half asleep. Suddenly a flare would light up the darkness and be followed immediately by the whistling of bombs, and not knowing where these were going to fall was pretty rotten. All you could do was lie flat on your stomach and hope for the best.

To make matters worse, enemy E-boats made a daring attack in the middle of the night and torpedoed a cruiser, but she did not sink. The E-boat is not a submarine, by the way, but a sort of small torpedo-boat.

What I thought was the worst attack of all came the next morning about ten o'clock, when the enemy sent over his famous Stuka dive-bombers in force. We all wondered if the enemy never got tired, because we could hardly stand, we were so tired.

The usual barrage and deafening noise went up, and this time the enemy directed his attack at the escort, making us personally his main target. I was watching this when I saw five Stukas directly above us. I had no sooner reported them than they came straight down at us in a practically vertical dive. Everything we had opened up – 4-inch guns, pom-poms, and all. Tracer bullets, shrapnel and smoke filled the sky, and the noise was like hell itself.

German parachutists, Suda Bay, Crete. (G Nash)

I saw a black object coming out of one plane. At first I thought the plane had been hit, then I heard the whistle and I fell flat. I think I nearly said my prayers backwards. The explosion and vibration of the bomb were terrific. One of them I thought had hit us, but after all the bombs had fallen I somehow managed to get to my feet and found that there was practically no damage at all; most bombs had been very near-misses. You can imagine how relieved we all were that that part was over.

After that the Italians had their turn at high-level bombing, but did no great damage to the ships. Later, however, the Italians made a really good effort at low-level torpedo attack and that gave us a lot of trouble. I can still see one of those torpedoes coming straight at us and just missing by a few feet.

Was I scared! Didn't I wish I was back somewhere in Cape Town! And yet I would not have missed it for all the world and I was proud to be there helping. I think you know, Dad, I am only seventeen but I feel I am ever so much older now. It was a pity in a way that we had to turn round.

What a wonderful service the Navy is. Everyone was so cheery with it all, and we did have a laugh at times.

We got back to Alex and although we had lost lives and ships we were willing to go straight back again. There is one thing I can draw from this trying action, and that is that the spirit among us all was wonderful. Courage is what you realise is there.

I could not but feel sorry for one Italian bomber. He burst into flames above the ship and came down clattering above us before he could release his torpedo. It was a magnificent sight, but I hope you never see anything like that over Cape Town.

After all these four days of continuous bombing I think I will be able to stand anything in the way of bombing. The Stukas put the wind up us at the start the way they come down in a loud screaming noise just like a vulture about to devour its prey. But I don't seem to have the same fear now, and I know we can give them as much, if not more, than they give us.

Well, I hope I will hear from you soon. It seems so long since I last heard from you and yet I have only been away four months. I have seen so much in that time Dad and Mum, I think quite sufficient to last me a long time.

To any former Navy man reading this it must occur to him that this boy's letter was a pretty stout effort since it was probably written in the crowded mess-deck of a cruiser on active service. Letter-writing was more common in those days than it is now; it was virtually the only means of contact during the war years. Outgoing mail from ships was always censored by the ships' officers, and the author has happy memories of some letters that passed through his hands.

One of the most memorable was from a sailor who had been away from home for five long years, yet whose wife had recently given birth. There had obviously been some earlier acrimonious correspondence over the event, but one sentence of this particular letter was memorable. 'You say it should be patched up. I think it should have been patched up before I left home!'

9

The 'Flat Tops'

South Africans served in aircraft-carriers, as pilots, observers, air-gunners or in various capacities on the ships themselves. If any one of those ships were to be singled out for special mention, perhaps it should be HMS *Hermes,* for she carried a greater complement of South Africans than most. And since sixteen of those naval volunteers lost their lives when their ship was sunk in the Indian Ocean she is, if only for that sad reason, the best remembered.

HMS *Hermes* was unique in that she was the first vessel specially designed by the Admiralty as an aircraft-carrier; earlier carriers had been adapted from other types of warships or merchant vessels. Of 10 850 tons' displacement and with a length overall of 598 feet and a beam of 90 feet over her flight deck, which was designed for twenty aircraft, a figure that was doubtless increased in time of war. She was laid down in the Armstrong, Whitworth yard at Elswick-on-Tyne in

Typical World War II aircraft-carrier. (Shipfotos)

1918 and launched in September 1919, when she was towed to Devonport for completion. While there she received her main armament which consisted of six 5,5-inch guns, backed up by three 4-inch anti-aircraft guns and some eighteen smaller weapons which also no doubt grew in number.

Her power-plant consisted of geared turbines developing 40 000 shp giving her a speed of 25 knots. Her peacetime complement totalled about seven hundred officers and men.

After trials and a period with the Mediterranean Fleet, she served on the China Station before refitting at Chatham in 1928. She then returned to China. She had another major refit in 1934, and once again she sailed for the Far East, and came back home in 1937.

On the outbreak of the 1939 war she was serving with the channel force protecting the transportation of the British Expeditionary Force to France. In October 1939 she arrived at Dakar and, with the French battleship *Strasbourg*, hunted German raiders on the trade routes. At the end of November she joined the South Atlantic naval units covering the passage of convoys.

In June 1940, after the fall of France, she was once again off Dakar, but this time policing her former allies. On 8 July one of her motor boats under the command of Lt-Cmdr RN Bristowe RN, succeeded in penetrating the harbour defence boom and dropped four depth charges under the stern of the battleship *Richelieu*.

The intention was to damage the big ship's propellers and steering gear so as to immobilise her. In the event, because of insufficient depth of water, the depth charges failed to explode. The motor boat, however, escaped and was picked up by her mother ship fifteen hours later and hoisted inboard. Meanwhile, aircraft from *Hermes* were plastering the French ships and dockyard.

Two days later the force was withdrawn and during the night of 10 July, in a sudden violent tropical rain-storm, *Hermes* collided with the armed merchant cruiser HMS *Corfu*. She suffered severe damage to her bows and to the fore end of the flight-deck, but managed to reach Freetown under her own steam. Next month she left for Simon's Town to undergo more permanent repairs. This refit took till November 1940.

Her next assignment was to the Persian Gulf where her aircraft helped the British and Indian forces to frustrate any German intervention in Iraq. From May to November she was employed on the protection of commerce convoy escorts, and the interception of enemy shipping in the Indian Ocean.

After another refit in Simon's Town, she sailed from there on 2 January 1942, being attached to an Australian squadron for operations in the Anzac area, but returned to the East Indies Station in February, being temporarily retained in the Colombo area while another carrier, HMS *Indomitable*, was busy ferrying aircraft to the Far East.

View along flight deck HMS *Khedive*. (Karstel)

At the beginning of April, Intelligence reports indicated an imminent Japanese air attack on Colombo. That was followed early on 9 April by a heavy air raid on the naval base at Trincomalee by a carrier-borne force of Japanese aircraft. The first warning of trouble brewing had been received the previous day when a patrolling Catalina aircraft had sighted Japanese surface vessels about five hundred miles away. Since there was little air cover over Trincomalee, the commander-in-chief ordered the harbour to be cleared.

That night *Hermes,* in company with HM Destroyer *Vampire* and other vessels, was ordered to sail, to keep inshore, and to be at least forty miles from Trincomalee by dawn on 9 April.

It was as well that the precaution was taken, although as it turned out the exodus of warships was in vain. At 0725 on that day about ninety Japanese aircraft attacked Trincomalee and made direct hits on several dockyard buildings. The monitor HMS *Erebus* was damaged by a near miss and suffered several casualties including six killed.

While this raid was going on *Hermes* and *Vampire* were about sixty-five miles from their base and about five miles offshore. At 0900 they altered course with the intention of returning by late afternoon. The weather was fine, the sea calm and visibility good. A report from a Japanese aircraft intercepted by the radio station at Colombo was interpreted as an enemy sighting report of *Hermes* and she was accordingly ordered to return to Trincomalee forthwith.

Both ships increased to full speed and by 1025 they were opposite the port of Batticola. Ten minutes later about fifty Japanese aircraft were sighted diving out of the sun from a height of ten thousand feet. The air attack was skilfully and fearlessly carried out and direct hits were scored almost at once.

During the next ten minutes attacks developed from every angle and bombs fell with devastating effect. *Hermes* was quickly sunk, and the enemy aircraft immediately turned their attention to HMS *Vampire*, which received a rapid series of direct hits and broke in two. The forward section sank immediately. Soon afterwards her after magazine exploded and the stern half sank at 1105. Two minutes later there was a heavy explosion under water, possibly the detonation of her depth charges.

The ill-fated HMS *Hermes*. (Unknown)

Before sinking, *Hermes* listed heavily to port with the flight-deck awash and large numbers of men scrambling overboard. Even after the ship had sunk, bombs continued to rain down and burst in the sea; after which the aircraft machine-gunned the swimmers, killing many of them. Fortunately for the survivors of *Hermes* and *Vampire* , they were not fated like those of *Cornwall* and *Dorsetshire* to spend long hours in the water. The attack had been witnessed by the hospital ship *Vita*, which immediately set about rescuing and treating the survivors. Nevertheless Captain Onslow, nineteen officers and 288 ratings lost their lives in this brief action, sixteen of them South Africans.

It was a day of gloom for the Royal Navy. About an hour after the sinking of the *Hermes* and *Vampire*, HMS *Hollyhock* and the Royal Fleet auxiliary *Atherstone*, having left Trincomalee at the same time as the other ships, were heading south in company when they too were attacked by Japanese aircraft. Five direct hits were scored on *Atherstone* which sank almost immediately. *Hollyhock* attempted to close the sinking *Atherstone* to render assistance but she herself was hit, and sank in a few seconds. Sixteen of her crew were rescued by one of *Atherstone*'s boats, but two officers and forty-six ratings lost their lives.

The reader may wonder why *Hermes* launched no aircraft to oppose the air attacks. Unfortunately her squadrons of Swordfish had been left behind in Colombo.

In 1986 survivors of *Hermes* held a reunion in Cape Town and recalled how Geoff Jardine of Fish Hoek and three others swam twenty-two miles to the south-east coast of Ceylon after the sinking.

'It took us about twenty-four hours', said Mr Jardine, 'and we only just made it. After we had recovered we foot-slogged sixty miles to the naval base at Trincomalee - only to be put under close arrest for desertion in the face of the enemy! They wouldn't believe our story at first, and it took some time to verify that we were in fact survivors of *Hermes*.'

Another survivor was Lt-Cmdr DPP Brimble of Kenilworth in the Cape. He wrote: 'Don't tell me there were seventy-one Japanese aircraft. Seventy-two were there. I counted them one by one! *Hermes* was an old ship and we were unable to elevate the main armament directly overhead to fight off modern dive-bombers. It was not a battle. Just carnage. 365 [sic] killed, let alone wounded. They even fired on the

HMS *Searcher*. (Unknown)

swimming survivors. Three and a half hours later I made it to the *Vita,* which had been sent from Colombo. Even the Japs didn't fire on hospital ships.'

A word or two here about the medical teams in HMS *Hermes* as published in *The Chief Naval Events 1942-43.* There were three medical officers in HMS *Hermes*: a surgeon-commander RN, a surgeon Lt-Cmdr and a surgeon-lieutenant RNVR. Only the last survived, and it is on the basis of his report that the following was compiled. For his services on that occasion he was given an OBE.

When the air attack [on the *Hermes*] developed, the medical personnel were at their action stations.

The junior medical officer was employed in a first-aid post on the ship's flight-deck, where he was assisted by a sick-berth attendant and the ship's master-at-arms. The first three bombs dropped were near-misses on the port side amidships, but soon afterwards there was a heavy explosion and a huge mass of metal [believed to have been the platform of the lift by which aircraft were raised to the flight deck from the hangar below] was thrown across the flight deck and ended up outside the entrance to the first-aid post.

The MO filled a syringe with morphia in preparation for casualties and instructed the SBA to do likewise. Almost at once the first casualty appeared, a seaman with a lacerated wound to his foot. The man was given morphia and his wound was dressed to the accompaniment of a series of explosions in various parts of the ship. The MO removed the casualty from the first-aid post and at once saw that the port side of the flight deck was awash and that the ship was heeling rapidly with large numbers of men already jumping into the sea. The MO inflated the patient's lifebelt as well as his own, and they entered the sea together.

The MO himself was caught and carried under water by the ship's boom and ropes hanging from it, but fortunately he was able to wriggle free and reach the surface. He found his patient still there, and together they swam away from the ship. Bombs were still exploding in the water and the MO has recorded that each explosion gave him the impression of a severe blow in the abdomen.

After *Hermes* had sunk, bombs still continued to drop and one exploded about 25 yards from the MO. Aircraft now opened fire on the survivors in the water, and several were killed, including a sick-berth attendant.

The MO still had his patient with him, but he eventually left him in the care of some survivors on a raft. He then swam to an officer who was suffering from severe burns and managed to bring him to the comparative safety of a float. He then swam to two other casualties, both of whom were in obvious difficulties, one being a non-swimmer. One of these men was not being supported very adequately by his lifebelt so the MO removed his own lifebelt and put it round the casualty. He then conveyed these men to a float.

On this float the MO attended to several seriously wounded men, and he then swam to other floats and rafts and dealt with such casualties as he discovered. Some of the rafts had fresh water, but others had none. On each raft survivors were instructed to remove their overalls and to use them as shades to protect men suffering from burns against the rays of the sun. No sharks were seen.

Further reference to aircraft-carriers will be found later in these pages recounting the experiences of a man who served in the so-called Woolworth carriers.

HMS *Illustrious*. (SANMMH)

CHAPTER
10

Small Fry with a Vicious Bite

Harbour defence motor launches (HDMLs) and a later enlarged version named Fairmile were turned out in South African boat-building yards and manned largely by crews drawn from the SANF, and more particularly those of the former RNVR(SA) who had chosen secondment to the Royal Navy.

Soon after the outbreak of the Second World War, a committee chaired by Mr Peter Payne was formed in Durban to send to the Admiralty an offer to build a flotilla of motor torpedo boats (MTBs) for the Royal Navy. The other members of the committee were Cmdr EL Bingham, Sub-Lt WL Hancock, and a boat-builder, Mr Fred Nichols.

Typical Fairmile motor launch. (G Nash) *INCORRECT : A POST-WAR COASTAL-DEFENCE SHIP-'OOSTERLAND'?*

Launching HMS *Insizwa*. (Seven ratings from Durban RNVR base.) Standing: L/Sto King, PO Gardiner, AB Main, Chief Motor Mechanic McMurfy, Lt-Cmdr Bingham, S Lt WL Hancock, LS Stead, Leading Seaman Espitalier. Extreme right kneeling: AB Scott.

The Admiralty was slow to respond to the offer, but eventually asked for HDMLs rather than MTBs. By then the Speed the Planes Fund had caught the imagination of the Durban public and few people had much money left for the Navy. Nevertheless the three hundred letters typed by Cmdr Bingham and the generous response of those canvassed by the committee raised enough money to build two 72-foot HDMLs.

The first boat to be completed, HDML 1098 was with the permission of the Admiralty and named HMS *Insizwa*. The name is a Zulu word for a young warrior. Mrs Claire Ellis-Brown, wife of the Mayor of Durban, himself a former member of the Durban RNVR, presided over the naming ceremony.

Two Gardner 8-cylinder, 300 hp diesel engines giving a speed of 11½ knots were installed in the fitting out, and later an establishment of eight depth charges was loaded and armament consisting of a 3-pounder gun, one 20mm Oerlikon, one Vickers (or two Lewis guns) were mounted.

The first commanding officer of the *Insizwa* was, appropriately enough, Lt-Cmdr Bingham himself. He had dropped rank to accept command of the 112th ML Flotilla. Both the two officers and seven of the HDML complement of nine ratings were from the Durban RNVR base.

In February 1942 *Insizwa* sailed for Simon's Town to get her Asdic gear installed. The weather report received on sailing was by some mischance that of the previous day, and the little ship ran into a howling gale off Port St John's.

Conditions became so bad that only Lt–Cmdr Bingham and Leading Stoker Roberts were not incapacitated by seasickness and were still able to remain on watch. A long ordeal without food or sleep followed although some relief was provided by the seasick men who did half-hourly tricks at the wheel with instructions to hold the course until relieved. One wonders how many of these young men subsequently saw fit to request drafts to larger vessels!

Despite the gale and heavy seas *Insizwa* reached East London safely where temporary repairs to weather damage were made. Next day she sailed for Port Elizabeth and on to Simon's Town.

After the installation of the Asdic gear, *Insizwa* returned to Durban, where she was joined by HDML 1086, commanded by Sub-Lieutenant LW Lockhead of the Port Elizabeth RNVR, the same man whose experiences have been related in these pages in connection with the loss of the AMC, HMS *Comorin*.

After further repairs and modifications the two HDMLs sailed for Colombo, a long and trying voyage for such small vessels. When they arrived at the Kenyan port of Mombasa seven days later they were ordered to escort two boom defence vessels (maximum speed six knots) to Addu Atoll in the Maldives.

Commander EL Bingham VRD RNVR (SA). (SANMMH)

Their course was to take them via the Seychelles, and while they were at Port Victoria Lt-Cmdr Bingham was ordered to sail south to the island of Coetivy to collect stranded US Air Force personnel. These consisted of five officers and two warrant officers with all their gear, altogether six tons of equipment! After returning to Port Victoria *Insizwa* resumed her interrupted voyage to Addu Atoll, where she made fast alongside a depot ship.

It was at that time that HMS *Cornwall* and HMS *Dorsetshire* were sunk by the Japanese on 5 April 1942, and it was *Insizwa*'s sad task to bury at sea two of their chief petty officers who had died of wounds.

Soon afterwards, while in company with an anti–submarine trawler escorting the water-boat *Singu* to Colombo, *Insizwa* narrowly missed an encounter with Japanese warships. Later in Trincomalee, Lt GCM Brown of the Durban RNVR was appointed First Lieutenant of *Insizwa* and later succeeded Lt-Cmdr Bingham as Commanding Officer. This change of command was occasioned by the onset of tuberculosis caused by mustard and phosgene gases, a legacy of army service in the First World War which compelled Bingham to relinquish command. Lieutenant Brown was still in command of HDML 1098 in October 1944.

★ ★ ★ ★ ★

Fortunately for the naval historian the activities of the Fairmile flotillas were given ample coverage by sources besides the official war histories. The records kept by the men who manned them and who were obviously proud of the distinguished service given by their small craft, especially in the Burma campaign, are of special interest.

Former Leading Seaman DE Lagerwall remembers those days well. The following is a slightly edited version of a detailed account of his own experiences in those craft during the Second World War.

> In 1942 the county-class cruiser HMS *Shropshire* was handed over in Simon's Town to the Australian Navy to replace HMAS *Canberra*, which had been lost through Japanese action. South African ratings in *Shropshire* were drafted to other ships and into barracks. Most of us, mostly ABs with gunnery and torpedo rates, joined the old training ship *General Botha* moored in Simon's Bay. By then she had resumed her former name of HMS *Thames*. The routine observed on board was strictly Royal Navy, but it included the old *Botha* practice of watering ship from the shore by means of a grass-line supporting lengths of canvas hose, all handled by a cutter under oars. Not a pleasant operation in cold Simon's Town.

Leading Seaman (later Midshipman) DE Lagerwall who served in MLs. (SANMMH)

A number of *Shropshire* ratings, including myself, volunteered for small ships; preferably motor torpedo boats in the English Channel as we were young and craved excitement. Our request was approved and we were transferred to HMS *Afrikander* in Cape Town. However, when we asked about our draft to MTBs we were told that MLs – 'Fairmiles' – were being built in Knysna and were almost ready for sea. There was a buzz that they were to be used in the Mediterranean, so we decided that that was the next best thing. We were then billeted in the Mount Nelson Hotel in Cape Town, where we enjoyed life for a while.

The MLs of the 49th Fairmile Flotilla were launched on 12 September 1942 and commissioned on 6 November. They were numbered 380, 381, 382 and 383. Later, up north, two were replaced by 829 and 846, but I cannot remember which two had engine trouble.

When the MLs arrived in Cape Town we were transported daily from the hotel to the docks to form crews for the four MLs. Lt Vic Bartholomew took command of my ML – 234 – with Lt Doug Hollis second in command. We had a crew of fourteen consisting of a coxswain, a PO ERA, an Asdic rating, a telegraphist, a torpedo-man and a stoker, the rest being gunnery ratings. With the crews sorted out we did sea trials and left Cape Town for Simon's Town, where we did gunnery shoots and so on.

The 49th Flotilla sailed from Simon's Town in March 1943, called at Cape Town and then headed for Port Beaufort to fuel. We were the first naval vessels to enter the Breede River. There we stretched our legs and sailed next day for Knysna where we tied up at Thesen's jetty, sailing again the following day for Port Elizabeth, my home town. Spent two days ashore there, and then left for East London. At all these stops we bunkered with high-octane fuel. On arrival at Durban we berthed in pairs at Maydon Wharf, and we were soon sorry to report that misfortune struck when we lost an AB from East London.

While painting the bulkheads between the coxswain's cabin and the radio room below decks, falling drops of paint had spotted the deck. The AB volunteered to clean up the spots with high-octane fuel, forgetting that we had a paraffin fridge with a naked light underneath. In a flash the octane ignited. That in turn set fire to the fresh paint, and the AB was trapped in the cabin. He had no option but to dash out through the flames, got badly burnt in the process and died later in hospital.

During the fire the captain shouted to start the engines so that we could run the ML on to a sandbank in the channel in case we blew up. But we managed to put out the fire and the rest of the crew

Camouflaged *Insizwa* in Eastern waters. (Bingham)

HDML 1098 (HMS *Insizwa*) was paid for with money donated by the citizens of Durban and was built there. (SANMMH)

cleared the ammunition from the forward locker. Next day workmen patched up the damage and we sailed for Lourenço Marques.

It was a neutral port so we had to go ashore in hockey shirts and No 6 white trousers. It was there that disaster almost struck again. Four of us found our way to a 'hotel', where we watched shapely dancing girls parading their half-clad bodies. After a while we realised that we were in a flashy brothel, and the Madam told us that if we had no money – which of course we hadn't – we would have to leave. After a few lighthearted feels and pinches by the *matelots*, whistles were blown and huge guards in red fezzes chased us down the road, where we found the gates locked. However, we managed to scale the walls commando fashion, and we were glad to get back on board in one piece!

Next day we sailed for Tullear in Madagascar, taking each other in tow for 'x' number of hours on one engine to save fuel. Then up the coast to Majunga where we bunkered and replenished supplies.

We found the people in Majunga were short of clothes and material, so we began to barter our vests, underpants, engine-room rags, etc., and ended up with two pigs, which we intended to slaughter later. But as we were leaving the jetty an English-speaking gent shouted to us that the pigs had worms – so we gently pushed them over the side.

From Majunga we had to cross back to the East African coast and fuelled at Lindi. That done, we then went on up the coast to Zanzibar, Mombasa, Malindi, Kismayo, Brava, Mogadishu, Masira and Muscat. By that time we realised that we had said goodbye to our hopes for the Mediterranean.

Our next stop was Khor Kuwai at the entrance to the Persian Gulf where we spent six months dropping charges and patrolling to deter submarines from entering the Gulf. We also called at Bahrein and from there ferried some Arab dignitary, complete with bodyguards, to Bandar Abbas and other places in the Gulf. The scorching sun produced temperatures of 158 F. At times, after depth-charging, fish would be blown to the surface (never sharks) and we would lower the dinghy and collect enough fresh fish to supply other ships living on tinned pilchards and herrings. Sometimes a New Zealand destroyer would call us alongside and lower a sack of bread and tinned butter. What a treat they were after weevily biscuits.

We all suffered from heat exhaustion and septic prickly-heat. Our daily bath was a bucket of salt water from over the side, or sometimes a swim. We had a few moans too, about fuelling from barges. For that operation we formed a human chain passing four-gallon tins to pour into our tanks. Apart from the heat we got 'high' on the fumes. Yet another affliction was the presence of yellow wasps, which usually got nasty while we were trying to drink our tea. Their stings were painful.

We had our daily issue of Pusser's rum (neat) which we drank at sundown. Since I played the ukelele and another man the accordion, our ship was dubbed 'Showboat' and we arranged concerts with other MLs tied up alongside. The only other music was provided by a wind-up gramophone with records, given to us by a Jewish Women's Association when we left Cape Town. The only 'comfort' we received was a tin of chocolates from Ouma Smuts. Mail deliveries were few and far between. My dear old Mum sent me a fruit-cake which by the time I received it was all crumbs.

Then came the Burma Push. Lord Louis Mountbatten wanted all the small ships for operations in Burma, and so we sailed for Chittagong in East Bengal.

Royal Marine piper on board ML 382 in Burma campaign. (Bartholomew)

We left the Persian Gulf on 15 October 1943 bound for India, and duly arrived at Karachi. Then we sailed onwards down the Indian coast to Bombay which we left on 27 February 1944 bound for Calicut, Cochin, Mamdapam, Colombo, Trincomalee, Madras, Vizagapatam and up the River Hooghly to Calcutta. The Indian pilot taking us up this dirty muddy river on an 8-knot flood tide steered our ML with his feet!

After a short rest we left for Chittagong from where the MLs began patrolling the Arakan coast. Our ML (382) carried out pre-invasion beach drills with Royal Marine commandos and their ca-

160

noes. These exercises were all done at night. There was not the slightest sound and waiting for the commandos to return was nerve-racking and unpleasant. We rolled for hours in the sea and swell. Everything was lashed down and there was no cooking, and even talking aloud was forbidden.

Once they were safely back on board we would start up and get out at full speed, heading for home and landing the marines with their test results. I remember the commandos having a good gulp of rum from their dixies before setting out in their canoes. They were a very brave bunch of men. One commando man was bald and with the black face-cream that they used he drew a face on his head saying that if he came across a Jap he would take off his woollen cap and 'frighten the buggers to death.'

During this time some of the RNVRs realised that their time was up. They had signed on for four years or the duration, whichever was the less. Soon there was a signal from General Smuts that that had now been changed to the full duration of the war. Everyone was quite happy about that for we had moulded ourselves with our RN shipmates into an efficient 49th Flotilla.

Burmese country craft identifying itself as friendly. (Bartholomew)

The highlight of the Burma campaign for us was sailing up the chaungs (riverlets), hiding under the mangroves by night and waiting for the Japanese supply boats. They had diesel engines and we could hear them coming. Our favourite spot was known as Hellfire Corner. The chaungs were like a four-way stop street. At a given signal we would open up and sink the barges and escorts, and go back the next day to inspect the damage. On one occasion Murphy and I asked permission to inspect one of these gun-boats which was damaged. We rowed over in the dinghy and as I hauled myself up and looked over the side, hoping to find a Jap sword, I saw a Jap's head split in half. At that moment the small-arms ammunition began exploding like a firework display and caused us to speed back to our ML – much to the amusement of our shipmates.

The RAF supported us in daylight, but they were a little trigger-happy, so we painted a broad white stripe across the upper deck and down the sides. When we had time we used to challenge the Royal Indian Navy and the Burma Navy MLs to games of hockey and soccer. The Indians beat us at hockey and I think we were on a par with the Burmese at soccer.

After the liberation of Akyab in January 1945 we pressed on up the Kaladan River, led by the Indian sloop *Narbarda*. All of a sudden we found ourselves being shelled by Japanese batteries ashore. In a flash *Narbarda* hoisted a five-flag signal – 'S-C-R-A-M!' We realised that we had to move fast and no time could be spared for coded signals. *Narbarda* had to go full speed astern as the river was too narrow for turning, but between them the Royal Indian Navy ships *Narbarda* and *Jumna* soon silenced the Jap guns.

On D-Day, 12 June 1945, we invaded Myebon, followed by Kangan. Later we were relieved by the 36th Flotilla from South Africa bringing with it the SA ratings Ralph Stewart (Coxswain) and K Cockroft, both RNVR (SA).

Commandos landing at Myebon, Burma, after softening up of target by aircraft. (Bartholomew)

During the Burma campaign the war virtually stopped during the monsoons, and we were sent back to India for refitting and a rest. Our ML crews were sent inland to Jubbapore, where we were entertained by the townsfolk and by the British, who had an army base there. Later we were sent to Diyatalawa Rest Camp in Ceylon. It was in the midst of the tea plantations, and there we met tea planters who could speak Afrikaans.

During our stay there we discovered graves and a monument to Boer war prisoners who had died there. Since they, like ourselves, were South African volunteers and far from home, we were happy to clean up some of the graves. It is hard to believe that these graves were later flattened. [*Author's note*: In February 1980 it was reported in the *Natal Daily News* that the South African War Graves Board had confirmed that it was aware that the entire Boer prisoners' cemetery at Diyatalawa in Sri Lanka (formerly Ceylon), except for the main monument, had been bulldozed by Sri Lankan soldiers. In this operation the grave markers of 141 Boer POWs who died there between 1900 and 1902 were flattened and later buried. 'We had no choice but to fall in with the decision to raze the cemetery', said Mr SCJ Joubert, Secretary of the Board. 'The markers had been removed on a British request that both the British and Boer cemeteries adjoining each other there should be levelled.']

The 49th Flotilla was the first to paint green and yellow bands round the funnel and we were proud of being South African lads in Burma. We got on very well with our English shipmates and in no time at all they were singing 'Sarie Marais' and 'Daar kom die Alabama'. The Indian and Burmese Navy lads were equally friendly, and never a word of politics was ever spoken. We all had one thing in common, and that was to finish the job and go home.

In the course of time we left our MLs in India and were transported to Durban in the aircraft-carrier HMS *Ameer* (formerly SS *Robin Kirk*) and then on to Cape Town to be demobbed.

★ ★ ★ ★ ★

Another account of this maritime 'jungle warfare' was given by former Sub-Lieutenant C Stuckey of the SANF. The following version has been extracted from an article entitled 'Chaung Chasers' published in the *Dekho* Issue No 100 of 1986. Mr Stuckey was the First Lieutenant referred to and also the Navigation Officer.

We were once patrolling up one of the chaungs and all seemed quiet and serene, when a bullet from out of the blue smashed through the forward window of the wheelhouse, missing my quartermaster by a hair's breadth. I immediately increased speed and brought all our guns to bear on the spot whence I had thought the bullet had come.

I was not left in doubt for long. Other bullets followed, puncturing the hull and exhaust pipe, and slashing through cushions in the wardroom and the first lieutenant's suitcase.

I had completed my training in the SATS *General Botha* when at the age of seventeen I joined the Royal Naval Reserve as a midshipman. After serving in several ships I then joined an ML of the 49th ML Flotilla at Mombasa on its way to the Persian Gulf, and was promoted to Sub-Lieutenant.

I also transferred to the South African Naval Forces and was seconded to the Royal Navy. The 49th ML Flotilla consisted of eight MLs which had all been assembled in South Africa. Four of these had served in the Persian Gulf for five months before they met the remainder of the flotilla in Bombay in November 1943, the latter having arrived there direct from South Africa.

The flotilla was originally designed for anti-submarine purposes. In Bombay, however, the Asdic and most of the depth charges were removed so that the MLs could operate in inland waters. To replace them they were equipped with assorted weapons such as a 3-pounder, an Oerlikon and other light machine guns, mortars, and later a Bofors.

The flotilla left for the Arakan coast at the beginning of 1944 and was based in the Tek Naf River which at that time marked the boundary between India and Burma. While there it took part in several operations. During the monsoon period, when operations were not possible, it withdrew to Ceylon and returned to the Arakan towards the end of the year for the final assault on the Japanese in that area as described in the booklet *Five Navies Fight for Burma*, published by the Inter-Services Publications Directorate, New Delhi.

I was in ML 380, which was the flotilla leader and carried the senior officer, Lt AG Milne, and had a crew of twenty. Before the final assault began we took part in several operations, such as escorting commandos in minor landings, and patrolling the coast in search of Japanese craft. The whole flotilla bombarded Japanese defences as far south as Diamond Island off the Irrawaddy Delta, and returned to Tek Nef on Christmas Day 1944.

I well remember some of the incidents mentioned in the article 'Chaung Chasers'. ML 380, in company with an ML from another flotilla under the command of Lt RN Harris, also a South African, was ordered to patrol at night along the Mayu River, north of Akyab. This river, like nearly all the other inland waterways, was shown as blank spaces on the the charts. A partial survey of the mouth of the river had revealed that there was a way through the sandbanks by lining up on two trees. We were thus able to enter the river without difficulty.

12-pounder gun. Gun's crew on board ML in Burma. (Bartholomew)
3

I was in the wheelhouse reading the echo-sounding machine when the bullet 'missed the quartermaster by a hair's breadth'. When the engagement was over we had difficulty in getting out of the river. It was not possible to pick up the same trees from inside the river, and we got out by moving at the slowest possible speed, taking constant soundings on each side of the ML. We eventually made it without mishap after much manoeuvring among the sandbanks in the dark.

ML 380 led the assault on Myebon and I was one of those who had to keep awake for over thirty hours. Such things are possible when one is young.

After that we were required to patrol the chaungs, first at night and until the Japanese found that they could no longer use these waterways. Listening in the absolute silence of the dark to the bloodcurdling cries of the Japs dying in the mangroves was something that I think we all remembered for a long time.

Both at Akyab and Myebon the Japanese made air attacks on us, and I heard that their planes were shot down by the Royal Air Force. After Myebon the 49th Flotilla returned to Vizagapatam in India, where it was taken over by the Indian Navy, and we all went our various ways.

Life in an ML was not always easy. There were no facilities for storing fresh food for any length of time, so while we were at sea and when serving on the Arakan Coast and in the Persian Gulf food

165

was always tinned or powdered. Water was scarce, and we had to wash out of a bucket on the deck. On the Arakan Coast we dressed informally. Many of the crew grew beards, which we shaved off on returning to civilisation. We operated for long periods in malarial areas and had to take tablets, which were not always effective.

It would seem from the *Navy News* of August 1989 that South Africans seconded to the Royal Navy whose citations were traced and who served in the light coastal forces on the Arakan Coast received more mentions in despatches than those in other war zones, a total of twelve, four Distinguished Service Crosses and three Distinguished Service Medals.

After the take-over by the Indian Navy I was transferred to a tank landing ship built in the United States. She was one of the ungainliest ships I had ever seen, but at least one could have a proper bath; and as there was an ice-cream machine on board we had a few things to make life more pleasant.

We returned to the Arakan Coast and also took part in the landings at Rangoon. The ship also played a part in the next phase of getting the Japanese out of South East Asia, namely, the invasion of Malaya.

Arakanese POW being interrogated on board ML 391. (Bartholomew)

We were part of a large invasion convoy, but while at sea heard that the Japanese had surrendered. Nevertheless the landing went ahead as planned, but without any untoward incident. We then proceeded to Batavia [now Jakarta]. Since there were no occupation troops, conditions there were chaotic. It was amazing too, to see how docile the Japanese troops had become. Previously they had been known as fighters to the death, but on command of their Emperor their attitude changed completely.

There were large numbers of women and children who had been interned by the Japanese still living in the camps. We arranged ice-cream parties on board for the children, and for many it was the first time in their lives that they had experienced such luxuries. Being able to speak Afrikaans I was able to talk to many of these people, although many of them spoke English.

While I was in Batavia I was told that I was being returned to South Africa. That took about two months by way of Singapore and Colombo, and I reached Durban just before Christmas 1945, by which time I had been promoted Full Lieutenant.

★ ★ ★ ★ ★

In the foregoing the reader will have noticed references to a publication called 'Chaung Chasers'. It is an apt name for those employed in this pursuit, the following description of which appeared in the December 1986 issue of the MOTH magazine *Home Front*; the contributor is Mr K Button of Plumstead in the Cape, who served in the ML flotillas, and quotes the author, JGH Gritten:

'Half the officers and men described in the article were South Africans, reminding us that in those far-off days the Union of South Africa was one of the Dominions of the Crown . . .'

He also wrote: 'The narrow chaungs that gash Burma's coast are the hunting grounds of our motor launches (MLs). It's a small scale but deadly warfare in which the fighting spirit and camaraderie of the little ships get full play.'

The following is likewise quoted from 'Chaung Chasers': an article written by JGH Gritten which was first published in the *Ceylon Review* of 28 April 1945.

Camouflaged, the motor launch, bristling with guns, nestles among the gaunt roots of the mangroves growing out of the soft ooze. To the commanding officer and his crew any movement other than the sluggish motion of this Burmese chaung means only one thing . . .

They are more than twenty miles from their natural element, the open sea. Many of them are veterans of full-blooded scraps in the English Channel, in E-boat Alley, and in the Mediterranean. But this is a totally new type of warfare for light coastal forces. Stealthy and unpredictable. Everyone is tense and alert.

Suddenly a mangrove branch sways – almost imperceptibly. But the gunner has seen it. It might have been just a breath of wind, but the orders are to open up on anything in the jungle that moves. The gunner presses the trigger and the gun spits a short burst. The branch sways again, there is a snapping of twigs and a thud. That is

MLs 438, 441, and 477 at Kiuakpyu. (Bartholomew)

all the crew see or hear, but they know that another Jap sniper will snipe no more.

Over-dramatised? No, this incident actually occurred and was repeated a dozen times and more when flotillas of the light coastal forces operating in the Arakan penetrated the Burmese network of inland waterways, time and time again, disrupting the Japanese lines of communication and supply and cutting their escape routes as they retreated before the 14th Army.

Some flotillas are manned by personnel of the Royal Indian Navy, or the Burma Royal Naval Volunteer Reserve, but in the Royal Naval flotillas all the commanding officers are South Africans who in peacetime were clerks working in a variety of offices.

The Senior Officer of the flotilla for instance, Lt AG Milne SANF(V), was treasurer to the East London Town Council before he joined up in 1940. Of the crews, half live in South Africa and half in the United Kingdom.

'Even they seem to be composed of peacetime office workers,' says Lt Lockhead, who was a shipping clerk in Durban. 'My crew includes two chartered accountants; the coxswain was a post office clerk. I have a former insurance salesman and a shipping clerk who man the guns alongside a Yorkshire policeman and a bricklayer. But I couldn't pick a more efficient crew if I had the whole navy to choose from! Springboks and the men from the Old Country work in perfect accord.'

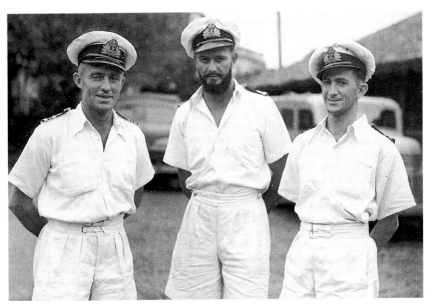

Lt-Cmdr AG Milne DSC RNVR (SA) of Port Elizabeth and East London. Senior Officer 49th ML Flotilla, Sub-Lt Herbert Twine RNVR (SA) (later chairman of WP Cricket Association) and Lt RLJ ('Bungy') Williams DSC RNVR (SA) of Port Elizabeth. (Bartholomew)

'The only bone of contention used to be that the Springboks preferred coffee to tea, the Englishmen tea to coffee. A compromise was finally agreed upon: the whole crew drank tea one day and coffee the next!'

Even the construction of the MLs themselves is part South African, part British. Prefabricated parts shipped from the United Kingdom were assembled in South African ports.

After a six thousand mile passage from the Cape (it was the first ML flotilla to accomplish that), the MLs served for some months in the sweltering temperatures of the Persian Gulf. The flotilla then carried out patrols in the Indian Ocean before operating in the Arakan. Perils in the Burmese chaungs abounded: from Jap motor gunboats, from snipers hidden in the mangroves, and from uncharted rocks and mud-flats. This was the first ML flotilla to engage and destroy Japanese motor gunboats – eight of them.

To prevent waterborne supplies from reaching the Japs, who were being hard-pressed by the Army at Myebon, Lt Milne, as senior officer onboard an ML commanded by Lt Whitehead (Cape Town) and accompanied by another craft under Lt RLJ Williams (Port Elizabeth), steamed up an uncharted chaung and lay doggo under the mangroves.

After a long vigil their patience was rewarded. Four Japanese landing barges, full of supplies and heavily gunned, hove in sight. Unsuspecting, they steamed well on to the beam of the camouflaged

MLs until, making the most of surprise, the guns of the two British craft tore the stillness of the Burmese jungle. The tornado of fire blew the Japanese craft out of the water. All that night the crews of the MLs were kept awake by the blood-curdling cries of the coxswain of one of the boats dying in the mangroves.

Later two more MLs under the command of Lt HH Brown and Lt HJ Bird (both of Durban) came up the chaung. Again the Japs sent down support craft, probably to investigate the non-arrival of their unfortunate comrades. This time the Japs opened fire first, at the spot where they expected our MLs to be lying and to draw their fire. In that they were unsuccessful, and a ding-dong battle began. But they were no more fortunate than their predecessors had been and four more Jap launches were sunk.

Troops disembarking into landing craft. Burma campaign. (Bartholomew)

On another afternoon units of the flotilla were anchored with two sloops up the Kaladan River. They were operating in close support of the Army. Shots suddenly fell near to the sloops which immediately opened fire on a village on the east bank. Lt Williams and Lt Hollis patrolled up the opposite bank until a dozen armed figures were seen running up a hill from the village. Holding his fire until he was quite certain that they were the enemy (for our own troops were known not to be too far away), Lt Hollis let fly with all his armament and the Japs were obliterated. Soon afterwards the Burmese villagers, invariably friendly and co-operative, rowed out to the MLs with white flags and told how they had been forced at bayonet-point to row the Japs across the river in their sampans the previous night.

Uncharted shoals and rocks are an ever-present menace and the depth of water in the chaungs can change from 18 to 2 fathoms within a comparatively short time. The chaungs are tidal up to twenty and thirty miles inland. Lt Lockhead's craft once got stuck on an uncharted rock in the middle of a chaung. There was a very real danger of the ML capsizing when the tide receded. For hours the crew strove to get off the shelf by violent manoeuvring of the engines and by placing all the ship's company first on one side of the craft and then the other.

'At last, with a grating that set all our teeth on edge, we slid off the brute,' said Lt Lockhead. 'That night we secured alongside another ML in safe waters. Next morning we found chalked on our funnel the word *Rock-Leaper*. I don't know to this day whether one of our crew was responsible or whether somebody from our sister craft was trying to take the mickey out of us!'

On another occasion Lockhead ordered a seaman to take a sounding. After some minutes he called to the seaman from the bridge to ask his findings. No reply was forthcoming – the seaman was still concentrating on his job. More minutes passed before Lt Lockhead, more impatiently this time, repeated his question. 'What is the sounding?'

'I can still see the top of the lead, Sir!' came the reply.

In spite of the intense strain, morale is high and with plenty of humorous relief. This often takes the form of gramophone records played over the ML loud-hailers as a comment on their misfortunes. Sometimes a boat limps back into harbour, damaged after a severe scrap, blaring 'On a Wing and a Prayer' or, for a late arrival unable to find a berth, the soulful strains of 'I'm Nobody's Baby Now.'

Everyone is mustard-keen to go on every possible operation, and if one boat has the misfortune to be ordered to stay in harbour a special record is played by all her sister craft as they steam away. The record consists of peals of ironic laughter!

56th ML Flotilla arriving at Akyab in daylight. During 1944 they had paid many visits during the hours of darkness. (Bartholomew)

To Leading Seaman JC Hannah of Port Elizabeth, one of the crew of this flotilla, came the honour of being the first man to step ashore in Akyab. With an officer from an Australian destroyer he rowed ashore in a dinghy and planted a Union Jack on the jetty. Lt Williams' ML was the first craft to enter the harbour.

But these colourful incidents are the exceptions that provide relief for a job of almost unparalleled strain. Not only does every movement, every sound, mean the possible presence of the enemy. When one night someone switched on a fan inside one of the MLs without telling anybody, the whole crew were at action stations for an hour before the sound was traced. That perfectly exemplifies the ever-present tension. No chances can be taken, and fire first and investigate afterwards is the invariable rule.

★ ★ ★ ★ ★

While still with the 'Chaung Chasers' the following report (which for its navalese alone should bring back memories for many) to the Senior Officer, Arakan Coastal Forces, HMS *Kedah*, was submitted by the Commanding Officer of HMML 854. It is dated 11 January 1945, and follows an operation to sound out the depth of water in a river. It illustrates the variety of tasks undertaken by Fairmile flotillas in Burma:

> In accordance with instructions from SOACF to contact HMIS *Narbada* (Capt St J Nott, RIN) for special duties, HMML 854 (Lt RN Harris SANF(V)) proceeded out of harbour and anchored off Akyab outer bar at 1735/8. Contact with *Narbada* was made at 1830. ML 854 closed her and formed Order One, speed 16 knots. Courses as requisite to enter Hunter's Bay, leaving Frederick Island close to

HMIS *Narbada*. Manned by Royal Indian Navy and co-ordinated with MLs in Burma campaign. (Bartholomew)

starboard. At 2255 *Narbada* anchored and ordered ML 854 to anchor in the vicinity and close her without further orders by 0600/9.

At 0600 ML 854 berthed on her starboard quarter, commenced loading Dan buoys and at 0810 slipped with Captain Nott aboard and proceeded on various courses in a northerly direction close to the eastern shore of Hunter's Bay, sounding constantly to find the deepest existing north channel. Dan buoys were dropped approximately every two miles. Average speed 12 knots.

At 1045/9 ML 854 entered the estuary of the Myebon and Thaygan Rivers. Soundings were irregular and speed was reduced, a course having been set roughly in the centre of the Myebon River. When approximately abeam of Myebon village a river steamer was sighted at the extreme end of the river's northern trend. It was decided to sink this as a blind for the morning's surveying, and accordingly fire was opened at about 5 000 yards with the 3-pounder, but all rounds fell short. Range was closed to 3 000 yards and fire resumed. It was then noticed that the target was aground and not in use. Course was altered 180 degrees and the Bofors opened fire for exercise until the target was out of range. Course was then set S10E and speed 12 knots to leave the river.

At 1148 an enemy battery opened fire from the pagoda on the Myebon Peninsula with what appeared to be a 37mm gun. The first three rounds were direct hits; the first passing through the wheelhouse between the helmsman (AB Smit SANF) and the rating and officer at the echo-sounder slightly wounding the rating. The second passed through the WT cabin and the POs' heads. The third passed right through the engine-room between the main exhaust pipes. None of these rounds burst.

The hands were at action stations and the layer of the 3-pounder (Ldg Sea R Stuart SANF) had pinpointed the target. Fire was opened at 2 000 yards with the 3-pounder and .303 Vickers; the latter to give the after guns the bearing. After the second round from the 3-pounder which hit the base of the pagoda, the enemy ceased fire. All guns continued to fire at the pagoda for three minutes. Speed had been increased to 18 knots at the beginning of the action and she touched bottom. Speed was at once reduced to 12 knots and she floated free.

The ship passed within 100 yards of the shore on the southern journey down Hunter's Bay but no further enemy fire was encountered. At 1245 ML 854 berthed on *Narbada*'s starboard quarter and transferred Capt Nott and two casualties. The latter returned on board at 1315. Orders were then received to return to Akyab independently and ML 854 arrived in harbour at 1700 and berthed at 1724/9.

RECOMMENDATIONS: HOPKINS, Neville C. Sub-Lt SANF(V) in that he stood in an exposed position controlling the gunfire in a very efficient manner with the result, in my opinion, that the enemy was put out of action.

SMIT, David JL. AB/SD SA67774. In that as helmsman and telegraph-man he stood at his post and obeyed orders promptly and correctly despite the fact that this compartment was hit and covered in splinters and flying glass. An error on his part in these waters, uncharted and dangerous to navigation, would have had serious consequences.

Leading Seaman David JL Smit with his parents after receiving the DSM for gallantry in Burma. (DJL Smit)

CASUALTIES: MITCHLEY, Robert, AB QMS SANF, slightly wounded by a .28 bullet in the left upper arm while engaged in loading the 40mm Bofors during the action.

WOOD, Reginald G. AB ST. Flesh wounds in the back while on duty in the wheelhouse on the sounding machine when that compartment was hit. Presumably from flying glass.

DAMAGE: Port and starboard forward wheelhouse windows broken and fittings blown over the side. R/T plug, telephone and switch smashed beyond repair. Barometer smashed. Woodwork and internally fitted drip-tray on side of wheelhouse torn and broken. Hole in ship's side both sides of W/T cabin. Watertight bulkhead between mess-deck and galley-flat gashed open for 4 feet. All electric leads to wheelhouse and forward circuits severed in galley-flat. Holes through both sides of engine-room. Oerlikon R/U locker stand damaged. One guard-rail stanchion severed.

This was the ship's second encounter with enemy shore batteries within a few days and it is gratifying to see the speed at which the guns found their target. The encounter also confirmed the theory experienced before, that the enemy allow a quiet passage into these rivers and do not attempt to open fire until the return journey has begun, probably to lure one into a false sense of security.

The Fairmile in which David Smit won his DSM with a close up of damage caused by Japanese gunners. (DJL Smit)

Liberators and Mitchells bomb Myebon in softening up prior to landings. (Bartholomew)

And what did those who came into contact with the Springbok sailors in Burmese waters think of them?

In a letter written to the MOTH magazine a New Zealander, formerly seconded to the Royal Indian Navy, quotes this tribute paid in the pages of a book *From Trombay to Changi*, compiled by one of the officers (presumably an Indian) with the co-operation of commanding officers and their juniors of the Combined Coastal Forces.

'The original 49th Flotilla crews did not leave [Burma] until the first atom bomb was dropped on 5 August 1945. The South Africans were flown home. They were as tough and fit a bunch of men as could be found anywhere in the world. They had stuck three months on the Arakan Coast in 1943/44 and a further stint of three months in 1944/45. They were liked and admired by everyone as a very fine flotilla.'

★ ★ ★ ★ ★

More praise came from an unidentified source and appeared in May 1945 when the war was drawing to its end:

Motor launches of the Royal Navy, manned by mixed British and South African crews, have been operating with Arakan coastal forces off Burma since February last year. They have carried out several close range bombardments of Japanese coastal defences. South Africans were the first sailors to enter the recaptured port of

Akyab on 4 January, and they were in the vanguard of the combined assault on the Myebon Peninsula eight days later.

They have taken part in the destruction of a large number of armed Japanese launches. These enemy craft were trying to sneak through the mangrove swamps east of Myebon with food, ammunition and oil for the Japanese troops now cornered by Indian and West African Divisions of General Sir Philip Christison's 15th Corps.

When the Springboks first arrived at a jungle base on the Indo-Burmese frontier the Japanese were on the offensive. The demands of other theatres had severely limited the naval and air support available, and the MLs – small heavily-armed motor gun-boats – were the only representatives of Allied naval power that could then be spared for the Burma front. Royal Indian Navy flotillas already operating were reinforced by five MLs, all commanded by South African SANF(V) officers.

Two important bombardments in which South Africans took part soon after their arrival earned a special signal from Admiral Sir James Somerville, C–in–C Eastern Fleet, who congratulated 'all concerned on the good planning and spirited execution of these operations.'

In the first of these bombardments, Springbok and Indian MLs started fires on the west coast of Akyab Island and completed their

ML 437 at Akyab with Army reconnaissance plane. (Bartholomew)

task despite machine-gun and heavier fire from the shore. In the second, two nights later, Springbok and Indian MLs set a Japanese Company HQ and barrack buildings ablaze by pumping four thousand shells into a wooded hill 20 miles behind the enemy lines.

There can be no doubt that Arakan coastal forces helped to thwart Japanese plans. In fact, it was later established that the little ships' patrols and bombardments, by threatening an amphibious assault on his flank, had persuaded the enemy to hold a large force in reserve well south of the fighting line.

During the monsoon the South Africans were withdrawn to Ceylon, where they carried out patrols in defence of the Eastern Fleet base, work at which they were joined by the rest of their flotilla and by other MLs manned by Burmese sailors.

The writer records that he had recently spent six days on board one of these MLs commanded by Lt TV Bartholomew of Johannesburg.

The ship was typical of the whole flotilla. She was built in South Africa in 1942 and had seen service in the Persian Gulf before coming to Burma. The ship's company were drawn equally from the Union and the United Kingdom. The Captain was a South African. Most of the South African ratings lived in Durban, Johannesburg or Port Elizabeth.

Rarely had I sailed with such a happy company. The South Africans insisted that they were serving in the Royal Navy, while the Englishmen were equally insistent that theirs was a South African ship, and they were proud of it.

When the British commandos and troops of the 26th Indian Division were landed on the Myebon Peninsula to cut off the Japanese force in the Kaladan Valley, South African MLs were entrusted with a Zero Hour patrol in the Myebon River. I accompanied Lt RLJ (Bungy) Williams of Port Elizabeth in the leading ship.

As the first wave of assault craft hit the beach, we entered the river on their starboard flank, giving the enemy a good plastering as we steamed past. Two of the palm trees lining the waterfront were cut down by our fire and hundreds of shells whistled into the township, flashing as they exploded and making a din like a thousand milk churns running amok.

Farther up the river we located and blasted two Japanese fox-holes, lobbing several shells straight through their front door. It was only when we penetrated about five miles northward, shooting up targets of opportunity, that we came under accurate shell-fire from Japanese 75mm field guns. The nearest burst missed us by about ten yards. Our river patrol was maintained throughout D-Day, although shells fired intermittently from the neighbouring hills fell uncomfortably close.

Several times in recent weeks the South Africans have come under Japanese fire, a measure of the impression they have made on the enemy, but there have been no serious casualties, and the boys are in fine fettle. Many of them will soon be returning home, having completed two years' overseas service. They take with them the good wishes of the Indian and Burmese flotillas with whom they have co-operated so effectively. Sailors are not given to flattery, but whenever South Africans are mentioned on this coast they are talked of as 'damned good types' – which is praise indeed.

★ ★ ★ ★ ★

Lt Lord DSC who won his decoration for service in Burma. (SANMMH)

Mr R Stuart was a Port Elizabeth man. He was called up for peacetime training in the RNVR (SA) in 1929. In the course of his training, during which he made several voyages in RN and SANS vessels, he passed for Leading Seaman in HMSAS *Immortelle* and later as a Seaman Gunner in HMS *Carlisle*. He volunteered for extended service in the hope of getting to the United Kingdom, but in the event that never happened, at any rate in peacetime.

When the war broke out he was among the first of the war reserves to be called up in February 1940, and after a month's refresher course at the RNVR base in Port Elizabeth he was drafted to Froggy Pond in Simon's Town awaiting a draft to the cruiser HMS *Shropshire*.

On qualifying for a higher gunner rate he and two other South Africans, PO Robinson from East London and Leading Seaman Masters from Port Elizabeth, were earmarked to go to the gunnery school at Whale Island, but since *Shropshire* was a Chatham ship they never got to Portsmouth.

HMS *Barracouda,* coastal forces depot ship. Built in Japan in 1940 as Danish *Heinrich Jessen.* She was the last ship out of Hong Kong, Singapore, Rangoon and Akyab in 1942. As HMS *Barracouda* she was the first ship back in Akyab, Rangoon and Singapore in 1945. (Bartholomew)

He served in HMS *Shropshire* for about five months and one thing he vividly remembers was the ship's mascot, an Alsatian called Rex. When *Shropshire* was in Simon's Town the famous Great Dane, Able Seaman Just Nuisance boarded the ship, as was his practice with all arrivals. He was met at the top of the gangway by Rex, and after a good deal of growling Nuisance retreated. They both later had three fights on shore. Nuisance won the first, Rex won the second and lost the third and last. Rex was buried in Simon's Town possibly as a result.

Stuart left *Shropshire* in Chatham and after about four months in barracks volunteered for HMS *Mauritius,* a Crown colony-class cruiser with a tonnage of about 8 000, a crew of about seven hundred, and carrying four triple turrets of 4-inch guns as main armament. The three SA seamen might have been at Chatham for ever if they had not volunteered, since apparently their service papers had ended up at Portsmouth!

After being commissioned at Newcastle, where she was built, *Mauritius* spent some time at Scapa Flow. There were three South Africans in her complement, and they saw a great deal of convoy work after her trials and working-up. In fact they experienced what might have been one of the longest convoy voyages of the war. Sailing for Scapa Flow and collecting and discarding ships along the way, they steamed to Freetown, Cape Town, Durban, Mombasa and Bombay, and they finished their escort duty off Rangoon. They lost not a single ship, although after they handed over one convoy to a battleship off Freetown sixteen ships were lost in just over an hour.

Mauritius was attached to the Far Eastern Fleet and engaged in a great deal of secret work such as carrying out surveys for landing bases for Catalinas in the Nicobar and Andaman Islands. She was in Singapore when the Japanese arrived and had to leave port in a hurry.

Ralph Stuart left HMS *Mauritius* in January 1943 at Mombasa and took passage in the battleship HMS *Revenge*. He spent five months in her before disembarking at Simon's Town. There he landed up in HMS *Thames*, (formerly *General Botha*).

While he was there he volunteered for motor launches and joined HMML 854, later known as Q854, as Coxswain, and sailed for Burma. The crew of sixteen were a mixture of SANF and RN ratings, with two officers. A good crew.

In Burma they had a busy time patrolling and landing parties on the beaches. While he was there, in June 1945, he got his draft chit for demob. That took him to HMS *Mayena*, a drafting base at Colombo, and finally to the destroyer HMS *Roebuck* for passage to Durban, where his arrival marked the last day of his sea-time. It also happened to be his birthday, 9 August 1945.

When he is asked why he joined the RN he says, 'I guess I wanted to see the world. I certainly saw quite a bit while I was in the service, and as far as I know the South Africans got along pretty well with the RN chaps. Just one big happy family.'

11

One Man's War

Douglas K Green formerly of Port Elizabeth remembers coming home
on 3 September 1939 to find his mother quietly sobbing. War had been
declared. There was good reason for her tears for she had lived through
the siege of Kimberley and her seventeen-year-old brother had served
in Flanders in the 1914 – 18 war.

In the prevailing excitement of the day young Douglas felt that he
had to get to Britain to join up. But wiser counsel prevailed and instead,
at the age of fourteen and a half, he was entered on the books of the
training ship *General Botha* to undergo two years of basic nautical
training.

He recalls the discipline, the wonderful comradeship, and the fact
that all were equal with no favouritism tolerated. In his second year he
was made Cadet Captain in charge of the ship's bugle band.

The course ended in December 1941 and one by one his term mates
left home to join either the Merchant Navy or to receive appointments

Some of the intake 1940/41 on the ropes and wall bars
SATS *General Botha*. (D Green)

as midshipmen in the Royal Naval Reserve (RNR). Douglas Green was one of the latter, and it was while awaiting a draft that he had his first glass of beer in the Lord Nelson pub in Simon's Town. He and two others then joined the troopship *Oronsay* for passage to Freetown, Sierra Leone.

On arrival he was drafted to the old Union Castle mail liner *Edinburgh Castle*, which was serving as a stationary depot ship. Next morning he had the unpleasant experience of seeing a seaman detailed to clean the wash basins cut his throat from ear to ear. The shocked Douglas spent ten minutes running about the decks seeking someone to whom he could report the incident. It was his first taste of life in the raw.

On 3 February the same three lads joined the armed merchant cruiser *Pretoria Castle* in which they were welcomed into the gunroom by yet another former cadet from the *Botha*, Bill Power.

Green taking a noonsight on *Chitral*.
(D Green)

He had a lot to learn. On being summoned by the call of 'Snotty!' he protested that his name was Green. Snotty is, of course, the time-honoured Royal Naval term for a midshipman. Next morning he cheerfully greeted the commander and received a blast in return. He was told that the commander would decide whether he wished to be greeted, but that a salute would be more appropriate.

Douglas takes up the tale: 'The sub-lieutenant in charge of the gunroom was a very arrogant Fleet Air Arm officer who seemed to spurn any colonials, as we were called. He was pilot of the Sea Fox seaplane that the ship carried and was catapaulted when needed. On one patrol we received a report that a German raider, described as having a structure amidships and a squat funnel, was in our area. We went to action stations and flew off the Sea Fox. A few hours later it was decided that we had been looking for ourselves! I still have a strong suspicion that it was a fake message put out by one of our radio operators.' *Pretoria Castle* carried out many patrols while based at Freetown. While at anchor in the port the *Nelson* and another battleship with attendant escorts anchored nearby. Soon afterwards a stoker on board *Nelson* came up for a breath of fresh air and fell asleep just in front of the stop-block on 'B' turret. When the ship went to dawn action stations the turret was swung through its arcs and the stoker ended up as flesh spattered on the foreside of the bridge.

Typical of the trials and tribulations that beset a young midshipman was the time when Douglas was in charge of the ship's pinnace employed on a continual round of taking his captain on official and social calls to other vessels. On one occasion he was called at 0200 to fetch his captain from a battleship, at the same time embarking the captains of the *Edinburgh Castle* and *Philoctetes*. On approaching *Philoctetes* the bowman seemed to be asleep and the pinnace rammed a buoy and began to make water. The pump was started, but the three captains got their feet wet. Douglas' captain asked if they could get back to the *Pretoria* and was assured that they could. They did, and the accident was duly reported to the officer of the watch. The chastened young coxswain was told to secure the boom and clambered into his hammock about 0330. Summoned to man his boat again at 0500, he found that it had sunk at the boom with only the top of the canopy visible. The ship's crane hoisted it out of the water, but for his sins Midshipman Green had to spend sixteen hours in the crow's nest, to be worked off in harbour, and had his shore-leave stopped for two months.

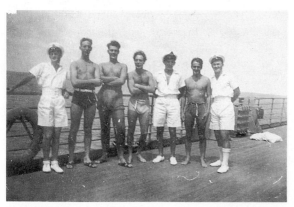

Some gunroom members of *Pretoria Castle*. Maxwell on left. Green on right. (D Green)

The *Pretoria Castle* continued her Atlantic patrols searching for raiders; but since one of their guns was dated 1895 they all wondered what would happen if they actually came across the enemy. This was a 6-inch gun with worn rifling, and at one practice shoot the shell only travelled a thousand yards. On another occasion there was a misfire, and after waiting the required period of time the breech was opened with the result that there was a great whoosh and a rating was seriously hurt.

One day, about 250 miles north-west of Freetown, the ship came across a beautiful schooner, the *Reina Marie Stewart*, 187 days out of New York, carrying a deck cargo of timber and lying becalmed in the doldrums. The AMC did not stop, but in passing warned the schooner of U-boats in the vicinity. A few days later, 4 June 1942, smoke was sighted on the horizon and on closing the position the cruiser found the burning hulk of the *Reina Marie Stewart*. She had been gunned by a U-boat, but of her crew there was no sign.

On another occasion three or four Vichy French ships were shadowed for a day or two bound for Dakar, but no action was taken.

In Bathurst, Gambia, with several other warships present, a soccer match was arranged between South Africans serving in *Pretoria Castle* and the Rest. The South Africans won 2 – 1, and in the resultant celebration Green's officer's cap was taken away and he was entertained in the ratings' canteen. The beer flowed; and later, while trying to negotiate the gangway, he fell overboard and was nearly drowned. Duly hauled before the commander he was ordered to be given five strokes of

Over the boom. (D Green)

the cane, to be administered by the unpopular Fleet Air Arm pilot. Refusing to bend over a chair, he told the sub who laid it on heavy and hard, that he hoped the latter would crash his plane. His wounds were soaked in hot sea water – not the best of treatments, and for the next ten days Mister Midshipman Green hobbled about with a very sore arse. He received a lot of sympathy from most of the officers, who were RNR and therefore Merchant Navy, and not in favour of naval physical punishment.

Eventually *Pretoria Castle* arrived at Greenock on the Clyde, the seaplane having taken off earlier for some Fleet Air Arm base in Scotland. They heard that it had indeed crashed, but never received news of the fate of the pilot.

The ship then went on to Newcastle-on-Tyne where she was paid off on 31 July 1942, and the crew were sent on leave. The *Pretoria Castle* was converted into an auxiliary aircraft-carrier, and of her former complement the South African Bill Power qualified as a pilot in the Fleet Air Arm and was later killed in a crash.

For the first half of August 1942 Midshipman Green was attached to HMS *Pembroke*, the naval establishment at Chatham, and then reported for duty at the Royal Naval College at Greenwich. He was overwhelmed at the thought of being at an institution so steeped in tradition and through whose portals so many great men had passed. He found the

The HMAMC *Chitral's* officer complement taken in Bermuda in 1944. Myself (Green) sitting front row extreme right. (D Green)

discipline rigorous; with no one allowed outside the grounds after 2200. But there was ample opportunity for sport of all kinds and at a pawnbroker's shop near the entrance he bought a cornet for £1.5.0.

Meals were eaten in the famous Painted Hall, approached through an underground tunnel; where Green managed to scratch his name for posterity under the table allocated to snotties. While at the college he was approached, as the only South African there, by the lieutenant-commander in charge of midshipmen and asked if he would care to dine with General Smuts. He was duly fitted out with mess-dress and joined the party.

It must have been an intimidating experience for a youngster since, apart from the 'Oubaas', included in the party were such famous names as Lord Gort, Admiral of the Fleet Sir Dudley Pound, Admiral Sir Bruce Fraser, and so on. A photograph was taken of the gathering on the steps of the Painted Hall and South Africa House in London had a copy sent to Mrs Green in Port Elizabeth.

After the dinner, and before the intended Cabinet meeting, Green invited Field Marshal Smuts into the gunroom for a pint of beer. The famous statesman, sitting in one of the black leather chairs, settled for half a pint!

After completing the Greenwich course the class was sent to the gunnery school at Chatham where everything was wet and dreary – which was in keeping with the rigid gunnery discipline typical of all such establishments. Whilst on the gunnery course young Douglas had a Springbok's head encircled by a wreath over the words 'South Africa' tattooed on his left forearm for the princely sum of 2/6! His pay was 5/- per day.

The course included all the rigours of commando training and when it ended on 19 December 1942, Midshipman Green left for Liverpool to join the SS *Bodegraven* destined for HMS *Tana*, the naval base at Mombasa.

He was not comforted to find the 'B' flag flying, indicating 'I am loading explosives'. On boarding they were shown to their cabins and told that under no circumstances were they to close the cabin or bathroom doors in case the vessel should be torpedoed and they should become trapped.

There were fourteen in the naval draft on board and after the hatches were battened down, the ship loaded a deck cargo of crated aircraft and tanks secured with massive chain lashings. Joining a convoy in the Irish Sea and being placed on the starboard wing because of the 4 500 tons of explosive in her holds, the ships encountered one continuous gale. Whether the convoy became scattered, or whether the Dutch master of the *Bodegraven* just 'got the hell-in' and elected to sail independently is not clear, but in the heavy weather the deck cargo took charge and over the side it went.

There were two Dutch stewardesses on board who made up the beds and changed the linen. It was hinted that they spied on the occupants when the latter were bathing and hence the restriction on closing doors!

The passengers had no idea where the ship was and they were never told. They did see icebergs and they knew they had sailed down the American coast and then across the Atlantic to Walvis Bay. A young Dutch apprentice was in the habit of walking around with a Luger stuck in his belt and brandished this in ordering the naval party off the upper deck at sunset when, so he alleged, a U-boat could see the glowing ends of their cigarettes. The midshipmen then held a council of war and told him that if he ever did that again they would throw him and his Luger over the side. It did the trick.

Despite offers to stand watches, or serve as back-ups on the DEMS gun-deck, these were refused and in fact the Dutch crew hardly spoke to them. The ice thawed a little after the ship suffered engine trouble in which the four Royal Naval engineer officers lent a hand.

South Africans on board the HMAMC *Carnarvon Castle* 1940.

Meanwhile, having only been allowed to take £5 out of England they all ran short of cash. No credit was allowed and they were reduced to following the crew around, picking up their 'stompies', and rolling the secondhand tobacco into cigarettes with Rizla papers.

Three days out of Walvis Bay the ship shed a propeller blade but fortunately a sister-ship in Cape Town was able to provide a replacement – the naval draft enjoying a much-needed visit to the naval paymaster.

The ship arrived in Durban in mid-February and Douglas managed a week's leave at home in Port Elizabeth before returning to Durban to join the cruiser HMS *Frobisher* for passage to Kilindini (Mombasa). *Frobisher* was an old 7,9-inch gun cruiser carrying far too many passengers. Douglas Green recorded his impressions thus:

> I had to spread my camp stretcher in the tiller-flat and all night when off watch I bounced around between the steering gears until I found some codline or spunyarn to anchor my stretcher. I was always late for my watch because I could never find my way around all the watertight doors that had to be opened and closed.
>
> When we left Durban we escorted a big troop convoy up to the Suez Canal. In the convoy was a Polish passenger ship carrying several hundred ATS girls. Fresh water was at a premium on board *Frobisher* so when a rain squall was sighted off we dashed to the pipe of 'All hands to bathe'. This was the signal for every officer and man who could manage it to run out on deck, naked, and each with his piece of soap to have a good shower and soak. When the ship emerged from the rain squall we were no more than 200 yards from the *Poluski*. The screeches and cat-calls from those ATS girls was quite something to hear and many of the naked sailors on the upper deck enjoyed the interlude, marked as it was by many ribald and lewd signs and signals. *Frobisher* was certainly the envy of the convoy!
>
> There were also some army officers on board, one of them being a very large overweight major with a colossal girth. At action stations his place was down below in the officers' flat. The big square hatch had to be closed leaving only a round manhole to be negotiated. The major got stuck in the hatch and blocked it for the whole exercise. To free this chap was a major (no pun intended) operation involving block and tackle, tins of grease, and having to cut off all his uniform. The services of the ship's surgeon, who had stood by during the operation were needed once it was completed.

Douglas Green left the *Frobisher* in Mombasa and was transferred to the battleship HMS *Ramilles*. He describes it as akin to being put in a snake-pit. He never knew where he was, and all he wanted was to get

Gunroom members on *Chitral* 1943. The Sub/Lt on left had just received his stripe. Green is standing next to Robinson on right of picture who survived the sinking of the *Prince of Wales*. (D Green)

off. Fortunately for him, after only a week on board, he was, on 15 May 1943, transferred to the AMC, HMS *Chitral*.

Chitral was a former P & O liner employed on the Australian service before the war. She was a sturdy ship and well loved by all who served in her. The midshipmen were comfortably housed on the afterpart of the boat-deck in the charge of an RNVR officer, a namesake, Lt Green. As an AMC *Chitral* was employed on convoy work between Kilindini, Aden, Bombay and Australia. The ship never had a major breakdown and apart from one boiler-clean in Bombay, never laid up.

One young midshipman on board *Chitral* was a Canadian named Robinson. He was a survivor from the sinking of HMS *Prince of Wales* and told of how he had swum out of the sinking ship from three decks down. He was understandably jumpy.

There was also a handful of South African RNVRs on board. One of them was an Afrikaans lad named Scrooby, brother of the Springbok and Transvaal rugby player Chris Scrooby. One day, when victualling ship, young Green spotted Scrooby walking by with two crates of potatoes, one under each arm and carrying these up the gangway. The rest of the working party were either standing marvelling at this, or picking up one crate between two of them. Both Green and Scrooby subsequently played rugby for the Navy in a competition in Bombay, the former on the right wing and the latter as a forward.

The U16 rugby team 1940. M Bisset on the left.

During a submarine alarm whilst escorting a convoy to Bombay the *Chitral* dropped patterns of depth charge which, however, appeared to have damaged the packing around the propeller shafts rather than any potential U-boat. This necessitated drydocking in Bombay and opportunity was taken for the aforementioned boiler-clean.

Whilst in Bombay most of the crew went down with 'Bombay Guts'. It was decided to send the midshipmen to a hill station named Deolali and there they went, generously equipped with case of whisky and gin from the wardroom mess. As Green has dryly recorded, 'We were popular with the Army wives because we were so young and fresh and had plenty of gin!' Deolali was a training camp for soldiers bound for the fighting in Burma and at the end of their ten-day stay the midshipmen noted a contingent of American soldiers arriving for training.

After the break in Bombay it was back to convoy duties. At one time they found themselves back in Mombasa to move the Eastern Fleet base from Kilindini to Trincomalee in Ceylon. That entailed emptying No 2 hold of empty 44-gallon petrol drums carried in all the holds to

Concert party of crew and Wrens at concert on board *Chitral* 1943 when shifting base to Trincomalee. (D Green)

give added buoyancy if the vessel were attacked and in danger of sinking. An enormous amount of work went into the transformation of the hold into living quarters for a contingent of Jenny Wrens (Women's Royal Naval Service). The chippies (shipwrights) did plenty of moaning, and the real 'pusser' old RN types did not much like the idea of a warship going to sea with women on board.

Let Douglas Green tell the story in his own words.

Eventually 125 Wrens, leading hands and POs came on board – and that did not include the officer complement. The crew could not believe their eyes when all these women came aboard, and sentries were placed all over the ship where easy access could be gained to their quarters.

I have the names of those 125 Wrens, listed alphabetically from Annereau L/WRN to Whitlock L/WRN. I had to collect these names for berthing and watchkeeping purposes.

We put to sea, and about the second night out I had the middle watch and while walking down aft on the starboard gun deck I heard some funny sounds coming from the turret of No 3 gun. I investigated and found one of the sailors 'having it off' with one of the Wrens in a very compromising position on the righthand side of the turret. She had somehow got her foot jammed in the turning gear. They had to stay like that until daybreak, when the engineers could cut the metal with acetylene torches and release her foot. On arrival in Colombo she was flown back to England. There were many other such incidents; but I withhold comment.

After a passage of eleven days the *Chitral* reached Colombo, and Douglas was sent for and ordered to report to Coastal Craft stationed in Chittagong. He hated the idea of leaving *Chitral*, but at least he had the satisfaction of knowing that although he would have to go in the first instance signals would be despatched to try to get him back.

In Chittagong he joined an ML as First Lieutenant under training and off they went down to the Arakan coast, popping into rivers behind the Jap lines and setting up ambushes. After ten days of that the ML returned to Chittagong and Green was delighted to find that a signal had come through ordering his return to *Chitral*. His delight was partly due to the fact that, as he says, he could not see himself spending much time behind the Jap lines in a hostile jungle with snakes in his sleeping bag while carrying offshore patrols!

One incident of that time he does remember: coming out of the mouth of a chaung and finding hundreds of Japs swimming from a beach. The ML cruised up and down with guns blazing. Some of the Japs were wearing their glasses in the water!

Back on board *Chitral*, the AMC went up to the Persian Gulf to escort some tankers. There was much lower-deck humour when the crew learned the name of the river: Shatt-al-Arab.

At long last the good ship *Chitral* took her leave of the Eastern Fleet and steamed through the Suez Canal into the Mediterranean. From Port Said she escorted a convoy bound for Port Augusta in Sicily, which had just been liberated by the Allies. There was still quite a lot of activity in the Mediterranean, and while they were on their way to Augusta a hospital ship was attacked and sunk. In Augusta with the easy-come, easy-go, wartime way of life the midshipmen of *Chitral* swapped a couple of bottles of gin for an army jeep in which they explored some of the country, intrigued by all the scattered debris of war.

In Catania our young hero had himself photographed in front of a vast billboard that Montgomery had ordered to be erected in the town square, giving warning of the prevalence of VD in the town and exhorting the troops to exercise caution. Emblazoned on the front were the large letters VD, ominously dripping blood, and advising infected men to seek out their nearest prophylactic centre, then run by the Canadian medical services. When Green got home after the war he was 'closely questioned by my mother over this photograph.'

From Augusta the *Chitral* sailed for Gibraltar and onwards to show the flag at Bermuda, the first big British 'warship' to visit the island for a long time. Their visit included a twelve-hour flight in a big seaplane in which the crew were served steaks and hamburgers while keeping a look-out for U-boats.

The next port of call was yet another Augusta, this time in the Gulf of Mexico where they were paid off and put on a train for New York. They spent a night there and then went on to the Navy Yard at Norfolk, Virginia, where Douglas was appointed to a LSD (landing ship dock). This ship was in effect a floating drydock with engine-rooms on either side.

Tanks were flooded and she settled down in the water when the stern gate lowered and landing craft could enter. Tanks were then blown and, hey presto! there was a drydock. Like many other wartime 'expendable' craft the bulkheads were only spot-welded, with the result that at sea the bulkheads 'worked' continually with a great deal of noise.

The name of this LSD was HMS *Northway*. After being loaded with some huge treetrunks she sailed for Bermuda to take on some very heavy and very old guns from the naval dockyard and then set course for the Canary Islands and the United Kingdom. Douglas had bought two very large bunches of bananas at the islands, but in the train from Plymouth to London were a lot of school children who had never seen a banana. The result was that he arrived at the Springbok Club empty-handed. The *Northway* then sailed on convoy duty to Murmansk, which was described as 'not very pleasant'.

At that time Portsmouth and the Solent were the jumping off points for the coming invasion of France. Douglas left the LSD there on 5 December 1944 and reported to HMS *Hornet*, the base for MLs. The same morning he was appointed to MTB (motor torpedo boat) 212 – a Vosper 71-foot craft. Let Douglas once again take up his story:

The captain was Mark Arnold Foster, DSC RNVR, and I was most disappointed when I met this officer, since there was no hint of ego or emphasis on rank with him. He was small, with very drawn features. What a change from officers in the big ships! He told me to report at 1600 in sea-going kit. I returned to the Quonset huts that were our quarters ashore – we never lived on board in these boats. At 1600 I duly reported on board dressed in my usual blue uniform, complete with collar and tie. The captain looked at me, shook his head and asked why I had no sea-going kit. I told him that what I had on was normal wear on big ships.

After attending a briefing we cast off and with two other boats carrying mines headed for the French coast in the Cap du Havre area. We were the cover and escort for the minelayers and we got right in under the cliffs. On completing the minelaying the other two boats crash-started main engines and screamed back to England. All of a sudden there was an almighty flash above us. It was the 12,9-inch coastal batteries opening up on the fleeing MTBs. It took us the best part of an hour to get out of their range but our captain certainly knew what he was doing and we got safely back to Portsmouth. I was so shaken that I could hardly speak.

Next day the captain made sure that I was fitted out with oilskins, sea-boots, and two thick, white, greasy woollen jerseys, the standard dress for coastal forces. I stayed with Arnold Foster till after the D-Day landings on 6 June 1944.

While the invasion fleet was coming over we made a recce round the Baie de la Seine between Cherbourg and Le Havre. While we were sitting off the latter the RAF came over, bombed the invasion area, and dropped paratroops. The invasion fleet was really something to see. Before D-Day we had also been dropping and picking up commandos on the Normandy beaches. I could write sheets about what we did on those beachheads. Between MTBs 212, 208, and 246, I spent three weeks on the beachhead with our depot ship, the same HMS *Frobisher*. She provided us with quarters during the day and supplied fresh water, bread and provisions

Lt-Cmdr Bradford RNR, who had a flotilla of 'D' boats, did sterling work in and around the area where the Americans landed on Omaha Beach and Cherbourg, shooting up pockets of Germans offering resistance. This officer had his boats painted with gaping sharks' mouths in bright red with big white teeth. Obviously they became known as the 'Shark Flotilla' and, judging from reports of captured prisoners, they were much feared by the German E-boat crews.

On 11 April I left HMS *Hornet* and reported to MTB 772 on the River Hamble outside Southampton where she was receiving her final touches. She was brand new and we had to victual before going round to Holyhead to work up. We swung the compass, carried out torpedo trials and were on our way.

My captain was Lt 'Shiner' White DSO RNVR, the First Lieutenant Sub-Lt NGB Sampson, RN, and the navigator was Midshipman D Green RNR! The captain had had lots of experience in MTBs and had been first lieutenant of an MTB on the Dieppe raid. He was a great favourite and very popular with the ladies, but when in his cups always called me a South African bastard. He worked the engines beautifully, looking after them to Holyhead and after, until we returned to HMS *Mantis* (Lowestoft), where we joined the 53rd MTB Flotilla under the command of Lt-Cmdr Stuart Marshall, RNVR.

Lowestoft was full of minesweepers and MTBs. We had a big Canadian flotilla, and those Canucks were really fearless. In the afternoons, just after being given orders, the boats would start engines to warm up. No one could hear anything and when we slipped lines and headed out to sea past the breakwater the local population would come down to the pier and wave to us.

There were several other flotillas based on Great Yarmouth to the north of Lowestoft, and Felixstowe (HMS *Beehive*) to the south of us. Harwich harboured all the destroyers and frigates working with us on Z patrols. From Lowestoft we worked nightly on two patrols guarding E-Boat Alley. We also went over to the Texel, doing patrols down the coast from Ijmuiden to the Hook of Holland. I was able by devious means to keep my working logbooks of this MTB, and I shall quote some of the action later.

We had many short encounters with E-boats, sometimes lasting only a few minutes, and at a very short range of between 150 and 400 yards. The fire-power was very concentrated, but because it was at night and over open sights not always accurate.

In early September we had been fitted with some very hush-hush navigational equipment, and I was sent on a course to familiarise myself with it. It was something like the modern Decca system. By switching on a little box you got readings that were plotted on special charts and pinpointed the position.

On Sunday, 17 September 1944 we left Lowestoft at 0555 at a speed of 20 knots, passed down the swept channel off the East Coast, and at 0950 stopped off the NF3 buoy. This placed us about sixty miles out in the North Sea about equidistant from Ramsgate

Lowestoft harbour 1944 with some of MTBs and MGBs of 53rd flotilla. MTB 774 just coming alongside. In background 1013 wooden built minesweeper. (D Green)

and the Dutch coast. At 1136 MTBs 607 and 673 passed us and at 1142 MTBs 684, 683 and 723 steamed along the flight path course. At 1150 we spotted aircraft approaching and up to 1238 we counted 558 aircraft passing overhead. These were mostly Dakotas towing Horsa gliders.

Some were towing two gliders, and some crashed into the sea near us when other MTBs and rescue craft would go to their assistance. After passing us the aircraft turned towards the Dutch coast. This was the famous parachute operation at Arnhem.

The following signal was received from C-in-C, The Nore. 'Credit is due to 53rd Flotilla and base staff for their part in an operation which imposed considerable strain on both crews and maintenance staff. Their good work ensured that marker boats were also in position when needed.'

On our way back to Ramsgate we passed several gliders floating on the sea, whereupon we cut open the canvas sides of one or two and 'lifted' as many cases of provisions as we could. Among these were vast quantities of cigarettes, which we later sold to the rest of our flotilla at a profit.

On returning from our second operation on 18 September there was a terrific dogfight going on overhead. I can remember seeing a Hurricane shot down and flying very low over the houses on the cliffs of Ramsgate. The pilot had activated his parachute, which

MTB 772 doing about 28 knots off Lowestoft 1945 just before end of hostilities. (D Green)

pulled him out of the cockpit; but I saw his body smash into one of the chimney pots.

After all this we returned to our base at Lowestoft and resumed Z patrols. On Saturday, 23 September we saw some flying bombs headed for England and the Thames. We opened fire, hits were observed and the engine flame was extinguished, followed by an explosion. This victory was credited to our Oerlikon gunner.

The next assignment, out of Felixstowe, introduced a new method of MTBs working with frigates. The latter, with their superior radar, could vector the MTBs on to approaching E-boats. This was generally carried out with two frigates and eight MTBs working as a single force.

During one such operation, on 31 October, the force headed for Ijmuiden and patrolled down the Dutch coast to the Hook of Holland. There they met some German H-class minesweepers and were shelled by shore batteries. Next morning they observed a V2 weapon being launched and then proceeded to cover the landing of commandos invading the island of Walcheren, where the dykes had already been breached by the RAF.

The monitor HMS *Erebus*, with her colossal 15-inch guns was softening up the beachhead. They could clearly see the shells flying overhead. The sea was dead calm, but a heavy mist hung over the water. Douglas was sitting on the top of the charthouse, from where he could see only the top halves of the figures of the coxswains steering their landing craft in towards the beaches. The landing craft were nearly all destroyed but some managed to get through and the German defence was eventually overcome.

The Allies now had control of the Scheldt estuary and the port of Antwerp. The eight MTBs returned to Lowestoft that night, having been at action stations for thirty-two hours.

A so-called Coastal Mobile Unit was then established at Ostend to patrol the swept channel along the Belgian coast and the Scheldt estuary, and they had some fun shooting up Germans who were operating radio-controlled explosive boats. They also depth-charged midget submarines and rescued crews from sinking ships.

Douglas was put on board one of the ships that had sunk in shallow water and was accessible. There he collected about five hundred frozen chicken, thousands of packets of Camel cigarettes, many pieces of good linen, innumerable boxes of tools, and much dental and medical equipment.

'You name it, we had it,' he says. Much of this was later sold to less fortunate vessels in the flotillas.

On returning to harbour in the mornings the MTBs would drop a 100-pound depth charge while running over the fishing banks. The crew would then man their small dinghy and collect the stunned fish. These would be sold to army messes in and round Ostend. They also acquired a jeep from American troops who off-loaded their supplies near the MTB berths.

The end of the war in Europe was marked by a colossal binge at the officers' mess of HMS *Mantis* in Lowestoft. Douglas Green was then appointed to an Australian base for Pacific service, but the war with Japan ended and he returned to South Africa in the SS *Drottningholm*.

When he arrived at Cape Town he joined HMSAS *Rondevlei* and when she was paid off he became Transport Officer at HMSAS *Bonaventure 1*. An application to join the SA Navy having failed, he became a railway policeman in Port Elizabeth for a short while, but transferred to the Post Office and retired as postmaster on 31 May 1985. He now lives in retirement at Onrusrivier.

Before we leave Douglas Green there are one or two other memories from his amazing variety of wartime experiences which are worth passing on to the reader. For example:

First Lieutenant Sampson and I got a weekend off together for the captain wanted the boat to himself because he was having a torrid affair with a Canadian nurse from one of the field hospitals outside Ostende.

Sampson and I caught the mail truck, a big Bedford, to Antwerp. We were really going to burn it up. When the truck stopped I got out of the back and Sampson was handing me my suitcase, when there was an almighty explosion. I came to sitting with my back to the wall opposite, still clutching my suitcase. The truck had been moved about fifty yards down the road and Sampson was underneath it.

I staggered up and went over to him. He was unhurt. A V2 had fallen down the road at one of the roundabouts. The truck driver was unhurt. Sampson would not stay and went on with the mail truck to Brussels. My belief was that a bomb never falls in the same place twice, so I went on to the NAAFI Hotel for officers. There were two hospital trains in the station loading wounded, and there was an 11 p.m. curfew in Antwerp.

The bridge of MTB 772. Christmas day 1944. Note the New Zealand Tiki emblem on front of bridge. On the left is S/Lt Sampson RN, 1st Lt and Gunnery Officer. (D Green)

I met up with a contingent of troops who were Hollanders conscripted in South Africa and now in the Princess Irene Regiment. We gave it a big wind and to hell with the curfew and V2s. In the morning, when I surfaced and went outside the station was a shambles, having been hit by another V2. One of the hospital trains was also hit.

When I saw Sampson on the mail truck on his way back he was very bleary-eyed, having spent the whole night standing in the doorway of a building in Brussels with German fighters strafing the streets.

SUPREME HEADQUARTERS
ALLIED EXPEDITIONARY FORCE

Soldiers, Sailors and Airmen of the Allied Expeditionary Force!

You are about to embark upon the Great Crusade, toward which we have striven these many months. The eyes of the world are upon you. The hopes and prayers of liberty-loving people everywhere march with you. In company with our brave Allies and brothers-in-arms on other Fronts, you will bring about the destruction of the German war machine, the elimination of Nazi tyranny over the oppressed peoples of Europe, and security for ourselves in a free world.

Your task will not be an easy one. Your enemy is well trained, well equipped and battle-hardened. He will fight savagely.

But this is the year 1944 ! Much has happened since the Nazi triumphs of 1940-41. The United Nations have inflicted upon the Germans great defeats, in open battle, man-to-man. Our air offensive has seriously reduced their strength in the air and their capacity to wage war on the ground. Our Home Fronts have given us an overwhelming superiority in weapons and munitions of war, and placed at our disposal great reserves of trained fighting men. The tide has turned ! The free men of the world are marching together to Victory !

I have full confidence in your courage, devotion to duty and skill in battle. We will accept nothing less than full Victory !

Good Luck ! And let us all beseech the blessing of Almighty God upon this great and noble undertaking.

Dwight D Eisenhower

This is one of my (Green's) most prized possessions. On our way out of Portsmouth Harbour on 6 June 1944 after passing Fort Blockhouse the captain opened his sealed orders and one of these was in it for each member of the crew. (D Green)

And this:

One of the frigates, either *Torrington* or *Thornborough,* stopped to pick up survivors from one of the E-boats that we sank. They put scrambling nets over the side and their searchlight was switched on. We came up close to help to pick up survivors. I saw an SS officer pull himself up the scramble net on to the quarterdeck, both his legs had been taken off at the knees. He walked on to the deck on his stumps, gave a Nazi salute, and keeled over.

Referring to a Christmas snapshot taken on board his MTB he wrote:

We are lying in a creek in front of the Ostend cathedral used by all the MTBs – about thirty boats could berth there. It could have been January or February 1945 when some Canadian MTBs pumped out their bilges of 100 octane fuel, which was against regulations. A soldier walking along the road threw a cigarette end into the water and Woomph! the Canadian boats began to explode.

I don't remember how many boats went up. A lot of the big D-boats were still coming in from patrol. We were already in and refuelling from a coastal tanker up river. We stopped fuelling and screamed down river, because the whole area was alight with burning 100-octane. Many of us steamed round Flushing. Broken and half pieces of boats were flying right over the signal tower in the background. One or two torpedoes and depth charges also exploded. Windows were shattered in the cathedral, but the sides of the creek were not damaged.

And finally, dealing more fully with the high jinks in *Chitral* when she carried a contingent of Wrens:

Doing my rounds I went up the port side to No 2 gun but could not find the sentry. I felt about in the turret for the earphones, but only found the cord which was extremely long, so that the sentry could walk up and down the deck and stay awake.

I had this cord in my hand and I followed it in the dark right to the door inside the black-out curtains of the commander's cabin. A sailor was sitting with his eye to the keyhole giving a running commentary on the commander seducing one of the WRNS officers.

I shot up to the bridge and told the officer of the watch. We put on the gunnery earphones and listened in to a most detailed, step by step, account of the scene taking place on the commander's settee which was facing the door. It was absolutely hilarious, until his light went out.

The next day everyone greeted the commander with knowing smirks, but I don't think he ever found out.

UNION DEFENCE FORCES

To 330801V S/LT D. GREEN

Now that you are returning to civilian life, I wish to express to you the thanks of your country for the part you have played in this great world struggle. . . You volunteered for military service: you made the sacrifice for South Africa and for the wider cause of world freedom. . . You and your comrades upheld the honour and the interests of South Africa. . . For all this I express our warm thanks to you.

The aftermath of war and the process of readjustment are likely to produce many difficulties and problems. . . Patience and tolerance will be needed and the demands upon your courage and spirit of service will remain as great as ever. . . I am sure you will be prepared in the tasks that lie ahead to render your country and your fellowmen equal unselfish service.

With all good wishes for your future.

Q
TORIA

15. 9. 46

J.S. Smuts

Minister of Defence

CHAPTER

12

The Submariners

Submarines are not everybody's cup of tea. Whether friend or foe they are awe-inspiring machines and their activities, conducted largely unseen, are sinister and stealthy. They are not regarded with favour by the men manning surface craft, yet there are few who would not confess to admiration for those who man these crowded, machinery-packed cylinders in which mere survival must seem something of a gamble.

It takes a very special breed of man to volunteer for these submersibles; and by and large they are all volunteers. And of course a state of war adds enormously to the ordinary hazards. They ventured into dangerous situations and still carried out attacks, no matter what the odds might be. Yet volunteers were never lacking and a seaman who could sport an HM Submarines' cap tally was (and still is) entitled to admiration and respect.

One such man was Alan Harold Maccoy, the first South African to command a submarine. He was born on 9 September 1916, and, like so many of his generation, he realised at the time of the Munich crisis in 1938 that war was inevitable and responded by joining the RNVR in Durban early in 1939.

He was commissioned as a Temporary Probationary Acting Sub-Lieutenant by Captain JT Borrett, RN, of HMS *Amphion* on the Cape Station, and attested for full-time war service in HMS *Afrikander IV* at Durban, in which he carried out routine minesweeping and examination service duties, and flying with the SAAF as an observer on sweeps over the Indian Ocean on anti-surface raider patrols.

When the Seaward Defence Force was established in January 1940 he was one of those who elected for secondment to the Royal Navy and he was accordingly drafted to HMS *Afrikander* at Simon's Town for a gunnery course and general duties at Klawer Camp.

After the occupation of Norway he was drafted back to Durban with a petty officer and four ratings to act as an armed guard on board the Norwegian merchant vessel *Elin K* under orders to sail for Baltimore via Freetown with a full cargo of manganese ore.

When the ship arrived in Freetown early in May 1940 she was declared loyal to the Allied cause and permitted to proceed independently to Baltimore. Sub-Lieutenant Maccoy then joined the armed guard pool in the depot ship *Edinburgh Castle*. This old mailship lying at permanent moorings was reputed to be resting on an accumulated reef of empty gin bottles!

Lt AH Maccoy DSC SANF (V). (SANMMH)

For successfully conducting the safe passage of the *Elin K* to Freetown the Lords Commissioners of the Admiralty were pleased to grant Sub-Lt Maccoy six months' seniority.

On 5 May 1940 he was appointed to the armed merchant cruiser HMS *Pretoria Castle* engaged in routine convoy escort duties between Freetown, the United Kingdom and Cape Town. When the ship underwent a major refit at the end of 1940 he was appointed Group Officer to a flotilla of four trawlers that had been equipped as anti-invasion minelayers. The group was attached to the Flag Officer-in-Command, Falmouth, and operated out of the little fishing port of Newlyn near Penzance and carried out nightly patrols off Land's End, the Scilly Isles and the Lizard.

Up to that time service in submarines had been restricted to Royal Naval and Royal Naval Reserve personnel, but in April 1941 an Admiralty fleet order invited RNVR officers to serve in what Winston Churchill had described as 'the most dangerous of all the services'. Sub-Lieutenant Maccoy was one of the first to volunteer, and he was appointed to the submarine base HMS *Elfin* at Blyth, Northumberland, in May 1941.

On completion of a six-week course he was assigned to HMS *Sunfish*, an S-class submarine, then under refit at Wallsend-on-Tyne as Fourth Hand and Navigator.

In September 1941, the refit completed, *Sunfish* was moved to the wet basin at North Shields for diving trials and 'to ensure that the dockyard maties had replaced all the rivets'. During an air raid that night *Sunfish* was badly hit for'ard by a bomb and sunk. Fortunately, most of the crew were ashore, but four stokers playing cards in the after mess-deck were slightly wounded. The first lieutenant and Maccoy were on the bridge at the time of the attack and went down the main hatch into the control room where they donned breathing apparatus because of the chlorine gas fumes from the batteries and helped the stokers out. For that Alan Maccoy was commended by the Lords Commissioners of the Admiralty.

His next appointment was to HMS *Pandora*, a P-class submarine refitting with HMS *Parthian* in the Portsmouth navy yard at New Hampshire in the United States under the Anglo-American lend-lease agreement. Escorted by three corvettes, he went to America in the comparative luxury of a troopship that had been on the Pacific run to New Zealand in pre-war days. In mid-Atlantic convoy protection was provided by the US Navy, and this although the United States was still neutral. These escorts even included a battleship.

After rectifying minor defects in Bermuda, HMS *Pandora* sailed for Gibraltar, where spare torpedoes and aviation fuel, stored in the amidship ballast tank, were loaded for discharge at Malta.

Pandora arrived at Malta on 31 March and berthed at Delimara Point. That night, while the fuel was being discharged, there was an air raid on the fuel depot. Next morning the submarine shifted to Grand Harbour and berthed in Boilermaker's Creek alongside a drydock that contained the destroyer HMS *Lance*. Later that morning, while discharging torpedoes for the 10th Submarine Flotilla, a very severe air raid developed over Grand Harbour. The main targets were the cruiser *Penelope* in drydock ahead of *Pandora* and the *Lance*. *Pandora* received a direct hit through the engine-room hatch, caught fire and sank within a

Lt Maydon (later Lt-Cmdr) DSO (and Bar) DSC, Commanding Officer of HMS *Umbra*, Lt Clark RNR, Lt AH Maccoy SANF and Lt Collins RN (First Lieutenant) (SANMMH)

few minutes. Everyone inside the submarine was killed, with the exception of an ERA who had a miraculous escape and crawled out unhurt.

On the bridge, which was temporarily engulfed in flames from the explosion, the first lieutenant and Lt Maccoy were unharmed, but the navigator and engineer officer had both disappeared. They may have jumped or been blown overboard. The navigator's body was washed up some days later. Several ratings on the bridge likewise jumped into the water, whereupon the first lieutenant and Maccoy went down the outer casing and pulled them out of the sea which, just before the *Pandora* sank, was a hissing inferno of exploding shells and flying bomb splinters.

Having had two submarines sunk under him by aerial attack, Alan Maccoy was next appointed to the U-class submarine P35, which was part of the 10th Submarine Flotilla operating out of Malta and commanded by Lt SLC Maydon, son of the Natal senator after whom Maydon Wharf was named. This time, while still a Fourth Hand, Maccoy was now Torpedo Officer. P35 was later renamed *Umbra* and operated very successfully out of Malta and, for a brief period, from Alexandria and Haifa.

Four months later Maccoy was appointed First Lieutenant of another submarine. But, having second thoughts, he chose to remain in HMS *Umbra* and very tentatively suggested that the appointment might be given elsewhere. It was in fact given to the Third Hand, Sub-Lt des Vaux. This submarine was torpedoed and sunk by an E-boat off Cape Maritimo on her next patrol.

On 15 June 1942 HMS *Umbra* took part in a memorable action against two Italian Littorio-class battleships, their escorting cruisers and destroyers, which were threatening a British convoy from Gibraltar to Malta. An unexpected attack on the Italian ships by American Liberator bombers forced the squadron to scatter, and that denied Lt Maydon the opportunity of a relatively easy attack. Nevertheless the heavy cruiser *Trento* was severely damaged and forced to return home escorted by four destroyers.

With the Italian squadron now out of range HMS *Umbra* pursued them at maximum speed and, successfully taking up an attack position, fired a full salvo. One torpedo struck the battleship *Littorio* severely damaging her. Coming across the already damaged cruiser *Trento* in mid-morning, Maydon decided to attack. By then two other British submarines were also closing in on their prey and were present when *Umbra* fired two torpedoes, which hit the cruiser. The *Trento* sank within three minutes.

On the afternoon of 27 September 1942, *Umbra* intercepted a convoy of two Italian ships, *Francesco Barbaro* and *Unione*, which were carrying urgently needed supplies for the Afrika Korps. The convoy was escorted by six destroyers. One of *Umbra*'s torpedoes disabled the *Francesco Barbaro*, which was then taken in tow by a destroyer. After eluding the destroyers Lt Maydon then attacked the *Francesco Barbaro* again that night and sank her. Her cargo included 547 tons of oil, 21 tanks, 151 vehicles and 1 217 tons of ammunition.

Lt Maccoy's submarine HMS *Umbra*. (SANMMH)

After the Battle of El Alamein and the Operation Torch landings in November 1942, HM submarine *Umbra* carried out two or three very spirited patrols off the North African coast. On one she narrowly escaped being sunk when she ran aground early one morning just north of Hammamat harbour in Tunisia. She was still aground at dawn, but was not spotted by enemy forces ashore and eventually got off in broad daylight. By then the code books had been burnt in a bucket in the wardroom heads!

In December 1942 *Umbra* assisted in 'severely handling' an enemy convoy in the Mediterranean and on 25 May 1943, Lt Maccoy was awarded the DSC by HM King George VI at Buckingham Palace. The citation reads: 'For devotion to duty, coolness and cheerfulness as Torpedo Officer and Navigating Officer in His Majesty's Submarine *Umbra* in highly successful war patrols in the Mediterranean in the last five months of 1942'.

In March 1943 *Umbra* returned to Devonport for a refit. Lt Maccoy was then appointed First Lieutenant and Acting Commanding Officer of

HMS *Porpoise*, refitting at Portsmouth. But when it became obvious that the refit would be extended he asked the Staff Officer Appointments at Northways, Swiss Cottage (the wartime submarine headquarters) for a sea-going appointment. His request was approved, and in June 1943 he was appointed First Lieutenant of the submarine HMS *Tantalus* in Northern Ireland, where she was employed on training with the Atlantic anti-submarine escort groups commanded by the legendary U-boat killer, Capt FJ Walker, CB DSO (three bars), RN.

After an immensely long patrol off Spitzbergen *Tantalus* was withdrawn and fitted in Portsmouth with long-range fuel tanks, and sailed early in February 1944 for Trincomalee to join the 4th Submarine Flotilla. In yet another very long patrol, down the Malacca Straits to Penang, she chased and sunk a Japanese supply ship of 3 165 tons bound for the Andaman Islands.

Lt Maccoy was then flown to England in a Sunderland flying-boat which called at Bombay, Bahrain, Cairo and Gibraltar *en route*. On arrival in the United Kingdom he went on a two-month course for submarine commanders, the Periscope Course or 'perisher'. He passed and was duly appointed Commanding Officer of the submarine L27 (HMS *Seaborne*) in Bermuda, with orders to sail in company with L26 to Halifax, Nova Scotia, where the submarines were to be fitted with dummy schnorkels for training exercises with the Royal Canadian Air Force. While on passage both submarines encountered what Lt Maccoy described as a 'particularly unpleasant hurricane', which caused so much damage that both craft had to be scrapped.

He then returned to Bermuda to take command of HMS *Unruffled,* attached to HMCS *Somers Isles*, which was the working-up base of the RCN for their corvettes, destroyers and frigates, particularly with regard to anti-submarine warfare ('ping running'). Two other U-class submarines were attached to this independent command, which remained operational until the end of the war. In September 1945 they returned to the Clyde, where the submarines were decommissioned and laid up at Lisahally in the River Foyle.

Alan Maccoy returned to South Africa in the troopship *Ile de France* in November 1945 and was released from full-time service later that month. He was the first South African naval officer to command a submarine and his gallantry and fine war record have earned him a very special place in our naval history.

★ ★ ★ ★ ★

Although he was born in Durban, Goodwin Felton ('Joe') Gower was brought up in the small Free State town of Tweespruit, and went to St Andrew's College in Grahamstown before joining the SATS *General Botha* for the 1938 – 39 term.

He passed out of the training ship with excellent examination results and was awarded the Max Sonnenberg Scholarship which entitled him to join the Royal Navy as a cadet. On his arrival at the Royal Naval College at Dartmouth he found that because of the exigencies of war the course had been shortened from a year to eight months.

After passing he was sent all the way round the Cape of Good Hope in a Union Castle troopship to Alexandria, where he was appointed to the battleship HMS *Malaya* as a midshipman.

That was in September 1940. Early in 1941 *Malaya* took part in the bombardment of Genoa. From there she went into the Atlantic escorting seven-knot convoys between Freetown and Gibraltar. At Gibraltar she took over outward bound convoys from HMS *Renown* and the aircraft-carrier *Ark Royal*.

It was on one of those convoys that she sighted the powerful German units *Scharnhorst* and *Gneisenau*. *Malaya* turned to defend her convoy, but the enemy retreated, calling up U-boats as they went. Two days later the U-boats were in position and picked off five merchant ships the first night. From then on they attacked continually and sank eighteen vessels. These submarines could actually be seen lurking on the horizon, but they always managed to evade the slow corvettes harassing them.

In one of these U-boat attacks *Malaya* herself was struck by a torpedo, and the convoy scattered. The battleship pressed on to Trinidad and later to New York for more permanent repairs. Incidentally, she was the first British warship to undergo repairs in the USA under the new lend-lease agreement.

The bright lights of New York were wisely considered an unsuitable environment for young midshipmen, so all the *Malaya*'s complement of young gentlemen were sent to Bermuda to join the light cruiser HMS *Diomede*.

They remained there for four months before rejoining *Malaya* in time to search for the *Prinz Eugen* during the *Bismarck* chase. *Malaya* then returned to the Mediterranean to join Force H on the dangerous Malta convoy runs.

In 1942 Joe Gower was promoted Acting Sub-Lieutenant and took passage to the United Kingdom in the corvette *Stonecrop*. In the big ships he had never suffered from seasickness, but *Stonecrop* soon sorted the men from the boys!

In the United Kingdom he took a lieutenant's qualifying course, on completion of which he was appointed to yet another battleship, HMS *Revenge*. Feeling the need for a change, or from sheer desperation, he volunteered for submarines and was sent to Fort Blockhouse and later to Blyth in Northumberland for a course lasting four months.

He was again successful, joined the submarine HMS *Tactician* as Fourth Hand and went back to the Mediterranean, where his submarine operated from Gibraltar, Algiers and later from Malta, mostly off the west coast of Italy. She was a big submarine and therefore slow in diving, so she was kept off-shore in the so-called 'deep field'.

In her early patrols she favoured attack by gunfire rather than by torpedo. Most of her victims were caiques and small coasters, and such action was confined to the end of the patrol to avoid giving warning to shipping. On occasion, when short of targets, she would shoot up railway trains.

When the Germans had their own Dunkirk in North Africa they seized on anything that would float, and the submarines had a field day in observing the signal to 'Sink, burn and destroy. Let nothing pass.' After any sinking HQ would always signal, 'You were sighted at such and such a time in such and such an area.' One cryptic signal came through which caused some bewilderment until light dawned. It was addressed to the submarine ace Ben Bryant (now retired as a Rear-Admiral with the CB, three DSOs and a DSC). It read, 'Ben Ben very naughty, sighted again at 1640!'

At one stage there was a gathering of submariners in Malta. Obviously something was brewing (it turned out to be the imminent invasion of Sicily) when an officer returning on board said he had seen men in strange uniforms with Air Force wings. They were an SAAF unit flown to Malta from North Africa. Among their number was one Nicholson who, like Joe Gower, came from Tweespruit!

Most submarine patrols at that time consisted of three weeks at sea followed by ten days in port. *Tactician* sailed from Malta to take station on the western side of the Gulf of Taranto. It was assumed that with their country being invaded the Italian fleet would put to sea, and even if there was no chance to attack at least their movements could be reported. On this cruise the submarine stayed at sea for thirty-eight days. Joe recalls that after a spell in port the first three days at sea were unsettling, but after that one fell into a familiar routine. He described himself as 'lazy', and the routine suited him since a shortage of water prevented shaving and if off duty one was encouraged to sleep rather than use up valuable air!

On one patrol off Bari and Brindisi the submarine nearly came to grief. The practice was to lie off a port to await ships and they soon got to know the swept channels. One day they noticed that the minesweeper came out farther than usual to meet a very sleek three-masted steel caique following astern of her escort. It was customary for the submarine to surface astern of the target and, with gun crew at the ready, to open fire with the minimum of delay while the escort was still ahead of the target and some way off.

On this occasion things went wrong: the submarine surfaced between the two vessels. As she fired at the caique on the starboard bow, the escort came in to attack. The captain yelled to shift target left.

The gunlayer failed to hear him, but the trainer did and promptly began to train the gun on the new target, the escort. Meanwhile the gunlayer, observing the original target disappearing from view, let off one last round. It hit the submarine's jumping wire and exploded. There was much shouting and yelling from the startled gun-crew, but they maintained their rate of fire and forced the escort to turn away. The crew of the caique had by this time abandoned their vessel and were rowing for all they were worth – but out to sea and not towards Italy!

After this little shake-up HM submarine *Tactician* moved to the Albanian coast where she sighted a 10 000 ton ship in the exact position where Intelligence had said she could be expected. The sea was flat calm – dangerous for periscope work – but the ship appeared to be unescorted, and the submarine fired a spread of four torpedoes, one of which scored a hit. Suddenly the hydrophone operator reported loud HE coming in from dead ahead. The captain ordered a dive to a hundred feet but before this could be achieved a depth charge exploded. Joe recalls that it felt as if someone had hit the deck under his feet with a ten-pound hammer. The lights went out and the gyro compass went 'off the board'. Altogether sixteen depth charges were dropped, all of them singly, and it was assumed that they were from small craft such as E-boats or MTBs. The first one was the nearest and the others were obviously being dropped at the end of the torpedo track.

The submarine remained submerged for an hour, then surfaced to periscope depth when it was observed that the ship had beached herself. They fired a torpedo at the wreck, and although it exploded it was doubtful whether it had hit home because of the shallowness of the water. Back in Malta they later heard that the RAF had been over their victim on a bombing run and found cargo being salvaged.

Their next patrol was in the Aegean. Off the island of Rhodes, Joe, now Navigating Officer, was in his bunk one afternoon when he heard his brother officers discussing a new and strange form of radar antenna on shore. He went to the control room to have a look through the periscope and, much to his amusement, saw that his shipmates were contemplating a windmill such as were common in his home town of Tweespruit. The British officers had never seen one!

On one operation out of Beirut in 1943 their mission was to land three Greeks, a soldier, a diplomat and a businessman, with radio sets to establish clandestine radio stations in Athens. The landing had to be done at night in complete silence, with an RAF rubber dinghy. All went well.

However, back in Beirut an officer named Harry Tate of the submarine *Taurus* which had been on a similar mission, had a different story to tell. Because of a mistake in inflating the rubber dinghy it exploded with the noise of a four-inch gun. Until then everything had been conducted in whispers. A second dinghy was got ready, and as the three cast off, none of them speaking any English, they stood upright in their rocking boat, gave three rousing cheers and burst out into 'Rule, Britannia!' All this when close inshore under cliffs in enemy territory!

Tactician was in Beirut during the Italian surrender and armistice and sailed almost immediately for Colombo to operate in the Malacca Straits. For Joe it was a different sort of war. In the Mediterranean they never surfaced in daylight, whereas in eastern waters they enjoyed a run of five days on the surface.

Apart from bottling up German and Japanese submarines in Penang, their main task was to intercept and examine passing junks. In one they found a heavy load of ammunition under a cargo of tea. From then on the order came to sink all junks, and that was done by ramming, to save four-inch shells for more serious business.

Early in 1944 Joe Gower was promoted First Lieutenant and appointed to the submarine HMS *Rover*. This vessel had an unfortunate record. She had been lying alongside the cruiser HMS *York* giving her power when she was sunk in Suda Bay. *Rover*'s hull whipped and the batteries were shattered. The submarine was then sent to Singapore for a complete overhaul which was just about to begin when the Japanese invaded. She was them towed to Sumatra, Colombo, and ultimately Bombay, where the dockyard had to carry out extensive repairs and alterations with no plans available.

The submarine had not dived for years and on completion of the refit she carried out diving trials. She simply would not submerge! It was back to the drawing board; and the sums indicated that nine tons of iron should be distributed throughout the boat. This time she went down like a stone, and the main ballast tanks had to be blown. It was all the fault of an engineer who would not confess to having miscalculated the ballasting needed.

Rover duly joined the submarine flotilla at Trincomalee, but Joe Gower was taken out and sent to the depot ship *Maidstone* as 'spare crew'. While he was there he joined the submarine *Tantivy*, and in her he sailed back to the United Kingdom, where he arrived in time for V-E Day. Recalled from leave, he was sent with other submariners to Londonderry to accept the surrender of eighty-five German U-boats. These were divided into groups of ten, with one British and one German officer responsible for each group. The British feared a repetition of Scapa Flow after World War I. The Germans were all convinced that forces would be joined to fight the Russians!

Joe Gower received his first command at this time; a German U-boat! With the engine-room manned by Germans giving all orders in German, the deck crew consisting of Royal Navy men, and a civilian pilot who insisted on full speed ahead – 17,5 knots, the fifteen-mile trip up the Foyle to Londonderry was an exciting experience.

As Joe put it: 'Here I was, a little *outjie* from Tweespruit in the Orange Free State, in command of a German submarine with a German engine-room staff requiring the orders to be given in German, a discontented and unhappy coxswain who had to have helm orders in English, a British upper-deck staff and an Irish pilot whom I could hardly understand!'

In the peacetime navy Joe Gower served in several submarines, and in 1947 he sailed for South Africa in the destroyer HMS *Wessex* (later to become the SAS *Jan van Riebeeck*). Not having been home since 1940, he received three months' well-earned leave which he spent in the Orange Free State where he decided that farming was the life for him. Accordingly he resigned from the Royal Navy, and until 1956 he farmed in the Westminster and Ficksburg areas of the Orange Free State before returning to sea on being commissioned into the SA Navy. In 1979 he retired as Chief of Naval Staff (Intelligence) with the rank of Captain and holder of the Southern Cross medal.

★ ★ ★ ★ ★

There were many other South Africans serving in submarines, both in the larger types and in the so-called midgets. Even under ordinary conditions, life in these latter craft was dangerous. In time of war conditions were appalling. It is surprising that men could be found to man these little submersibles. Yet there was no lack of volunteers. One of them was Temp Lt Alan Bonnellie. Here is his story:

Alan was a lower-deck member of the RNVR(SA) when he joined up for active service on the outbreak of war. That was in Durban, where he underwent three months' training in minesweepers.

In December he was drafted to Simon's Town and two months later (February 1940), with several other South African boys, he joined HMS *Cornwall*, an 8-inch county-class cruiser. They patrolled the Atlantic and Indian oceans with occasional convoy escort duties.

At the end of August 1940 six South Africans, Bonnellie himself, Harris (the author's younger brother), Hartready, Lewis, Parker and Stanbury had been selected as CW (commissions and warrants, i.e. officer) candidates and transferred to the troopship *Moreton Bay* for passage to England. In this ship they were joined by Turnbull and Stephens, eight of them altogether. On arrival in the United Kingdom they were drafted to Portsmouth and then to HMS *King Alfred*, the officers' training establishment at Hove in Sussex.

After being commissioned, Alan Bonnellie was sent with Stephens, Turnbull and Hartready to Combined Operations at HMS *Tormentor* where he was to be stationed for eighteen months with a break of three months when, with Roy Turnbull, he was employed on sea rescue work at Littlehampton on the south coast, and a couple of months spent training army units in landing craft procedures at Inverary in Scotland.

On returning to HMS *Tormentor* he was moved to complain about the 'same boring and frustrating routine of training in landing craft and having proposed and planned operations suddenly cancelled'.

It was small wonder, then, that when asked by a recruiting officer from HMS *Dolphin* if he would like to volunteer for 'hazardous service', he replied in the affirmative and duly entered his new sphere on 1 June 1942. He was not told what it was about, and indeed it was not until he had done his DSEA drill and a diving course with a helmet and shot-line down to 120 feet, that he was told that he had volunteered for 'chariots'.

By this time he had come to the conclusion that this was not his scene at all. Ever since his prep school days he had suffered from claustrophobia.

However, being young and naive, he thought that if he made any sort of protest the authorities would assume that he was afraid and he would lose face. He therefore decided to brazen it out and put on as good an act as possible. At that point he was joined by three other South Africans at HMS *Dolphin* (the submarine school) – Sub-Lt John Mc-Carter, Sub-Lt Jack Grogan and Leading Seaman Tom Yates.

While they were at *Dolphin* his party was sent to the Siebe–Gorman diving school at Surbiton to undergo an endurance test which entailed being placed in a tank of water which was pressurised to a depth of thirty feet in which they had to survive by breathing oxygen for thirty minutes. A diving instructor sat in the tank above water level carefully

Sub-Lieutenants Bonnellie, Jack Grogan and McCarter, all of whom volunteered for midget submarines. (SANMMH)

watching his charges. If one seemed about to pass out he just shouted 'Up!' Pressure was immediately released, the hatch opened, and the tail-end of a block and tackle hooked on to a safety ring on the shoulders.

John McCarter suffered what was described by Commander Fell as 'Oxygen Pete'. This affliction caused blackout and convulsions, with frothing at the mouth. Alan did not find this a pretty picture, especially as he was next in turn. In the event he passed the test.

From *Dolphin* the volunteers were sent to Loch Cairnbawn on the Isle of Lewis, where they joined HMS *Titania* for training in the 'chariots'.

Beginning with a wooden model towed by a skiff, they learned to steer, submerge and surface, until they became quite accomplished, but nevertheless they were glad when the first of the real chariots was completed.

John McCarter, his number two, Leading Seaman Yates, and Alan Bonnellie made their first mock attack on *Titania* from a submarine fitted with a big cylindrical 'garage' on the forward casing housing the chariots. When the attack began the door of the cylinder was opened with the submarine on the surface, the chariots were pulled out, and their crews climbed on board while the mother submarine slowly submerged for'ard and the chariots floated off.

While they were at the Loch training was intensive. That resulted in several casualties who were then transferred elsewhere. John McCarter suffered a complete breakdown, which did nothing to ease Alan Bonnellie's peace of mind, especially as he was still acting a part. McCarter elected to stay with *Titania*, but in an administrative capacity.

Alan's sense of impending doom was not allayed when he suffered a perforated eardrum and indeed he had Leading Seaman Yates to thank for saving his life. When they attempted to pull their chariot under an anti-torpedo net at low tide, there was a mass of net lying on the bottom. Alan slipped in the mud, and the weight of the net pinned him face down. Yates lifted enough net to allow him to get on to his knees.

Soon after that horrifying experience, and after six months of mental agony, Alan told Commander Fell about his doubts whether he was temperamentally suited to that type of service. The commander was sympathetic, and he was offered a post similar to that occupied by McCarter; but since he was not feeling prepared to make others do things that he was unwilling to do himself, he declined the offer.

A few days later Jack Grogan was doing his last night dive in a mock attack on the battleship HMS *Howe* and Alan was standing by on skiff duty. He sighted a flare from the anti-submarine net, and when he got there he found Jack's number two holding him up. When they got Jack into the skiff and cut his suit open they found that he had burst both lungs. 'It was not a pretty sight,' recorded Alan Bonnellie. It is worthy of note here that Jack Grogan's elder brother, Basil, was lost when HMS *Gloucester* was sunk during the evacuation of Crete in May 1941. Both were from Walmer, Port Elizabeth. Another local family, like the Thorps, to lose two sons at sea.

There were in fact three Grogan brothers serving in the Navy, Graham, Bill, and Jack. On one occasion Bill was in London on a fortnight's leave. Unknown to him, his brother Jack was there too. Each day Bill cabled home for money, signing only as Grogan and asking that the money be sent to him c/o South Africa House. Jack also visited South Africa House daily, but ahead of his brother Bill, and he was duly handed the money.

One morning while Bill was having a shower he heard singing from the next cubicle. It was his brother's voice. Jack said that the family must have gone crazy. 'They are sending me money every few days,' he said. 'Let's go and have a party!' The family knew that Jack was in London and assumed that the cable was from him. Bill soon put him right!

Soon afterwards the team were all sent on leave. Alan was drafted back into general service and saw the war out attached to DEMS in Freetown and Lagos. John McCarter and Leading Seaman Yates went on to the Mediterranean with the chariots and carried out a couple of successful operations against the enemy.

★ ★ ★ ★ ★

Lt Peter H Philip whose exploits in midget submarines earned him the MBE. (SANMMH)

Another midget submariner was the late Peter H Philip. Together with the late Lieutenant J V Terry-Lloyd (brother of the late Rear-Admiral MR Terry-Lloyd) he played a vital part in the daring midget submarine attack on the German battleship *Tirpitz*.

A remarkable feature of Lt Philip's subsequent career was that at the age of twelve he was stricken with polio. Despite that handicap he got a blue as cox of the Oxford University Eight. Later, with an MA degree, he was the famous Uncle Peter of the 'Children's Hour' on the SABC. It was he too, who on the outbreak of World War II announced this historic and momentous fact to South Africa's listening radio audience.

Somehow Peter Philip managed to pass his medical examination for entrance into the Navy, and was drafted to HMS *Cumberland* at Simon's Town. After service in the Atlantic he was commissioned and appointed to HMS *Blackfly,* an anti-submarine trawler destined to escort convoys on the dreaded Arctic route to Russia. These convoys are described more fully elsewhere in this book.

When unmarried officers were called for to undertake hazardous secret work he felt he would be letting himself and his country down if he did not volunteer. Only after being accepted did he learn that he was being drafted to HMS *Varbel 11* for training in X-craft, or midget submarines.

The most memorable episode in a brief naval career packed with action was his share in the attack on the German battleship *Tirpitz*. This daring attack necessitated the towing of the midget submarine from Cairnbawn Loch in the north of Scotland to Altenfjord in Norway. Lieutenant Philip and Lieutenant JV Terry-Lloyd, both of the SA Naval Forces, were selected to command X7 and X5. X7 was towed by HMS *Stubborn*, an S-class submarine. The seven-day ordeal of the passage crews was described by Admiral Sir Max Horton:

'The long approach voyage in unparalleled conditions . . . called for and produced the highest degree of endurance and seamanship skill.'

On the evening of the seventh day, fresh crews took over to make the actual attack on the *Tirpitz*. But for their part in the operation both Philip and Terry-Lloyd were decorated with the MBE. Service in midget submarines in the Pacific followed, but it was cut short by the Japanese surrender.

Among others to serve in submarines was an Old Grey's boy, Brian Phillipson, who in the school magazine of the day revealed that he had circumnavigated the globe in HMS *Dorsetshire* and was in the ship when she took part in the memorable action against the German battleship *Bismarck*. He then qualified as a submariner, and a later piece reveals that he was Second-in-Command of the submarine HMS *Seraph*.

Yet another, a former Selbornian, Lieutenant David Nicol, either through a natural modesty or an awareness of the lurking wartime censor, wrote to his old school confiding that he was 'engaged in submarine work'.

There were many others, unmentioned in this brief résumé, but who nevertheless shared the honour of belonging to that most exclusive of bodies, the submariners. All strength to them.

CHAPTER
13

The Frigates

While in the last chapter submarines were briefly discussed, the vessels designed to hunt them down will be specifically looked at here. That was primarily the task of the destroyers, but their numbers were insufficient, and the Admiralty ordered the building of a much smaller type of escort vessel and in so doing they restored a time-honoured designation: the corvette. Later yet another class was revived, that of the frigate.

In 1944 the British Government struck a bargain with General Smuts by offering him three of the latest Loch-class anti-submarine frigates, then under construction, to be at the permanent disposal of the SA Naval Forces. The SANF, for their part, undertook to supply three thousand South Africans for service with the Royal Navy over the next twelve months. The offer was acceptable to both parties, and in the long term this generous offer was surely the inspiration for the introduction of a permanent navy in South Africa after the war.

The sea-going rank and file of the SANF received news of this offer with great pleasure and eagerness. Since the outbreak of war most of those who had not been seconded to the Royal Navy had had to serve in small converted whale-catchers, trawlers and motor launches. Now, at long last, they were to be given the opportunity of serving in real warships.

The frigates handed over to the SANF were HM ships *Loch Ard*, *Loch Boisdale* and *Loch Cree*. They were renamed HMSA ships *Transvaal*,*Good Hope* and *Natal*.

Since these were the first major war vessels operated by the SANF, some details are in order. With an overall length of 307 feet, a beam of 38,5 feet and a maximum draught of 15 feet, they had a standard displacement of 1 610 tons and a full-load displacement of 2 450 tons. Main armament consisted of 1 x 4 inch gun, 4 x 2 pdr pom-poms and 10 x 20mm anti-aircraft guns (*Transvaal* had 6 x 40mm Bofors and *Good Hope* 2 x 40mm Bofors). Saluting guns, in Good Hope only consisted of

4 x 3 pdrs. Anti-submarine weapons included two squid triple DC mortars and two DCT throwers plus the usual set of depth charges.

Main propulsion was two sets of triple-expansion engines of 5 500 ihp, driving two shafts giving the vessels a speed of 19,5 knots. Bunker capacity was 724 tons and the normal complement ten officers and 153 ratings. The ships were a development of the earlier river-class frigates, of which more anon.

The first of these new ships to be commissioned was HMSAS *Good Hope* and the honour of commanding one of South Africa's first 'big' ships went to Lieutenant-Commander RP Dryden-Dymond (now Commodore, SM ED SAN Retd) in November 1944.

HMSAS *Good Hope* on convoy escort duty in Icelandic waters, January 1945. (LV Snell)

After an intensive workout at Tobermory in Scotland under the stern ministrations of the redoubtable Commodore 'Monkey' Stephenson, *Good Hope* set off to escort a large troopship to Iceland.

When she was two hundred miles from her destination she encountered a fierce north-Atlantic winter gale for which that region is notorious. So severely was she battered that on her return to the Clyde she spent five weeks undergoing repairs to buckled bottom plating and other storm damage. The story was also told of how the important sphincter muscle of at least one burly officer failed in its retentive function!

She resumed her escort duties, mainly in the Irish Sea and between Portsmouth, Cherbourg and Le Havre. The ship's company of HMSAS

Good Hope had the distinction of being the only South African unit to serve in North West Europe and so to qualify for the France and Germany Star or clasp.

The second of the frigates to be commissioned was HMSAS *Natal*, whose remarkable story will follow. Suffice it to note here that she was the only one of the three frigates to cross the Indian Ocean. The war had ended by that time, but on 20 August 1945 she sailed from Durban for Singapore where she took part in the Allied occupation of Malaya and Singapore, carried out escort duties through Japanese minefields, mainly on the route between Singapore and Port Swettenham, and for a while she was guard-ship over the former Japanese island base of Sabang at the northern end of Sumatra.

She returned to Durban on 30 November 1945 and for the next few months she joined her two sister frigates in transporting time-expired army and air force men from Egypt back to the Union.

The third of the three, HMSAS *Transvaal* (Lt-Cmdr HE Fougstedt) was commissioned just after V-E Day on 15 May 1945, and therefore took no active part in the war. She arrived in Cape Town on 28 July, a month after *Good Hope* and *Natal*.

In addition to these frigates, agreement had been reached with the Admiralty for two Royal Navy river-class frigates, HM ships *Teviot* and *Swale*, to be manned by South Africans but remain the property of the Admiralty. These two ships were already in South African waters, so there was little delay in putting the transfer into effect. Of the two, HMS *Swale* had been blooded in the North Atlantic, having shared in several successful attacks on U-boats.

HMS *Swale* which together with HMS *Teviot* were Royal Navy frigates manned entirely by SANF. (Unknown)

HMS *Teviot* (Lt-Cmdr AS Bowyer) was recommissioned with a South African crew at Cape Town on 10 June 1945, and sailed for Colombo to join the Far Eastern Fleet. She arrived there on 2 July, but later struck an uncharted wreck in Burmese waters. After undergoing repairs she returned to Durban to be paid off from wartime service in January 1946.

The second RN frigate to be recommissioned with a South African crew was HMS *Swale* (Lt-Cmdr EV Brown) on 1 August 1945 at Simon's Town. Likewise destined for service in the Far East, the war ended before she could be usefully employed as a fighting ship. Instead she remained for a few months based at Mombasa, showing the flag at various East African ports in what was the first of such cruises in those waters. It was a time of exhilarating social life for the officers but there was some discontent among the crew, many of whom were impatient to resume their interrupted civilian life.

The author was serving in the ship as Navigating Officer at that time and recalls that they gave passage to a much-decorated British army officer, Brigadier Philip Myburgh, CBE DSO★ MC Croix de Guerre, whose task it was to close down various military establishments along the East African seaboard. There were also some riotous reunions when the three South African frigates bunkered at Mombasa on their repatriation voyages between Egypt and Durban.

HMS *Swale* left the Kilindini area on 14 December 1945 and steamed through the harbour to the strains of 'Sarie Marais' played by the Royal Marine Band of a battleship moored off the port. She was paid off to a South African care and maintenance party in Simon's Town in January 1946, and returned to the Royal Navy in March that year.

The Unique Feat of HMSAS *Natal*

HMSAS *Natal* was commissioned in Britain on 14 March 1945 and her first captain was a large and cheerful extrovert, Lt-Cmdr DA ('Stoker') Hall, who had earlier won the Distinguished Service Cross while in command of the *Southern Maid* in the Mediterranean in 1941. 'Stoker' Hall had been trained as a cadet in the SATS *General Botha* and served at sea in the Clan Line steamers before swallowing the anchor and working at the mines on the Reef. The outbreak of war brought him back to the element for which he had been trained and in which he was to win distinction.

In his commissioning speech, the High Commissioner for South Africa, Mr Heaton Nicholls, said of *Natal*: 'She is a true frigate – the old hunter of the enemy and pirate destroyer, brought up to date to deal with the pirates of today.'

Sailing with Lt-Cmdr Hall were men who had had much experience of war. The First Lieutenant, LTF Alexander (now a retired medical practitioner in Knysna) conned his ship through flames to rescue survivors in the Mediterranean, while Stoker Petty Officer J Mooney of Cape Town won the DSM for gallant work on the Tobruk Run.

Chief Petty Officer DB Blackshaw of Cape Town was wounded in the *Southern Maid* at Tobruk. So was Petty Officer Telegraphist Randall during a dive-bombing attack on the same port. Stoker T Henry of Springs was rescued by Lt-Cmdr Hall in *Southern Maid* after his ship had been sunk. Leading Seaman DM Glen of Durban and formerly of the Merchant Navy was a survivor from HMS *Cornwall*. The ship's surgeon, Surgeon-Lieutenant RL Skea of Bloemfontein, served under Commander Kenneth of Cape Town at the storming of Westkapelle in the attack on Walcheren. Able Seaman KM Duke of Cape Town had the unusual record of having served in all three branches of the armed services, first in a bomber squadron, then with the Fourth Armoured Car Regiment, the Desert Rats, and lastly with the SANF.

They were a good team.

Natal was earmarked for operations 'in the North Sea and all waters to the eastward between Southend and the Shetland Islands'. An extract from the official Admiralty publication, *The Battle of the Atlantic* says:

On March 14th His Majesty's South African ship *Natal*, which had been only a fortnight in commission, was on passage from Newcastle-on-Tyne to the Firth of Forth. Early in the afternoon she was informed that a ship in convoy had been torpedoed about five miles to the northward, and a few minutes later her look-outs sighted a lifeboat and rafts. The *Natal* was ordered to carry out a search and within twenty minutes had an unmistakable contact. Her

HMSAS *Natal* – the U-boat killer. (SANMMH)

attack brought up more oil and a small metal tank, after which contact was lost. Three days later, however, other ships confirmed *Natal*'s success by finding and plastering her target with depth charges, which yielded up a considerable quantity of wreckage.

This was only four hours after leaving the builders' yards and after her captain had asked for a two-day postponement on the grounds that his ship was newly commissioned with a crew 'new to this type of vessel'. She had sailed from Tyneside at 0900 and by lunchtime had a kill to her credit!

The official German record of U-boat losses compiled after the war confirms the loss: 'U-714, Nordsee vor Firth of Forth/brit *Natal*.' Her captain's name was Schebke, and the official position given is latitude 55,57N, longitude 01,57W. There were no survivors.

For a firsthand account of this encounter we can do no better than to quote an edited version by Roger Williams who was serving in *Natal* at the time and who later became Chief Reporter of the *Cape Times*:

March 14, 1945, was cold and blustery, a typical winter's day in England, and for those who had the misfortune to be afloat in the North Sea. U-714 had just torpedoed and sunk a merchant vessel, and this was reported to *Natal*, which was on her way to Tobermory, where the ship's company and their brand new ship were to be subjected to the rigorous working-up exercises. With a ship that was still shaking down, and with only a half-trained crew, her Captain, Lt-Cmdr 'Stoker' Hall, DSC, wished to keep out of trouble.

The urgent signal changed all that and action stations was sounded on the alarm rattlers and an all-round Asdic sweep was started by a team led by Lt S Richards, who in peacetime had been on the veterinary research staff at Onderstepoort. Forward of the bridge, Sub-Lt John Moir of Cape Town and his Squid team checked their six loaded depth-charge mortars and stood by.

Suddenly the lifeboats, with their thinly-clad occupants flailing their arms and with their feeble cries for help carrying plaintively across the water, came in sight, and a few minutes later a sharp metallic echo was picked upon the Asdic.

Lt Richards turned to the captain: 'I like that one,' he said. 'It must be a submarine.'

The big blue submarine flag was run up on the bridge, and *Natal* closed in for the attack. A lethal pattern of six Squid charges was fired ahead of the frigate at a range of about 150 yards. There was a shuddering crash as they exploded at the recorded depth of the submarine.

The frigate swung away from the turbulence, took a short run seawards and then turned for a second attack while the mortars were hurriedly reloaded. Six more charges whistled over the bows into the depths where U-714 already lay in her death agony.

This time an oilslick appeared on the surface and a couple of cylindrical drums could be seen bobbing in the flurry of foam in the frigate's wake.

But no sign of the U-boat. The Asdic operators reported 'contact lost', and although a wide sweep was made of the area it was not regained. In the meantime the merchantman's survivors were picked up by the Royal Navy destroyer HMS *Wyvern*.

Natal patrolled the area till dusk, when she was relieved by *Wyvern* and after picking up one of the cylinders and a sample of the oil the frigate made for the small anchorage of Methil in the Firth of Forth. On the way the mysterious piece of wreckage was scrutinised by ship's officers and technicians. There was a small circular door at one end, and when it was opened, a peculiar bellowing sound came from within.

'It's a time bomb,' someone shouted, and everyone withdrew to a safe distance. But after a while Surgeon-Lieutenant Skea, overcome by curiosity, walked boldly up to the Thing and applied his stethoscope to the outer casing to find out whether the bellowing continued when the door was shut. It did not. The Thing was landed at Methil amid sighs of relief.

Natal resumed her voyage to Scapa Flow and after a brief stop in the Home Fleet anchorage she went on to Tobermory. It was while the ship was standing on her beam ends with everyone holding on for dear life that a signal was received from the Admiralty confirming that U-714 had been destroyed, and expressing their Lordships' pleasure at *Natal's* early kill.

But with their own ship seemingly on the point of taking its final plunge, no one appeared to be particularly elated. And there was no time for celebration at Tobermory. Commodore Sir Gilbert Stephenson, the tough little commander of the training base, was not a man who was easily impressed, not even by a ship that had despatched a U-boat on her maiden voyage.

He boarded *Natal* as soon as she dropped anchor in the sheltered bay from which so many little ships had gone to join in the Battle of the Atlantic, and told the assembled officers and men that, although they were to be commended for their early success, they were not to get the idea that it entitled them to sit back and relax.

'Let me assure you – you haven't even started yet!' he bellowed. And it was not long before the South Africans found this dapper white-haired martinet meant what he said. The story has often been told how Stephenson boarded a ship in the small hours of

HMSAS. NATAL.

Ship's company of the *Natal*, 1945. (SANMMH)

the morning expecting to find everyone relaxed and, throwing his gold-braided cap to the deck, yelled to the sleepy quartermaster, 'Incendiary bomb – what are you going to do about it, man?' Legend has it the quartermaster sprang into action at once and kicked the cap over the side. All present waited in awe for an outburst from Stephenson. Instead he commended the quick-thinking quartermaster but added, 'It's now a man overboard. Go and rescue him.' That on a cold November night.

It was while at Tobermory that they learnt that the Thing had been identified as a German container for collapsible dinghies, with automatic bellows for inflation when needed.

After the departure of *Natal* from the attack area, bodies and more wreckage were recovered from the sunken submarine. The evidence included a small blue hand-carved shield with a gold-painted U-boat superimposed and the number U-766 below the emblem, which indicated that, since the numbers differed, it was probably a trophy from another U-boat. This was sent to Lt-Cmdr Hall and became one of *Natal*'s most prized wardroom trophies. Sadly, nobody now knows what became of it.

After service in Western Approaches with the 8th Escort Group, *Natal* was sent to the Far East.

On her return to South Africa several awards were made by the Admiralty to mark her successful anti-submarine attack and 'Stoker' Hall received a bar to his DSC. With regard to that, it is interesting to note that in the early days of the war the sinking of an enemy submarine

SOUTH AFRICAN FRIGATE SINKS U-BOAT ON TRIAL VOYAGE

FEAT UNIQUE IN RECORDS OF THE NAVY

SOUTH AFRICA'S SECOND FRIGATE, Natal, performed a feat unique in the records of the Royal Navy when it sank a U-boat while on its trials recently, states a Sapa message from London. The news has just been released by the Admiralty. The ship's commanding officer is Lieut.-Commander D. A. Hall, D.S.C., who in civilian life is a mining official at Krugersdorp.

The voyage was made to enable some senior officers to study new features of lighting.

The London correspondent of The Star cables that the action was started when the submarine was picked up by Able Seaman E. S. Scott, who is number one of the Asdic team commanded by Lieut. A. Richards. Scott was a jockey before the war, riding for Mr. Bradley in Durban and Johannesburg and for Mr. Sid Garrett in Cape Town.

"I have operated Asdic for three and a half years," he said. "So when I heard the signal I knew at once it was a submarine, but it was the first time I've had it followed by a definite kill." Before joining Natal Scott served in South African waters under Lieut. Richards, who was a physicist at Onderstepoort and used to live at Deelfontein, O.F.S.

Once the hunt was on members of the Asdic team had to concentrate on separate tasks on their

This is how *The Star*, Johannesburg, reported HMSAS *Natal*'s unique feat on the front page of its edition of 26 April 1945 – more than one month after the event. HMSAS *Natal* sunk U-714 in the North Sea on 14 March of that year. The officer depicted was Lieutenant-Commander DA ('Stoker') Hall, DSC, *Natal*'s Commanding Officer. The picture was taken when he was still a lieutenant.

brought immediate recognition in the form of a DSO. Later, when anti-submarine methods and measures became more sophisticated, failure to destroy a target resulted in a 'please explain' letter!

Lt–Cmdr Hall (who died in 1958 at the age of forty-eight) attributed his successful attack to 'a colossal piece of luck'.

Nevertheless, *Natal* made history by being the first warship to sink an enemy submarine while still on trials and for the exploit she received two battle honours, as listed in an Admiralty Fleet Order issued in 1954.

Natal was to carry out yet another U-boat attack in 1945, but it has been described as 'the one that got away'. The following signal was sent to the leader of the 8th Escort Group, HMS *Loch Achray*, on 26 April 1945 and records the fact that *Natal* had gained contact with a U-boat, first on the surface and then submerged. But because of a last minute technical hitch (in fact more human than technical) the submarine got away. It might well have been *Natal*'s second U-boat kill.

On 14 March 1990 – 45 years after the sinking of U-714 – 18 members of HMSAS *Natal*'s original ship's company of 140 forgather in Durban to commemorate the commissioning of their ship, at Newcastle-on-Tyne.
Standing, from left: Ex-AB (Coder) now Rear-Admiral (Rtd) SC 'Fanie' Biermann; ex-Lieutenant Ron Pedley; ex-AB (Tel) Mick Allen; ex-AB (Tel) Willy Sardinha; ex-AB Don Allport; ex-Sub-Lieutenant Bryan Bates; ex-AB Roger Williams; ex-PO (Yeoman of Signals) Percy Wolfaardt; ex-AB (radar) Alan Cuzen; ex-AB (SD) Terry Scott, DSM; ex-Lieutenant (E) Douglas Swan; ex-AB Cecil Jansen and ex-L/Wireman Buller Louw.
Seated: ex-AB (Coder) Bernie Carroll; ex-AB Neil O'Shea; ex-AB (SD) Mike van Breda, DSM; ex-AB Derek Bradfield and ex-AB (QR3) Roy Wilkinson.
On the extreme right, pouring tea, is Councillor Arthur Morris who deputised for the Mayor of Durban, Councillor Derek Watterson, who had had to fly to Cape Town at short notice.
After the civic reception, the HMSAS *Natal* men attended a 45th-anniversary reunion dinner at SA Naval Base, Durban, on Salisbury Island.

To: SOEGS.   From: *Natal*

Initial contact gained by Radar Type 277, Range 5800. 'A' display gave indications of surfaced sub. Initial course of submarine 175 degrees for 4 mins, then 095 degrees for 4 mins. Estimated speed 12 knots. Echo faded 3 900 yards. 30 mins later gained A/S contact 900 yards. Extent 12 degrees. Contact bearing 125 degrees 2 500 yds from diving position. Course submerged 020 degrees 3 knots. Recorded depth 60 feet. Range track indicated sub with wake. Could not attack. Lost contact on opening out.

   TOO 1300/26/4/45.

CHAPTER

14

An Interlude in the Midst of War

War is apt to produce the unexpected and when in the second half of 1942 volunteers were called for to go to the United States to take delivery of a flotilla of five new minesweepers intended for the SA Naval Forces, the prospect was attractive and the roster was soon filled.

Commander LE Scott-Napier DSO RN (Retd) was selected to command the contingent. He was a man with a remarkable career. He had been a term-mate and personal friend of King George VI at Dartmouth and from 1921-1931 Commanding Officer of one of the first little South African warships, HMSAS *Immortelle*. He resigned in 1931 and in 1934 became in turn a traffic officer in Cape Town, a farmer, and a senior official in the Automobile Association. When he was called to active service on the outbreak of the Hitler war he was for more than a year Deputy Director of the SDF before choosing secondment to the Royal Navy. After the war he joined the Merchant Navy and served as Master of Coasters plying between Cape Town and South West Africa.

Scott Napier, accompanied by two prospective commanding officers and an engineer officer, sailed direct for the United States in mid-October 1942, followed a little later by the other three commanding officers and two engineers. The main body of the crews arrived much later, having sailed direct from Cape Town to New York in the mail liner *Cape Town Castle*, at that time serving as a troopship.

The second contingent, of which the present writer was a member, sailed from Cape Town on 29 October 1942 in a former Belgian cross-Channel vessel, *Prince Baudoin*. This handsome little vessel was capable of 24 knots but having been designed for short cross-channel passages and thus with minimum bunker capacity, fuel had to be conserved and speed kept down to around 10 knots or so. Very frustrating when in the submarine zone, just when that particular form of German *Schrecklichkeit* was at its peak. Although we were living in some luxury – reputedly in a cabin once occupied by the King of

Belgium – we had to live out of suitcases, for there were no wardrobes, such furniture having been considered unnecessary for the short Channel crossing.

Prince Baudoin bunkered at Walvis Bay, Takoradi, Bathurst, Freetown and Las Palmas. At the last a portly gentleman puffing down a hill was pointed out to us as the German consul hastening to the post office to cable news of our arrival to his masters.

MV *Prince Baudoin* in which the author's party sailed on the first leg of their voyage (Cape Town to Londonderry) to USA, October 1942. (Author)

That night we headed south for some hours before swinging back to a northerly course. Arriving off the northern coast of Ireland our party was transferred to a destroyer and taken to Londonderry from where, after a few days, we went on to the Clyde by sea and to Liverpool by train. While we were there the senior member of our party, Lt-Cmdr RP Dryden-Dymond (now Commodore SAN Retd) was summoned to London to explain who we were and to draw the necessary identification documents.

After several days of frustrating delay in bomb-blasted Liverpool, our party embarked through a covered gangway to board the Royal Mail line freighter *Deseado*. Seventeen days later we disembarked in New York by the same method and thus never got an outside view of the ship or of her silhouette.

As befitted a naval contingent, Dryden-Dymond offered our services as look-outs; but much to his disappointment it was declined. The captain furthermore refused to give us the ship's daily position. After some argument he relented to the extent of allowing us the previous day's noon fix.

Deseado was on her maiden voyage and was 'light ship', in ballast with empty holds. The library intended for the ship had gone astray because of the bombing and the only reading matter on board was a set of books on Pelmanism, the property of the chief engineer. We all became highly observant of things around us. The only other passengers (she carried twelve) were British shipmasters bound for the States to take delivery of new tonnage from American yards.

It was a cruel crossing. Winter in the North Atlantic is no picnic at the best of times, and the clerk of the weather really threw the book at us. For the whole voyage *Deseado* punched her way through mountainous seas in freezing weather. If there was one redeeming feature it was the hope that it would keep the U-boats down. In fact the passenger liner *Ceramic* was torpedoed at that time leaving only one survivor, who was picked up by the attacking submarine. Many South Africans lost their lives in that sinking.

Peering through unbreakable glass windows at the endless procession of huge walls of cresting water bearing relentlessly down on the ship, we wondered how our little minesweepers would fare in such conditions. Later, we heard that *Deseado* was drydocked in New York to receive treatment to her bottom hull-plating, which had been corrugated by the heavy pounding.

Royal Mail Line's MV *Deseado* in which they completed the voyage – Liverpool to New York, December 1942. (NMM-Greenwich)

On our arrival we were met and escorted by Scott-Napier and his party consisting of Lt 'Stoker' Hall and Lt 'Lammy' Taylor, to our quarters at the White Ensign Club in the Barbizon Plaza Hotel on the corner of 57th Street and Fifth Avenue. We also learned to our surprise that the ships that we had come so far to fetch, were still on the drawing board.

In discussions with senior naval officers Scott-Napier expressed the opinion that the most suitable minesweepers for our use were those of Russian design and asked for ten of them. General Smuts, however, considered that the Admiralty's need was greater than ours and refused them. Instead we accepted British yacht minesweepers (BYMs) which were not quite what we wanted.

Meanwhile the officers already in New York settled down to a demanding round of exhausting but very enjoyable social activities. These included a semi-private tea party with Eleanor Roosevelt, wife of the American President, and meetings with various stars of stage and screen. American hospitality was overwhelming and we received the full treatment.

This idyllic life in time of war was occasionally interrupted by various short courses on the gyro compass, the echo sounder and whatnot, interspersed with brief spells as duty officer at either Asbury Park in New Jersey or the Brooklyn navy barracks. The engineer officers were sent off to Cleveland, Ohio, for instruction on the type of engines that they would have to work with.

After several weeks of this Shangri-La existence, we were ordered to stand by our ships. My BYMs and another commanded by Lt Doug Tweedie of Chaka's Kraal in Natal were a-building at the little seaside resort of Greenport, Long Island. There I stood by her until she was ready for trials and eventually steamed her to Brooklyn navy yard. On arrival there we were greeted with the news that the BYMs had been declared unsuitable for use in South African waters and so we reluctantly took leave of our new vessels and once again went back into the Barbizon Plaza. Our stay was for only a few hours and it ended with our being bundled into blacked-out motor coaches and taken by road, rail and sea to Norfolk, Virginia, there to man a flight of landing craft infantry LCI(L) for delivery to the Mediterranean.

In the course of time a flight of eighteen of these craft was assembled and the crews inspected by Col Frank Knox, Secretary of the US Navy, and by Anthony Eden, the British Foreign Secretary, who happened to be in the States at the time. The crews were a mixture of British RNVR and SANF. The latter, many of whom had been Merchant Navy officers, were probably the only ones with previous experience of deep-sea navigation.

On 25 March 1943, after having spent three months in the States, the 'flight' sailed for Gibraltar via Bermuda. At this remove I seem to recall that we had no armament and at the pre-sailing briefing were told that our best protection lay in the fact that with our long low hulls and conning tower-like bridge, we closely resembled submarines!

Apart from engine-room breakdowns, seasickness among many of the raw crews and the odd collision due to the unwieldy craft being in inexperienced hands, nothing untoward happened to mar our Atlantic crossing. I was told that one merchant ship had been sighted and that she, presumably observing what could easily be mistaken for a U-boat wolf pack, promptly made smoke and disappeared over the horizon. Apart from a gap in mid-Atlantic, comforting air cover was provided for the greater part of the crossing. We were indeed fortunate, for the month of March 1943 saw the most bitter fighting in the long Battle of the Atlantic.

When we reached Gibraltar all but a handful of the South Africans were taken off and sent home via the United Kingdom by troopship.

I thus found myself Senior Officer of the flight for the onward passage to Algiers and from there to Didjelli, Bone, Bougie and other ports very much in the news at the time.

On sailing from Gibraltar we got tangled up with a cruiser squadron approaching the port. 'Out of the way Little Ones,' signalled the leading cruiser, 'before you get trampled on!' Didjelli was the main landing craft base and subject to frequent enemy air attacks. It was while we were there that the Afrika Korps was surrounded and trapped on Cap Bon and we received the signal from the C-in-C to 'sink, burn and destroy – let nothing pass.' It was 'Dunkirk time' for the Axis.

One of the landing craft ferried from the USA to the Med in 1943. (P James)

On one coastal voyage we embarked army units, and I was very impressed at how these men, veterans all, without any prompting, built themselves gun emplacements on the upper decks with kitbags, boxes and any other things at hand. Our call for fighter protection was Cornhill 3. We called – and we are still waiting!

Another memory of those days is of receiving a signal that a cargo of beans had been delivered and that mess cooks were to draw rations. Such a come-down after living in the lap of luxury in New York!

In due course my turn came to be relieved, and I was posted to the AA light cruiser *Carlisle*, a ship that I had known well on the Africa Station in more peaceful times. In her I sailed from Algiers to Alexandria. Then came a move to Cairo and later a flight home in a SAAF shuttle-service Lodestar (Capt G Behn, SAAF), in the course of which we touched down at Luxor, Wadi Halfa, Khartoum (night stop), Malakal, Kuba, Kisumu, Nairobi (night stop), Dodoma, Kasama, Ndola (night stop), Lusaka, Bulawayo and finally Swartkops airport in Pretoria on 18 June 1943.

That long flight was notable for the fact that it was election time in SA and *en route* we loaded bags of soldiers' votes and, of even more importance, a large consignment of privately bought rolls of lavatory paper, which commodity was in short supply on the home front at the time.

The obliging and friendly Capt Behn flew low to stampede elephant and other herds of wild game. On board were two civilian representatives of the Douglas Aircraft Corporation, who wore sun-helmets with all their many stop-overs inscribed under the brims. Learning of my dislike of flying, they suggested to the pilot that he should put my feet in a bucket of water to make me feel more at home!

The most remarkable aspect of that particular overseas draft, entailing as it did thousands of miles of travel by land, sea and air in the midst of a global war, was that it was accomplished (apart from air raids in North Africa) with no enemy interference. We never even got our feet wet.

The authorities to whom I reported in Pretoria must have been aware of that and when I applied for foreign service leave I was told, severely, that since I had enjoyed a good time in New York at government expense I could forget it! They were a bit upset too, by the fact that all our paybooks had gone adrift. We were told to assess our cash withdrawals over a period of eight months, with the net result that the less scrupulous among our number did very well out of the whole deal.

CHAPTER

15

The Sinking of the Battleship
Barham

On the outbreak of the Second World War it was obvious to all but the die-hards among senior naval officers that the day of the battleship was over. That had been amply proved years earlier by an intrepid American aviator who, despite a practical demonstration, found himself in disfavour and retired into comparative obscurity with his naval career ruined.

Few very senior officers fully appreciated the importance of air power. They were to be brought up all-standing with the loss of *Repulse* and *Prince of Wales*; both great ships sent to the bottom of the ocean by a handful of Japanese aircraft.

HMS *Prince of Wales,* lost together with HMS *Repulse.* Their loss spelt doom for the battleship class of ship. (Author)

Before that stupendous blow the Royal Navy had already lost two of its big ships: *Royal Oak*, torpedoed in Scapa Flow and *Barham* in the Mediterranean. But those losses were the result of submarine attack and considered to be all part of the wages of war.

There were isolated actions by big ships such as the destruction of *Bismarck*, but perhaps the main function of the battleship in Hitler's war, apart from acting as a deterrent to opposing capital ships, was the bombardment of enemy territory. At a lecture on landing operations the author well remembers the lecturer, an army officer and a VC, impressing on his audience the boost to the morale of troops landing on hostile beaches given by the sight of a great ship belching forth destruction on enemy positions with her huge 15-inch guns. Its imposing presence instilled more confidence that any number of bombers overhead.

The old battleship *Barham* ploughs her stately way. (Fourie)

The first HMS *Barham* was a 74-gun ship of 1 761 tons launched in July 1811 and scrapped in 1839. The 31 000 ton *Barham* of our story was the fourth to bear the name. Launched on 31 December 1914 and commissioned with a crew of 1 100 officers and men, she fought at Jutland along with her sister battleships *Malaya, Valiant* and *Warspite*, all of which gave excellent service in the second of the great wars.

HMS *Barham* had a few South Africans in her crew. One of these was former Able Seaman Fletcher Evans, RNVR(SA). He happened to be in Mauritius when the war broke out and returning to South Africa in a cargo vessel, he joined the 2nd Natal Mounted Rifles.

Frustrated at not being sent 'Up North' he then joined the RNVR. After a month in the Fleet Mail Office in Durban and a month's refresher course he was drafted to HMS *Barham* as an Ordinary Seaman. There were ten South Africans in the ship's complement of whom seven were to lose their lives when she was sunk.

In due course *Barham* sailed from Durban to join the Mediterranean Fleet. On 25 November 1941 she was at sea in company with the battleships *Valiant* and *Queen Elizabeth* escorted by the customary screen of cruisers and destroyers. The object was to try to entice the Italian battle fleet out and into action.

Evans had just completed the first dog watch and was drinking a mug of tea in No 1 mess two decks below the fo'c'sle when he felt three tremendous explosions, and the whole ship shuddered violently.

One of the chaps shouted, 'We've been tin-fished!' whereupon they all made a bee-line for the gangways, and Evans managed to get to the upper deck, where he found the ship listing to port at a steep angle. Instinct told him to get off the stricken ship via the starboard bow, but the angle was so steep that the port 4-inch guns were already awash. Nevertheless he managed to slide down the side into the sea getting some very bad cuts from marine growth along the way.

He swam under water as far as he could to get away from the ship. When he surfaced it was to find about ten inches of oil on the water, and it seemed to him that the ship had blown up and capsized. The time between being torpedoed and sinking was only about four minutes.

Fletcher Evans managed to tread water for a time until, together with four others, he managed to hold on to a broken piece of mast.

The fleet put back to Alexandria but the destroyers *Nizam* and *Hotspur* stood by to rescue survivors. While awaiting rescue those in the water sang 'Roll out the Barrel' and 'There'll Always be an England'.

Fletcher Evans and 'Bungy' Williams, HMS *Barham*. (F Evans)

It was getting dark when he was picked up by a motor boat from the Australian destroyer HMAS *Nizam*. Once on board they stripped off their oil-soaked clothing and were given fresh gear by the generous Aussies.

After a spell at a rest camp for survivors Evans was drafted to another battleship, HMS *Valiant*, as a member of the gun-crew on the multiple pom-poms. Some time later, when he got back to Durban, he was put in hospital and later discharged from the Navy as medically unfit.

HMS *Barham* had been torpedoed by the aristocratic *Kapitänleutnant Freiherr* Hans-Dietrich von Tiesenhausen, commander of U-331. Altogether 866 officers and men lost their lives in the sinking. Of the thirty boy seamen (mostly from Dr Barnado's Home) only six survived while of the 168 Royal Marines on board 134 were lost. Altogether there were about two hundred survivors. The ship's chaplain, the Rev FT Burnett, is said to have given up his life by staying behind and encouraging members of the crew to get to the upper decks as quickly as possible.

Every year, on 25 November, a memorial service is held in Westminster Abbey in memory of the dead. An HMS *Barham* Survivors' Association was formed and a few years ago the man who sank their ship asked if he might attend the annual dinner. He was welcomed as an honoured guest.

★ ★ ★ ★ ★

Another account was given by another survivor, Midshipman HT Bailey, a former cadet of the *General Botha*.

It was a perfect day, I remember, with a calm sea and excellent visibility. It was about midday on 25 November 1941, and I had just been relieved after a long strenuous watch. After lunch I crashed my skull on a couch in the gunroom and was awakened at 1620 by a steward telling me that it was time for tea.

Bleary-eyed I sat down at the long oaken table in the gunroom and began my tea. At the after end of the gunroom I noticed a number of midshipmen listening to the radiogram, among them Midshipman WSW Maplesden who had been a shipmate of mine on various ships after our time together in the *Botha*.

I was chatting to a midshipman RN when the ship was shaken by a violent explosion. This was at approximately 1625. It immediately flashed through my mind that we had escaped a near-miss by high-level bombers which we had been expecting all day. Split seconds later another two explosions followed in quick succession. The lights went out and there was uproar and confusion.

The ship gave a heavy lurch to port and I barely escaped being crushed by the heavy table as it crashed into the bulkhead. It was then that I realised that we had been torpedoed and as the ship increased her list rapidly I realised that she was doomed. My only aim was to get out on deck before I was trapped below.

Leaving the gunroom, I dashed up the first companionway that I came across, but I found to my horror that the watertight door was locked. Having no time to waste I slithered through a man-sized porthole, clambered over on to the starboard side, and found my way along the upper deck to below the bridge superstructure.

By this time she was listing at an angle of almost 45 degrees. About one minute had elapsed since the first torpedo struck her aft on the port side and there had been no time for taking up abandon ship stations. It was a case of every man for himself and God for all.

Not having my lifebelt on, I decided to divest myself of all my clothing before jumping over the side. A number of seamen were trying to cut loose some of the Carley floats and other life-saving gear, but time was against them.

The ship gave a violent lurch to port and began capsizing. I felt myself slithering over the high side amongst a number of other men. Then I hit the water with a terrific thump and struck out away from the ship to avoid the suction. It must have been about ten seconds later that I heard, and felt, a violent explosion behind me.

I seemed to be going right down to the bottom with the ship. When I could hardly stand it any longer I found myself beginning to rise. My lungs were nearly bursting when I felt myself able to suck in fresh air.

Everything was pitch-black, and I wondered whether I had crossed the Great Divide. A little while later I could see quite clearly

The *Barham* lists heavily to port after being torpedoed . . . (Fourie)

. . . and blows up. A wonder any escaped. (Fourie)

and knew that it was only a thick pall of black smoke that covered the whole scene of the disaster. All round me men were struggling in the water, clinging to bits of wreckage and anything that floated; all were covered in thick black oil.

I swam towards a small Carley float with a number of men on it and clambered on board. Darkness was rapidly approaching, and as the destroyers were quite a distance away we thought we might not be picked up in time, so, grabbing bits of wood, we began paddling our way towards the nearest destroyer.

She turned out to be the *Hotspur*, busy picking up other survivors. She was forging slowly ahead, and when she approached quite near us a seaman dived over the side with a heaving line round his waist, which he made fast to the raft. In no time we were alongside and clambering aboard – thankful to feel a deck under our feet once more.

The grand old *Barham* had gone to join many another fine ship in Davy Jones' locker, where all good ships go in the end. With her went 865 officers and men. Out of her complement of ninety officers, twenty-four lived to tell the tale. She had carried twenty-six midshipmen, and eight of them survived. Maplesden, the only other *Botha* boy (to my knowledge) had made the supreme sacrifice.

We subsequently learned that we had been torpedoed by a German U-boat that had somehow evaded the screen and fired a salvo of three torpedoes at extremely close range. Each one had taken full effect. The 27-year-old battleship could not stand up to the punishment and blew up and sank within three and a half minutes.

★ ★ ★ ★ ★

Another survivor was Alfred Duffell-Canham, whose brother's exploits in the Mediterranean have been noted elsewhere in these pages.

A Duffell-Canham (right) and shipmates HMS *Barham*. (SANMMH)

Duffell-Canham's watch was due to close up at 1600, and they spent the time after the midday meal writing letters, reading and washing clothes, or trying to get forty winks. Tea was at 1530, and twenty minutes later he prepared to go up to his gun station.

About two minutes later there came a tremendous explosion, followed by several others, and the ship seemed to lift bodily. Their first thought was that these were near-misses from a high-level bombing attack, and within seconds their gun was loaded and the gun-captain scanning the sky. Then they realised that the great bulk of HMS *Barham* was rolling over and that torpedoes had torn holes in her port side.

They climbed up the now sharply sloping deck to the starboard side to avoid any boats or loose hamper that would roll down the port side. Here is Alfred Duffell-Canham's account in his own words:

> Everything happened so rapidly. I can recall our immediate group of three – John Smith, Hamish Cuthbert and myself – first sitting together trying to persuade Hamish, who said he could not swim, to jump to avoid being sucked down by the ship. Then sliding on our backsides to the bilge keel which had now come into view. We had seen several men hitting, and probably killing themselves, against that keel by jumping too early.
>
> I cannot remember actually jumping, but do recall hearing the explosions inside the ship which I thought were the boilers but were actually the magazines.
>
> My next recollection was being swept along head over heels in the water and instinctively striking out for the surface as I was near to drowning. When I stopped trying to swim – I was heading down – I rose to the surface.
>
> There was an eerie silence, and for a while I thought I was the only survivor. After clearing my mouth, nose and eyes of oil fuel, which covered a large area, I looked about. Then I heard a voice calling 'Anyone alive?' and response coming from all quarters. We gradually got together in groups making use of wreckage, timber, and a couple of Carley floats. Our piece of timber supported five men, although it was submerged most

Lt Fourie. He was drafted off the ship and so lived. (Fourie)

of the time. A half Carley float came near at one point, but we could not bring ourselves to use it, as it contained the top half of a torso.

During the hours that ensued several gave up through injuries or exhaustion. Eventually we observed two destroyers, HMS *Hotspur* and HMS *Nizam*, approaching from opposite directions. They were slowly making their way through the debris and, with the boats and scrambling nets, picking up survivors.

I was picked up by HMS *Hotspur*. Our oil-soaked clothing was discarded overboard and in my case was replaced with a football jersey kindly given me by one of *Hotspur*'s men. We were then given rum, which made me sick but got rid of a good deal of fuel oil.

Next day we disembarked at 44 Shed, Alexandria. Our oil-grimed ragtag group was greeted with a remark from an ignorant dockyard matey – 'Are these Eyetie survivors then?'

At a rest camp they learned that Vice-Admiral Pridham-Wippell, whose flag was worn by *Barham*, had survived, but that Captain Cook and the

ship's Commander had both gone down with the ship with 868 others including six of the twelve South Africans who had joined her in Durban only four months earlier.

Nemesis caught up with U-331 on 17 November 1942, when she was attacked and sunk off Algiers by aircraft from the carrier HMS *Formidable*. Tiesenhausen was taken prisoner.

LV Snel, SANF who survived the sinking of HMS *Barham* and later joined HMSAS *Good Hope*. (SANMMH)

CHAPTER
16

Was he the Youngest?

The author believed he could do no better than quote a letter received from Mr SJ Munton of Port Elizabeth, who at his enlistment must surely have been the youngest seaman in the SA Naval Forces.

Mr SJ Munton. (SANMMH)

My decision to join the armed forces during World War II was not prompted by any sense of patriotic duty or other emotion of that nature. The motive was an urge for excitement and adventure. The prospect of leaving school was also a very strong incentive!

Late in 1941 the recruiting centre in Johannesburg was at the Union Grounds between the city centre and Hillbrow. Huts were situated round the perimeter. I was not particularly concerned about what I joined, just as long as I could get in.

I began with the infantry, but was asked to produce my birth certificate. I was then fifteen and a half years old and seventeen was the minimum age. I then tried the Artillery, the Signals, the Tanks, and finally the Medical Corps, but they all wanted that birth certificate. The last hut was the SA Navy, next to the exit gate!

I said that I was seventeen and a half . They did not ask for a certificate, and I was in! If the Navy still has its 1941 records they will see that Munton SJ No 71731V was born on 21 May 1924. In fact the year should be 1926.

I went to Cape Town by train with about thirty other naval recruits and ended up on a windswept piece of ground near Woodstock. This was our home for the next four or five weeks while we underwent training. We also spent a day on a minesweeper and this was the first and last time I was seasick.

After our 'training' we were assigned to ships. I went to Durban and joined HMSAS *Rondevlei* as a stoker. Duty consisted of about three days' patrol off the coast followed by two days at Maydon Wharf.

In November 1942 a signal came calling for volunteers for the Royal Navy. The tedious routine in *Rondevlei* made up my mind for me, and I volunteered immediately. I had a week's leave with my family, and that was the last time I saw them for four years.

I reported to Simon's Town, where I spent three weeks in Klaver Camp and was then transferred to the *General Botha* to await assignment to a ship. That turned out to be the destroyer HMS *Express*. I was the only South African on board and in her we sailed as escort to the battleship HMS *Valiant* to Durban. That would be in January 1943. While I was in Durban my two elder brothers arrived, the eldest in a hospital ship having been severely wounded at El Alamein with the RLI. My other brother was on his way to the Mediterranean to join HMSAS *Bever*. Fortunately he left her just two weeks before she was mined and sunk.

Escort comes alongside to take bunkers. (Munton)

We sailed from SA with a convoy that included HMS *Valiant* and arrived in Liverpool early in February 1943. It was my first glimpse of England. The crew were paid off and given a fortnight's leave which I spent with a shipmate's family at a picturesque little village in Surrey.

My next draft was to Portsmouth barracks, where life consisted of boiler-cleaning ships in the harbour and sweeping up the parade ground. Worse still was the watery beer in the NAAFI canteen!

Eventually orders came to report to the parade ground with full kit. There we piled into navy trucks and were taken to the station to entrain for Greenock in Scotland – reputed to be even wetter than Manchester, which I can well believe. There we embarked in the 85 000 ton liner *Queen Elizabeth*. With only about six to eight hundred on board she was practically empty, yet the Navy crammed us into what had been the ballroom, now fitted with bunks six tiers high. It was a pleasant trip though and we arrived in New York on 21 May 1943, my 17th birthday.

We had a wonderful reception from Americans in all walks of life. Their kindness and generosity was overwhelming and something I shall never forget. We were billeted at Asbury Park, New Jersey, in converted hotels suitably enclosed in barbed wire!

It was there that I had my first 'run in' with the authorities. It was a nasty experience. Just before leaving Portsmouth I had telephoned the daughter of friends of mine at her insurance office

Capt Colquohoun RN, Captain of HMS *Trumpeter* addresses ship's company on 4 August 1943. (Munton)

and told her that there was a possibility of my leaving for the States in the next few days. We then discussed personal and family matters. Of course the telephones had been tapped at the Navy barracks – I never gave it a thought. My name was called over the speaker system at Asbury Park to report to the commander's secretary. On complying I was told to remain in barracks and report again next morning.

Then I appeared before a panel of three officers, a stenographer and two men in civilian clothes (security officers). The presiding officer read out my telephoned conversation verbatim. They took a serious view of my giving confidential information over the telephone, etc., etc. Then followed a discussion as to whether my offence justified a court martial! Eventually it was decided that the tone of our conversation contained no 'evil' content on my part and I was given two weeks' confined to barracks. The young lady that I had telephoned also had an unpleasant shock when two detectives arrived at her office the day after we had spoken.

From Asbury Park we went to the Philadelphia navy yard where we trained for eight weeks on simulated catapult and arrester gear as fitted to aircraft-carriers. I was most impressed with the American instructors. It was there that we were told we were to commission a new aircraft-carrier and that my job would be to handle the control gear on the flight deck.

HMS *Trumpeter* dives into a heavy head sea. (Inset) HMS *Trumpeter*'s crest. (Munton)

From Philadelphia we went by train to Canada. Through Ottawa, Winnipeg, Calgary and Banff, in the beautiful Canadian Rockies. Then south again to Portland, Oregon, and to the shipyard where our ship, HMS *Trumpeter*, was being built. She was still in the throes of construction and swarming with welders, both male and female. It was the first all-welded hull that I had seen.

Trumpeter was commissioned on 4 August 1943 and we steamed down the Columbia River and up to Puget Sound for sea trials.

From Seattle we went down the west coast through the Panama Canal and up to the US navy yard at Norfolk, Virginia. Then on to Newark, New Jersey, where we loaded and lashed down American fighter aircraft for delivery to the United Kingdom.

For the next four months we shuttled back and forth in North Atlantic convoys between the United Kingdom and the USA bringing across fighter aircraft. Apart from a few depth-charge attacks on suspected submarines by our escorts, the trips were uneventful.

From February to the end of May 1944 the ship underwent modifications at Dundee in Scotland before becoming fully operational. One of the alterations demanded the complete stripping out of the American soda-fountain and ice-cream vending equipment in the main mess deck. Such fripperies were not for the Royal Navy!

After the refit we were posted to Scapa Flow where, apart from two or three visits to Greenock, we spent the last year of the war on North Sea patrols with our aircraft making shipping strikes off the Norwegian coast. We also made one convoy voyage to Murmansk.

Trumpeter's Avengers returning from raid over Norway. (Munton)

Trumpeter's Avengers attacking shipping in Norwegian fjord. (Munton)

In August 1944 a large carrier force was assembled for a strike against the German battleship *Tirpitz* holed up in a Norwegian fjord. The force consisted of the carriers *Formidable, Furious,* and *Indefatigable*, and of the escort carriers *Nabob* and *Trumpeter*. During the operation *Nabob* was torpedoed. She had been steaming about a quarter of a mile from *Trumpeter* and on the same course. An escorting frigate, *Pinkerton*, was also hit, presumably by the same submarine, and she suffered heavy loss of life.

Nabob did not sink but was well down by the stern. During her passage south she actually flew off one of her aircraft on anti-submarine patrol.

HMS *Nabob* after being torpedoed. (Munton)

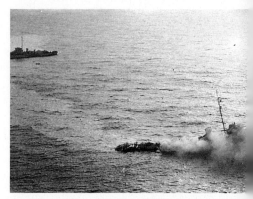

HMS *Pinkerton* sinking. Probably victim of same U-boat that torpedoed *Nabob*. (Munton)

The Russian convoys to Murmansk were notorious for the bitter cold and severe weather. That, along with submarine and air attack, made these runs the most arduous of all naval operations. Rough seas and poor visibility made flying conditions particularly dangerous. When the Fleet Air Arm pilots flew off, their carrier would not be in the same position on their return, so that it called for navigation of the highest order.

Since my job was to work the catapult for take-off and the arrester gear on landing, I had to stay on deck as long as we had aircraft in the air. Our ship's speed was 18 knots, and with headwinds of about the same velocity we had cross flight-deck air velocities of up to 40 knots, with temperatures well below freezing. Despite thick layers of protective clothing the cold still penetrated. I shall always remember how welcome was the cocoa that was brought up to us, thick and steaming hot.

The ship was equipped with American Wildcat fighters and Avenger torpedo bombers, about twelve of each. Once a Wildcat fighter was on the catapult at full throttle with the pilot's head held back on the headrest waiting for the signal to be fired. I was standing on the catwalk below the wing. The cable tensioner at the back of the aircraft suddenly broke. The pilot was unaware of that and

HMS *Trumpeter* icebound in Murmansk with Russian tug in attendance. (Munton)

slowly moved towards the bows of the ship. Fortunately the propeller torque pulled the aircraft to the right and he went over into the sea off the starboard bow and was picked up by the escorting frigate.

Trumpeter's crew numbered about eight hundred. Apart from myself there was only one other South African on board, Roy Christianson from Durban. We were both on the arrester and catapult team.

One of our duties was to pump aviation fuel up to the hangar deck. To do so we had to go right down into the bowels of the ship. Ventilation was bad and we had to wear rubber boots and gloves to prevent sparks from igniting the fumes.

I had to go down a twelve-foot vertical ladder into a shaft to open valves, and once when I had difficulty in handling a valve I stayed down longer than usual. I climbed back up to where Roy was working the pumps. He saw my head appear above the coaming, and a minute later when he turned round I had disappeared! Overcome by the fumes I had fallen down the shaft. Roy Christianson somehow carried me up that twelve-foot vertical ladder in a shaft no more than three feet square; and he undoubtedly saved my life. It took me twenty minutes to recover.

On V-E Day, 8 May 1945, we were off the Norwegian coast again when the news of the end of hostilities was broadcast over the ship's speakers. It was a clear sunny day, and we flew off a few of our Wildcat fighters, and they did low level runs over us and performed other aerobatics – it was a great feeling that day! Two German JU 88s appeared in the distance but did not approach us. No doubt they were also aware of the cessation of hostilities.

On our return to Greenock my fellow South African and I were asked if we would care to volunteer for service in the Far East. We both declined.

Leaving *Trumpeter* was a sad occasion. We had been together for two and a half years. After celebrating ashore in a suitable manner boarding the London train in Glasgow was but a hazy memory!

Back in Portsmouth I took leave of friends and sailed for Cape Town in January 1946 in the Dutch liner *Ruys* with the last of the repatriated SA prisoners of war, and I was duly discharged from active service at Hector Norris Park about my twentieth birthday. My official designation was Stoker 1st Class.

17

Return to the Med

South African ships performed many outstanding feats during the Mediterranean campaign, not the least of which were the operations carried out by the salvage vessels *Salvestor* and *Gamtoos*.

It was in Naples in August 1944 that Lt-Cmdr TF O'Brien was transferred from *Gamtoos* to *Salvestor* in command. She had been provided by the Admiralty, but at their request was manned by a South African crew. After service in the Aegean which lasted until the end of hostilities in that area, *Salvestor* then sailed for Durban before joining the Far Eastern Fleet.

She was to do much steaming in the next few months. After leaving Durban she went to Trincomalee via Mauritius and Colombo, and then south again making for Fremantle, but orders diverted her to Onslow and thence to Port Darwin. She sailed again on 19 June with two tugs and a floating dock in tow escorted by two Australian fleet sweepers for Milne Bay in New Guinea. After meeting bad weather, which damaged the dock, and a call at Thursday Island they reached their destination on 8 July, and waited for the dock to be repaired.

On 8 August *Salvestor* went to the assistance of a merchant ship, took her in tow and brought her back to Milne Bay. On the 14th she sailed for Manus and finally arrived in Hong Kong, where her first salvage job began: to raise a Japanese tug. By now the war had ended, and the South African crew were gradually replaced, one of the earliest being the commanding officer, who had broken his arm during salvage operations. By the end of 1945 *Salvestor* had severed all connection with South Africa.

Meanwhile, as early as April 1942, it had been decided that South Africa should equip a salvage vessel to carry out rapid clearance of newly captured harbours in the Mediterranean. Accordingly the Durban coaster *Gamtoos* was requisitioned and converted for her new task, and she sailed under the command of Lt-Cmdr RD Cruikshanks on 19 November 1942.

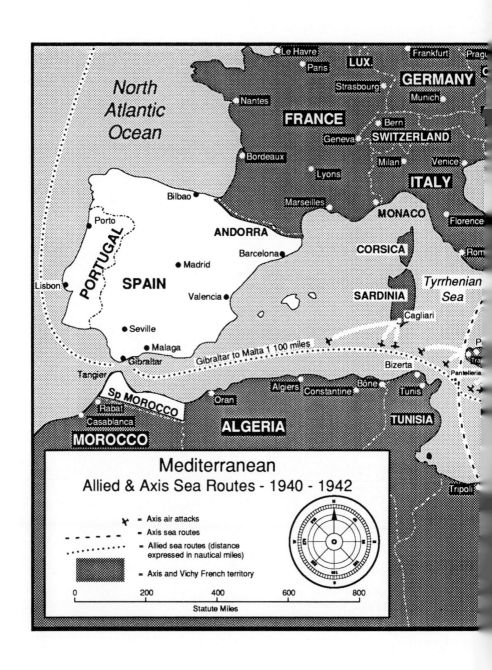

North
Atlantic
Ocean

Le Havre
Paris
LUX.
Frankfurt
Pragu
Strasbourg
GERMANY
Munich
Nantes
FRANCE
Bern
SWITZERLAND
Geneva
Bordeaux
Milan
Venice
Lyons
ITALY
Bilbao
Marseilles
MONACO
Florence
Porto
ANDORRA
CORSICA
Rom
Barcelona
Madrid
SPAIN
Valencia
SARDINIA
Tyrrhenian
Sea
Cagliari
Lisbon
PORTUGAL
Seville
Malaga
Gibraltar to Malta 1 100 miles
P
Tra
Gibraltar
Bizerta
Pantelleria
Tangier
Algiers
Constantine
Bône
Oran
Tunis
Sp MOROCCO
ALGERIA
TUNISIA
Rabat
Casablanca
MOROCCO
Tripoli

Mediterranean
Allied & Axis Sea Routes - 1940 - 1942

✈ = Axis air attacks

— — — = Axis sea routes

· · · · · · = Allied sea routes (distance
expressed in nautical miles)

▓ = Axis and Vichy French territory

0   200   400   600   800

Statute Miles

HMS *Salvestor*. Manned by South Africans, she served in the Med and the Far East. (SANMMH)

When she arrived in Port Said on 20 December she was immediately given her first job, which lasted until 4 January 1943. On the 17th she sailed in convoy to Benghazi where she arrived on the 21st, and left a few hours later, by herself, for Tripoli, where she arrived on the 23rd, to find the minesweeper HMSAS *Boksburg* and her consorts already at anchor awaiting the outcome of the land fighting.

Tripoli fell on 24 January, and after waiting for the minesweepers to clear an approach channel, *Gamtoos* entered harbour on the 26th and

The work-horse of the Mediterranean – HMSAS *Gamtoos*. (SANMMH)

made fast alongside the wreck of the SS *Ngoma* which, with other sunken ships, submerged hawsers, boom-nets and other obstructions, completely blocked the harbour entrance.

After delays caused by bad weather, *Gamtoos* cleared a gap wide enough for her to enter harbour on 29 January, and was thus the first Allied ship to do so. The wreck of the *Ngoma* was patched so that she could be raised and swung clear of the channel. A sunken concrete ship and large sheer-legs were broken up by blasting and removed piecemeal.

By 3 February *Gamtoos* had widened the gap to a width of ninety feet and a depth of three fathoms, which allowed merchant ships to enter. A few days later General Montgomery visited the harbour, boarded the *Ngoma* and sent a message to *Gamtoos* : 'I congratulate you and all concerned in the great achievement of opening Tripoli harbour to Eighth Army supplies. Today is the date by which you stated a depth of 25 feet would be reached. You have, in the intervening period, progressed the work at a greater rate than I expected and the supplying of the Army has benefited accordingly. Well done!'

Unfortunately space does not permit a full account of the many salvage undertakings performed by *Gamtoos* under her various captains, but her record was second to none and won the gratitude of the Army which was so dependent on ports being cleared rapidly and efficiently.

Perhaps the best-known of her commanding officers was Lt-Cmdr HH Biermann (now Admiral, Retd) who assumed command in Naples in 1944. Biermann, like so many others, was trained in the *General Botha* (1932 – 33) and served an apprenticeship with the Prince line of steamers before transferring to the fleet operated by the SAR & H. In 1938 he applied for a war reserve commission and was commissioned into the RNVR war reserve. When war broke out his ship, SS *Dalia*, was passing Singapore bound for Manila. In Sydney he received his call-up papers, and on returning to Cape Town he reported to the Castle where he was given the choice of serving either with the RN or the SDF. He chose the latter and, again like so many others, he served first with local minesweepers. He could scarcely have foretold at the time that he would end his nautical career as the first full South African Admiral and Chief of his country's Defence Force.

Wrecked ships dealt with by *Gamtoos* clearing harbours in North Africa. (G Nash)

One of the most noteworthy achievements of *Gamtoos* under Biermann's command was the clearance of Marseilles harbour, the entrance to which was blocked by the wreck of the cargo vessel *Cap Corse*. Inspection revealed that salvage would be a waste of effort, and accordingly her stern was cut away as far as the mainmast. When that was done a 300 pound demolition charge was exploded under her counter. That in turn detonated a mine on her port side; fortunately without casualties, but it blew a gap wide enough for small minesweepers to enter the harbour and set about clearing the area of mines.

Lt-Cmdr HH Biermann CO HMSAS *Gamtoos* in the Med. (SANMMH)

Mines were also widely scattered outside the harbour and *Gamtoos* ran considerable risk, anchoring to seaward at the end of each day's work awaiting their clearance.

Work continued with divers placing charges, and lifting craft removing bits and pieces until the gap was big enough for light vessels to enter. On 12 September *Gamtoos* was herself able to enter and berth in the harbour; as in Tripoli, the first ship of her size to do so.

Demolition of the *Cap Corse* continued until 8 October when a gap of 130 feet had been made. Meanwhile work had begun on the wreck of the scuttled *Morialta*. Divers also inspected the wreck of the *Sidi Aissa* blocking the entrance to the neighbouring port of La Coitat, in which there was a much-needed graving dock. The holds of the *Sidi Aissa* had been filled with gravel to a depth of six feet; there were two large holes about twenty feet square in her port side, and adjacent bulkheads had been destroyed. Despite that, and the presence of magnetic mines in the vicinity, the ship was pumped out, refloated, and towed clear of the entrance by 14 December. For that exploit Biermann received the OBE.

Lt-Cmdr HH Biermann and ship's company HMSAS *Gamtoos*. (SANMMH)

On 4 January *Gamtoos* left her berth in Marseilles and entered the dry dock she had so recently freed at La Coitat. From there she went to Ajaccio to work on two ships, one of which was made seaworthy while the other was handed over to HMS *Sea Salvor*. On 24 February *Gamtoos* sailed for Malta via Naples to refit. While that was in progress she sent a salvage party to work on the wreck of the destroyer *Maori* which had been sunk in an air raid in the Grand Harbour during February 1942.

On 28 April 1945 *Gamtoos* sailed from Malta, and after calling at Augusta, Syracuse, Palermo, Naples and Leghorn, she arrived at Genoa on 12 May. There she raised and towed clear the block-ship *Sterope,* patched up another, and returned to Malta, where she raised another ship and completed work on yet another in early November. That was the last of her jobs in the Mediterranean and she sailed for home, arriving in Durban on 11 December. After a period of moving stores from Durban to Cape Town she was finally paid off on 15 February 1946 and handed over to the Ministry of Agriculture. She was a modest little ship with a proud record. She ended her long life humbly employed in collecting guano from offlying islands.

★ ★ ★ ★ ★

While still in Mediterranean waters let us rejoin Lt McWilliams who was a survivor of HMS *Hecla.* The following slightly edited version of his personal account presents a vivid picture of the invasion of Sicily, from which many lessons were learned and put to good use in later operations:

> I have never in my life spent such a hectic ten days as those after our arrival off the Sicilian coast; the *Hecla* affair was child's play compared with the bombing attacks and the constant alarms we had during the first three days of the operation. I find from records that there were twenty-seven air attacks during that time alone, but I have lost count of the raids we had since our arrival.
>
> I was Senior Naval Officer on board a merchant ship adapted for the transport of motor vehicles, and responsible for liaison between the master of the ship and naval personnel on board indirectly for the unloading of vehicles and stores and the working of landing craft doing that job. It doesn't sound much, but it kept me busy for forty-eight hours, to the extent that not only had I no time for more than five hours' sleep in that time, but I never had a moment to realise that I was going without rest or meals. It is remarkable how one's body reacts to emergencies. I never felt hungry, and when food was available I only pecked at it. It must have been the same automatic stimulus that kept everyone going, from troops unloading the ship to the sailors manning the landing craft, all of whom carried on cheerfully and energetically without any break until the job was done; and yet they still found time for laughing and joking.
>
> The drama began with the conference, which was held in secret in the fortress at Alexandria the day the convoy sailed. All ships' masters, their SNOs and other important officers were present. We were protected against breaches of security by marines and shepherded into a large hall where places were marked for everyone at long

tables down the middle. Big important-looking sealed envelopes and rolls of charts were handed out. Up to that moment I had no idea where we were bound, and I don't think many others had either.

It wasn't long before the Admiral got up and announced, 'The time – July 10; – the place, gentlemen, Syracuse in Sicily.' We were then given various instructions. The plan of assault, etc. was explained, and we were then escorted down to the pier and sent off to our ships. The convoy sailed at noon; and what a sight it was! The harbour was densely packed with shipping, and it must have been obvious to everyone that an expedition had been mounted. About thirty MT ships like ours left the harbour strongly escorted by destroyers, corvettes and a monitor. Permanent air cover was given by aircraft based on airfields on the North African coast.

Since the convoy was a slow one we spent a week at sea. The air of expectancy was tense and rose to fever pitch when on the third day one of the ships three columns away from us was torpedoed and fell behind. Eventually she caught fire and burned furiously. We little realised what a common sight such a spectacle would become – I even made a drawing of it!

As D-Day approached we got very restless and couldn't settle down to anything. The constant air screen was a great comfort, especially when, on the afternoon of the preceding day, we joined another convoy twice the size. Ships every three hundred yards in every direction, right to the horizon, or apparent horizon, covering each sector of the compass. In addition to ordinary steamers and warships there were curious invasion vessels of special design and small craft towing strange contraptions intended for landing.

We were due to arrive at the release position off the coast at first light the following morning. The actual assault, which was to take place in darkness, would by then have been carried out. We formed the second wave and we hoped that the coastal batteries and other forms of resistance would have been silenced by the time we got there.

When night fell the weather worsened and, with all the ships labouring heavily, we cursed our luck. There was a bit of a moon and we were stirred by the fantastic sight of our bombers flying overhead towing strings of gliders. They were to land airborne troops and surprise units behind the enemy lines as a diversion. The air seemed filled with those enormous bat-like monsters, flying low and making a strange whistling sound.

The first sight of Sicily was thrilling; it looked very like a chunk of South Africa. The low mountains might have been those of Humansdorp, with limestone cliffs about twenty feet high along the shore. The olive groves and vineyards gave the impression of the vegetation around Constantia – olive trees and silver trees are very similar in certain lights.

Offshore a big naval battle was in progress but we couldn't follow it because destroyers were laying smokescreens, so a lot of the action was hidden. The progress of the army on land could be seen, however. Gunfire, explosions of all sorts, and clouds of dust marked their advance. As we made our way to our anchorage we could see enormous fires in some of the villages, and there was one spectacular explosion caused no doubt by an ammunition dump going up. Our planes were much in evidence so we felt fairly safe as we began to get our stuff over the side.

All went well until 1530. Planes had been overhead all day so we were not particularly surprised to see a formation of about a dozen coming over. 'Spitfires!' said everyone. Our gun crews, although permanently at action stations, hardly bothered to look up. The two cruisers and the destroyers patrolling to seaward didn't open fire or make any warning signal. Suddenly the 'Spitfires' peeled off in pairs and dived, and we could actually see the bombs, shining silver in the sun, fluttering down from them.

The transformation from peace to pandemonium was instantaneous. Every ship had at least half a dozen small high-angle guns and one large one, while the cruisers and other warships were able to put up a terrific barrage. Before I could stuff cotton wool into my ears I was deafened by our own guns. I felt awfully vulnerable for I was wearing only a pair of shorts because of the heat. One doesn't feel very secure in shorts and a tin-hat! Every time a bomb fell I could feel its scorching breath on my body.

That was my first experience of dive-bombing but I can tell you it doesn't need much practice to fling yourself flat on the deck when you hear the whine and screech of a falling bomb. We had two near misses, one fell ten yards ahead of the ship and another only about twenty yards off the port quarter. This latter peppered our ensign with splinters so that it looked like a piece of open-work lace. It also punctured the ship's side in many places: some holes were six inches across. The whole ship was lifted bodily by the explosion, and the noise was astonishing. After that there was so much acrid smoke and general mess that for a while I couldn't see what was happening. Then it cleared, and I saw one of the cruisers straddled by bombs and hidden from sight by spray and smoke. But she was not damaged, and we all cheered when we saw her alter course with all guns firing.

The sky was filled with the white and black puffs of bursting AA shells and flying streams of scarlet tracer bullets, of which there is one in four in the jet of fire from the Oerlikon guns.

The surface of the water was broken by white splashes caused by the fragments of bursting bombs, falling fragments and other debris, and our steel decks resounded to the clang of falling splinters, like handfuls of acorns on a corrugated iron roof.

I suppose the whole action lasted only about ten minutes, but it seemed ages until silence reigned again and we could stand up and look about us. High up we saw one of our fighters pursuing an enemy plane and then, to our delight, shoot it down. Four little parachutes appeared in the sky and the plane slid down in alternate streaks of orange flame and black smoke until it crashed over the hills on shore.

Only a few minutes later the alert signal went. This time a large number of twin-engined German bombers appeared, very high up. They dropped their loads indiscriminately, but actually achieved better results than the dive bombers, as the latter were obviously put off their aim by the tremendous barrage of fire that met them. The ship astern of us had a near miss, so near to her stern that her plates were stove in and she immediately filled in No 5 hold. She was soon low in the water with her bows cocked up in the air, but she didn't sink and, miraculously, no one on board was hurt.

Most of the bombs fell some distance from us. One hit a ship and immediately set it on fire. Unfortunately she was filled with oil and petrol. By the time the fighters had climbed to the height of the bombers they were far away and we couldn't see what happened.

After all that we were very much on the alert. Apparently the enemy had used captured Spitfires to lead the first attack and some Italian planes that looked rather like them. But the planes used in the second wave were German. They had a specially vicious look, heavy-headed like dragon-flies, and when they opened their bomb flaps the bombs appeared like handfuls of confetti twinkling and fluttering through the sky. They seemed to come down very slowly, until the whistling noise of their descent could be heard, by which time they were actually travelling so fast that they could no longer be seen.

Work went on, and the blazing ship filled the sky with thick black smoke, turning the sun into a dark red ball. We expected enemy planes to use the smoke as cover and pounce on us out of it at any moment. A destroyer tried to tow the burning vessel into the wind so that the fire would not spread, but the tow parted. Finally all the neighbouring ships were moved away and they torpedoed her.

What a sight! Flaming debris flung high into the air, great tongues of fire and jets of coloured steam and smoke shot out in every direction. After it was all over huge patches of burning oil still floated on the sea. Of course the water was filled with all sorts of wreckage; cargo, parts of the ship and rafts, boats, etc. All survivors were taken off before the ship was sunk and only a few were killed by the bomb explosion.

I must tell you about the night raids, since they are altogether different. There was a faint moon, which was all we had to work by, but the unloading went on just the same with the men in the holds using torches fitted with blue shades. They hardly stopped for raids, except when bombs were actually falling. The alarm went, as flares suddenly appeared overhead and the menacing throb of the bombers' engines could be heard.

In daylight one can sometimes see the planes, or at least see in which direction the ship's AA guns are trained, but at night with their dazzling magnesium flares coming slowly down on small parachutes you feel so helpless lying at anchor, lit up and yet unable to look up. Some of the gunners tried shooting down the flares but they were so blinded by the glare they were unable to aim at anything for some time afterwards, so I forbade the practice.

Their technique appears to be to demoralise by means of flares, and after keeping one in suspense for a quarter of an hour, suddenly to swoop down and drop the bombs. One can only fire blindly towards them and hope for the best.

We had four of these nerve-racking attacks before dawn, when yet another ordinary high-level raid was made. In all cases the bombs missed the ships, some by only yards, but thank goodness none came nearer than half a mile from us. Still, you never know where they are going to fall and you live through an agonising twenty seconds as the wail of the blasted thing warns you to keep under cover.

The flares take nearly ten minutes to come down, and the relief as they sizzle out on falling into the sea is indescribable. The darkness seems like a tangible protection and confidence is restored again.

The unloading went on all next day and until moonset the next night, about 0300. At dusk we saw a horrible spectacle. A large three-funnelled hospital ship closed in, with her lights blazing and at least four enormous crosses picked out in red lights. She lay about a mile from us while various small craft sped out to the anchorage with the casualties of the day. Suddenly five dive bombers swooped down with a vicious whine like a bunch of ill-tempered mosquitoes. Simultaneously five columns of water shot up. There were two direct hits on the forepart of the hospital ship and all her lights went out.

For a few moments nothing could be seen but a mass of haze and spray from which pieces of wreckage occasionally dropped with a splash. When it cleared the ship was already sinking with her entire bows under water and her stern, with its twin propellers, sticking high in the air. The whole thing happened so quickly that hardly a shot was fired and the dive bombers were out of range before anyone realised what had happened.

We could see the boats being lowered and numerous destroyers and other craft racing to the scene. Presently two of the three funnels were under water, and I don't think a quarter of an hour elapsed before the ship disappeared in a cloud of coloured steam. Everyone was enraged and shocked. I still think it was unnecessary to have all the lights on. If the ship had been blacked out, it might never have happened.

A few days later, after a series of intermittent raids, the next ship to us received a heavy bomb amidships, a dive bomber having suddenly nipped over the hill behind the beach and dropped it before any warning could be given. The troops were having their tea. The bomb hit the ammunition, which immediately went up, and the whole ship was hidden in an immense explosion that knocked us all flat.

For quite a time afterwards large objects fell out of the sky. Ventilators, eighteen-inch pulleys, blocks and so on. Some of it quite a long way off. The remains of the ship blazed furiously and only about a couple of dozen survivors could be taken off. She had to be blown up and sunk and once again the sea was covered with burning oil and wreckage, amongst which were limbs and entrails.

After the fifth day our planes kept all hostile craft away, but with the exception of two nights, we had air raids every night during the thirteen days after the first landings. Several ships had been hit, but on the whole the losses were absurdly small. We had expected to lose far more. In our sector only three large ships and one smaller ship were lost.

The oil fuel and wreckage have entirely ruined the beaches. Oily scum and planks and rubbish all over them. The debris of many camps and the havoc of bombing have altered the appearance of the shore above the high-water mark. Now and then a small cove or projecting rock can be found free from oil, and when we want a swim we look for those. The water is still in such places, and unexploded bombs and other instruments of destruction can clearly be seen lying on the bottom.

★ ★ ★ ★ ★

Another man who has recorded his wartime experiences in unpublished form was Lt JN Barfield, DSC, who joined the RNVR in 1930 and did his training at sea in the original HMSAS *Immortelle* in 1933.

He volunteered for active service in the middle of 1940 and was appointed to the heavy cruiser HMS *Cumberland* as an Ordinary

Lt JN Barfield DSC. (JN Barfield DSC)

Seaman. He was in her when she sailed from Simon's Town in mid-November with the famous dog Just Nuisance shanghaied on board. Nuisance was usually intelligent enough to know when a ship was sailing and to keep clear, but this time he was caught napping. But he was landed by tug off Roman Rock while still in False Bay, so all was well.

In due course Barfield and Ernest Brackley from East London were selected by the ship's captain, the Hon Guy Russell, DSO (later knighted) as suitable material for commissioned rank. During a spell of leave in London before joining the training establishment *King Alfred* at Hove, he met Group Captain 'Sailor' Malan whom he described as 'a fine, quiet and unostentatious man'.

On 30 October 1941 Barfield assumed the uniform of a sub-lieutenant RNVR and embarked in the Polish troopship *Batory* for passage to Gibraltar, where he received his first sea-going appointment as an officer: First Lieutenant of HMML 126, commanded by Lt GW Stead RNVR.

HMML 126 was a Fairmile motor launch and one of a flotilla of eight such craft that had been operating in the English Channel on anti-submarine patrols, which duty they continued to perform, criss-crossing the Straits of Gibraltar.

Enemy spies abounded in the Gibraltar area, and when ML 126 and a sister, 130, were selected

MLs 126 and 134 alongside at Malta, 1942.
(JN Barfield DSC)

to undergo a secret refit for what gave every evidence of being a cloak and dagger operation, false clues were scattered about, such as charts covering the West African route as far as Simon's Town.

In fact the MLs were bound for Malta, and they were given French and Italian ensigns in case they had to bluff their way through. They had been camouflaged to look like Italian ships and the crew were instructed to look as scruffy as possible!

Wearing the Italian ensign they passed along the North African coast, and were challenged in the process by a number of gun-sites and an inquisitive Italian float plane which dropped smoke floats but otherwise took no action. When they arrived at Kerkenna Island off Sfax they made for some hulks lying in the shallows about which Gibraltar Naval Intelligence had informed them and sheltered there for the remainder of the day, before making the final crossing to Malta by night. The 'hulks' turned out to be an entire convoy that had been destroyed by the guns of HM cruisers *Aurora* and *Penelope*.

There were Arabs on board the hulks helping themselves to whatever they could find. The naval party searched for documents, manifests and so on. In the holds they found nothing but burnt-out tanks and guns.

Wary of lurking Italian MTBs from the islands of Lampedusa and Linosa, the MLs were favoured by a heavy mist during their night crossing to Malta, where soon after arrival they had their first experience of the many air raids to which the George Cross Island was being subjected.

Once Barfield's two-ship flotilla had reached Malta safely, it was planned that others should follow from Gibraltar, sailing in pairs, until the entire 3rd Flotilla was grouped at Malta. Unfortunately MLs 129 and 132 sailed too early and were attacked by Italian aircraft. 129 blew up with severe loss of life, and ML 132 suffered engine-room damage. Survivors of 129 were interned in Bône, and so were the crew of 132 when she put into Bône for repairs, claiming the 24-hour stay permitted by international law. They derived some satisfaction on being told by their French captors that one of their attackers had been shot down and a second had force-landed on a beach nearby.

With the loss of MLs 129 and 132 there was little in the way of operations that the original pair could perform; so, having been ordered to vacate their ships during raids, they burrowed holes in the sandstone to provide accommodation for the crews. The men were in the habit of bathing from the ship's side until it was tabooed by the Vice-Admiral, Malta, who considered that, as a result of the bombing, the creeks had become polluted by damage to the sewerage system.

Air raid on Luqua Aerodrome, Malta, 1942. (JN Barfield DSC)

In April 1942 it was suspected that mines had been laid by Italian coastal forces, and despite the shortage of aviation fuel on the island MLs 129 and 132 were ordered to mount dusk-to-dawn sea patrols. On the third night ML 130 went out and was never seen again, although it was learned later that at least two wounded survived an action in which the ship had been blown up and half the crew were lost. Next day a fishing boat brought back a lifebelt. That ended those patrols.

At that time the submarines based on Malta were finding life trying because of minelaying by Italian small craft. Minesweepers were overburdened with work and decreasing in number, so with the discovery of surplus minesweeping gear in stores that had been used by motor boats and pinnaces in the 1914 – 18 war, the remaining ML was fitted out as a minesweeper with Lt Phillips RNR serving as instructor in the art.

On their first trial run to see if the gear was correctly calibrated there was a sudden terrific vibration along the wire, and a mine popped up to the surface! The gear had not even been properly rigged when, a little farther on, a second mine was cut. Phillips said: 'You have swept two mines. On our way back to harbour I will show you how to rig your kite and then you will need no further instruction from me!'

Now since she was neither an anti-submarine vessel nor an E-boat, 'The Asdic dome was removed and she was equipped with limited minesweeping gear. A ship with a compass, two officers and a ship's company with a sense of humour and a will to beat the Iti and the Hun at this game of sowing and reaping mines, we took on the role of minesweeper.'

Soon after that Lt Phillips' ship, the last of the minesweepers, was blown up by a mine, and he spent many months in plaster with a broken back. Meanwhile the 10th Submarine Flotilla had to be withdrawn from Malta, leaving the humble ML 120 with one lieutenant RCNVR and one sub-lieutenant RNVR(SA) as senior ship afloat under the command of Vice-Admiral, Malta!

Day after day ML 120 streamed her gear and swept the searched channel at a sedate 6 knots, and it was not long before they had notched up a total of fifty mines, all of the same type and obviously laid by Italian E-boats. The little ML continued her task whenever the weather was favourable and petrol stocks were adequate.

Then came the day when they had cut two mines and had a third tangled in the sweep gear when three enemy fighters dived at them and from a low-level altitude blazed away with machine guns. Fire was returned, but the fighters, except for one which had apparently been damaged, roared in from all angles. The ship still had the mine entangled in her gear and there was no alternative but to cut the precious sweep loose. In the meantime they scored another success and saw one of the attackers head for the horizon belching smoke.

Motor torpedo boat salvaged – but only just. (Fourie)

The wounded ML made her way back to harbour with remarkably little damage, although five ratings were treated for shrapnel wounds. The motor mechanic and his two stokers spent a few hours meticulously examining the engine-room for possible damage, and when the MM had finished he found that he couldn't sit down since his backside was peppered with shrapnel. Not until he arrived at the hospital did he show signs of shock! Sub-Lt Barfield had broken a bone in his right hand and was excused sea duty until the medics gave him the all clear.

June 29th was a great day for Malta when, almost down on her knees, the remains of a convoy arrived. Only four of the original twenty supply ships had got through. As part of the escort came the remainder of the 3rd ML Flotilla, MLs 121, 134, 135, 168. MLs 462, 459 arrived, too, as replacements for the interned 129 and 132. They all came equipped with minesweeping gear and spares, so obviously the Admiralty had been favourably impressed by the performance of 120 in her new and unaccustomed role.

Sub-Lt Barfield was now appointed Flotilla Minesweeping Officer, and his ML underwent a refit with the new equipment and then continued to serve as before, when weather and stocks of petrol permitted.

In a raid in June, apparently directed at the 3rd ML Flotilla, an unexploded 500-lb bomb dropped from a very low level; missed the berthed little ship's stern by a few yards, shot through a garage door and came to rest harmlessly against the rear wall of the garage.

There followed a busy period of minesweeping and escorting Malta-bound convoys and, on 30 January 1942, Barfield was promoted Lieutenant, and on 1 June that year, in common with all other SA RNVRs he was transferred to the SANF. Because of the higher rates of pay of the SANF his ship was promptly christened 'The Bullion Ship'.

In January 1943 the flotilla sailed for North Africa to sweep a channel from Homs to Tripoli. No mines were swept. However, they were fired upon by the 8th Army, who later apologised. It was at Tripoli that they encountered the *Gamtoos* busy clearing obstructions and were honoured by the presence of Winston Churchill, Montgomery and other top brass on board for a tour round the harbour. Churchill was asked by one of the seamen to autograph a Mussolini postcard and did so, scrawling his signature across the dictator's likeness with the comment, 'That will give him a nasty taste in the mouth, won't it?'

There followed many months of sweeping, patrolling, cloak and dagger operations and other duties between North Africa and Malta until the African campaign ended. Meanwhile Lt Barfield had been appointed to command of HMML 134. In the New Year Honours List for 1943 he was awarded a mention in despatches. His ship took part in the invasion of Sicily. While they were there a SAAF captain boarded from a RAF dinghy to collect Barfield's vote. Smuts was making certain that nobody escaped his civic responsibility.

ML 134 took part in the Italian landings and during an interlude in Capri met Lt-Cmdr Douglas Fairbanks Jnr, USN, who was most intrigued to find the MLs functioning as minesweepers and not as anti-submarine vessels.

On 1 October Naples fell and Barfield was told that he would be getting home leave. In the celebrations that followed he lost the port side of his carefully cultured beard! The voyage home from Port Said in a troopship was uneventful except that he shared a cabin with a man whom he never saw, although his baggage was in the cabin and the bunk had been slept in!

On returning to Durban after his leave in January 1944 he met a Miss Reilly, who later became headmistress of St Anne's Preparatory School at Hilton Road, and soon after they became engaged he was drafted to a troopship for return to the Mediterranean.

On a flight from Alexandria to Malta via Tripoli the plane touched down at Mersa Matruh, where he met his younger brother serving with the SAAF as an observer. Instead of Malta, he found his flotilla at Ischia Island on the north-west corner of Naples Bay. ML 126 had been hit by a circling torpedo and blown in half, surprisingly with no casualties.

Space precludes a detailed account of the operations described in Barfield's *My War 1939 – 45* which are of absorbing interest. They included training American minesweeping crews and the waging of marine warfare over the length and breadth of the Mediterranean. When hostilities ended he received congratulatory signals from senior officers and was asked to stay on. But home and his fiancée beckoned.

He took passage to Alexandria in a new frigate, arranged for his heavy luggage to be shipped home in a SA minesweeper and then waited in Cairo for a shuttle service flight to South Africa. He shared a tent with Captain FJ Dean, who later became Director of the SANF. Dean tried to persuade him to stay in the Navy, but Barfield had other ideas, and he was demobbed in Cape Town on 7 November 1945. He had fought an intense and demanding war and must have derived a great deal of satisfaction on opening the *Rand Daily Mail* of 30 January 1946 to learn that he had been awarded the Distinguished Service Cross.

He did not know the exact number of mines swept by the MLs in the Mediterranean, but he estimates it at something like five hundred. His own score was ninety-five.

★ ★ ★ ★ ★

Lt W Neilson. (W Neilson)

Another South African who saw his fair share of war in the Mediterranean was William Neilson of Port Elizabeth. He was born in Cape Town on 21 February 1921 and was educated at the Grey High School in Port Elizabeth. While he was there pupils were invited to choose one of the three services for ACF training after leaving school. He chose the Navy and in 1939 he received call-up papers to appear before a selection board at the RNVR base.

His appointment was approved and he underwent training at the Port Elizabeth base, then under the command of Lt-Cmdr Russell Paterson, with Lt Jack Rice as his First Lieutenant. Both were RNVR (SA) officers.

In January 1940 he began his war service as an Able Seaman attached to the office of the Naval Officer in Charge, Port Elizabeth, who at that time happened to be Commander DE St M Delius RN and whom, it may be remembered, was the first captain of HMSAS *Protea* on the formation of the original SA Naval Service in 1922.

His duties included coding and decoding signals, driving vehicles and generally acting as a courier for the delivery of documents and what-not. Later he was drafted to the heavy cruiser HMS *Shropshire* in Simon's Town to get sea-time as a prospective CW (Officer) candidate.

In October 1942 he was sent to the Royal Naval Training College HMS *Good Hope* at Seaview, Port Elizabeth, as a member of the first class to undergo training there. Of the twenty-eight officer candidates he passed out fourth and was commissioned as a Sub-Lieutenant in February 1943.

The next month he was posted to HMS *Stormwrack*, a magnetic and acoustic minesweeper then lying at Port Elizabeth. This ship, like so many others of her kind, was a converted whale-catcher; and after final refitting at East London and Durban she sailed for Port Said. On the way she encountered a severe storm in the Red Sea that lasted six days. The ship was flooded below decks, the galley was out of action, and they spent most of their time hanging on to stanchions on the bridge or upper deck!

After an extensive refit at Port Said, HMS *Stormwrack* began sweeping operations in the approaches to the port and in the Suez Canal, where the local people had reported seeing magnetic mines parachuted from enemy aircraft; but none was found.

The ship was then relieved of minesweeping duties and given the task of escorting small weekly convoys from Port Said to Haifa, Beirut, Tripoli, Turkey and Cyprus then back to Port Said.

In March 1944 *Stormwrack* was attached to HMS *Prometheus,* the minesweeping base at Alexandria. With the Allied forces now busy moving from North Africa to the Continent, the ship was sent to Piraeus in Greece to sweep mines in the Aegean Sea. Soon afterwards William was promoted Full Lieutenant and transferred to HMS *Cumbrae*, an Admiralty Scottish Isles-class minesweeper equipped for Orepesa sweeping of moored contact mines. Sweeping was carried out throughout Greek waters, and he remembers the valuable assistance given to his flotilla by the South African ships, which laid Dan buoys for them as they swept. It was while sweeping off Southern Greece that HMSAS *Bever* struck a mine and sank within a minute or two. Neilson's ship rescued seven survivors from a total crew of twenty-six.

In December 1944 they swept the Gulf of Salonika for moored mines while other ships searched for magnetic and acoustic mines. Many were found and destroyed. They then swept the approaches to Heraklion in Crete for the six weeks before V-E Day. There was a fourteen-thousand garrison of Germans still on Crete that had been cut off by the advance of the Allied forces into Europe.

On V-E Day the ship sailed into Suda Bay, in Crete, where Neilson introduced himself to some sullen German officers on the quayside. He then went on board one of the SA ships that had been laying Dans for them off Heraklion to thank her commanding officer, Lt H van Eyessen MBE, SANF.

In May 1945 the ship returned to Piraeus to help to put down the Communist rising in Greece. There they patrolled to Kavalla in the far north of Greece, stopping caiques and boarding them to check for arms and ammunition being smuggled to the rebel forces (ELAS, ELAN and KKE). If arms were found, the caique was seized and towed to Piraeus.

In Piraeus itself, rebels came down from the hills to attack the port, and HMS *Cumbrae* was ordered to stay in harbour and head them off

HMS *Cumbrae* – Lt Neilson's minesweeper in the Med. (W Neilson)

with her main armament, a 4-inch gun mounted for'ard. All other ships were ordered out to anchor in the roadstead. But Neilson found himself being mortared from behind a bombed-out power station, and so, being unable to respond, he withdrew to rejoin the rest of the flotilla outside. Much good-natured jeering came from the sister ships, which had been listening-in to his R/T reports to base HQ.

In September 1945 Lt Neilson was ordered to Alexandria for onward passage to South Africa and discharge. He had been invited by the Admiralty to remain with the RN for a further two years to conduct mine clearance operations, but he declined.

On his arrival at Alexandria he and another member of his flotilla, Lt Bryan Cross, RNVR, received letters from the Commander Mine-sweepers and Staff congratulating them upon 'the well-deserved honour bestowed upon us by His Majesty the King'. A few days later Lt Cross received the DSC but there was nothing in the bag for William Neilson, and all enquiries have drawn a blank. He did receive a mention in despatches, but that was during his time as a Sub-Lieutenant and had nothing to do with later more exciting experiences with the minesweeping flotilla during the last stages of the war in Europe.

He returned to South Africa in the *Carnarvon Castle* and was discharged at Simon's Town on 12 December 1945. William Neilson may have been disappointed at not receiving the DSC, but nevertheless he gained an impressive array of campaign medals. These included the 1939 – 45 Star, the Africa Star and clasp, the Italy Star, the Defence Medal, the British War Medal with oak-leaf clasp, the Africa Service Medal and the Efficiency Medal.

★ ★ ★ ★ ★

Mr WS Adams of Kimberley wonders why he was awarded the Burma Star. He *was* posted to Burma, but by the time he reached India the situation in Burma had deteriorated to such an extent that the posting fell away. His only contact with that theatre of war was joining an LCA flotilla that had just returned from Burma!

Stewart Adams joined the RNVR(SA) in January 1942 and after basic training did guard duty at the old Union Castle building in Cape Town docks which had been taken over by the RN, before being drafted to the Hunt-class destroyer HMS *Exmoor,* which had arrived *en route* to the Mediterranean and needed a hand. That was in April 1942, and he and a fellow OD, Roger Hartley, tossed a coin for the one vacancy. Stewart won, and a few weeks later found himself in the Mediterranean.

There was plenty of high-pressure work there: Malta convoys and an unsuccessful raid on Tobruk, in the course of which the destroyers *Sikh* and *Zulu,* the AA cruiser HMS *Coventry* and a couple of others were lost. They were operational pretty well continuously, and they even did a spot of coastal bombardment to back up the El Alamein offensive.

He returned to South Africa in January 1943 and did an officers' qualifying course at HMS *Good Hope* in Port Elizabeth and with one other he was retained to do an extra navigational course. They were told that they were being sent to Burma. The reason was unspecified, but they suspected that perhaps it was thought that they could help the army to find its way out!

When they arrived at Bombay in a troopship they found that the posting was impracticable, and Stewart was appointed to No 1 LCA Flotilla. For a couple of months he lived in great luxury in a sea-front flat backing on to the Cricket Club of India, the Bombay equivalent of Kelvin Grove!

In December 1943 the flotilla was hoisted on board the Bibby liner *Derbyshire* and sailed for Naples, where they were worked-up for the Anzio landing which took place in January 1944.

There followed a spell of trooping in the Mediterranean, enjoying the relative luxury of *Derbyshire*'s first-class passenger accommodation, most of which was shared by the twelve officers under full peacetime conditions, being served by a lascar crew and Goanese stewards.

On one voyage they carried a large proportion of the SA 6th Division to Italy. Stewart put up a notice inviting any ODs in for a drink, and from that there evolved an OD deck-hockey team. There was another South African in the flotilla, G Pedlar from Matatiele.

The flotilla was next hoisted into several merchant ships and RN auxiliaries including HM ships *Glengyle, Keren, Brassard* and *Royal Scotsman*. That was followed by a long spell in a camp in an idyllic setting in Corsica, working up for a planned landing on Elba.

It was a well-defended action in June 1944, during which Stewart's flotilla landed Free French African troops. They were Goums, 'clad in dressing gowns – a fearsome bunch who soon had the German garrison looking for whites to surrender to.'

More Mediterranean cruising in *Derbyshire*; then came the landings in the South of France. Stewart's flotilla went in at St Tropez, which apart from a few air attacks was virtually undefended.

That was in August 1944, and after it the flotilla was sent to the United Kingdom, where they arrived in September, having in their wanderings lost their No 1 flotilla status and were now renumbered 573!

After some well-earned leave came a great deal of exercising with Combined Operations units, largely run by the Royal Marines. The flotilla was split up, and Stewart was drafted to a new type of landing craft, LCN, fitted with every known navigational device to ensure pinpoint landfalls for future assault landings.

They were then moved up to HMS *James Cook*, a remote base in the west of Scotland to which the only access was by sea. There they had an intensive work-up, and their only neighbours were a two-man submarine group doing the same.

But once again their off-duty hours were spent in luxurious surroundings, in a castle placed at their disposal.

Stewart 'made the tactical error of annexing the commanding officer's girl friend [the administration staff were Wrens and Wren officers] and he retaliated by sending me off on every possible course to get me out of the way – Tropical Hygiene, Underwater Demolition, Breaking and Entry – you name it, I did it!'

By that time V-E Day had come and gone, and they were told that they were to go East to lead assaults on islands held by the Japanese. But here too they were foiled by the dropping of the atomic bomb. There followed the inevitable waiting to see what would happen next, and lectures to potential immigrants. At last it was back to Cape Town by troopship in time for Christmas 1945, and out of uniform in February.

Stewart Adams sums up his war service thus: 'I think I was lucky in having more comfort and luxury than some.' Many would agree, but it is obvious that he has played down the beach landings, which were, to use an expression of the time, 'Operation Fraught'.

CHAPTER

18

Some Notable Wartime Personalities

A man who became something of a legend in his own lifetime was the late Vice-Admiral James ('Flam') Johnson, SSA,SM,DSC,KSt J, SAN (Retd), former Chief of the South African Navy.

Flam, as he was always affectionately called, was born on 10 February 1918. He left Potchefstroom Boys' High School in December 1932, having matriculated at the tender age of fourteen, and joined the training ship *General Botha* in January 1933.

He left the ship two years later having completed his course with distinction, and became a cadet with the prestigious P & O line. He was also made a Midshipman, Royal Naval Reserve.

In 1937 his cadet training was interrupted when he reported to the Royal Navy and joined the battleship HMS *Nelson*. In *Nelson* and *Fearless* he took part in watching the course of events in the Spanish Civil War.

On the outbreak of hostilities in 1939 he was called up for full-time service and appointed Assistant Navigating Officer to the cruiser HMS *York* serving in the North and South Atlantic, Norway, and the Mediterranean. He survived the sinking of HMS *York* in March 1941 off Crete.

He made his way across enemy-occupied Crete, hiding in olive groves by day and marching by night, and was taken off by the cruiser HMS *Orion* in which he had a dangerous passage to Alexandria, being constantly attacked by aircraft and suffering serious damage.

There had been so many ships sunk that the rest camps in Egypt were crowded with survivors who had nothing much to do but swat flies. That did not suit Flam who was thoroughly bored, and he called on the Captain of the Fleet at Alexandria and volunteered for 'anything that was going'. Old sailors will always tell you never to volunteer. Perhaps Flam should have heeded this advice, for he was appointed to the command of a broken-down Admiralty tug whose task it was to pick up lighters of ammunition and supplies towed by destroyers and berth them at Tobruk, occasionally doing the towing himself along the stretch known as Bomb Alley between Alexandria and Tobruk. The harbour at Tobruk was littered with wrecks and during air raids his tug would shelter under the lee of one of them.

Vice-Admiral James Johnson. (Mrs Johnson)

After six months of that he was returned to Alexandria for a break and transferred as Executive Officer to a small tanker, *Toneline*, whose Merchant Navy crew had flatly refused to go back to Tobruk. Air attacks were constant and once when, they were being escorted by HMSAS *Protea* (Lt JK Mallory), a torpedo was seen coming straight for his ship. He yelled to the bridge, blocked his ears and froze. To his astonishment the torpedo porpoised, dived, missed the ship by inches, reappeared and headed for *Protea*. Flam would never forget seeing the bright yellow nose of that torpedo.

His ship was employed in transporting high-octane petrol to Tobruk, and when attacked by bombers off Mersa Matruh a shell splinter penetrated the ship's side and emerged through the upper deck, miraculously without sparking off their highly dangerous cargo.

After nine months of an extremely dicey existence on his little tanker he was relieved at the news that Rommel had captured Tobruk! He was then transferred from the Mediterranean and took passage to Durban in the troopship *Mauretania*, which was crowded with Polish troops. On arrival they were greeted with the news that they were to be transferred to Oribi camp at Pietermaritzburg and put in quarantine for three weeks. When the quarantine was over he managed to wangle a few days' leave.

His next posting was to Liverpool in the *Durban Castle*. On arrival he spent two or three months doing intensive anti-submarine courses, and he realised that there were actually two wars, anti-aircraft in the Mediterranean and anti-submarine in the Atlantic.

Flam's next appointment (he was by then Lieutenant RNR) was to the brand-new frigate HMS *Jed* commanded by Lt-Cmdr RC Freaker RNR, an officer of the Blue Star line who, after the famous anti-U-boat ace Captain FJ Walker, RN, was the next most successful anti-submarine officer. Freaker, who had sunk nine U-boats, held a double DSO, a double DSC, and the Polar Medal for service in Antarctica in the research ship *William Scoresby*.

Like all new frigates *Jed* underwent the rigorous training pro-gramme at Tobermory under the renowned 'Monkey' Stephenson and then she set off for the Battle of the Atlantic. Of the nine U-boats sunk by Freaker, Flam shared in three of the successes. One U-boat that they stalked on the surface was sent to the bottom. Seventeen of her crew, including the captain, were rescued. Flam described them as being 'jolly good chaps'. The submarine captain was given the run of the ward-room, and one afternoon on coming off watch Flam found him studying the *Illustrated London News, Sphere,* and other glossy maga-zines. The German looked up with a grin. 'They're really pulling the wool over your eyes in England aren't they?' he said.

Flam served in *Jed* until the Atlantic war ended and was then transferred to the East Indies Squadron, taking passage from Colombo to Durban in the aircraft-carrier *Ameer* in which he was appointed to the command of the corvette *Rose Bay*. In her, and later in HMS *Verbena*, he was occupied in seeking out Japanese submarines in the Indian Ocean, without in the event ever seeing one.

The Japanese war ended, and Flam steamed his *Verbena* back to the United Kingdom via a now peaceful Mediterranean and so to Milford

Haven to pay off. But for him active service had not quite ended. Appointed to command HM landing ship (tanks) 416, and now with the rank of Acting Lieutenant-Commander, he shuttled between Chatham, Sheerness and Antwerp recovering damaged vehicles and tanks and generally clearing up the debris of war. Finally, six months after the war ended, and having been awarded the DSC, he returned to South Africa in the troopship *Alcantara* and in 1946 he joined the South African Navy, dropping a rank to do so. He soon regained it and his subsequent naval career was a record of success.

★ ★ ★ ★ ★

Lt Victor P de Kock, MBE, DSC
The Most Decorated War Hero in the South African Navy

There always seems to be some controversy about the award of decorations for valour. No one would grudge such recognition to those so favoured, but of course there were innumerable acts of bravery that were unrewarded by any official recognition.

During the war it was generally accepted that the British were far more liberal in their distribution of honours than those who controlled the destinies of South African forces. For example, of the four South African winners of the Victoria Cross in the Second World War, three were seconded to British forces. They undoubtedly deserved that supreme honour; but surely there were others no less deserving, yet who were overlooked by a certain diffidence on the part of their commanders?

Victor P de Kock MBE, DSC, as seaman. (SANMMH)

If this was indeed the case then perhaps the most-decorated SA naval hero should have been entitled to even higher distinction.

Lt Victor Pieter de Chatillon de Kock was the only officer in the SA Naval Forces to win three awards for gallantry during the last great war. They were all earned while he was serving with the Royal Navy. Because of his secondment, there is little information concerning his naval career in the SADF Archives. Fortunately, however, some letters, an incomplete diary, his photograph albums and press cuttings were preserved by his brother, Mr PH de C de Kock, and it is through these and other sources that it has been possible to compile the following account.

Victor de Kock was born on 1 August 1919 and educated at Caledon and Graaff-Reinet. In Caledon his favourite recreation was scouting, and Mr Pieter de Kock recalls that the Scoutmaster, Mr Rodney McGregor, 'imbued the boys with a lively sense of adventure and a fine responsible outlook.' After sitting his matric Victor joined the SA Reserve Bank in Port Elizabeth in 1938, and in the next fateful year was transferred to Cape Town.

South Africa declared war on Germany on 6 September 1939, and on 27 October 1939 Victor de Kock joined the Royal Naval Volunteer Reserve (SA Division) as an Ordinary Seaman.

On 15 March 1940, after service in the RNVR base and at the Castle and the SA Naval Service HQ, he was drafted to HMS *Shropshire*, a London-class cruiser. By June 1941 no fewer than 143 South African ratings had served in that particular ship. The personal adventures of some others are recorded in these pages. One, Lt DR Stephens, says that Victor encouraged him and a number of his shipmates to join Combined Operations.

In 1940 he was transferred to the Royal Navy barracks at Chatham with a view to selection for a temporary commission. He was accepted, passed all the qualifying courses and was commissioned as a Temporary Sub-Lieutenant on 1 November 1940. On 27 December he was appointed to HMS *Glenearn*, a fast 10 000 ton cargo liner converted into a combined operations assault ship. By 31 January 1941 she was bound in convoy for the Middle East via the Cape, together with three other big ships and an escort of six destroyers.

On 1 March 1941 *Glenearn* reached Suez and three days later anchored in the Great Bitter Lakes opposite Fanara, where all the troops were disembarked.

Training with the troops followed. Sub-Lt de Kock commanded a fifty-foot MLC (landing craft mechanised Mk1) with a displacement of 25 tons. Like the others he soon discovered that there were compensations for the irritation of sandstorms and prickly heat in the form of picnicking, aquaplaning and swimming. It proved to be a pleasant interlude in the hardships of war.

Three weeks later, on 28 March, 'on a night hop in hellish weather', he lost the fourth finger of his left hand while trying to put fenders over the boat's side. The MLC broke adrift and was only recovered and towed in an hour later.

By the middle of the following month he was again fit for duty, but he declared himself fed-up when a raid on Bardia was cancelled because the weather was considered too rough for landing craft.

Germany invaded Greece on 6 April, and by the 21st the main Greek army had been surrounded and forced to surrender. The Greek Government, realising that further resistance would be impossible, now requested that the British, Australian and New Zealand forces should be withdrawn.

Accordingly *Glenearn* sailed in convoy on 24 April to help in taking off soldiers from Nauplia Beach in Morea. While they were on passage the ship was struck by bombs dropped from two Heinkels, but her landing craft escaped damage. At Nauplia the *Ulster Prince* grounded and blocked the entrance to the harbour, which made use of the MLCs more important and urgent than ever.

De Kock's MLC (MLC 10) which was overloaded with up to 8 to 10 men during the evacuation of Crete. (SANMMH)

Fortunately the sea remained very calm, and Lt de Kock took off nearly two hundred men on each trip. *Glenearn* reached Crete safely the following afternoon and returned to Greece next morning. Although the convoy had been seen by enemy aircraft as early as noon, no attack developed until the sun was setting at about 1800 when Junkers 87 and 88 dived on the ships from a high altitude.

Although *Glenearn* survived the attack, a thousand-pound bomb that had narrowly missed the ship exploded alongside, holed her starboard plating and flooded the engine-room. HMS *Griffin* was detached to tow *Glenearn* back to Alexandria, and her landing craft were lowered and ordered to make for the beach at Monemvasia. By then the swell was heavy and the small craft were about thirty sea miles from the land.

When they managed to reach their destination it took some time to find suitable hiding places. They remained until 0400 the following morning, then sailed farther up the coast.

After lying low for another day, two of the three landing craft (No 10 – Sub-Lt de Kock; No 11 Sub-Lt Lloyd) made contact with the army on the evening of 28 April and began ferrying troops from the beach to offlying destroyers and the cruiser HMS *Ajax*. A period of furious activity followed, and the ALCs were overloaded with up to eighty men per trip. These assault craft, 25 feet in length and with a displacement of eight tons, were designed to carry forty-five!

When the troops had all been taken off Lt de Kock returned to make sure that Lt-Cmdr Best (later Cmdre DSO, RNR), who commanded the *Glenearn*'s landing craft, had not been left behind. The ALC ran aground and, when boathooks failed to shove her off, Lt de Kock and a man called Somerville jumped into the water and bodily pushed her clear.

The ALC then went alongside HMS *Ajax* and the crew removed most of their gear. The ALCs should then have been blown up, but the ships were too dangerously exposed to risk further delay. Lt de Kock returned to Crete sleeping the sleep of utter exhaustion on the deck of *Ajax*. From Crete the ALC crews were returned to Alexandria.

In the weeks that followed Lt de Kock was drafted first to HMS *Glenroy* and then, on 28 May, to HMS *Glengyle*. He was bitterly disappointed at being separated from two of his friends (Mike and Hank) who were drafted to the Australian cruiser HMAS *Perth*.

He was amused to learn that he and three others had been recommended by Lt-Cmdr Best for the Distinguished Service Cross for their services in Greece.

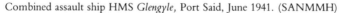

Combined assault ship HMS *Glengyle*, Port Said, June 1941. (SANMMH)

Next night he played an important part in the evacuation of Crete. Assisted by two MLCs from HMAS *Perth*, the MLCs from HMS *Glengyle* ferried over six thousand troops from Sphakia beach to the ships by 0320 on 30 May. *Glengyle* and the seven warships that had accompanied her then sailed, leaving three landing craft behind.

The crews of these craft were ordered to hide in caves until 2000 the following night when, so they were told, they would be taken off. When the time came, however, De Kock was told to lie low for another day or two, with the somewhat demoralising message that there was no guarantee that they would be taken off at all!

On 31 May he received the following handwritten order, which has survived among his papers:

'Request you proceed at once to Franko-Kastelli to report on beach there which may be used for evacuation. There are reports of offlying dangers there. Please give your report to Lt Cox RM. Also report on the anchorage there for destroyers or other transports.'

His worst fears concerning the perilous nature of the mission were soon realised and he later wrote that his MLC and crew were 'bombed and machine-gunned by enemy aircraft which kept up a continuous patrol. About three miles off the town the enemy opened fire from shore . . . they kept this up for quite a time hitting my boat several times.'

The beach and anchorage proved unsuitable, and it was only by great good fortune, narrowly avoiding two low-flying Stukas, that De Kock's MLC returned safely to the caves.

Lt de Kock ferried about 1 500 to 2 000 servicemen to the ships, but later reported that the three MLCs at Sphakia beach could have evacuated another 3 000 if the organisation on the beach had been better. The other two MLCs were commanded by Lt JH McDowell and Lt GA Dixon.

At 2030 on 1 June, De Kock and his crew flooded all tanks and smashed the engines of their MLC before boarding the fast minelayer HMS *Abdiel* in which vessel they returned to Alexandria.

De Kock was later rewarded with a mention in despatches 'for outstanding Gallantry, Fortitude and Resolution during the Battle of Crete'.

On the morning of 7 June 1941, he collected a newly arrived assault landing craft and at noon the same day sailed for Syria, where commandos were to be landed. When the surf proved to be too dangerous the operation was abandoned. After a well-deserved break on shore he was then given command of A17, an A lighter (tank landing craft Mk1 – length 150 feet, displacement 350 tons and speed 10 knots).

By the end of June 1941 the cost in losses and unserviceability of escorts protecting convoys to Tobruk had become unacceptably high and it was decided to replace them with eight A lighters working in pairs.

De Kock sailed on his first Tobruk run on 6 August, his crew having been augmented by four South African anti-aircraft gunners lent to give extra protection against enemy aircraft. His account of their experiences on the Tobruk Run show how lucky he and the crew of his tank landing craft were to have survived the ordeal.

The normal complement of these A lighters was two officers and twelve ratings. They have been described by those who had the misfortune to sail in them as the most uncomfortable craft afloat. On the credit side it was thought that their buoyancy tanks made them virtually unsinkable, but the cold fact is that five of the ten such vessels employed on the Tobruk Run were sunk.

The slow speed of the A lighters, 10 knots, was greatly reduced in adverse weather, and their proneness to engine breakdowns made them easy targets for enemy aircraft. Their fuel tanks carried eight thousand gallons of 87-octane petrol, and besides the vulnerability of their slow speed and highly volatile fuel, there was the even greater danger of their cargoes, which usually included ammunition and petrol.

The following entries in De Kock's diary give some idea of conditions over this period:

10 August 1941. One thousand pounder landed on the jetty (at Tobruk) not ten feet away from the ship – buckled ship's side – what a shaking! Fortunately it landed in soft earth.

17 August. Everything all right until about 1930 when thirteen Junkers 87 attacked us. I had five near misses all round us.

11 September. Attack by single Junkers 88. Dropped nine light bombs (delayed action), landed ahead of us and as we went over them they exploded. Shook starboard engine off its bed. Also machine-gunning.

15 September. Both engines stopped ... *Southern Sea* towed us until 1520, when we managed to get one working.

On 17 October while HMS *Gnat*, A13, A18 and A17 (De Kock) were on passage, a torpedo was fired at A18. It missed and passed just ahead of A17 causing the two landing craft to collide. Fortunately neither suffered damage.

Three days later he was relieved to write that it had been decided to take them off the Tobruk Run altogether. 'I think we were all very pleased.' In fact the news was premature, for on 30 November A17 was to sail in convoy to Tobruk yet again.

At 0900 on 27 December 1941 Convoy TA6 sailed from Alexandria. Besides the A lighters A13 and A17, the convoy was protected by a destroyer screen and a corvette. At 0250 the next morning the store carrier *Volo* was torpedoed off Sidi Barrani by the German submarine U-559. As De Kock wrote later, 'She went down in three minutes. Terrific flash and explosion.'

While the convoy escorts frantically hunted the submarine the rest of the convoy sailed on, with A17 remaining behind until nearly 0600 searching for survivors. While they were so engaged, Able Seaman RW Knott dived over the side and rescued the second officer of the *Volo*, whose leg had been broken. Sub-Lt Pullen likewise dived overboard to rescue a seaman struggling in the water. De Kock reported that A17 had picked up eleven of *Volo*'s crew.

'For courage, determination and fine seamanship in rescuing men from a torpedoed merchant ship in a lighter when the weather was rough and the enemy near', Lt de Kock was awarded the MBE.

On 5 January 1942, A115, A111 and De Kock's A17 sailed for Tobruk again escorted this time by HMSAS *Protea*. On a night that was 'so darn dark we couldn't see the bows' A17 narrowly escaped being rammed by a Greek destroyer.

By the end of May 1942 De Kock guessed that the fall of Tobruk was imminent, and he confided his fears to Lt (now Cmdr) Charles Curtis, pointing out that his cargo on the return voyage had changed from wrecked motor transport for cannibalisation to 3,7-inch heavy anti-aircraft guns and their crews. His fears were justified when Tobruk, by then no longer the fortress that it had once been, fell on 21 June. From 11 July to 25 October 1941 the ten A lighters had carried 2 800 tons of stores, forty-eight heavy and seven light tanks and an unknown number of guns and vehicles from Alexandria to Tobruk.

Later that year Lt de Kock and another SANF officer seconded to the Royal Navy, Sub-Lt AH Crossley of Durban, joined the Combined Operations Pilotage Parties. This elite naval commando unit was established to carry out dangerous missions, which included the collection of vital information needed by the planners of amphibious landings.

Although he arrived a little late for the commando course, De Kock soon demonstrated that he could 'outdistance and outstay the rest of the officers quite easily'. Great emphasis was placed on the handling of collapsible two-man canoes, and of course members were required to

De Kock's collapsible canoe. (SANMMH)

assemble them in the dark in stormy conditions, right them when they capsized and paddle them at speed for considerable distances.

The course included parachute-jumping, and the demands of that led to a temporary ban on alcoholic drinks. To solve that problem Lt de Kock invited other members of his course to tea in his tent (named South Africa House) every evening. These tea parties were a great success.

His last task was to carry out a survey of the southernmost tip of Sicily with Sub-Lt Crossley, Lt Davies and Ordinary Seaman McGuire, to obtain information for the planners of the invasion. They were taken in to the beach in the U-class submarine *Unrivalled*. De Kock and Crossley paddled inshore alone on 7 March 1943 and were never seen again. Three of the others taking part in the beach reconnaissance elsewhere in Sicily were killed, and Davies and McGuire were captured. Two failed to rendezvous with HM Submarine *United* and paddled their flimsy craft all the way to Malta!

Lt SL Amsden who knew Lt de Kock well, described him as an officer 'who inspired devotion among the most miscellaneous collection of men thrown together in Greece, Crete, and in the heartbreak of Tobruk; generally in the most wretched conditions and who had extended his will when those under him could see nothing ahead.'

He was well thought of by his superiors also. Capt RKC Pope RN, wrote, 'You have always done consistently well and kept a fighting spirit among our chaps.' Commander JW Best DSO RNR, in a letter congratulating De Kock on being awarded the DSC wrote, 'I cannot remember one that I consider better deserved.'

De Kock, Crossley and those who followed them into Combined Operations established the amphibious fighting tradition of the South African Navy. The fact that Victor Pieter de Chatillon de Kock earned three awards for gallantry at the age of twenty-three while seconded to the Royal Navy makes his achievements all the more impressive.

★ ★ ★ ★ ★

Chief Petty Officer R Sethren, CGM

René Sethren, a Transvaaler from Johannesburg, joined the Seaward Defence Force as a stoker in 1940. In those early days of the war the personnel of our naval force consisted of a thin sprinkling of professional Royal Naval officers mostly pulled out of comfortable retirement. They were backed up by RN men on secondment and members of the RNR and RNVR (SA). But by far the largest number of volunteers were ordinary civilians eager to take part in what was to be the greatest adventure of their entire lives.

One of those was René Sethren. He was educated at Springs English-medium school and had served as a gunner in the pre-war

Special Service Battalion which had been established by the then somewhat controversial Minister of Defence, Oswald Pirow. His object was to provide an opening for young men who had been hard hit by the unemployment caused by the Great Depression of the 1930s. It was probably the best thing that Pirow did in his entire political career.

Chief Petty Officer R Sethren CGM. (SANMMH)

In a less professional sphere Sethren was making something of a name for himself as an amateur boxer. He was, in fact, a good all-round sportsman. He was highly disciplined, intelligent, and dedicated to the Navy.

Shortly after his initial training he was promoted to Leading Stoker. At that time the young Navy had only a certain number of converted trawlers and whale-catchers, the former used mainly on minesweeping duties while the whale-catchers were earmarked for anti-submarine operations for which they were well suited.

At first they worked only off the South African and South West African coasts but when Italy entered the war the situation changed.

When the four modern whale-catchers, the 'Southerns', were earmarked for the Mediterranean, carefully selected crews were appointed; and among those joining *Southern Isles* was René Sethren.

The four 'Southerns' sailed from Durban on 15 December 1940 under the command of Lt–Cmdr AF Trew (later to make a name for himself as a novelist) as the 22nd Anti-Submarine Group of the Mediterranean Fleet. The passage to Alexandria, with calls at Mombasa and Aden, was a useful opportunity for conducting concentrated evolutions and for the training of the largely inexperienced crews. It soon became obvious, even at that early stage, that Sethren would turn out to be a most useful member of the ship's company. Without fail he was always 'calm, cool and collected', no matter what the circumstances. He learned quickly and soon displayed marked qualities of leadership.

With René Sethren in *Southern Isles* there were two other keen amateur boxers, Sub-Lieutenant Ribbink and Petty Officer 'Paddy' Mooney.

Sethren was the right type of man to be trained as a reserve machine-gunner and by the time the little ships had reached Alexandria he was able to carry out this extra duty with confidence and, as will be shown, with great courage.

Very soon the 'Southerns' were in the thick of things, escorting convoys and patrolling the Libyan coast. Very soon, too, the crews became skilful fighting men with more than enough action to round off any rough edges.

A month after their arrival in the Mediterranean the flotilla, now part of the Inshore Squadron, lost its first ship when, as has been told elsewhere, HMSAS *Southern Floe* struck a mine and foundered with the loss of all but one man.

Until the fall of Tobruk when the remaining 'Southerns' reinforced their armament with captured Italian anti-aircraft weapons and machine guns, the ships had been inadequately armed for the part that they were called upon to play. Even so, the twin Lewis guns on the fo'c'sle head were kept and Sethren was detailed as reserve crew for the port Lewis.

The Tobruk Run, Bomb Alley or Hell's Alley as it was variously called by the press, and in even stronger terms by those who endured its misery, was an exhausting, action-packed voyage. Practically all the fighting was against German and Italian aircraft and at times Allied air support scarcely existed.

René Sethren was awarded the Conspicuous Gallantry Medal. He was the only South African to receive it for his great courage in one of these actions. The citation for this very rare decoration – since 1855 only 243 have been issued – describes his gallantry:

'For his steadfast bearing when HMSAS *Southern Isles* was attacked by an enemy aircraft which machine-gunned the deck. Though eleven times wounded, he stood to his gun and turned a steady fire on the aircraft until it fell in flames into the sea.'

That is only the bare bones. Lt Louis Ribbink, who was also serving in *Southern Isles* (and who himself was awarded the Distinguished Service Cross) takes up the story:

On 29 June 1941, 'being in all respects ready to engage the enemy', we sailed from Mersa Matruh for Tobruk with HMS *Flamingo,* an anti-aircraft sloop, convoying SS *Antiklea* and SS *Miranda*. Also in the convoy was HMS *Cricket*, a China river-gunboat that was going to bombard a German battery which shelled ships entering or leaving Tobruk harbour; the Afrika Korps having taken over the port.

The following day, 30 June, we intercepted a signal from HMAS *Waterhen*, which had been hit near Tobruk and was under tow by HMS *Defender*. We knew that our convoy would also be receiving considerable attention. At 1350 came the first attack on us by about eight Stukas.

From then on we were under frequent attack and at 1630 between forty and fifty enemy planes launched a determined assault. A stick of bombs fell just ahead of us and the ship plunged into the water crater, washing the fo'c'sle gun's crew down on to the foredeck. The bridge had been set on fire but our dousing quickly extinguished that.

Then the casualties began and Sethren was rushed up to replace the men on the twin Lewis. We shot one Ju-88 down, and *Cricket* and *Flamingo* were also scoring, but the convoy was suffering. *Cricket* was hit and *Miranda* and *Flamingo* were damaged by near misses.

With Leading Seaman Tillis, I manned the 4-inch gun, the original crew all being casualties. Our starboard 20mm jammed and bullets were flying everywhere. We saw yet another Stuka going down and then a Ju-88 flew in at us, just above sea-level, machine-gunning as he came.

I saw Sethren go down in a welter of blood and shouted to him: 'Get up and fight your gun.' The Ju-88 was inside the fuse setting of the 4-inch gun so we had to wait for him to come very near in the hope of a direct hit. Somehow Sethren dragged himself up to his gun and went on firing at the roar of the 88. We fired the 4-inch at the last minute and scored a very lucky hit on his port engine. Suddenly the attack was over and the skies were clear. I was the only unwounded man on the fo'c'sle.

We carried Sethren and the other wounded men down below and I was sure that Sethren would die. The citation said he was hit by eleven bullets; we attended to twenty-seven wounds in one arm, both legs and his side. How he climbed that machine-gun stand and went on firing I shall never know. Just before dark he recovered consciousness and asked me to write to his mother for him; 'But sir,' he pleaded, 'please don't make it sound too bad.'

We transferred our wounded to *Flamingo*, which, although badly damaged, took *Cricket* in tow and returned safely to Alexandria. The convoy limped in with our ship towing *Miranda*, and arrived at Tobruk in heavy shelling the next morning.

I went to see Sethren in hospital in Alexandria and wrote a second letter to his mother telling her that René's main regret was that his boxing days were over which, he said, would please her no end!

René Sethren never went to sea again, but he remained in uniform for another two years. Between surgical operations he trained others. He was always very modest about his CGM.

In 1943 the Navy released him from service because of the constant attention that his wounds demanded, and continued to demand. For twenty-five years after the day of the fateful action he was still undergoing surgery for the removal of splinters and what he called 'patching up'.

He is gone now; but he should be remembered as a very gallant gentleman.

★ ★ ★ ★ ★

Lt DR Stephens DSC
Dieppe, D-Day and the Rhine Crossing

It really is remarkable how young men, drawn from all walks of life and attracted to the Royal Naval Volunteer Reserve, adapted themselves to their new calling and left their mark in the annals of the war at sea.

Lt DR Stephens DSC, who took part in the Dieppe raid, D-Day and the Rhine crossing. (SANMMH)

Such a one was Dennis Rupert Stephens who joined the RNVR at the Castle in Cape Town in 1935. So well did he acquit himself that only a year later, on 29 August 1936, he was recommended for future appointment to commissioned rank and rated able seaman the following day. Before the outbreak of war he underwent the customary training periods, which included sea-going experience in the Falmouth-class minesweeping sloop HMS *Milford*.

In November 1939 Dennis Stephens volunteered for full-time war service and reported to the Castle on 1 March 1940. On 9 May, together with another wartime hero, Alfred Winship, whose story will also be told in these pages, he was drafted to the heavy cruiser HMS *Shropshire*.

He remained in *Shropshire* until he joined the armed merchant cruiser HMS *Moreton Bay* for passage to the United Kingdom. On arrival there he was drafted to the shore base, HMS *Victory*, before being transferred to HMS *King Alfred* to undergo officer training. On 10 January 1941 he put up the single wavy stripe of a Sub-Lieutenant RNVR.

By that time a Directorate of Combined Operations had been established in July 1940 by the Prime Minister, Mr Winston Churchill, and Sub-Lt Stephens had the distinction of being among the first South Africans to serve with this élite company.

Having been accepted, he was first appointed to HMS *Tormentor,* a Combined Operations shore base at Warash, a village on the Hamble River. (As a matter of interest the ship's badge of an earlier *Tormentor* represented the common flea as its centrepiece. The Lords Commissioners of the Admiralty were not greatly pleased.)

At HMS *Tormentor* training took place in the waters of the Solent and the English Channel on the use of various types of landing craft. Dennis Stephens and a colleague, John Lewis of East London, were sent first to Newhaven and then to Shoreham on air – sea rescue duties for about three months. Then Stephens was sent back to *Tormentor* to train infantrymen in preparation for reconnaissance raids on the French coast. The first of them ended in disaster, but there was nothing unduly eventful about later raids.

Training and preparation for the great Dieppe raid was then begun and in January 1942 Sub-Lt Stephens was promoted Lieutenant and appointed Flotilla Officer of the 2nd LC Flotilla (Personnel). In August 1942, when it was decided to attack Dieppe, he carried No 3 Commando, whose job it would be to subdue the heavy batteries to the east of Dieppe harbour, while Lord Lovat's commando would do the same to the west.

The commando set off to the skirl of pipes, and by midnight, as Lt Stephens' flotilla was passing through the swept channel about seven or eight miles from the French coast, they were illuminated by star-shells fired by German trawlers inshore of their position.

The Germans then very quickly set about wrecking and destroying the vulnerable landing craft, and in a mere ten minutes they had succeeded in putting the escorting gunboat out of action.

Stephens rounded up what was left of his flotilla and set course for Dieppe, where they arrived off their allocated beach in broad daylight and proceeded under heavy fire to land the commando and beach party.

After withdrawing from the beach the craft again came under fire from coast batteries farther to the east. This decided them to close the beach again, but once more they ran into a barrage of mortar and heavy machine-gun fire, which forced them to keep on the move.

When Lt Stephens closed the beach again to pick up survivors he found only the beach party remaining. The next move was to go to the main Dieppe beaches and help take off soldiers. When that was done, they returned safely to Newhaven about 1900, seven out of the original flotilla of twelve landing craft having been lost.

For gallantry, daring and skill in the combined attack on Dieppe Stephens was decorated with the DSC on 2 October 1942. When he returned to HMS *Tormentor* he embarked on a training programme in preparation for the big one: D-Day.

In May, despite professing an earnest desire to return to general service, he was again appointed Commanding Officer of the 2nd Landing Craft Flotilla, which was then being converted into a fleet of smoke-makers. A tank containing CSA was fitted in the troop space and a pipe was laid aft along the deck to the stern, where it curved up for about three and a half feet and ended in a fine spray nozzle. Acid was forced out under air pressure and on contact with the air it formed dense clouds of whitish-grey smoke. With about twelve craft pumping out this mixture the resultant screen was very effective.

But it was wicked stuff to work with for everything had to be done in a confined space and of course the ratings generally ignored standing orders on the wearing of protective clothing. As long as the wind blew from ahead to just abaft the beam, everything was fine. But when an alteration of course was suddenly made, and the flow was not stopped, everybody got a blast of the concentrated acid; which was pretty painful.

In September 1943 the flotilla operated out of Dover in company with fleet sweepers which were gradually sweeping a cleared channel towards Boulogne. On D-Day the flotilla would be responsible for smoke-screening the anchorage at Sword beach and for looking after the Duplex-drive tanks after they had been launched from their tank-landing craft (TLCs). The flotilla did a great deal of training with these tanks, mainly at night to preserve security.

It had been decided, in the interests of fuel conservation, that the flotilla should be towed across the Channel; and so on 5 June they moved into the Solent and joined the TLC carrying the tanks. Being towed by those wallowing monsters was no joke as there was a heavy following sea and the speed of the TLCs was about five knots. As a result the lighter craft overran the towing vessel and then had to fall back till the tow-line tightened again. That resulted in a sudden jerk, often severe enough almost to dislocate one's neck.

The flotilla arrived off Sword beach (the extreme left flank of the landings) at dawn and took charge of their tanks, together with an LCA (landing craft assault) fitted with a coiled hose, which was supposed to be shot over the beach by means of a rocket and then pumped full of liquid TNT, with an explosive charge fitted, and the whole lot would be dumped overboard into the sea. The intention was to blow a clear lane to the beach, either by detonating or exposing mines and then to lead the landing craft to the beach. They were happy to get rid of that one!

The flotilla then spread out round the bombarding ships and made smoke to cover the anchorage, making it difficult for the German gunners to get definite fixes on individual ships among the massed vessels.

In the days immediately after D-Day the flotilla, although always on stand-by to make smoke, busied themselves on various tasks in the area and were particularly busy rescuing survivors after the first dropping of parachute mines by the *Luftwaffe*. On the first day that that happened these mines alone put about seven ships in the Sword area out of action: one destroyer, three Liberty ships carrying troops and vehicles and three landing craft. One of the last, a headquarters ship, rolled completely over and trapped her crew.

The whole area was immobilised for the rest of the day while means were sought to deal with this new menace. This type of mine, which became known as the pressure mine, operated on the principle of water displacement depressing a cushion at the top of the mine which in turn triggered off a detonator. At the time no counter-measure to this mine was found, and it is doubtful whether a solution to the problem has been found to this day. The mine was activated by any ship that moved over it, regardless of size.

The flotilla returned to HMS *Tormentor* on 9 July and all the craft underwent an extensive and much needed refit, at the same time they were fitted with Orepesa-type sweeps similar to those used by the fleet minesweepers but much smaller.

On completion of trials at the end of August the flotilla returned to Normandy, where it was immediately assigned to an operation that entailed sweeping the Seine approaches to Le Havre.

Their main objective was to ensure the removal of a type of moored mine with a trigger device to which was attached some 20 fathoms of very light braided rope, which floated with the tide, either on or just beneath the surface, and since it was tinted sea-green, it was very difficult to detect. There was no dearth of volunteers for look-out duties!

This type of mine, simple yet very effective, was generally laid in estuaries and in approaches to harbours where any passing craft was apt to pick up the trailing rope in its screws and wind it up and so trigger off an explosion.

The minesweeping provided an impressive spectacle. In the vanguard was Lt Stephens' flotilla in arrowhead formation. They were followed by motor-launch minesweepers, BYMs (both magnetic and acoustic sweeps) and lastly by the larger fleet sweepers.

That meant that Stephens' landing craft had the honour of being the first British vessel to enter and sweep Le Havre harbour. It also meant that it stood a good chance of being the first to touch off an explosion. For gallantry displayed in this work he was awarded the bronze oak-leaf signifying a mention in despatches.

The 'smokers' were now detached from the flotilla and replaced by American LCVPs which could carry vehicles as well as men. The remaining landing craft now joined a dockship off Portsmouth, were taken on board and launched just off the mouth of the Scheldt from where they made their way up-river to Antwerp.

There they spent about three weeks while tank transporters were modified to accommodate their landing craft. It was a miserable period for the crews, made memorable by the V1 flying bomb and the V2 rockets.

After launching trials at Nijmegen the flotilla set off for Germany where the transporters and their cargo of landing craft were to be hidden in the Reichswald forest near the town of Kleve. A suitable launching site was found at the town of Xanten and during the night they made their way to Emmerich to join up with troops for the crossing of the Rhine.

When they arrived they co-operated with the army in constructing a Bailey bridge and for their help in that task they received letters of appreciation and thanks from the Supreme Allied Commander and the Colonel Commanding the 1st Canadian Army.

The hard-worked flotilla was then briefed for an operation involving setting up a bridge across the River Ijsel to allow the passage of troops who were to take part in the final assault on Arnhem. Since it was necessary to get this bridge up in the shortest possible time, the army engineers decided that each landing craft would carry a span of bridge athwartships. These were numbered in sequence with Stephens' craft carrying No 1, and so on.

With the span extending about ten feet on either side of the vessel, navigation, manoeuvring and ship-handling generally became difficult, especially in the fast-flowing current. At Emmerich the army removed a span of the existing bridge and the flotilla passed through.

They then had to proceed down the Rhine and into the Lower Rhine and make a wide sweep to starboard to enter the Ijsel. There was a German strongpoint at the junction of the Lower Rhine and the Ijsel, and although they had been assured by the Army that it would have been taken care of by the time they arrived on the scene, they soon discovered that it had not. There was nothing that they could do about it and the bridge was put up in record time!

Once again the landing craft found themselves loaded on to transporters and the procession set off for Ulzen, via Osnabruck, Hanover and Celle. There Lt Stephens reported to the US Army, and he was sent to the Elbe, where the flotilla helped with the bridges and patrolled the river till the end of hostilities.

Back on board the transporters, the unit set off on the homeward journey via Nijmegen, Antwerp and Ostend, where they were picked up by a dockship and finally discharged at Portsmouth. Altogether the distance that they had been transported while on shore was about twelve hundred miles – no small feat.

Lt Stephens has the distinction of being the only South African seconded to the Royal Navy to have taken part in the Dieppe raid, the D-Day landings and the Rhine crossing.

It is even more remarkable that he was so often in the thick of some of the fiercest fighting of the war, yet returned home unscathed.

★ ★ ★ ★ ★

Lt-Cmdr AH Winship, JCD, DSC
More Action in the European Theatre

Another of the keen young South Africans to win fame and bring credit to their country was Alfred Harvey Winship.

Lt-Cmdr AH Winship, DSC SANF (V). (SANMMH)

On 1 July 1937, having just turned eighteen, Alfred Winship joined the Royal Naval Volunteer Reserve in Durban, reporting to what is now SAS *Inkonkoni*.

Within a few of months of enlisting he was detailed to attend a continuous training camp at Simon's Town in September 1937, and in the next two years, underwent sea training in the Falmouth-class sloop HMS *Milford*, then serving on the South Atlantic Station, in which he qualified as a Seaman-Gunner.

When war was declared on 3 September 1939 he immediately volunteered for war service; and indeed his name was the very first in the paybook of the Durban RNVR base. Soon afterwards he was one of those seconded to the Royal Navy for the duration of hostilities.

After serving for a while in both Durban and Simon's Town he was (like Dennis Stephens) drafted on 9 May 1940, to the London-class cruiser HMS *Shropshire*. This ship was a unit of Force T, which bombarded the coast of Italian Somaliland in support of the South African offensive. From the intense heat of tropical East Africa the cruiser then sailed direct to the waters off Iceland.

After only a year's service in the *Shropshire,* Winship was selected for a commissioned officers' course and followed the usual route via HMS *Victory* (naval headquarters at Portsmouth) to undergo mandatory training in the shore establishment HMS *King Alfred* at Hove and was commissioned Sub-Lieutenant on 30 October 1941.

His next appointment was to Singapore. He sailed on 3 December 1941, only four days before the Japanese attacked Pearl Harbour.

By February 1942 Singapore had fallen, but by that time Sub-Lt Winship was in Colombo, where he served as an Assistant Gunnery Officer until April 1942. He was then appointed Officer Commanding Boom Defence Protection at Trincomalee, with three large commandeered motor boats under his command.

He was moved again on 19 August 1942, when he was drafted to the Flower-class corvette HMS *Aster* as a watchkeeping officer. During his period on board *Aster* the ship took part in the salvage of SS *Martaban* which had been torpedoed in the Bay of Bengal by a Japanese submarine. The *Martaban* was on fire and had been abandoned but, providentially, a heavy tropical downpour helped to put out the fire, and despite very bad weather, which probably saved them from further attentions of submarines, HMS *Aster* successfully towed her prize to Trincomalee, though at the excruciatingly slow speed of only one and a half knots!

Alfred Winship was certainly kept on the move; for on 14 July 1943 he was again transferred; this time to the boom carrier HMS *Kirriemuir,* as Assistant Navigator. They visited Madagascar and various African ports. Alfred also benefited from expert tuition and encouragement from his Commanding Officer, Commander Montague.

It was at this time that he read in an Admiralty fleet order that qualified navigators who were good swimmers were required for hazardous duties. This intrigued Winship, who had been a volunteer lifesaver in Durban for about two years before the war; and he accordingly volunteered.

Approval of his application was made conditional on his passing a navigation course at HMS *Dryad* in England.

He was promoted Temporary Lieutenant on 1 January 1944 and left the ship a month later to attend the course. His commanding officer described him as 'a very competent and energetic young officer', and recommended him for accelerated promotion.

By 31 May he had passed the course, and he was then drafted to HMS *Copra* for duty in combined operations pilotage parties. This élite band in which two other South Africans, Lt VP de Kock, MBE, DSC and Sub-Lt AH Crossley, had served, was based at the yacht club on Hayling Island near the great naval base of Portsmouth. Lt Winship was on stand-by there on D-Day. In the meantime he had been trained to land from a submarine on a hostile coast and that was oftimes an extremely dangerous business.

In October 1944 he left for Italy to relieve the Commanding Officer of Combined Operations Pilotage Party No 5 (COPP5) who had been wounded in Yugoslavia. After much searching he found the unit in Piraeus. On 4 October 1944 the unit sailed for Salonika in the Greek destroyer *Kriti*.

Mines at the harbour entrance delayed the landing, in the course of which Lt Winship acted as beach-master to the landing craft of the 5th Battalion of the Parachute Regiment. He described this episode as 'a very quiet and short affair', because the Germans had left and the unfriendly Greek ELAS guerrillas were still trying to get control.

The unit returned to Piraeus at the end of November 1944, but by then a communist rising had plunged the country into civil war, and Winship's unit was often under heavy fire. His coxswain was killed in the fighting.

COPP5 was flown back to England by the RAF in time for Christmas leave on 2 December 1944. It was a purely private arrangement, greatly appreciated by members of the unit.

By March 1945 the hard-fought war in north-west Europe was drawing to its end, but one great obstacle remained: the Rhine.

This great river was between four and five hundred yards wide at low tide on Field Marshal Montgomery's front. That, in addition to the stiff resistance put up by German troops in the lower Rhine, promised heavy losses and a difficult crossing.

Before it could be done it was necessary to find out whether there were mines or other obstacles in the river and it was that vital task which Winship and his unit were now called upon to perform.

At 1330 on 20 March 1945, members of COPP5 were told by telephone that their leave had been cancelled, and they were ordered to prepare for a short operation for which wet-suits would be needed.

After spending the night preparing and packing stores the unit left the depot in three trucks for Down Ampney aerodrome from where they were flown to Nivells. A punctured tyre delayed the departure of the second aircraft and it was not till the early morning of 22 March that all members of the unit reached Kapellene, where Lt Winship met the GOC 12 Corps, Lieutenant-General (later General Sir Neil) Ritchie, under whom many South Africans had served in the Western Desert. It then turned out that General Ritchie had requested the services of a COPP unit six weeks earlier!

A few hours later Lt Winship was instructed by GSO 1 (Operations) of 15 Division and then spent until 0120 on 23 March arranging artillery support (mixed smoke and high explosive) to reduce the chances of detection by noise or change of wind. He personally visited each of the batteries concerned.

The 'Most Secret' operations order by the Chief of Staff 12 Corps dated 22 March 1945 stipulated that the special reconnaissance team would operate on the night of 22 – 23 March only, and that they must reconnoitre three separate points and three more later that same night. The operation was codenamed 'Plunder'.

Particular care was to be taken to ensure that the team was not to be given detailed instructions but simply given definite tasks. They were taking considerable risks, and it was necessary that they should not know anything that would compromise the general situation if any of them should be captured.

Incorrect information on the time of moonset, combined with the ineffectiveness of the smokescreen, delayed the start of the operation until 0430 on 23 March when the three two-man canoes set out. The teams were Lt Winship paddled by PO WJ Young, Lt AG Hamilton paddled by Sub-Lt TH Turner and Lt RF Preedy paddled by Sgt Page. The two last were Royal Engineers.

Winship's landing craft used for the Rhine crossing. (SANMMH)

The crossing through the dense smokescreen was most difficult and precluded all possibility of making an accurate landfall. A further drawback that might easily have put paid to the whole mission there and then now overtook them for, despite all the care with which Winship had instructed the gunners, the barrage, which had been started before they set out, landed uncomfortably near and not fifty yards ahead of the canoes as planned.

As the canoes reached their objective each swimmer got out of the cockpit. This was a dangerous operation because of the possibility of being trapped there if any noise attracted the attention of the enemy.

While swimmers carried out their reconnaissance the paddlers waited in the dark for their return. This was real cloak and dagger stuff with a vengeance.

General Ritchie had ordered that the first three points that the swimmers should reconnoitre were in the Bislich sector in the middle of the 12 Corps front, and in the Vynen sector. At least one of these was not a point of assault.

As mentioned previously, the main purpose of their mission was to establish whether there were any mines or other underwater obstructions. In addition they were to establish whether the exit gradients were suitable for the special equipment of the Army and whether there was any other information to be discovered concerning conditions under water.

Although enemy movement on one beach hindered reconnaissance work there, and although an obstacle believed to be upended railway lines blocked the entrance to one small bay, no other major obstructions were found, and the reconnaissance was completed by 0530, and the last member of the unit was just clear of the river bank by daybreak.

Lt Hamilton had the misfortune to become separated from his canoe and was carried downstream. Fortunately for him he came ashore in the American sector and was brought back to his companions by jeep. Most of the team had been able to snatch only six hours' sleep between the night of 20 March and the beginning of their mission.

At 1000 Lt Winship handed in his report to the Brigadier-General, Staff of 12 Corps who was delighted with the information that it contained and thanked the officers of the team for their work. Winship and the COPP5 team later left Kapelenne to visit the GOC 2 Army General, Sir Miles Dempsey, who also thanked them. By Sunday night the whole team, in understandably high spirits, had been flown back to England.

In a letter to Lieutenant Winship, Lieutenant-General Ritchie wrote: 'I rate the reconnaissance that you carried out as a very fine piece of work for it undoubtedly added to the confidence we all had in our ability to carry out the Rhine crossing successfully. This not only applies to the Higher Command, but also to those in the rifle companies who had to do the initial assault. And it is those people who really matter in an operation of that nature.'

From 31 May until 11 July 1945, Lt Winship served as Navigating Officer in HMS *Prinses J Charlotte,* a large Belgian ferry, spending most of the time transporting troops from Dover to Ostend and Antwerp and taking home personnel who had been wounded or were going on leave.

After the war he returned to Durban and was released from active service on 27 May 1946. Some months later he rejoined the Durban SA Naval Reserve Base (SAS *Inkonkoni*) and was later promoted Lieutenant-Commander and appointed Executive Officer of the base.

He served on shore during the 1960 state of emergency and was placed on the Citizen Force Reserve on 14 February 1963.

Lt-Cmdr Winship's gallant exploits on the Rhine and his long and distinguished naval career have earned him a special place in the annals of SAS *Inkonkoni* and the South African Navy.

★ ★ ★ ★ ★

Two Very Gallant Gentlemen
Able Seamen Adlam and Smithers

Decorations were awarded not only for bravery in action. At least two members of the SA Naval Forces received awards for saving life. One of these, Harold Sydney James Adlam, must surely be numbered among the bravest of the brave.

Although he served afloat in the war zones during the Second World War, the deed for which he was decorated was performed far away from the sound of the grumbling guns, and in fact only a day before his discharge from naval service was authorised.

Harold Adlam was born on 6 February 1905 and served in the SA Division of the Royal Naval Volunteer Reserve for four years before the outbreak of war. Since his parents lived in Durban, it is reasonable to suppose that he enrolled at the Durban RNVR base, now SAS *Inkonkoni*. It is known that on at least one occasion of annual sea training he served in one of the original SA naval service ships, the hydrographic survey ship HMSAS *Protea,* the first to bear a name honoured in the South African navy.

Able Seaman Harold Adlam. (SANMMH)

He was thirty-five when he volunteered for full-time naval service on 14 October 1940. Then, after the usual training periods at RNVR bases in Durban and Cape Town, he elected to join a defensively equipped merchant ship's (DEMS) class at Simon's Town on 27 November 1940.

He was then drafted to HMS *Cape Sable* on 4 January 1941 and served in her till 8 June that year. *Cape Sable* had been commissioned as the decoy ship *Cyprus* on 19 September 1939 and was converted into an armed merchant cruiser in 1941.

298

From 9 October 1941 till 31 December 1942, and again from 9 July 1943 till August 1945, he was borne on the books of HMS *President III,* and it seems likely that he served in defensively equipped merchant ships in the Atlantic and Mediterranean waters. His record card in the SADF Archives shows that from the RNVR base at Durban he was drafted as a DEMS seaman to the cargo vessel *Clan Maciver.*

The citation that follows describes the very brave deed that earned him the King's Medal for Gallantry (Silver). This award was later renamed the Woltemade Medal, and it depicts the hero Wolraad Woltemade on its reverse.

At Durban on 16 October 1945, this rating, with total disregard for his own personal safety, risked his life by diving fully dressed into a shark-infested sea – a fact which was known to him – and at full tide with exceptionally high seas running, in order to save the life of a labourer who had been stunned after having been washed off the breakwater by an overwhelming wave.

Able Seaman Adlam successfully brought the man to safety although at the time he was in danger himself of being dashed on the partly submerged and barnacle-covered concrete blocks strewn in the vicinity. The space between these concrete blocks into which this rating dived so gallantly was about four and a half feet wide and the slightest error of judgement, with the sea as rough as it was, would have spelt double tragedy.

His prompt and unselfish action was an exemplary display of bravery to the crowd that had gathered in the vicinity before he arrived on the scene.

The scene that the citation so vividly describes is easy to picture. AB Adlam was then forty years of age and had risked his life at sea during the war. He might justifiably have said that the sea was too rough and the chances of success too slim to attempt a seemingly hopeless rescue. Instead, he set an example that no sailor in the SA Navy should ever ignore.

He received his decoration from HM King George VI in Pretoria in 1947.

★ ★ ★ ★ ★

Another man who had to wait till July 1945 to be decorated for a rescue made three years earlier was Able Seaman PJ Smithers.

During the evacuation from Tobruk, Able Seaman Smithers courageously saved a soldier from drowning.

On 20 June 1942, when serving in HMSAS *Parktown,* then making a last minute departure from Tobruk harbour, Able Seaman Smithers saw a small tug belonging to the Royal Engineers capsize with seven men on board. Six of the men who could swim were hauled on board *Parktown*, but the seventh, who could not, came under heavy tommy-gun fire from the Germans closing in on Tobruk.

Without thought of the consequences and with complete disregard for his own safety, Smithers dived overboard and swam to the soldier, who had been badly wounded and was unconscious. Smithers managed to support him for some time, and although a lifebuoy was thrown from *Parktown* it failed to reach them.

When he realised that he would be unable to get back to the ship, Seaman Smithers decided to make for the shore as best he could. He succeeded, and the unconscious soldier was taken to hospital.

Next day the Germans entered Tobruk, and the brave rescuer was taken prisoner. That probably saved his own life, for if he had regained *Parktown* he might well have lost his life when she was sunk by enemy action, as has been related elsewhere.

After eighteen months in an Italian prisoner of war camp, Seaman Smithers was moved to various camps in Germany until, with the Allied advance he was eventually released and, with other South African prisoners of war, sent to a rest and recuperation centre at Brighton in Sussex.

It was while he was there that he learned for the first time that he had been awarded the Bronze Medal of the Royal Humane Society for gallantry in saving the soldier's life.

Like most heroes Able Seaman Smithers was a modest man; it did not seem to him that his action was 'anything unusual', and he was greatly surprised at receiving the award.

One wishes that the story could be rounded off satisfactorily by learning who actually recommended the award and whether the man whom he rescued made it safely to the end of the war; and whether they ever made contact with one another later.

19

Springbok Sailors in the Far East

Lt RF Scragg SANF(V), a former senior prefect at the Diocesan College (Bishops) in Cape Town, like so many others who went direct from the classroom to the grim realities of war, kept his old school informed about his wartime voyagings. Because of the strict censorship of the time the name of his ship is not recorded, but it would seem that it was attached to an American task force.

He reported as follows:

I am now in China. Our good ship, along with others, sailed into Hong Kong to accept the surrender. It had been knocked about a bit by the bombing, but not too badly.

I was very intrigued by all the junks and sampans, and by the Chinese women propelling them with long bamboo poles. They are all clad in black silk trousers with a coloured blouse or smock covering their upper-works. They wear straw hats shaped like large lampshades, beneath which swing long black pigtails. They are all bare-footed and their feet splay considerably.

The Japs are arrogant swine and although the 'higher-ups' were more or less resigned, *hoi polloi* were truculent. Most of them are more primitive than the backwood savage, to my mind. The filthy crimes that they have committed are too revolting to enumerate. Such things as public beheadings, burning alive, crucifying and gouging out the eyes are mere child's play compared with some of their foul atrocities.

A few nights ago the Chinese set on a bunch of them, dealt with them and then threw them over the dockyard. We are all armed, and have had to shoot a few Japs for throwing hand grenades or sniping. The other night they tried sniping but we floodlit the hills above the town and soon put an end to that.

We are slowly establishing order out of chaos, but there is still a fair amount of looting. The Chinese have suffered terribly at the hands of these barbarians, and I believe that over a million have died or been killed.

Yesterday a house ashore blew up as a result of combustion of cordite and two of my lads were killed. We buried them in Happy Valley. But there are lighter sides as well. Some of the ratings were taking their baths in a large gold fishpond amid the lilies and the fish!

When the prisoners of war saw us, there were many touching scenes, and scarcely an eye was not dimmed by tears as the Union Jack was hoisted in the prison camp, 'God Save the King' played, and the Last Post was sounded in memory of the gallant dead. It was a most impressive and inspiring spectacle. Everyone was hugging each other irrespective of rank, class or creed.

They are all absolute heroes to have withstood the dire treatment handed out to them. The Indians came off worst at the hands of these celestial face-saving monstrosities. They [the former POWs] were all painfully thin, but in excellent spirits. I have had many of them on board to dine with me, and it is pathetic to watch them eat, for after years on rice many cannot stomach meat yet, and up it comes. They cannot drink much, and they smoke only a few cigarettes – they had been smoking dried papaya leaves.

They are all overcome with joy and eagerly want to know all that has been happening in the world outside. They had only the Japanese version. I would willingly go through the past six years of war all over again if it meant freeing such grand men. Some of them have gained as much as 20-lb already.

Some of our lads have been taking the children in the prison camp for rides in a motor car and they are all having a good time honking the horn continually and climbing all over the seats. One car had fourteen in it yesterday. Most of them had never seen a car before. It is a treat to see their little eyes brighten when we give them sweets. We are hoping soon to get all these fine people on their way home.

In another letter Scragg tells of a visit paid to Japan:

We are at present on a cruise round Japan. Since leaving Tokyo Bay I have been ashore in Nagasaki to see the results of the second atomic bomb for myself.

Quite frankly, I felt humiliated and ashamed as I gazed at the woebegone faces of the remaining Japs, who are doubtless still wondering what hit them. There is no doubt of its being a fiendish weapon, and it seems a pity that mankind has had to stoop to such measures, despite the foul deeds perpetrated by the Japs.

All the newspaper accounts that you may have read are quite true. One cannot possibly comprehend that a single bomb could cause such utter havoc. The whole place is completely flat for many miles, and one could easily visualise that nothing living could survive within a radius of miles and that the immediate casualties would be scores of thousands.

In the centre of the 'atomic field', where the bomb burst above the ground, it is *so* flat that the Americans are using the area as a small aerodrome! The stench of decaying flesh still pervades the air even after two months, and on alighting from the bus I have to confess that I vomited violently and had to light up my big pipe.

There must still be thousands buried beneath the rubble, which is hardly more than a foot high. Nagasaki *was* situated in a valley, and the whole valley presents a scene of utter desolation. Amidst the rubble one can see skulls, skeletons, vertebrae, cups, china, pottery and glassware, all twisted into fantastic shapes by the heat, and there are no traces of buildings – no demarcation even to suggest its ever having been a city.

Several miles away the ghost steel frameworks of what were once factories reel drunkenly at precarious angles where the steel has been pushed sideways by the blast. It is a most distressing sight, but one that everybody should see, for the sight of it is enough to end all wars.

It took us an hour and a half to drive through the area, which will give some idea of the extent of the damage. I hope I shall never see anything like it again.

Although, unfortunately, at this distance in time his name cannot be traced, it is known that a young South African seaman who was serving in HMS *Exeter* when she was sunk in the Battle of the Java Sea actually saw the atomic explosions when he was a prisoner in Japanese hands.

★ ★ ★ ★ ★

Another South African sailor was present at yet another surrender, that of Rangoon. The July 1945 issue of *Nongqai* carried the following account of the capture of Rangoon as seen through the eyes of former Lt EW Turpin, SANF, of Bedford in the Cape, who served in the cruiser HMS *Phoebe* and left his impressions:

That 'buzz', or rumours, should have been the order of the day was only the natural outcome of events, for the ship was having a refit and half the ship's company was enjoying the first few days of a well-earned leave when they were suddenly recalled, and away we sailed to our base to fuel and provision and then proceeded to sea, again in the van of a carrier force.

Our destination was Kyaukpyu on Ramree Island and when we arrived the object of our journey became apparent: an invasion of seaborne troops, for we found the harbour packed with all the impedimenta of an assault force, troopships, assault ships, and landing craft of every description.

During the cruiser *Phoebe*'s activities off the Arakan coast our captain was called by the seamen 'Sam, Sam, the Arakan Man'. Now he had become Rangoon Ram, and when he was told of this he retorted, 'They'll be calling me Singapore Sam before I'm through with them!'

Several days elapsed before we left for sea again, this time with HMS *Phoebe* in the van of the main assault force and carrying with us Air Vice-Marshal the Earl of Bandon and General Sir Philip Christison, commanding the 15th Indian Corps, who were carrying out the landings. It was then that we heard that our objective was to be Rangoon Town. The convoy was to be taken to the mouth of the river and anchored there the night before D-Day, when during the early hours of the morning the assault would begin.

Towards evening, and while we were approaching the mouth of the Irrawaddy, a message was received from General Sir Oliver Leese and passed on to everyone: 'We are now going to capture Rangoon and complete our victory in Burma. We shall capture it by closing in on all sides in irresistible strength. I call upon every officer and man to do his utmost to take Rangoon and take it quick. Good luck to each one of you.'

The Japs were in a tight spot and knew it. The 14th Army was steadily advancing on the town, and the seaborne assault was merely the last touch to assure a quick victory.

At 1800 the ship went to action stations. The weather was moderately good, but towards 1900 that night heavy threatening clouds gathered on the horizon, and we knew we were in for a bad time, and all wondered how long it would last and how it would affect the landings.

As Action Officer of the Watch I had a ringside seat, which soon proved to be of little or no value, because by 2000 it seemed as if the heavens had opened up and nature was doing its damnedest to frustrate our efforts.

Small ships of the Royal Indian Navy had preceded us and, anchored at various points, they were to burn white lights at their mastheads and so guide us in. The whole convoy was now in line ahead with *Phoebe* at the head of the column. Whether everyone would anchor in the correct position depended on where we ourselves would anchor. The ships being only three cables apart did not make things any easier.

Long before the time came to anchor, visibility had been reduced to nil. At times even our forecastle head was obscured from view. The time came for anchoring, and it was later proved that we were only fifty yards from the position allocated – eloquent testimony of the superb skill of our navigating officer.

From action stations the ship reverted to two watches, which meant that half the ship's company was on duty for four hours while the others rested, four hours on and four off. Midnight found me once more on the bridge. The heavy downpour had ceased but the rain continued and until about 0300 the only thing that could be done was keep a vigilant look-out since there was always the possibility of attack from Japanese 'human torpedoes' or motor torpedo boats, which were known to be hidden up the river.

It was during the last part of the middle watch (midnight to 0400) that the assault craft began to assemble. Faint lights bobbed up and down on the water ahead of us, reminding one of glow-worms on a dark night. Beyond, in the drizzling rain, could be heard the deep throb of the larger landing craft. As the small assault craft were lowered from their parent ships, so did the number of tiny lights increase. There seemed to be no order until, quite suddenly, one craft switched on a red over white light display.

This was obviously the leader, for slowly the lights took up formation behind it, two by two, all the way down the line. As they were all very small stern lights they could of course not be seen from the shore. The formation then crossed our bows, not a stone's throw away. The captain, who never left the bridge, took up the microphone of the loudhailer and called out, 'Good luck you fellows; get a few Japs for us!' and the reply came back: 'Thank you. We'll be back!'

D-Day had begun, and during the next hour three waves of assault craft, supported by landing craft tank, infantry and guns, which are big landing craft mounting long-range naval guns, were to lay down a barrage and soften any resistance that might be encountered. We were always apt to think of our own discomfort; the appalling heat between decks and the incessant rain which prevented anyone other than those on duty from getting any fresh air without being drenched to the skin; but not one of us was blind to the still greater discomfort that our troops then going ashore would have to endure.

That there was little opposition does not detract from the magnificent management, down to the smallest detail, of the whole seaborne operation. And of course it adds to the glory of the British 14th Army, who were remorselessly pressing on to Rangoon and who at that time were not many miles away.

Resistance was expected at the town of Syriam to the south-east of Rangoon, and one of our objects was to bombard it until Japanese resistance ceased. But, much to our disappointment, our seaborne troops beat us to it and took the town on D-Day+2. That day also brought a signal from the GOC: 'Please convey to all ranks and ratings my congratulations on their splendid courage and seamanship. Well done. Keep it going and the best of luck.'

While no pitched battle ensued, many incidents occurred and we were kept in a state of constant readiness with dawn action stations at 0500 and again at dusk about 1830 in the evening.

The nearest Jap aerodrome was only sixty miles away with reinforcements two hundred miles beyond that and an unknown air strength in Siam itself. One of the first outstanding reports was that of the exploit of a Commander of the Royal Naval Fleet Air Arm who was out on aerial patrol. After being up in the air for some time he got bored, so he landed on an aerodrome near Rangoon and calmly walked into the town.

The first place he visited was the fort, which was also the local gaol. There he found fourteen hundred Allied prisoners. He then went down to a jetty where he either begged, borrowed, or stole, a sampan and headed out to sea where a motor launch was patrolling. He was thus able to pass on some extremely valuable information!

Another was that of a unit that reported that they had suffered one casualty so far: a man killed by a bullock! This may sound ridiculous but in fact cattle in certain parts of the East, while quite

Signing of Japanese surrender on board USS *Missouri* in Tokyo Bay on 2 September 1945. SANF was represented by Commander AP Cartwright who can be seen here to the left of General Douglas MacArthur (behind the microphone). (SANMMH)

tolerant of any amount of indignity and cruelty from local inhabitants will go mad at the smell of a European!

A couple of days later, with red flags indicating an air-raid warning, we went on up-river at a cautious speed, as many mines had already been found. As it was five mines were exploded by minesweepers preceding us. We were lucky, for when we left our base a mine was seen floating quite near to our starboard bow. Where it had come from nobody knew, and although its bottom appeared to be encrusted with barnacles, it still packed a terrific punch. We circled and opened fire on it with the Bofors gun. After the sixth round it exploded throwing a huge column of water into the air.

On D-Day+6, when Rangoon was indisputably ours, came news of the unconditional surrender of Germany. We were not aware of how the rest of the world took it, but on board there were no scenes of wild excitement. Rather, I think, men's minds turned towards their homes and the day when the war would end here too, and they could return to live happy normal lives.

★ ★ ★ ★ ★

While still on the subject of surrenders, many readers may recall the stirring signal sent by the C-in-C Mediterranean fleet on the occasion of the surrender of the Italian fleet. It was to their Lordships, and it begged to inform them that the Italian fleet now lay at anchor under the guns of the fortress of Malta.

Stirring stuff; but it was not quite like that. The former SANF Lieutenant Hilgard Bob Fourie was there, and in a letter home from Malta dated 11 November 1943 he described the event thus:

The most outstanding news of the moment is the arrival of portions of the Italian fleet. I do not agree with the BBC version of its arrival. In fact, I would say that their reporter handled the truth carelessly. Two battleships, two cruisers and a destroyer were the first to arrive. They were met some distance away, not by powerful units of the RN but by a single destroyer. This destroyer then led the procession in single line ahead and a corvette brought up in the rear.

On closing the island, seven of our MTBs, gunwales nearly under with sight-seeing Paybobs and sundry other base-wallahs, took up position on either flank of the line. These subsequently disengaged and lay off the entrance to Grand Harbour in case someone tried any funny business such as scuttling himself in the entrance. A Greek destroyer, either by design or accident, appeared on the scene wearing an outsize Greek ensign and made a trip down the line.

The Italians had their crews fallen in and lining the rails. Such powerful units of the RN as may have been in the vicinity were uninterested, or satisfied that there was enough force to handle the situation (good old MTBs!), or were going about their business of fighting a war. The Italian ships looked huge, with graceful lines. But I should say – never have such large ships felt so small!

A single aeroplane was buzzing about towing a drogue for AA practice at the range up the coast. The procession passed to an anchorage in St Paul's Bay. Other units arrived this morning to make a total of seventeen ships.

In his carefully prepared volume of unpublished wartime memoirs the same Lt Bob Fourie tells of another surrender: that of the macho image. At the time he was serving in the cruiser HMS *Aurora*.

As junior ship in the squadron we were sent to Algiers to pick up and transport the C-in-C's staff of WRNS to Naples.

The captain's day cabin was cleared for the officers, and the chief's and petty officers' mess for the ratings. Needless to say all this caused quite a flutter. Everyone became very gallant and we put on a Wrens Benefit firing the guns and conducting Wren tours all over the ship. The Wren officers were very decorative but decidedly up-stage, being accustomed to dealing with nothing less than a Commander or the Great Man himself. The ratings appeared to be far more fun and revelled in the trip.

I was Officer of the Watch when one of the conducted parties turned upon the bridge. The young officer took some pains to explain our radar system. A very bored Wren officer said, 'Yes, I know – but of course you are very much out of date – you should have the Mark – This for surface and the Mark – That for long range.' She had evidently had enough of the young man and came over to where I was. 'What is that thing for?' she asked in a refined and superior voice. 'I'm afraid you must ask someone else', said I – 'I am in charge of the ship at the moment.' Coward!

We entered the Bay of Naples in the forenoon and the captain ordered the fo'c'sle cleared of all male personnel and had the Wrens fallen-in in their place in two long lines as is the custom for entering harbour. We passed down a long line of Allied warships, and their crews crowded the railings and spontaneous cheers came across to us, with the odd signal such as, 'Brother can you spare a dame?'

CHAPTER
20

The Merchant Navy

While the armed forces stole the glamour and gained most of the kudos during the war, their combined efforts would have been in vain if it had not been for the ships of the Merchant Navy and the mostly unsung heroes who manned them. If it not been for the dedication of these men in their cargo ships and tankers, victory could never have been achieved. Winston Churchill himself confessed that nothing caused him graver concern than the progress and outcome of the Battle of the Atlantic.

There was good reason for that. During the course of the war the Allies lost 4 786 merchant ships of all kinds. An analysis shows that 2 775 were sunk by submarines, 521 by mines, 326 by surface craft, 2 828 by aircraft and 820 were lost through unknown causes. Some of the figures are hard to grasp. In May and June 1942, 269 ships were torpedoed by U-boats and in November the same year 117. In March 1943, at the time when the author crossed the Atlantic in landing craft (see Chapter 14), the losses were 108 ships. In the North Atlantic alone forty-one were lost in the first ten days of that month and fifty-six in the next ten days. After that slaughter the Allies gradually gained the upper hand, and the number of sinkings showed a marked and encouraging decline.

The men who manned these ships, some of them having suffered the distresses of attack, sinking and days in open boats over and over again, were a very independent breed. They stoutly resisted any form of regimentation, and seldom wore a uniform. To differentiate them from ordinary civilians they wore in the buttonhole a small metal badge with the letters NM encircled by a wreath and surmounted by the Tudor crown.

For several months before the outbreak of war, Merchant Navy officers and men had been encouraged to undergo courses in naval gunnery, convoy work and the like, while, since most of the vessels were coal-burners, firemen or stokers were trained to fire furnaces with the minimum of tell-tale black smoke. These courses raised an interesting point. Under the Geneva Convention any enemy unit sinking a merchant vessel was in duty bound to ensure that the crew were given proper warning and placed in a position of safety. Lifeboats were not considered as falling within that category.

Presumably when this convention was ratified it was assumed that merchantmen would be defenceless targets, whereas the quite blatant aim of these courses was not only to teach the merchant crews to defend their own vessel but to destroy their attacker either by gunfire or by ramming if at all possible. Both did in fact occur, and in some respects we can understand the response of German submarine commanders who in the early days at least, were prepared to act chivalrously towards their victims, only to find that an innocent-looking cargo vessel carried an unexpected punch and a sharp stem that, if they did not look nippy, could crush their very vulnerable submarine underfoot.

The convoy system was instituted early in the war, but it was not until 1941 that the Admiralty really concentrated on providing the strongest possible escorts.

Masters of ships, accompanied by their radio officers, would attend convoy conferences conducted by senior naval officers and the man who was to act as commodore of the convoy – usually a retired admiral called back to serve his country in time of need and dropping a ring or two to do so.

The author served in the very earliest of these convoys and in doing so gathered memories never to be effaced. The large collection of ships of all shapes and sizes, including a few neutrals (to whom most of the

Typical coastal convoy. Probably taken in the English Channel or North Sea. (ND Orpen)

convoy code signals had been denied), would be given pennant numbers and herded together in a close formation. This was hateful to most captains, who preferred the wide open seas and were in the habit of giving all other ships and headlands a wide berth. Now they found themselves beset on all sides by ships of varying tonnages and speeds, dogged and chivvied by officious naval craft.

A system of zigzags had been devised and each ship was issued with a cheap clock, round the outer rim of which would be placed small metal stops at selected intervals. When the minute hand reached this stop a bell would ring to signify an alteration of course to conform with the zigzag pattern. Alas, this warning signal frequently failed, and an officer of the watch, busily poring over the chart, would sense something amiss, look up and find the whole great armada converging on his ship. Sirens would bellow, bad language would be exchanged, and sweating engineers would adjust revolutions to regain station.

Station-keeping was often a nightmare. The time-honoured signal to the engine-room of 'Full away on passage' gave way to revolution adjustments 'Up 5', 'Down 10', every few minutes. At night all that one had to steer by was a dim blue light on the stern of the next ahead. In fog each ship would trail a small barrel astern, and the following ship would do its utmost not to lose sight of its splash and wake. Then coal fires had to be clinkered out, which meant a fall in steam pressure and loss of speed. Collisions were innumerable and the number of near-misses incalculable.

Until they were replaced by steel and concrete, all the vital parts of the ship such as the bridge, the radio room and so on, had been protected by a wall of sandbags against shell-splinters and bullets. The result was that in anything of a headwind the long-suffering officer of the watch and the bridge look-outs got generous blasts of sand in their eyes.

As the war progressed, experience produced a high standard of proficiency in convoy work and station-keeping. It became a way of life for many, since only the faster ships sailed independently.

It is perhaps appropriate here to mention the resentment felt by many Merchant Navy officers over certain books on the war at sea. Such books describe fast sleek destroyers rounding up stragglers from a convoy and exhorting them to keep station, as though the men in command of such ships were amateurs and idiots. What these authors apparently failed to appreciate was the great difficulty of handling some ships in bad weather conditions.

The average cargo vessel of the Second World War was a low-powered coal-burning vessel of about 5 000 tons gross. Most could make about ten knots at best, and many not more than eight. Outward bound across the North Atlantic to the United States and Canada these ships were light, in ballast, with no dead weight in their holds. In the atrocious weather of the North Atlantic in winter with hurricane force winds, blizzards with snow, sleet and mountainous seas, they were entirely at the mercy of the elements and at times altogether uncontrollable. With their high sides they sat like balloons on the water, and with their screws sometimes wholly exposed, plunged and reared like bucking broncos, answering neither helm nor engine. Inevitably they became scattered. They were beyond human control. Their captains were all experienced men who in normal times would ride out the weather as best they might, but to endeavour to keep station in a convoy in such conditions was to attempt the impossible.

We can of course appreciate the concern of the Navy. Any straggler from a convoy was a sitting duck for a lurking U-boat. They also knew that many a shipmaster, impatient of the restrictions of sailing in convoy would take advantage of the weather, fog, or simply some excuse to break away and proceed independently to his destination. Surprisingly, many such truants made it safely home, while their companions in the convoy were massacred by U-boat wolf packs.

On the outbreak of war many merchant ships were strengthened to take a defensive gun on the after deck or poop. These guns were of ancient vintage, and varied from a 12-pounder to 4-inch and even in the larger vessels to a huge 6-inch gun. In the early days, when they were clear of the submarine zone, these guns would be unshipped at a suitable port and transferred to a homeward bound vessel. The gun crews consisted mainly of the ship's own hastily trained personnel backed up by one or two professionals, usually drawn from the Royal Marines. Later, as more armament became available, they were manned by DEMS (defensively equipped merchant ship) crews drawn from Artillery and Naval Reserve units.

The war had been in progress for several months before the author's own ship, SS *Umona*, was fitted with a defensive gun. The ship was an aged (1910) veteran of the First World War. There had been speculation that her structure would not be able to withstand the shock of firing the gun and it was with some trepidation that we watched the installation of the mounting.

Our orders were to wait until we were well clear of all traffic before trying the gun out for the first time. Came the day when, well out into the Atlantic, the Chinese carpenter was told to make a target. He did so and, with Japan laying his own country waste in his mind, he painted a bull's-eye in the form of the Japanese rising sun flag!

The amateur gun crew closed up, loaded their ancient weapon, and on the order to fire from the bridge duly pulled the lanyard. There was a prodigious explosion as the shell sped on its way. The stove-pipe funnel from the crew's galley at once collapsed and covered the poop with soot, a potato locker burst open and spilled its contents, and the occupants of a chicken coop found themselves at large. A few more rounds were fired, and the comment from the bridge (once hearing was restored) was 'Jolly good shooting!' It seemed that we had actually straddled the target.

Our captain, who with his entire complement of crew and passengers, except for two survivors, was to lose his life a few weeks later, held the fighting navy in low esteem. There were, alas! many like him in the Mercantile Marine of those days, and the antipathy was no doubt mutual. As the war progressed this latent hostility gave way to mutual admiration.

The ship was steaming steadily southward in the blue South Atlantic when news was received of an encounter between a German commerce raider and an armed merchant cruiser, not so far from our own position and, since the raider had escaped, giving rise to some anxiety.

Next day, a beautiful calm Sunday morning, the look-out was alerted by an aircraft suddenly appearing overhead, a sight not to be expected in the middle of the South Atlantic. We soon saw, with much relief, that the markings on the aircraft were those of the Fleet Air Arm and, as the plane circled inquisitively overhead, the second officer seized the Aldis lamp and with the author lugging the heavy battery, we made a circuit over all the obstacles on the boat-deck, mainly chocks, since in wartime the boats were kept swung out, we attempted to identify ourselves. No one had thought of hoisting the Red Ensign.

Apparently satisfied, the plane flew off over the horizon leaving behind it an excited audience. Packing the Aldis lamp back into its stowage, the captain entered the wheelhouse. He regarded us in silence for a moment, and then observed that it was very gratifying to know that one of our cruisers was lurking somewhere just over the horizon! It was the first indication of a softening in his attitude to the senior service.

In passing, it may surprise the modern mariner to know that before the war smoking on the bridge was strictly forbidden. During the war officers were put on double watches, that is four hours on and four hours off. The captain therefore relaxed the prohibition, but it was so deeply ingrained that even with permission, cigarette ends were hastily stubbed if the captain was heard climbing the ladder to the bridge.

So far only brief mention has been made of defensively equipped merchant ships. According to the war orders for the Africa Station, arrangements were made to provide a number of gunlayers from the RNVR for that service. The total number agreed upon to be provided from South Africa was seventy-four, subject to the adequacy of local sources. Fifty seaman gunners were left from the total of those trained after requirements of M/S and A/S vessels had been met, and after two complements of volunteers for AMCs had been sent to the United Kingdom. Meanwhile the remaining seaman gunners who had volunteered were trained as gunlayers and drafted to DEMS as and when ships arrived at South African ports for fitting out.

TSS *Clan Lamont*. Typical of the modern fast cargo carriers used extensively on the Malta convoy run. (Author)

A report for the year ending 30 May 1941 shows that 103 ratings were serving as gunlayers in DEMS, most of them being in ships plying between South Africa and Britain, while at the request of the C-in-C Mediterranean a number of ratings had been trained and sent for duty in merchant ships supplying the fighting forces in the Mediterranean and the Middle East.

One of the South Africans to serve in DEMS was Bernard Watts (Watty) Johnson of Durban. He joined the RNVR in 1936 and went on active service on the outbreak of war as an Able Seaman Gunner. He was posted to the ill-fated *Comorin* whose story has been told. Surviving that disaster, he was rescued by the cargo vessel *Glenartney* and taken to Cape Town, where, after survivor's leave, he volunteered as a DEMS rating.

When he was asked why he had given preference to that branch, which, in view of the wholesale sinkings, was a rather dangerous occupation, he replied that since each merchant vessel carried only a couple of DEMS gunners he would be comparatively independent, free from naval regimentation, and that he had been told he would eat with the officers. That turned out to be a false promise.

After a six-week course he sailed as a passenger in the *Nieuw Amsterdam* for Port Said, where he was drafted to a Norwegian tanker, *Noordewind*. She was carrying high-octane fuel, and he recalls being 'not only scared, but utterly petrified'. He was interested to find that a captured Breda gun had been installed. His first job was to strip and clean the gun, full as it was of desert sand.

314

The ship got involved in some dispute when it was discovered that the radio officer was a Quisling, and Watty was drafted to another Norwegian tanker, this time a crude oil carrier, the *Sagona* on the Persian Gulf, Port Said and Haifa service. She happened to be in Alexandria harbour when Italian frogmen put the battleships *Queen Elizabeth* and *Valiant* out of action. They also attached bombs to the stern of his ship which promptly sank into soft mud off the quay and was later converted into a floating oil storage depot.

Rather to his surprise, he then learned that he had been selected for officer training, and he duly embarked in the *Queen Mary* for passage to Cape Town and from there to the United Kingdom in the *Stratheden*. This was in 1942, and although he attended the full course at *King Alfred,* he failed to pass in navigation, so that he did not attain commissioned rank.

Returning to the DEMS he joined the Dutch ship *Meerkerk* in Liverpool as gunlayer in charge of guns. In her he plied the North Atlantic and eventually, after some leave in Cape Town he joined yet another Norwegian tanker, the *Ehrling Brovig*. In a convoy of forty-eight ships in the Persian Gulf several were sunk, including his own. The torpedo split the ship in two, but surprisingly there were no casualties. He was picked up by the naval escort and landed at Suez and after some leave at a rest camp was drafted to a T & J Harrison line freighter as far as Durban and was then transferred to the *City of Chester*. He arrived in Liverpool on V-E Day. In the *City of Chester* they later passed through the Mediterranean *en route* for Karachi and on his return to Suez he was transferred to the troopship *Alcantara* for passage to Durban and arrived there on V-J Day. He was demobbed in October 1945.

An interesting point about his service was his refusal to accept the Burma Star awarded for his brief period in Karachi! On board merchant ships he was signed on at a nominal rate of a shilling a month as a supernumery. Whenever possible Royal Navy paymasters would make payment at ten shillings a week. If Watty has any resentment over his naval service – and he admits that he has no regrets, since 'you can't buy experience', it is that he feels he was conned by the RNVR. On the outbreak of war he was earning £9 a month as a bank clerk. The RNVR told him he would be getting £12 a month for seeing the world. Payment was made fortnightly, and his first pay was only £3. When he queried, it he was told that £6 would be taken off monthly for fuel, lights and furniture!

Ask any wartime merchant seaman for his recollections and he will be bound to mention the hazards of complete blackout at sea, especially in crowded convoys; and the accompanying discomfort. Doors were fitted with automatic switches to put out any light when opened. That meant that doors had to be kept shut, and in the tropics that could mean real discomfort, for few ships were fitted with any kind of through-draft ventilation or even electric fans.

They will also remember the prohibition on lighting matches on the open deck. They were told that the flicker of a match could be seen half a mile away on a dark night. Perhaps the precaution was necessary, but U-boats were equipped with highly efficient sonar systems that would pick up propeller noises long before a lighted match could be seen.

Unlike most wartime sailors who were 'hostilities only' men, the merchant seaman carried on his customary peacetime avocation, except that in addition to the ordinary hazards of his calling he now had to contend with all the dangers of armed conflict.

CHAPTER
21

The Russian Convoys

Much has been written of the horrors of the convoys to Russia: the constant threat of attack by aircraft, surface vessel and submarine; the cruel weather and the poor chance of survival in icy waters if your ship fell victim to a lurking U-boat or the suddenly appearing bomber.

South Africans serving in the Royal and Merchant Navies, accustomed to the bright sunshine of their own country, had to endure the hardships of a Far North winter. The very term 'Russian Convoy' was pregnant with danger, fatigue, misery, suffering and, more often than not, disaster and death.

One who had his fair share of the frozen north was William Douglas Hogg, now a retired Commodore, SA Navy. He grew up in Port Elizabeth and joined the training ship *General Botha* for the 1935 – 36 term. He was then apprenticed to the Ellerman & Bucknall line. He was also appointed Midshipman RNR, and in 1938 broke his cadetship to serve for four months in the cruiser HMS *Amphion*.

When war broke out he was summoned to naval duty, and he served actively in a variety of ships throughout hostilities; earning in the process a mention in despatches.

During the evacuation at Dunkirk the fleet minesweeper HMS *Hussar* was bombed and had her stern blown off. Bill Hogg joined her after she was repaired at Chatham, and he was to remain in her for two years as her navigator.

In September 1941 HMS *Hussar* sailed with the first convoy to Russia. On that voyage at least, they were unmolested, probably because of the almost continuous darkness of the high latitudes at that time of year. On her arrival at Archangel the ship became iced in, but with the help of the Russian icebreaker *Lenin* she broke free and made for Murmansk, where she remained, carrying out the lawful occasions of the Royal Navy, until January 1942 when she sailed for the United Kingdom carrying with her Spitfire pilots who had delivered aircraft to the Russian Air Force.

Commodore W Hogg SM SAN (Retd). (SANMMH)

In the Spring of 1942 *Hussar* once again escorted a Russian convoy but this time she suffered air attacks along the way. They passed lifeboats with their occupants sitting bolt-upright, frozen stiff in death. Once again they were compelled to remain in Russian waters, based in Murmansk until July that year.

During that time they carried out minesweeping and escort duties, and they were present when the cruiser HMS *Edinburgh* met her end. Readers may remember that divers recently reached the wreck of that ship and recovered gold bullion worth about £45 million. Two seconded South Africans serving in HMS *Edinburgh* were killed in action on 30 April 1942.

Hussar, Gossamer and *Nigel* formed a flotilla of minesweepers under the senior ship HMS *Harrier*. Although slow (14 knots) and lightly armed, they proved useful in times of escort shortages. They backed up a force escorting convoy QP11 of seventeen ships. The cruiser *Edinburgh,* wearing the flag of Rear-Admiral Stuart Bonham-Carter, a jovial character and a splendid seaman, was in close support.

The convoy was homeward bound and on 29 April 1942 the minesweepers turned back to Murmansk. The temperature was below freezing, with frequent snowstorms, low cloud and heavy seas. There was little darkness. Next day the minesweepers learned that the convoy had been sighted by the enemy and that *Edinburgh* had been torpedoed by U-456 (to be sunk herself on 13 May 1943 by HMCS *Drumheller,* HMS *Lagan* and a coastal command bomber in the North Atlantic – there were no survivors).

The U-boat scored two hits that tore off the cruiser's stern, which immediately sank, taking with it the rudder and at least one propeller. Amazingly, two screws were still working and *Edinburgh* steered an erratic course heading back to Murmansk – two hundred miles away.

At 2018 on 30 April, four hours after the attack, the minesweepers sailed to assist, and they spread out over a wide area searching for the stricken cruiser. *Hussar* brought up astern escorting a Russian tug, and it was she who first sighted the *Edinburgh* and a little Russian gunboat, *Rubin,* together with the two destroyers *Foresight* and *Forester* circling the cruiser on anti-submarine patrol. The Russian tug connected a tow-wire but had insufficient power for the job. *Gossamer* then secured to the cruiser's stern to help keep her on a steady course, while the big ship churned away making about three to four knots.

The next thing to cause alarm and despondency was the appearance of what was thought to be the battleship *Tirpitz,* but which turned out to be a German Z-class destroyer whose shells were already bracketing *Hussar*. The Admiral had ordered that if hostile forces were met, the sweepers were to retire under a smokescreen. But the senior ship *Harrier* headed straight for the destroyer at 14 knots, firing her single 4-inch gun.

Next, three more German destroyers appeared on the scene, making smoke and dodging in and out of snowstorms. All ships, including *Edinburgh* opened fire on the enemy who, however, remained at a range of four or five miles. The Germans must have imagined they had met a superior force. If they had only known it they could have sunk all the Allied ships with ease.

The British ships were being constantly straddled by gunfire; and then another torpedo was seen approaching the *Edinburgh* which by this time had cast off her towing cable and was steaming in circles. This second torpedo hit directly opposite the first, and only the upper deck plating and her keel were holding the ship together. It was obvious that she was doomed whereupon *Gossamer* and *Harrier* were ordered along-side to take off sick and wounded men, many of whom were being shipped home as survivors from earlier convoys. Once the wounded were off, the rest of the crew followed them. Altogether 440 were transferred to *Gossamer* and 400 to *Harrier*.

Meanwhile the sea had flattened out and with a list of seventeen degrees *Edinburgh* was still firing her B turret guns. While all this was going on the Russian *Rubin* attempted to come alongside *Harrier*, and caused some damage in the process.

At last the Admiral transferred his flag to the humble *Harrier*. In theory that was all very well, but minesweepers are not in the habit of carrying an Admiral's flag. But they had a white flag with a St George's cross in their flag-locker and the yeoman of signals marked in the two red balls of a rear-admiral with red ink. Later, when he was told of this, the jovial Admiral Bonham-Carter observed, 'Two balls! That's more than I expected to have this afternoon!'

The *Edinburgh* took so long to sink that the Admiral even contem-plated reboarding her. Despite shell fire from the minesweepers and depth charges dropped alongside her torn hull, she remained stubbornly afloat. Finally she was sent down with the destroyer *Foresight*'s last remaining torpedo.

About twelve hours after the *Edinburgh* went to her last resting place, *Harrier, Gossamer, Hussar* and *Nigel* returned to Kola Inlet. The *Edinburgh* and the destroyers *Forester* and *Foresight* lost between them seventy-four killed and forty-three wounded. The minesweepers es-caped unharmed.

As a postscript to this action, a letter is quoted from the Russian *Rubin* which had had a minor collision with *Harrier*. It was headed 'From Commander of Divisions, USSR Gunboat *Rubin*, 4th Day of May 1942' and reads (original style):

Dear Sir,

Soviets seamen was witness of heroic battle English seamen with predominants powers of enemy.

English seamen did observe their sacred duty before Fatherland.

We are proud of staunchness and courage English seamens – our allies.

I am very sorry what injured your ship by approach to board for what I must beg pardon.

Certain war histories have emphasised the fact that Stalin was dissatis-fied with, and critical of, the flow of supplies to the Soviet Union. He seems to have had little gratitude in his make-up. Now, a new generation of Russians are awarding a special medal to anyone who sailed in those grievously battered convoys.

One of those entitled to that medal was Lt Peter H Philip RNVR (SA) who described his experiences on a voyage to Russia in a letter to his parents, which was later published in the *Diocesan College Magazine* from which I have drawn this account.

At the time he was serving in the armed trawler HMS *Blackfly*, and he describes his voyage as quite the most exciting he had experienced at that time.

During encounters with pack ice they were attacked by enemy aircraft, and they were delighted to be officially credited with shooting down one enemy plane and damaging two others.

A and B gun turrets iced up on board HMS *Cumberland* on Murmansk convoy run. (E Redgrave)

The voyage was full of incident and the enemy remained in contact with them throughout most of the passage. To add to their difficulties a severe storm in the early stages caused the convoy to scatter, leaving only one merchant ship for *Blackfly* to escort. But she too was lost to sight when, sighting a U-boat on the surface, the warship went in to attack. The merchantman wisely retreated. Such were the conditions that to drop depth charges on their target, they had to break the ice with crowbars. The result of this unusual attack was not known, but they felt sure that they had given the submarine something to think about.

Next morning they sighted a Heinkel bomber overhead, but no attack developed. Next was a radio report that three enemy destroyers were only twenty miles away. It is as well that they were not sighted, for *Blackfly* was then entirely on her own. At the time she was searching for survivors from a torpedoed merchantman, and she actually sighted another U-boat, which was attacked, but again with inconclusive results.

By now the ship had again run into pack ice, from which she took three hours to extricate herself before making a run for Murmansk. Even in port there was no rest. There were on average three air raids a day, but to those seasoned veterans who had endured the London blitz they were not at all impressive.

There was to be no remission on the homeward voyage either. For the first three days the convoy was attacked by aircraft and U-boats, and for the next three shadowed by long-range *Focke-Wulf* reconnaissance aircraft.

The air attacks were carried out by several squadrons of Heinkel bombers. Once eight of them dived on the convoy from all directions. Nevertheless the hard-pressed crews were heartened to see several coming down in flames.

At first the Heinkels roared in at mast height to strafe the convoy, but after the gunners on the merchant ships had put up a terrific barrage and *Blackfly* had brought one down, they held off and contented themselves with releasing their bombs from a high altitude. That had its effect, for despite the fact that the convoy was almost hidden at times by leaping columns of water only one ship was hit in those first harrowing three days.

A sister trawler managed to rescue sixty-eight survivors from the stricken ship – forty-eight from the water – and then, with not a little danger to herself, she went alongside the sinking ship to take off twelve more. Despite the severe machine-gunning and bombing and icy water, only eight men were lost.

Besides all that there was the almost continuous rumble of exploding depth charges as attacks by U-boats were repelled.

On the second night out, a solitary plane suddenly dived on *Blackfly* out of the blue and nearly scraped the bridge with its wing-tip. Peter was on watch at the time, and he swore he could see the smile on the pilot's face as he flashed by. This aircraft bracketed the little ship with a stick of long yellow bombs. Peter was quite sure of that for he saw them coming all the way down! They landed about ten feet from the ship and he thought that the pilot ought to be ashamed of himself for missing. Needless to say, the ship was badly shaken by the series of near-misses and almost jumped out of the water. All the compasses were smashed, which added to their navigational difficulties.

A few hours later a merchant ship was torpedoed and *Blackfly* was detailed to rescue survivors. Of the ship's complement of seventy, she managed to rescue sixty-six including five women and two babies. One of the women, a stewardess, later died of internal haemorrhaging, which was beyond the medical powers of Peter Philip who also fulfilled the role of ship's 'doctor'.

Yet the babies, who had been sleeping when the ship was torpedoed, were still asleep when they were recovered from the lifeboats!

All these extra people on board stretched the little ship's resources to its limits. Quite suddenly their complement had been increased by 150 per cent. Water had to be strictly rationed and no one was allowed to wash for the next eight days. When they reached their destination they all stank. Accommodation was a problem too. The bunks and furniture had been smashed and soaked by the near-misses, and, in any case there were barely enough bunks for the crew, let alone any extra people. However, the petty officers' and stokers' messes aft were still more or less intact, so the women and children took over the chief's and coxswain's cabins while their captain dossed down in the captain's quarters on *Blackfly*. As for the rest they slept where they could, wherever they could find shelter and warmth. The radio room, the steering compartment, the engine-room casing, the wheelhouse, the chartroom, even the galley, were full of snoring bodies of men off watch at night. No one could have a change of clothes and Peter records that he never saw his shirt for eight days.

The near-misses had opened the ship up to the sea, and the pumps could barely cope with the flow. It was as well that nothing more happened to endanger them for the ship only had boat and float accommodation for twenty-five people. In the event they arrived safely at their destination, and the captain whom Peter described as 'a tower of strength, a fount of cheerfulness and confidence, and the only man he had ever met who could make a molehill out of a mountain,' was awarded the DSC for his devotion to duty on Russian convoys.

Among other South Africans to be decorated for service in those inhospitable waters were author Lt-Cmdr Anthony Trew, who was awarded the DSC when serving in the destroyer HMS *Walker* on Russian convoy duties, and Cmdr AS Pomeroy, RN, who received the DSC and a mention in despatches while commanding a destroyer on the dreaded Murmansk run.

On Land and Sea: The Royal Marines

About seventy-five South African officers were privileged to be seconded to the élite corps of Royal Marines. Many of them earned awards for bravery, yet few South Africans are aware of their achievements. However, thanks to a letter from one of them, Mr Peter Brooke, to Commander Bisset SAN, some light is thrown on the subject.

The writer reveals that at first, on the outbreak of war, applications from men in mining and its associated industries to join up were refused. The mines did, however, appreciate that some form of military training was desirable and mining brigades were formed all over the Reef to be trained by permanent force instructors. The training consisted, in the main, of weekend camps at which they were taught to build bridges over rivers, make roads, runways for aircraft and the like.

In early 1942 the mine management did an about-face, and large numbers of employees were granted permission to enlist for service up North, or for that matter anywhere in the world. Those who did so were drafted into the SA Artillery for training at Potchefstroom, where they were sorted out and a number were selected for an officers' training course. This was the longest ever: five months' instruction in all types of arms at Roberts Heights, followed by a further six months' gunnery training at Potchefstroom.

On completion of the course, and while awaiting posting, they were visited by a Colonel of the Royal Marines who, on returning from the Far East, delivered a series of lectures on the Jollies. That led to several of the former course to apply for secondment. Things moved rapidly after that, and those accepted departed for the United Kingdom a fortnight later. Arriving there they were first stationed at the Royal Marine barracks at Eastney in Portsmouth, where they received a final polish and were put through all the routines and duties required of an officer of the Royal Marines. On completion of this intensive training

New class stepping it out on the RNVR parade ground, Cape Town. (SANMMH)

period they were then all promoted full lieutenant and sent to various units such as the Commandos, Parachute Regiment, Small Craft and so on.

Peter Brooke was appointed Gunnery Officer on a specially designed landing craft. These were not of the usual design with dropping bow doors, but were built on the lines of more conventional ships. Each was armed with either a 17 or 25-pounder mounted amidships, and two anti-aircraft guns abaft the bridge. Crew consisted of a naval lieutenant as commanding officer, a sub-lieutenant as second in command, a coxswain and twelve ratings, a sergeant, two corporals and twelve gunners.

The purpose of these vessels was to form an artillery unit on the beaches by grounding the craft at full speed and then flooding the ballast tanks to make a firm gunnery platform. On the way in, a kedge anchor would be dropped to help to pull the ship off when necessary. Beaching was generally carried out after the beaches had been softened up with rockets from rocket-carrying craft and aircraft and their own guns whilst on the run in.

Records available reveal that forty-one South Africans seconded to the Royal Marines were awarded the France and Germany Star while another, Lt JH van der Walt, who acted as Air Liaison Officer, HMS *Emperor*, Naval Party 1746, in Germany, received the Atlantic Star with France and Germany clasp.

Among those who received awards for bravery were Capt LLA McKay and Lt CAD Bircher, both of whom won the Military Cross on D-Day. Their citations read as follows:

> Capt McKay showed qualities of initiative, energy and courage to a high degree by spotting and engaging enemy strong points, machine-gun positions and anti-tank guns from the beach through-out D-Day. In the course of the day he was wounded by a direct hit from a 75-millimetre shell which put the main armament of his Sherman tank out of action, but he nevertheless continued to engage the enemy with his .300 Browning machine gun until he was finally moved inland from the beach with only one of four Centaur tanks; the remaining three still being out of action through damage to tracks on landing.

The citation for the award of the Military Cross to Lt Bircher reads thus:

> Lt Bircher was Officer Commanding Troops in a LCT(A) carrying part of his troop. The craft engines broke down and it was towed to a position off the Isle of Wight to the assault area by an LCT and LCI. On 6 June 1944 when approaching the beach at Bernikres-Sur-Lier these craft had to cast off the LCT(A) which was left drifting in a strong tide about 150 yards from the beach. Although there was a heavy sea running and the beach was still under close-range fire, Lt Bircher, without hesitation plunged into the water and swam about a hundred yards to the shore with the beach lines. On arrival on the beach he secured the lines to some stakes, enabling his craft to beach, and disembarked his section of Centaur tanks. He subsequently led his section from the Canadian sector in which he had landed into the sector of the 50th (N) Division to which he was attached although the enemy opposition still persisted between the two sectors. Throughout the operation Lt Bircher showed personal courage of the highest order and unflinching determination in the most adverse conditions to get his guns into action at the right time and place.

Not all who chose secondment to the Royal Marines were decorated for valour, yet they all shared in maintaining the proud tradition of the corps in no uncertain manner as the following extracts, kindly provided by Mr MJ Schoeman, show:

Lt Thomas served with 45 Commando in Normandy. This commando, in the last Special Service (SS) Brigade, landed at Ouistreham ('Sword') on D-Day, on the left flank of the invasion. It made an unsuccessful attack on Franceville Plage on 7 June 1944, and then fought with the Brigade at Merville and took part in the holding of the eastern flank of the beachhead by 1 and 4 SS Brigades.

After the CO of the 1st Brigade (Lord Lovat) was wounded in action, Mills-Roberts took over the brigade which, unlike the other commandos manned by veterans with experience of Norway, Africa, Italy and Dieppe, had no experience and they had not, until then, been quite so steady as other units of the brigade.

He therefore suggested to the OC of 45 Commando that a night raid was in order, presumably to give the troops some experience of close-quarter combat and to instil in them a more aggressive spirit. Lt Thomas led the patrol, and they made a successful night attack on transport and reserve troops behind the German lines after crossing a well-defended sector of the front along a road. They attacked between two artillery concentrations and got into the enemy harbour area, setting six vehicles alight, and threw grenades into the German trenches as the confused enemy stood to. Thomas, although wounded, led his patrol back under cover of artillery fire. General Gale, the Commander of the Airborne Division, considered the raid to be 'a first-class piece of enterprise'.

Lt TD Wright of Johannesburg had already won the Military Medal while serving with the SA Tank Corps. As a trooper he had in 1942 been wounded three times in the back by a strafing Messerschmitt. He was seconded to the Royal Marines with 45 Commando and he was killed in action on 4 April 1945, the only casualty when 1 Commando Brigade took Osnabruck, 45 Commando having struck the only serious opposition after the first attack had been launched in the early hours. Lt Wright, only twenty-seven years of age, lies buried in the Reichswald Forest War Cemetery.

Three South African subalterns seconded to the Royal Marines joined 48 Commando. They were Lt Wally England, Lt SL Fouche and Major John Freeman. England was stricken with leukaemia, which at that time was considered incurable and fatal. However, he subsequently recovered, only to be killed by the enemy.

On D-Day 48 Commando landed on the beach at St Aubin sur Mer, just east of Courseuilles at the junction of Juno and Sword. Lt Fouche of Y-troop, on landing, concentrated on getting his men off the beach. Their landing craft had got stuck on one of the obstacles and had begun to sink. An LCT took Fouche and his men off and landed them. On the beach he was sorting them out from among the tanks when a mortar bomb exploded seriously wounding him in the stomach. His CO thought he had been mortally wounded, but he recovered.

Major John Freeman landed as a supernumerary with commando headquarters, but after the CO of Z-troop had been killed, he assumed command as they moved inland during the following days. As OC (a rank that he retained until September 1944) he spent two months in the line with 48 Commando at Sallenelles.

John Freeman served with the South African Infantry in the Western Desert and, being fully battle-trained, ran a patrolling course for commandos while in the line. In September he was transferred back to England for a training appointment in which his experience would have proved valuable, but, such are the strange ways of the military, he found he had nothing to do.

RNVR Communication branch ratings with Lt G Brunyee. (Brunyee)

About this time, Fouche having recuperated from his wounds and England having apparently recovered from leukaemia, both returned to their units in time to train for the Walcheren operation. The objective was to take Battery W13 to the south-east of Westkapelle. In the attack, which began at 1010 on 1 November 1944, Fouche with Y-troop went through Strong Point W285 to take W286. The attack on W13 failed and the troop leader was killed. The rest of the commando then came up and took the battery, whereupon Moulton deployed Fouche and the depleted Y-troop, of which he apparently acted as commander, forward to hold part of the perimeter that night. On about 8 November Lt England was killed together with eighteen marines and sappers (and another nine wounded) when their LVT Buffalo struck an eleven-inch shell laid as a mine at a crossroads while they were on a patrol. The battle for the island was almost over, and this patrol had been ordered to ensure that the whole of the western area was in British hands. Three LVTs had been despatched and they had just passed through Serooskerke when England's LVT, the second in line, was blown up at the road junction.

Lt WW Layman of Johannesburg was another who had chosen to be seconded to the Marines. He served on an LCG(M) on Operation Infatuate. During the attack on Westkapelle at the north-western tip of Walcheren, which was flanked by batteries W15 (North) and W13 (South), on 1 November 1944, the dyke had been breached and forces were to be landed on either side of the breach. The LCG(M)s were to beach on the shoulders of the gap, flood ballast tanks to provide a firm gun platform, and fire point-blank into the concrete emplacements with the two 17-pounder guns that each carried, using solid AP shot. Both LCG(M)s were heavily armoured but had not seen any previous action.

Layman's craft (102) was seen to be hit near the bridge just prior to beaching on the southern shoulder right on time at 0943. It fired at a concrete emplacement but could not penetrate it. At 1002 the LCG(M) was seen to be on fire although this was apparently brought under control. However, she was later reported to be broached to and in flames. Of the crew of forty-one there were no survivors and only one from an LCS(L) supporting her.

The captain of 102 was Lt DRV Flory RNVR. He had taken his command in under heavy fire, and drawn off much of the barrage, which would otherwise have been directed at the personnel craft and troops. 102 had been engaged at close range by batteries of 5.9-inch and 4.1-inch guns. Both LCG(M)s had been lost and the OC of the Support

Group of newly qualified RNVR (SA) Engineer Officers *en route* to the United Kingdom on board SS *City of Cairo*. (RK Aldrige)

Squadron, Commander KA Sellar RN reported: 'Theirs was a very gallant action. I cannot speak highly enough of the courage, determination and devotion to duty of these LCGs.'

Among others who served with the Jollies and who are perhaps better known to the general public, is Commandant Denys H Ranger, MBE, Officer Commanding the Kaffrarian Rifles from 1964 to 1969 and who, aged only twenty-three when he was serving in Normandy, was the oldest officer but one in his unit! JJK van Noorden, who by 1977 had risen to the rank of Major-General in the SA Defence Force, kept him company in his military career after the war. After serving with the 5th Field Regiment SAA in North Africa he was seconded to the Royal Marines and fought in Normandy, Burma, India and Malaya.

Only one, Major Gideon F Jacobs, has published a book on his wartime exploits, *Prelude to the Monsoon*. After serving in north-west Europe he was parachuted into Sumatra on an extremely dangerous peace mission. He was only twenty-three years old at the time, and he was awarded the OBE for ensuring the safety of Allied prisoners of war in Sumatra before the arrival of the liberation forces.

They were indeed a brave band of men, and in carrying out some of the cloak and dagger expeditions peculiar to commando units, they automatically and unconsciously continued the traditions inherited from their pioneering forefathers.

23

The U-boats Head South

Apart from the minefields laid off the Western Cape coast, a mild form of rationing, the semi-blackout and the presence of a Japanese aircraft reported over Durban, South Africa had been spared the immediate hardships and dangers of war. That was to change as the war entered its third year.

It must have been obvious to the enemy that with the virtual closure of the Mediterranean a huge amount of shipping must be building up at South African ports, and since all traffic was routed via the Cape of Good Hope there were rich pickings to be got. Through their agents in neutral Lourenço Marques, they must also have had some hint of the inadequacy of the local defences. On one occasion, when SA mine-sweepers were rescuing survivors, their pennant numbers were broad-cast from the German short-wave radio station at Zeesen, along with an order to refrain from any hostile action!

The naval authorities were well aware of the dangers to which vessels lying at anchor in unprotected roadsteads were exposed, and measures were taken to secure Saldanha Bay, the only large alternative harbour on the coast that could be made submarine-proof. At the peak periods of the closure of the Mediterranean, fifty or more (the maxi-mum was eighty) ships could be found at anchor awaiting berths off Cape Town and Durban, protected only by a handful of SANF A/S vessels, minesweepers and routine air patrols. They were extremely vulnerable to attack, and the fact was fully appreciated by both sides.

In October 1942, when the scene changed and the war became a matter of immediate local concern, the Royal Navy had only one corvette *Rockrose* (later to become in peacetime the hydrographic ship *Protea* of the SAN) on station. She was joined almost immediately by her sister corvettes *Thyme* and *Cyclamen*. However, by a fortunate chance, two destroyers, HMNZS *Nizam* and HMS *Foxhound,* had arrived for refitting, while another pair, *Arrow* and *Active,* had called in on their way to Freetown. At this time the SANF could muster seven A/S vessels at Cape Town, six at Durban and one at at Saldanha Bay.

HMS *Rockrose* played an active role in anti-submarine warfare in SA waters. She later became survey ship HMSAS *Protea*. (Mrs Hamilton)

These latter, while useful for harbour protection duties, were precluded by their modest speed of only ten and a half to thirteen and a half knots, from being effective U-boat hunters. Air patrols were carried out by modified Venturas and the older and simpler Ansons.

That was the situation when the Germans launched the first of their series of submarine attacks against shipping along the South African seaboard.

From October 1942 onwards, people living on the South African coast became more and more accustomed to the arrival of survivors from ships that had been destroyed. Altogether, within a thousand miles of the South African coast, German submarines destroyed 133 merchant ships and damaged six more. Surface commerce raiders captured or sank a further twenty, while two were sunk and two damaged by mines, making a grand total of 163. In addition, one warship was lost as the result of submarine attack and one suffered mine damage. South African warships rescued about four hundred survivors from sunken ships.

To inflict such losses, the German Navy at various times employed a total of twenty-eight submarines in operations off the coast. Despite several attacks carried out both by surface vessels and aircraft, only two submarines were lost. One of these, U-179, was sent down off Cape Town by the destroyer HMS *Active* and the other, UIT 22, by Catalina aircraft about six hundred miles south of Cape Point. UIT 22 was not

Crash boat ex Gordon's Bay approaching survivors from a U-boat sinking. (HC Woodhouse)

engaged in active hostilities; she was one of a group of former Italian submarines running much-needed raw materials to Germany from the Far East.

The submarine warfare in southern waters may be said to have begun with the torpedoing of the battleship HMS *Ramilles* by a Japanese midget submarine while she was at anchor in the harbour of Diego Suarez. From then on the Japanese were almost unmolested in the waters off the east coast during the months of June and July 1942. They sank twenty-one ships, mostly in the Mozambique Channel, one only 115 miles north-east of Durban.

On 7 October 1942, the American freighter *Chickasaw City* was torpedoed and sunk seventy miles west by south of Table Bay, followed on the same day by the cargo vessels *Firethorn, Boringa* and *Koumoun-douros.* The game was well and truly on. Only three days later the 23 456 ton liner *Orcades,* carrying a complement of crew and passengers numbering about a thousand was hit by three torpedoes about 250 miles west south west of Cape Town, having sailed only that day. The ship was still able to steam, but her captain wisely decided to get all unnecessary hands into the boats. Forty were lost when one of the boats capsized on launching, but the rest were picked up by the Polish *Narwik*. The master of the *Narwik* took a great risk in stopping, for the U-boat had surfaced only a few miles away. For some inexplicable reason, which can only be supposed to have been on humanitarian grounds, *Narwik* was not herself attacked, and she landed the survivors safely at Cape Town. *Orcades* was the largest ship to be sunk in those waters.

Another well-known vessel sunk by a U-boat (U-177) was the Union Castle liner *Llandaff Castle.* She was torpedoed 115 miles south west of Lourenço Marques on 30 November. Two days earlier, when only 155 miles north-east of Durban, the 6 796 ton transport *Nova Scotia* was torpedoed by the same submarine. In addition to her crew she had on board nearly eight hundred Italian internees and 134 SA soldiers homeward bound from North Africa.

Once clear of the sinking, the U-boat commander reported to his HQ: 'Sank auxiliary cruiser *Nova Scotia* with over a thousand Italian civil internees ex Massawa. Two survivors taken on board. Still about four hundred in boats and rafts. Moved away because of air.' He erred in two respects: *Nova Scotia* was not an auxiliary cruiser, and he had overestimated her complement. A reply was received three hours later: 'Continue operating. Waging war comes first. No rescue attempts.' Nevertheless the German HQ did inform the Portuguese in Lourenço Marques who despatched the sloop *Alfonso de Albuquerque* which, on 1 December rescued 192 survivors, among them many injured. Ninety-one South Africans were lost out of the total of 750 who perished. That was the worst loss of life in South African waters during the war. 120 corpses, carried inshore by the current, were washed up on Durban beaches. It brought the war to the very doorstep of South Africa.

The last merchant ship to be sunk during the submarine campaign within a thousand miles of the South African coast was the *Point Pleasant Park*, torpedoed on 23 February 1945 by U-532 when 587 miles north-west of Table Bay.

Needless to say, vessels of the SANF were kept busy throughout this period. The first of many rescues was made by HMSAS *Africana* when she picked up survivors from the torpedoed American cargo vessel *Anne Hutchinson* only thirty-four miles from East London. The ship broke in half, and the stern portion was towed into Port Elizabeth by the minesweeper *David Haigh*, which earned the MBE for her captain (Lt HF van Eyessen).

Survivors of a U-boat attack. (Author)

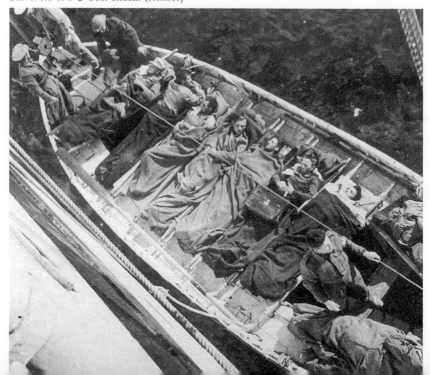

On 1 November 1942 HMSA ships *Rondevlei* and *Nigel* picked up eighty survivors from the SS *Mendoza* (see Chapter 6) which had been sunk only eighty miles east north east of Durban Bluff, the nearest sinking to Durban of the war. Once again *Africana* entered the picture when she rescued another twenty-five survivors from a ship sunk off Port Elizabeth.

Because of the congestion of shipping outside SA ports, few SANF vessels could be spared for actual submarine hunting, and with a few exceptions, they were mainly employed in protective operations round the anchored ships and in covering the approaches to the harbours.

The most difficult and dangerous rescue on the South African coast was carried out in November 1942, when the liner *Dunedin Star* beached herself after striking a submerged object near the mouth of the Cunene River on the border between Angola and South West Africa. HMSAS *Nerine* was despatched from Walvis Bay to find that sixty-three of the complement, including twenty-one passengers, had been landed on the desert beach. The story of their rescue has been told by John H Marsh in his book *Skeleton Coast* and is too well-known to be repeated here; but it is interesting to recall that yet another minesweeper from Walvis Bay, HMSAS *Natalia,* commanded by Lt JC Walters (who became Chief of the SA Navy from 1977 to 1980) floated rafts of water and provisions to the stranded survivors, only to see them swept away by the strong current. On a later expedition they succeeded in floating drums of water ashore, much to the relief of those suffering the hardships of that notoriously inhospitable beach.

With incursions by U-boats, all SANF vessels were constantly on the alert. On 16 December 1942 HMSAS *Hektor* reported sighting a submarine near Cape Point, but the sighting was considered unreliable. There were many false alarms, and the author remembers very vividly having his crew at action stations while his ship steamed at her maximum speed of 10 knots to ram a periscope sighted off Durban, which turned out to be a broomstick floating upright in the water!

The greatest individual success gained by a submarine was by U-160, which in one night torpedoed six ships in a convoy fifty-odd miles south of Durban. Two of the torpedoed ships managed to make it back to port. On 20 September 1943 the big Italian submarine *Ammiraglio Cagni,* which had in the previous November sunk the Greek ship *Argo* near Cape Point, entered Durban harbour to surrender after the collapse of Italy.

The minesweeper *Terje* carried out an attack on a submarine in 1943, but without any tangible result. Meanwhile, with the arrival of some British A/S trawlers in December 1942 it became possible to introduce what were known as 'group' convoys as opposed to 'through' convoys, which consisted of more important vessels, such as troopships, escorted by destroyers and larger warships. Until the end of the active submarine

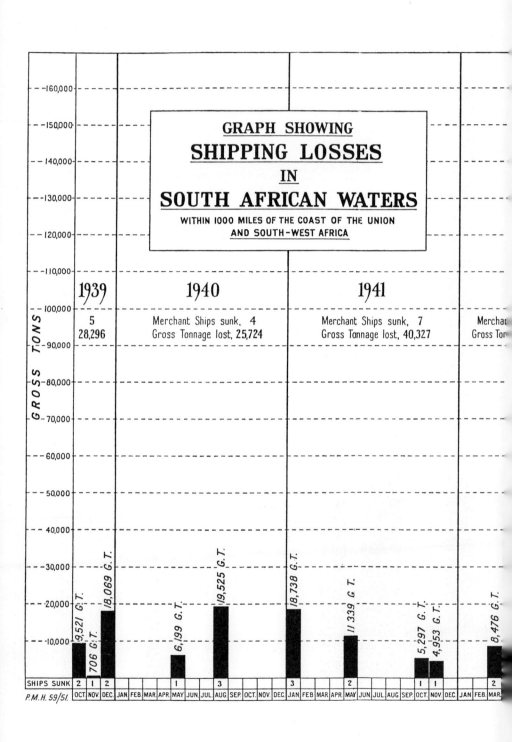

GRAPH SHOWING
SHIPPING LOSSES
IN
SOUTH AFRICAN WATERS
WITHIN 1000 MILES OF THE COAST OF THE UNION
AND SOUTH-WEST AFRICA

GROSS TONS

-160,000-
-150,000-
-140,000-
-130,000-
-120,000-
-110,000-
-100,000
-90,000-
-80,000-
-70,000-
-60,000-
-50,000-
-40,000-
-30,000-
-20,000-
-10,000-

1939
5
28,296

1940
Merchant Ships sunk, 4
Gross Tonnage lost, 25,724

1941
Merchant Ships sunk, 7
Gross Tonnage lost, 40,327

Merchan
Gross Tor

9,521 G.T.
706 G.T.
18,069 G.T.
6,199 G.T.
19,525 G.T.
18,738 G.T.
11 339 G.T.
5,297 G.T.
4,953 G.T.
8,476 G.T.

SHIPS SUNK	2	1	2	OCT.	NOV.	DEC.	JAN	FEB	MAR	APR	MAY	JUN	JUL	AUG	SEP	OCT.	NOV.	DEC.	JAN	FEB	MAR	APR	MAY	JUN	JUL	AUG	SEP.	OCT.	NOV.	DEC.	JAN	FEB	MAR
	2	1	2				1				3								3				2					1	1				2

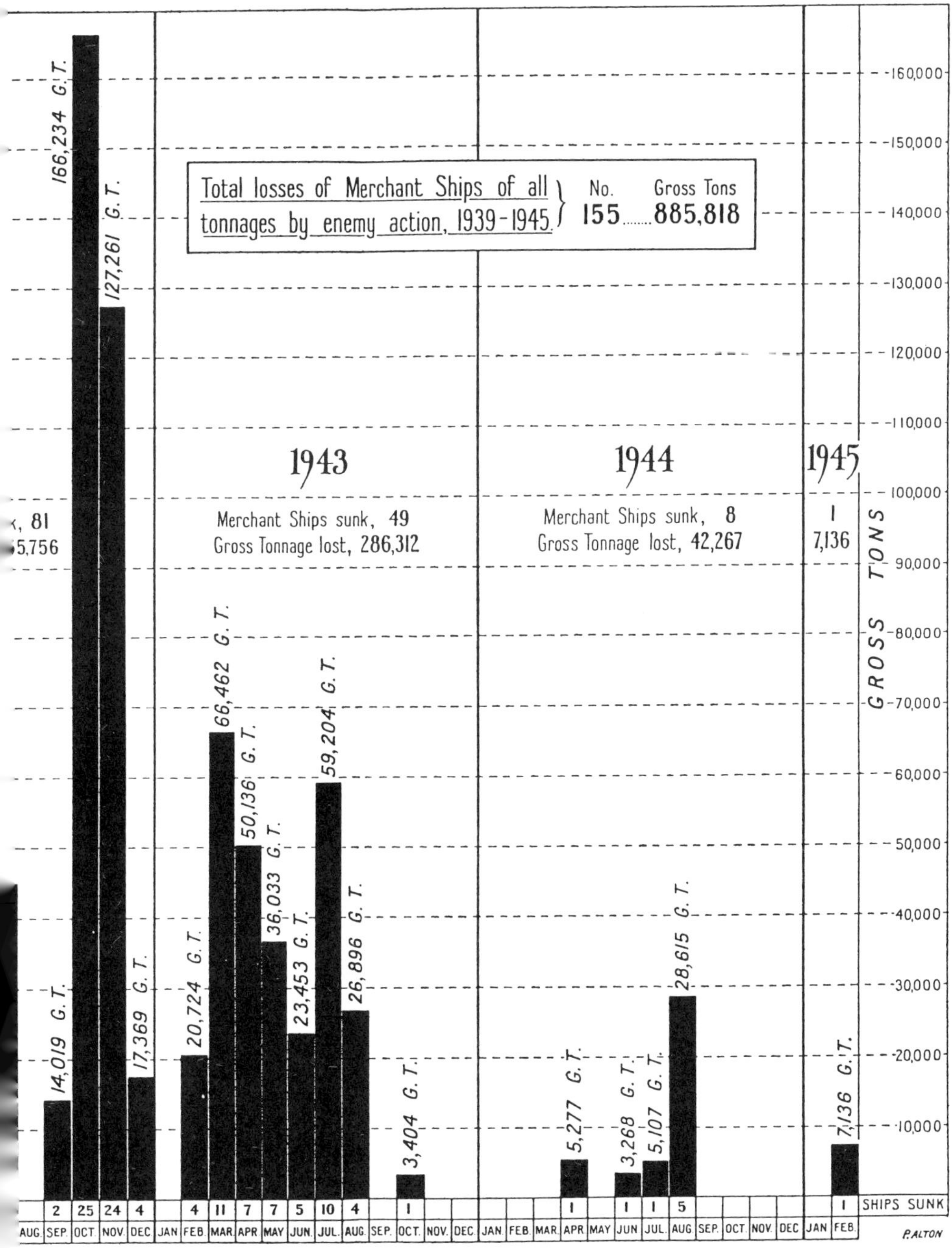

Total losses of Merchant Ships of all
tonnages by enemy action, 1939-1945.

No.	Gross Tons
155	885,818

1943

Merchant Ships sunk, 49
Gross Tonnage lost, 286,312

1944

Merchant Ships sunk, 8
Gross Tonnage lost, 42,267

1945

1
7,136

GROSS TONS

160,000
150,000
140,000
130,000
120,000
110,000
100,000
90,000
80,000
70,000
60,000
50,000
40,000
30,000
20,000
10,000

166,234 G.T.

127,261 G.T.

, 81
5,756

14,019 G.T.

17,369 G.T.

20,724 G.T.

66,462 G.T.

50,136 G.T.

36,033 G.T.

23,453 G.T.

59,204 G.T.

26,896 G.T.

3,404 G.T.

5,277 G.T.

3,268 G.T.

5,107 G.T.

28,615 G.T.

7,136 G.T.

| | 2 | 25 | 24 | 4 | | 4 | 11 | 7 | 7 | 5 | 10 | 4 | | 1 | | | | | | 1 | | 1 | 1 | 5 | | | | | | 1 | | SHIPS SUNK |
|AUG.|SEP.|OCT.|NOV.|DEC.|JAN.|FEB.|MAR.|APR.|MAY|JUN.|JUL.|AUG.|SEP.|OCT.|NOV.|DEC.|JAN.|FEB.|MAR.|APR.|MAY|JUN.|JUL.|AUG.|SEP.|OCT.|NOV.|DEC.|JAN.|FEB.|

P. ALTON

campaign in September 1943 one or two SANF ships sailed between Cape Town and Durban every week escorting 'group' convoys. For this type of operation the ships came under the control of the Royal Navy.

While all this promoted experience and gave the crews a real taste of active service, they had few contacts with the enemy. Coastal convoys became the focal point of only three attacks, on one of which no SANF vessel was in company. During two later attacks on the same convoy HMSAS *Vereeniging* was acting as rearguard when at 2353 two explosions were heard and two ships were seen to be falling astern. *Vereeniging* steamed ahead and carried out an A/S search, but without success. She did, however, rescue survivors from three lifeboats before resuming her search. On returning to the scene she picked up more survivors, making a total of ninety-seven in all, and while doing so one of the ships that had been abandoned, but was still afloat, was torpedoed a second time. Another A/S sweep was carried out but again without result. *Vereeniging* made no Asdic contact, nor did she sight a submarine. But the survivors had seen the submarine proceeding at high speed on the surface.

On 14 June 1943 the minesweepers *Steenberg* and *Brakvlei* were sweeping at the end of the searched channel in calm weather when, thirteen miles south of Saldanha, they sighted a trail of blue smoke about three miles away. Slipping their sweeps they closed the position and sighted a periscope moving south-east at about twelve knots, pushing a bow-wave a little ahead of it. Two minutes later the periscope disappeared and left a swirl marking the spot. Two depth charges were dropped by *Steenberg* but, despite an intensive aerial search, no target was seen.

On the morning of 2 July a similar incident took place. This time the minesweepers *Natalia* and *Krugersdorp* were running along the swept channel, when the *Krugersdorp* observed bluish-grey smoke inshore of the ships about two miles away. Five minutes later they saw the upper half of a conning tower moving north-east at about twelve knots in a cloud of diesel smoke. Soon afterwards the submarine submerged. The two ships circled the position and at 1005 *Krugersdorp* sighted a periscope at about nine hundred yards away, closed the position and dropped both her depth charges, but without any apparent effect.

Since this attack was carried out on the very threshold of Cape Town and a convoy was forming up only two miles away, Combined Operations HQ began to fidget with their worry-beads. Aircraft and A/S vessels were summoned to carry out a box search, and when that was proved negative Naval Operations gave the assessment a low rating of reliability. The Commanding Officer of *Krugersdorp*, however, insisted firmly that he had seen and attacked a submarine.

By September 1943 independent sailings had been resumed along the South African coast, although group convoy sailings continued north of Durban, partly because the route skirted neutral territory, and in any case it was considered to be exposed and vulnerable.

Escorts on these east coast convoys had consisted mainly of coal-burning RN trawlers. These now switched to oil-burning SANF vessels, which took over convoy duty while the coal-burners were used on coastal and offshore harbour patrol duties.

The first of the South African convoy escorts sailed for Kilindini (Mombasa) on 27 November 1953. This 4th Escort Group was made up of HMSA ships *Pretoria, Standerton, Odberg* and *Cedarberg.* The 3rd

HMSAS *Odberg* and sister A/S vessel alongside in Port Elizabeth. (F Neave)

Escort Group, consisting of HMSA ships *Turffontein, Vereeniging, Sonneblom* and *Immortelle,* followed on 19 December. By that time, unlike the early days of the SDF, the powers that were could now afford to allocate replacements in reserve. *Blaauwberg* and *Tordonn* were earmarked for that, although the former permanently replaced her sister ship *Cedarberg* in June 1944. Next to go, at the end of the year, were the *Vereeniging* and *Turffontein.* Both were replaced by the battle-scarred *Southern Isles* and *Southern Sea* recently returned from the Mediterranean. The last of these east coast convoys was completed on 11 May 1945, soon after V–E Day, when the Japanese threat had diminished. No certain submarine contacts had been made in their eighteen months of escort duties.

Meanwhile unsuccessful anti-submarine attacks and the rescue of survivors continued. On 30 March 1944 the cargo ship *Dahomian* sank eleven miles west south west of Cape Point, though whether by torpedo or by mine is not known. *Natalia* and *Soetvlei*, sweeping the Cape Town – Simon's Town channel, actually witnessed the sinking. *Krugersdorp* also arrived on the scene, and together with *Natalia* picked up forty-nine survivors from a total crew of fifty-one.

Another encounter was reported by the minesweeping trawler HMSAS *Arum* based at Walvis Bay. At 1355, when about twenty-three miles west north west off Pelican Point, she sighted and identified a periscope moving at the same speed and on a parallel course. *Arum* slipped her sweep, increased speed, headed for the target and opened up with her 6-pounder gun. She fired ten rounds before the periscope disappeared. *Arum* then dropped a depth charge ahead of where the submarine had dived and, together with her consort *Bluff*, which had now joined her, searched until after dark; but again without success.

The last of the search and rescue operations appears to have been carried out by HMSAS *Africana*, which by that time, February 1945, was based at Walvis Bay. Of all the small ships operating along the coast in time of war, she featured over and over again in missions of mercy, either plucking frightened and helpless men from the uncertain safety of lifeboats or saving them from a watery grave. There must have been many a merchant seaman with reason to be grateful to that staunch little ship.

As we have already noted, the *Point Pleasant Park* was torpedoed on the afternoon of 23 February 1945. She was hit by a single torpedo which killed nine men and was then shelled by the submarine. She sank two hours later. The first news of this last disaster off the coast was received when survivors were landed by a fishing boat on 3 March. *Africana* was immediately sent to search along the coast to the south and on the evening of the 4th she picked up the remainder of the crew, a hundred miles north of Luderitz Bay and who had been in their two lifeboats for nine days. They were all safely landed at Walvis Bay next day. U-532 had been responsible for the sinking, and she survived to surrender at Liverpool three months later.

This chapter would be incomplete without some mention of the aircraft that carried out often dangerous and tedious long-range patrols over the sea. Although strictly speaking the airmen have no place in these pages, their co-operation and comradeship with naval forces cannot be allowed to pass without mention.

To an outsider investigating the story of the offshore aerial patrols, it would almost seem as though those squadrons were the tail-end charlies of Air Force planning, at least in the procurement of up-to-date machines. That is a handicap they shared with the Fleet Air Arm.

On the outbreak of war eighteen Junker 86 aircraft were modified and prepared for coastal patrols. Although spares were a problem, squadrons consisting of three aircraft were stationed at the ports. Fully loaded, these aircraft had a range of about a thousand miles at a speed of 135 mph. The patrols became routine, and they usually carried a naval observer to assist in identifying any shipping sighted.

The squadron based at Cape Town, for example, flew deep-sea patrols to 140 miles south of Cape Agulhas and systematically searched the area east and west. By late 1940 the whole system had become better organised and the Avro Anson was introduced. These aircraft were quite comfortable with good visibility, but at 158 mph their cruising range was just over five hundred miles, and their bomb load was 300-lb compared with the four 250-lb bombs and eight 20-lb bombs of the Junkers.

By 1941 the Coastal Air Force, now designated No 6 Wing, was still flying Ansons, although Marylands occasionally joined in the flights. Many false alarms sent these aircraft off on wild goose chases, and it is known that, no doubt out of sheer frustration, at least two pilots fired on Allied ships forcing them to display their identification pennants. At the same time an order by the British Admiralty for ships to fire on aircraft not recognised as friendly caused some anxiety, especially since they had no means of identifying themselves other than by visual markings.

By late 1942 Venturas had made their appearance, and they were a vast improvement on the previous machines. With a cruising speed of 195 mph they had a range of fifteen hundred miles and endurance of up to ten hours.

It was later learned that a U-boat commander operating off the South African coast revealed that SAAF planes always flew too high and could be sighted well in advance by his look-outs. When taxed with that SAAF pilots admitted that the desert was their real operational area, and they seldom stayed long enough on coastal surveillance to absorb and master the techniques of this specialised form of aerial operations properly.

It is not possible in this brief account to give details of the many dangers to which the pilots engaged on coastal patrols were exposed. Engine failure over the sea was not uncommon, and the boisterous winter weather many miles south of the land caused trouble, and even the cancellation of patrol flights.

One man who flew coastal patrols in those days was Flight Lieutenant HC (Bert) Woodhouse of Johannesburg. When he was transferred from 25 Air School at Standerton to No 66 Air School at Youngsfield, Cape Town in 1942, he found that it had been formed primarily to train navigators for the SAAF, the Royal Hellenic Air Force and the RAF. Bert Woodhouse was an instructor in navigation.

The aircraft used were Avro Ansons with a cruising speed of a hundred knots and an endurance of about three hours. Crew consisted of a pilot, usually SAAF, a wireless operator and two pupil navigators under training. The normal routine was to fly exercises of half of each day over a fortnight, with alternate flights over land and sea. As course instructor, he flew with a different pair of pupils on each flight.

About August 1942, despite being under training, they received verbal orders to the effect that when they were flying over the sea they were to consider themselves an auxiliary coastal squadron of the SAAF. Subject to orders from Coastal Operations Room in Cape Town, they were to regard themselves as being on patrol and to watch out for anything unusual.

His logbook records that on 12 September 1942, piloted by Lt van den Linden of the SAAF, they carried out a practice square search and successfully located an Allied submarine that had been co-operating in the exercise. A similar operation followed on 21 September, when they intercepted the cruiser HMS *Newcastle*.

On 9 October 1942 Woodhouse notes the first entry of an explicit reference to an anti-submarine patrol carried out at an altitude of five hundred feet. Nothing was sighted, but four days later they saw and photographed two lifeboats and seven rafts. The logbook entries do not say whether they were occupied, but it is likely that the survivors had already been rescued.

There followed a quiet routine period until February 1943, by which time the Ansons had been equipped with depth charges. After many uneventful patrols, they heard whispers that the enemy submarine campaign was warming up and on 29 May 1943, flying with Capt Wheatley, SAAF, in Anson 1BJ, they had the good fortune to sight what turned out to be two lifeboats containing eight survivors from a ship sunk the night before. They gave the position by R/T and circled the lifeboats until a crash–boat arrived from Gordon's Bay. While they were circling they were joined by two other aircraft from the same navigation course.

Soon afterwards Bert Woodhouse looked round for the second of the new arrivals, only to see the crash-boat heading rapidly towards the tail-fin of an Anson protruding from the water. No explanation of the mishap was given, but it seemed to him that one engine had probably cut during the manual changing of petrol cocks, which had to be done by the pupil navigator sitting next to the pilot.

The crew were all killed outright except for one of the pupils, who was thrown clear – probably whilst taking pictures through the open window with an F24 camera – but he died in hospital three days later. His parents presented a picture to the pupil's mess at Youngsfield.

Regular patrols continued without much incident or any special assignment until 10 March 1944, when they received orders to try to find four fishermen reportedly blown out to sea after their engine failed. The search was unsuccessful, which is not surprising for the men

Air Observer's Course No 39, 66 Air School, Youngsfield, Cape Town, 29 May 1943. Pupil air observers, Clarence and Comyns (second and third from left, bottom row) were killed when their Anson crashed into the sea. (HC Woodhouse)

were later found safely anchored near the mouth of the Berg River, having got back inshore with a small sail!

In July 1944 they were again responsible for sighting survivors on a dinghy, who were duly rescued by the ever-ready crash-boat.

They were given an unusual task in June 1944 when, piloted by Lt 'Joe' Starling SAAF, they were ordered to take Lt-Col (later Lieutenant-General) Fraser to Windhoek to address a meeting. During that flight Bert carried out the only leaflet raid of the war over Southern Africa when, lying in the nose of the Anson, he threw out pamphlets urging the citizens of Windhoek to attend the meeting!

For the return trip the pamphlets were replaced with Windhoek beer, and Colonel Fraser was properly impressed with both the resources and resourcefulness of the combined SAAF and RAF crew when he was presented with a glass of beer on the way back to Cape Town!

Another veteran of wartime coastal patrols was George Young of Cape Town. He was the doyen of newspaper shipping columnists and he served in the SAAF, in which his knowledge of ships and his ability to recognise them made his appointment to coastal patrols entirely logical. In his book, *Salt in my Blood* he tells of some of the natural dangers facing these air crews other than enemy action.

The weather in the winter of 1942 was appalling, but since the authorities were most concerned about the vulnerability of the massed shipping lying in the offshore anchorage at Durban, the squadron of

Ansons in which George Young was serving were flown from East London to Durban as an emergency measure.

It was pouring with rain and blowing a gale when the six aircraft of the squadron took off for Durban from the then only partly-developed aerodrome at Collondale, East London. There were only two runways, one running NE-SW alongside the main road and the other NW-SE. One was intended for aircraft taking off towards the sea, and if they failed to get off the short field in time, they tumbled down an embankment. It really was no place for big aircraft. The longest runway had a bump in the middle, and after touching down the machine became airborne again at the very time they wanted to apply the brakes!

The Ansons had no trouble getting off in a fifty-knot wind, but it was a terribly bumpy exit; and by the time George had made the prescribed 129 turns of the handle to raise the undercarriage he was nearly airsick. Conditions were so bad that they had to signal the formation to break up and make their own way to Durban independently.

It was a wartime rule that all aircraft from the south had to make a circuit of Port Shepstone lighthouse for identification, but in poor visibility they could not find it; and in any case they were not too happy at the prospect of meeting any of the flight in the same restricted area. So they flew on without bothering to locate it.

Crossing the harbour entrance in pouring rain they headed for the small aerodrome at Stamford Hill abaft the Snell Parade barracks. The airfield was awash, and when they landed the wheels splashed up great fountains of water.

That night they were ordered to carry out a patrol; but such were the conditions that it was doubtful whether even a U-boat could have found the anchored ships. Nevertheless a flare path was made from oil cans with burning waste sticking out of the spouts, but the rain kept putting them out and some of the cans were actually floating away in the flood! The aircraft kept a wary eye on the lights of Durban and never ventured more than twenty miles away. They returned safely, to land on a bogged field with the aid of flickering hand-held torchlights.

Recalled to East London once the flap was over, they took off after some trouble with a defective plug-lead, and with a following wind they made good time back down the coast, despite rain, drizzle and bad visibility all the way home.

When they arrived over Collondale they were not too happy to find a strong cross-wind blowing over the runway. Coming in crabwise to land, the pilot shut off the throttle to put her down, when the port wing suddenly dropped. The Cheetah engines were given full boost, and with the ground flashing past under the drooping wing, the Anson tore across the road, skimming trees, and at last managed to gain height – to get back into the rain.

Ground crews later reported that, with the plane doing between eighty and ninety knots, they estimated the wing-tip as being only a half an inch off the ground.

The second time around the landing was successfully accomplished in spite of the cross-wind and a bounce on the airport hump that nearly sent them airborne again.

When they landed an RAF armourer opened the door and demanded the pins for the two depth charges 'before you put on any more flying circuses!' He then complained that only one pin had been handed in; the other depth charge must have become dislodged in the turbulence and fallen to earth or sea – who knew where?

Epilogue

In preparing a book of this kind one of the difficulties of the writer is the wealth of material that must be either curtailed or omitted altogether because of the limitations of space. That is as regrettable as it is unavoidable.

Another is that after a lapse of nearly half a century memories and the sequence of events grow dim. True recollections of incidents once so vivid become distorted with the passage of time and imagination tends to supplant or embellish them. As is well-known, stories relayed verbally from person to person are susceptible to variations of fact and sometimes become remote from the original. That is one of the penalties of frequent repetition. Strictly speaking, only a written record of events noted at the time or very soon afterwards bears the marks of authenticity.

With that in mind, and whenever possible, facts have been checked; but at this distance confirmation has not always been possible or available. The author regrets any misrepresentation of fact that may have found its way into the text and begs the reader's forbearance.

Another difficulty has been to select suitable extracts from a range of unpublished records submitted by those concerned, or borrowed from the SA Naval Museum. The memoirs of several naval veterans are in the form of quite bulky volumes, the contents of which would fill a dozen books of this size. Condensation, summarisation, and modification of content has been no easy task, and it is to be hoped that the original authors will not feel slighted because much of their extensive memoirs has had to be passed over.

Other omissions include mention of the Fleet Air Arm, the SA Women's Naval Auxiliary Service ('SWANS') and gifts and comforts organisations. That also is regretted, but at least many individual histories have been recorded elsewhere in detail.

Bibliography

Published Works

Goosen, Cmdre (SM, SAN) JC. *South Africa's Navy: the First Fifty Years*. Johannesburg: WJ Fleisch & Partners 1975.

Turner, LC; Gordon-Cumming (OBE, RN), Cmdr HR, and Betzer, JE. *War in the Southern Oceans*. London: Oxford University Press 1961.

Young, G. *Salt in my Blood*. Woodstock, Cape: JE Midgeley 1961.

Reader's Digest. *Reader's Digest Illustrated Story of World War II*. (Volume II, 5th ed). Cape Town: Reader's Digest Association of South Africa (Pty) Limited 1980.

Unpublished Works

Gordon Cumming Cmdr (OBE, RN), HR. *History of South African Naval Forces during the Second World War*. Union War Histories (Sea).

Burgers, Lt AP. *Short History of the South African Navy*. Directorate of Personnel, Naval Headquarters, Simon's Town: December 1967.

Duffell-Canham, J. *Seaman Gunner Do Not Weep*.

Barfield, Lt (DSC, SANF (V)) JN. *My War 1939 – 1945*.

Scott-Napier, Cmdr (DSO, RN) LE. *Autobiographical Notes*.

Fourie, H. *Second World War Memoirs*.

Bisset, Cmdr WM and MacCoy, Lt (DSC) AH. 'The First South African Naval Officer to Command a Submarine'. (Article to be published in *Navy News*.)

Articles in Periodicals

Author unknown. 'A Street in Paarden Eiland', *Safmarine House Magazine – Wheelhouse,* Jan – Feb 1990. (Article in journal.)

Bisset, Cmdr WM and De Kock, Lt (MBE, DSC) VP. 'The South African Navy's Most decorated War Hero', *Navy News,* Volume II, April – May 1988. (Article in journal.)

Bisset, Cmdr WM and Stephens, Lt (DSC) DR. 'Dieppe, D-Day and the Rhine Crossing', *Navy News,* Volume VII, September 1988. (Article in journal.)

Bisset, Cmdr WM and Winship, Lt-Cmdr (JCD, DSC) AH. 'Operation Plunder: The Rhine Crossing Reconnaissance', *Navy News,* Volume VIII, February 1989. (Article in journal.)

Bisset, Cmdr WM. 'South African Naval Personnel Seconded to the Royal Navy 1940 – 1942', *Militaria* 15/1, 1985. (Article in journal.)

Bisset, Cmdr WM. 'South African Personnel Mentioned in Despatches during World War II', *Navy News,* Volume VIII, August 1989. (Article in journal.)

Bisset, Cmdr WM. 'South African Naval Personnel during the Second World War', *Militaria* 12/1, 1982. (Article in journal.)

Bisset, Cmdr WM. 'Tribute to Mr Peter Philip, Midget Submariner', *Navy News,* Volume VI, June 1987. (Article in journal.)

Index